ADVANCES IN
LIBRARY ADMINISTRATION
AND ORGANIZATION

Volume 6 • 1986

ADVANCES IN LIBRARY ADMINISTRATION AND ORGANIZATION

A Research Annual

Editors: GERARD B. McCABE
Director of Libraries
Clarion University of Pennsylvania

BERNARD KREISSMAN
University Librarian, Emeritus
University of California, Davis

VOLUME 6 • 1986

 JAI PRESS INC.

Greenwich, Connecticut   *London, England*

CONTENTS

INTRODUCTION

As *Advances in Library Administration and Organization* moves into the second half of its first decade, it is, perhaps, premature to look backward—we shall save such an historical assessment for our tenth volume. Nonetheless, a few general reflections on the past five years are appropriate. Whether *ALAO* is to be considered a success would depend heavily on the personal attitudes of the individual making that appraisal. However, two signs of such success may be noted: (1) the articles in *ALAO* are increasingly cited in the profession, and (2) whereas the editors diligently searched for contributions for the first two or three issues, today contributors, in increasing numbers, seek out the editors.

Any estimate for the reasons for those gains would be clearly speculative, but again, two issues seem to be indicative. First, *ALAO* has never been trendy, indeed I believe the annual is regarded as downright old-fashioned. Whatever the prime issue of the day, be it databases, automated technical services, of conservation and preservation, it has always been welcomed by *ALAO*, but never to the exclusion of those other professional concerns which have not made that month's best seller list. Secondly, though we do not turn our backs on brief articles, *ALAO* has been particularly receptive of meritorious articles of greater length than can normally be accepted by the general periodicals of librarianship. As a scan of the length and nature of the articles in volume VI would disclose, those precepts continue to invigorate the pages of *ALAO*.

As for the future, the editors have discussed several ideas which may come to fruition in future volumes of *ALAO*. One or two of those considerations are confidential, but some others may be noted. We hope to expand internationally, to gain some views of foreign librarianship. Also, as Brian Reynolds' paper indicates, we are desirous of more articles from the public library sector. Finally, we hope to publish material on unorthodox subjects, procedures, and attitudes. We know that there are many feisty librarians out there. Why aren't more of them writing! The profession needs more gnats, more cross–patch and spitfire writing.

Welcome to Volume VI.

Bernard Kreissman
Series Editor

PROACTIVE MANAGEMENT IN PUBLIC LIBRARIES—IN CALIFORNIA AND IN THE NATION

Brian A. Reynolds

INTRODUCTION

This paper presents four interrelated areas of public library management. The emphasis throughout is on successfully managing a public agency— in this case, a library—during times of stable or reduced funding. The central theme of the discussion is that a new orientation to the challenge of retrenchment is required.

The new orientation is a shift in attitude and stance. Public librarians and public library supporters can no longer afford to provide, in a complacent and dependable way, reactive services that are managed by a traditional set of rules. The library management team, which would include library leaders, staff, supporters, and the public at large, must go into

Advances in Library Administration and Organization
Volume 6, pages 1–78
Copyright © 1986 by JAI Press Inc.
All rights of reproduction in any form reserved.
ISBN: 0-89232-724-3

1

their communities and "hustle". They must actively seek out support for a healthy library program by listening to the needs and demands of the public. By adjusting the service matrix accordingly, the public library will remain on the cutting-edge of our nation's cultural evolution in the years to come.

The information and ideas contained in this study are meant to provide practical alternatives for public librarians and their supporters in the struggle to cope with economic downturns, tax limitation initiatives, rapid technological change, and increasing mistrust of government by the governed. Public libraries today face unprecedented challenges.

Much of the data contained in the first two sections, "Politics" and "Finance," has a special emphasis on California. California, with its Jarvis-Gann property tax limitation initiative of 1978 (Proposition 13), was the first state to grapple with massive property tax cuts. Research shows that public libraries were among the local agencies hit hardest by the passage of Proposition 13. Sections 4 and 5, "Personnel" and "Leadership," are dealt with in a more general framework and are therefore applicable to all states. Pro-active public library management is the theme of the work before you. It is, I believe, a management orientation that will work in any fiscal climate.

The author has conducted an extensive survey of applicable ideas and material on this subject. In addition, the author relies upon ten years of professional experience, including two years as library director of a Northern California county library system. Agreement and assent to the author's opinions and research is not sought; rather, constructive comment and criticism to a somewhat narrow view of public library management is heartily encouraged.

POLITICS

Introduction

The California State Education Code gives county and city governments the right to establish free public libraries. In addition to a legal basis of existence, public libraries have enjoyed two other kinds of support, fiscal and moral, since their establishment. The fiscal aspect in California has meant that public libraries have received, on average, about 1% of local budgets for their operations. The moral support comes from the library's user community: benign approval from almost everyone, plus active use and involvement from a minority of the whole.

Times have changed. Property tax revenues, the historical bulwark of California public library funding, were cut 57% in 1978 due to Proposition

13. In the years subsequent to 1978, the state has provided relatively high levels of "bail-out" monies to local governments to replace the lost local tax revenues. Because of state support, local governments, including their libraries, have been able to operate in a more or less normal manner. In July, 1982, California faced an overall budget deficit, and severely reduced the local government bail-out monies. As a result, many local jurisdictions experienced budget shortfalls, causing confusion and cut-backs in both service and personnel. Mosquito abatement districts, schools, police and fire departments and jails all faced unprecedented reductions in funding. Already malnourished public libraries were affected most of all.

The tax payer revolt in California was the result of at least two events: overall economic recession, and citizen perception of "excessive" property taxes plus government waste. While it is beyond the scope of this paper to examine the causes and effects of the current economic problems, the mood of the citizenry must be probed. Americans have always maintained a skepticism of government. Since 1978, however, healthy skepticism seems to have evolved into unreasonable paranoia and cynicism. State and local governments in California have suffered repeatedly at the polls. Government revenues at both levels have been consistently denied by the electorate, while demanding that high levels of public service be maintained. This clash of opposing ideas requires a reassessment by government agencies at all levels, including public libraries.

Public Libraries in California: An Overview

Today, most of California's 58 counties have their own public library system, as do many cities. While public libraries have their legal basis firmly grounded in the State Education Code, the fiscal basis for the library's existence is not static.[1] Most public library budgets have shrunk since 1978. The concept of egalitarian, free public library service is being questioned both within professional library circles, and within the larger sphere of local government. Philosophical ideals are at war with fiscal reality. Even at its best, the property tax was an inflexible and inadequate funding mechanism for the public library.[2] Over the past four years, the local funding share of public library budgets has been decreasing, while the state and federal shares have been growing. In 1978, the state and federal shares were 0% and .06%, respectively. In 1980, the shares were 12% and .08%, respectively.[3]

Since the passage of Proposition 13, many local agencies have been forced to cope with leaner budgets by reducing staffing levels and services. From 1978 through 1980, the number of public library outlets in California dropped 22%. The number of public library employees dropped 18%, while the use of volunteers skyrocketed 282%. Based upon a 25% inflation rate for 1978–80, public library purchasing power decreased by 24%. Public libraries have, on average, been using 5% or more of their carryover and reserve funds each year to help meet their fiscal needs.[4]

In June of 1982, the State of California faced a deficit of more than two billion dollars. The budget finally adopted by the Legislature for FY 1982–83 substantialy reduced bail-out monies to local governments. President Reagan's proposed budget for FY 1983–84 proposed elimination of the most important federal aid to libraries programs: the Library Services and Construction Act, plus the library-aid portions of the Elementary & Secondary Education Act, and the Higher Education Act.[5] This means that the funds public libraries received from all governmental levels—local, state, and federal—are now under determined attack.

Public libraries were among the first agencies to bear the brunt of the tax revolt. Public library administrators were among the first explorers to tread into the dark, dank swamp of retrenchment. The future will undoubtedly take public libraries even further into this area. What can public library administrators and supporters do to counteract such pressures and continue to provide the level of services demanded by the community? Innovation and increased political activity can effect a safer, more sure passage through these difficulties. Phyllis I. Dalton offers some ideas on what, in her opinion, is the single most important activity for public librarians:

> The success of a library administrator depends largely upon an understanding and an ability to operate within the context of the political process. Library administrators have, in many instances, held themselves aloof from politics. . . . A failure to understand and utilize political processes has resulted in the lack of needed legislation and adequate tax support.[6]

While an administrative board or commission is the immediate governing authority for many public libraries in the Midwest and East, most public libraries in California report directly to either a Board of Supervisors or a City Council. Library political strength could well be augmented in California by establishing this kind of commission . . . an entity that would act as a buffer and a defender, made up of local "movers and shakers".[7]

As a profession, librarians have never been particularly organized or militant.[8] Library administrators are often afraid to enter the political fray. The political battle for funds and for recognition involves hazards and risks. Phyllis Dalton continues:

> The paucity of services and facilities, the poverty of library resources . . . are the results of the isolation of the public library administrator within the government . . . it is doubtful that most communities are best served by such timidity.[9]

One could conclude that the traditional public library administrator has been on the edge rather than in the center of the local political processes. This is no longer a safe position.

While public library managers have sat on the political sidelines, the tax structure that funds their institutions has been changing rapidly. Local services now depend more and more upon state-level aid, which means greater State influence in local affairs. Power follows money. It is ironic that California voters believed that Proposition 13 would reduce government waste and "power at the top". In effect, the opposite occurred. By reducing local tax revenues, the role of the Legislature in Sacramento has been augmented proportionally.

Problems unique to California have been compounded by Ronald Reagan's new-new Federalism. His plan is to turn over many Federal programs to the states, but with less funds than before . . . to move from specific, complex categorical grants to a scheme of general, block grants.[10] The states, in general, lack the infrastructure and the money to provide the same levels of service that federal aid programs have provided.

Public library management in times of retrenchment has its own peculiar characteristics. Planning, innovation, and political activity are all tricky and difficult in the best of worlds. The scarcity and confusion that accompany cut-backs are beset with paradoxes. Charles Levine, a management expert, opines that, "We know very little about the decline of public organizations and the management of cutbacks."[11] Retrenchment and scarce resources demand time to plan, innovation to be able to bounce back, yet the time and money to do so are typically not there. In an era of expansion, change, always a threat of some sort to employees and managers, can bring rewards of increased efficiency, pay-raises, and public acclaim. In an era of reduction, change brings only worker lay-offs and cut-backs of services. There are no clear pay-offs in cut-back management.

The requirements of cut-back management are several. Education is paramount. Groups such as staff, public, and government officials must be lobbied for understanding and support. Traditional services must be scrutinized carefully and priorities established. The above mentioned groups must be brought into this process so that they understand the reasons and buy into the results.[12] These activities require of the administrator skill, imagination, sensitivity, and political acumen. We now turn to this topic.

California Politics and Public Libraries

Politics. What is it? How is this amorphous term related to California public libraries? Politics and administration, value and fact, are two complementary halves of public library management.

Administration, with techniques such as personnel, bookkeeping, time management, and inventory control, are semi-scientific. These activities, in the words of Martin Landau, possess an internal criterion of correctness.[13] Administration, or process, is behavior conceptually distinct from politics. Decision-making is at the heart of administration, and decisions spring from premises. Landau argues that process (administration) and politics (policy) are based upon two different kinds or premises: factual and ethical. According to Landau:

> politics has to do with the expression of goals or ends, with the basic question of social policy, and, thus, with value judgements. There is . . . no scientific way of making such judgements.[14]

Administrative techniques can be empirically validated and tested. Policy questions are never right or wrong; they simply are. They involve complex ideas such as social equity. Policy is what governments do and do not do.[15] Public library managers both obey policy direction laid down by other entities, and generate their own policy. Public library managers are trained in process. Are they adept in policy (politics) as well?

Let us glance at the public library administrator as one actor upon a stage peopled with many actors. Among these other thespians, we find people associated with library schools; professional library organizations; library support groups; the California State Library; cooperative library systems; local, state, and Federal governments. All of these disparate entities have a real or potential effect upon public library policy in California. Do they exercise this power? Do they do it well or poorly? Are public libraries themselves in or out of step in the political dance? Some of these issues will be examined further.

First, who are public library administrators? They are people—mostly women—who have a Master's degree in librarianship, plus a certain amount of job experience which entitles them to assume management roles. Most of these librarians are trained, at the undergraduate level, in the humanities and the arts . . . very few in the sciences. A cursory look at the way they are trained—curricula of California graduate schools of library and information science—reveals no coursework which, by its title, names it as relevant to politics. Library schools are where librarians receive their professional training. They are taught to manipulate information—to order, receive, classify, process, and store it for public access. However, more and more, library schools are now called upon by practitioners to be more than they have been: to train librarians in outreach techniques, in active rather than passive librarianship. Library schools are also being urged in some quarters—for example, in the draft Master Plan for California Libraries—to become innovators and leaders in the world of library research.[16] These proposed areas of concern have at least two inherent goals:

service to patrons/abstract research value, plus political power. Library schools—the cradle of professional librarianship—must orient and train their students in the art of politics.

Since the 1970s, professional library organizations have become more active politically. The American Library Association (ALA) established a Washington office—as so many other interest groups have—to monitor and influence legislation affecting libraries. Recently, ALA prepared a 90 page rebuttal to the U.S. Office of Personnel Management's (OPM) study of Federal librarianship. This OPM report suggested a uniform downgrading of professional requirements of librarians working for the Federal government. ALA's Intellectual Freedom Committee finds its anti-censorship campaigns in ever increasing demand. In the Spring of 1982, Paul Simon (D-Illinois) held hearings around the country for his House Education Sub-Committee on the pros and cons of re-funding the Library Services and Construction Act. ALA and many state library associations, including the California Library Association, were in touch with Simon to make sure that informed library advocates were on hand at each site to make an impassioned plea for continued funding of LSCA.[17]

The California Library Association (CLA) established its own political action group, the Government Relations Committee, several years ago. This committee publicizes bill hearing dates (e.g., funding, censorship, etc.), target legislators for mail and telephone calls, and so forth. In February of 1979, CLA hired contract lobbyist Michael Dillon. This respected advocate worked closely with former Senator John Dunlap and his successor, Sen. Jim Nielsen, in promoting the first-ever State per capita funding bill for public libraries, SB 358. The bill, in a previous incarnation as SB 958, passed both houses of the Legislature overwhelmingly, only to have Governor Brown veto it. In the Fall of 1982, Governor Brown signed SB 358, authorizing a $23 million Public Library Fund. The Public Library Fund received an appropriation level of $6 million (about 25% of full funding) for FY 1983–84. This Bill would never have been successful without the inspired and consistent leadership of CLA, the talents of Michael Dillon, and a never-ending barrage of input by library supporters to their legislators and to the Governor.

In the Spring of 1982, ALA and CLA sponsored legislative days in Washington, D.C., and in Sacramento. Hundreds of librarians and library supporters traveled to these cities to lobby their hometown legislators in person. They were given orientations, pep-talks, and turned loose in the august hallways to lobby for libraries. All subsequent reports on these efforts indicated success. However, the message from legislators themselves was symbolized by the remarks of the keynote speaker to these library advocates, Assemblyman John Vasconcellos, Chairman of the Way & Means Committee. He emphasized, in strong terms, that legislators needed to hear the library message not so much from librarians, but from citizens-at-large who support libraries.[18]

As noted earlier, California public libraries do not generally have a library board (interested, influential citizens who act as administrators and advocates for their library district). Whether fiscally empowered, or simply advisory, these boards have political weight. The closest analogue to this kind of board is the Citizens' Advisory Board attached to each of the 15 cooperative library systems around the State. The Boards were established by the California Library Services Act of 1977. Local Friends of the Library groups have usually supplied the member from each county that sits on this Board. What is innovative about these Boards? Involvement. They are made up of influential, library-committed citizens. The mechanism of the Boards means that library users participate in regional library planning. The board members become informed advocates for library issues at the county, regional, and statewide levels. This idea dovetails nicely with one of the prime purposes of *California Libraries in the 80s:* to involve, as never before, the citizen/user in library planning and operation.[19]

Local Friends of the Library groups have been only marginally active in the political arena. Before the recent financial crises, Friends usually concentrated on book sales, author's nights, and so on . . . only occasionally feeling the need to pack the Supervisors' or Councils' chambers at budget time. Since 1978, this political awareness has increased. The statewide Friends group, Friends of California Libraries, is flexing its political muscles. Where a librarian's pleas might seem self-serving to government officials, a library Friend's arguments are taken seriously.

> As a citizen group, the Friends can play a major role in presenting the library's financial needs to the appropriate body or to the voters when the library is on the ballot.[20]

The California State Library is perhaps the single most important actor in the political drama in the state. The State Library's role duplicates that of the Library of Congress in the sense that it is the support library for the Legislature. But it is much more than that. The State Library disburses millions of dollars of the Library Services & Construction Act (LSCA) funds to California libraries for demonstration projects in the areas of cooperation, consolidation, and better serving the under-served. These dollars translate into political power and policy direction.

A draft Mission Statement for the State Library lists, under Goal C: Library Development, Objective #1: "To continue a leadership role in development and maintenance of library services for all Californians, working to overcome geographic, political, economic, and ethnic barriers within the state."[21] State Librarian, Gary Strong, in a telephone interview with the author, made the following points: The State Library has not always been active in the political arena . . . the changes have come since 1956, with the passage of the Library Services Act, and especially since 1977, with the passage of the California Library Services Act (CLSA). Since the State contributes, on average, only about 5% of local library budgets, it is difficult for the State Library to exert powerful leadership. Additionally, recognition of the State Library as an integral part of State government makes it difficult to lobby the Legislature. According to Strong, the Library must concentrate more on coalition building and in helping the relations between the Legislature and these coalitions to become more sophisticated.[22]

The California State Library played a pivotal role in sponsoring the local town meetings, regional and state conferences leading up to the White House Conference on Libraries and Information Science in the Fall of 1979. The State Library was instrumental in helping that process to be a success, and continues to be active in helping to keep White House Conference resolutions alive, among whose goals were passage of a National Library and Information Services Act.[23]

The State Library, CLA, and the California Library Authority for Systems and Services (CLASS) among others initiated a steering committee to develop a master plan for all California libraries. Nothing like it had ever been done before. *California Libraries in the 80s: Strategies for Service* has several purposes, among which political strength is explicit. The Plan seeks to improve library service to both users and non-users. This is the most important task. But, there is more: the Plan seeks to have libraries and the library support community speak with one powerful and integrated voice: to the user, to each other, and to government bodies.

> Each library will set up a program to educate people, including decision-makers, about the role and operation of libraries. . .[24]

> Each library, as appropriate, will regularly provide its elected state and Federal legislators with information about its accomplishments in meeting the needs of its community and about its needs for support.[25]

> The California State Library and the coalition (of professional library associations) will use information gained from surveying needs of the community to propose legislation to provide improved support for services and resources.[26]

The Plan stresses that the business as usual ideas of yesteryear are no longer adequate. Parts of this Plan—consolidation and mutual support—have been at work for years in the idea of regional, cooperative library systems.

Regional, cooperative library systems developed in California in the late 1960s. Receiving most of their funding from the State (about 70–30 State and Federal aid, respectively), these systems enable what is basically a locally operated and funded service to cooperate regionally.[27] The main areas of cooperation are in resource sharing and provision of sophisticated reference services. Via system newsletters, system members receive political information of importance to all California libraries. The system councils also work closely with the system advisory boards, as mentioned earlier. Finally, we need to discuss political activities at the source: federal, state and local governments.

The Federal government has always had a minor, but strategically important role in funding California public libraries. Through LSCA, the Feds have supplied less than 1% of local public library budgets. However, this small portion has been wisely invested in library innovation by the State Library. What may have been the most significant Federal action relating to California public libraries in recent years was the White House Conference on Libraries and Information Science. The process was overseen by a National Commission on Library and Information Science. The Conference prepared a document to be presented to the Congress and to the President for implementation. President Reagan's attitude toward the work of this Commission is intriguing. Inasmuch as most experts agree that our citizenry's information needs are more critical than ever, the President proposed zero funding for the Commission, for the 1983–1984 fiscal year, contradicting the spirit of a statement he made twenty years earlier: "government has laid its hand on health, housing, industry . . . education, and to an ever increasing degree interferes with the people's right to know."[28]

Few people would argue that the White House Conference process has set a precedent. Pursuant to Federal statute, each delegate above the regional conference level must be chosen in the following ratio: two library users to each librarian. This key requirement forced into the library planning process hundreds of concerned library users across the nation. California, alone, had several hundred of these delegates at its state-level conference. Most of them, of course, did not get to go to Washington, D.C., but for the first time ever, they participated. Librarians, who in the past had often been protective of their own domains like any other bureaucrat, now listened eagerly as users talked about their perceptions of California library service. These same delegates still form a potential cadre of library activists. These people are not forgotten; they are counted upon. Delia Martinez, chairperson of the White House Conference Task Force, makes the following assertion:

> Let me assure you that the WHCLIST members, and the more than 100,000 participants in the State and territorial conferences and the national White House Conference are not going to let libraries disappear. We are going to pursue the adequate support of the people's institution—our nation's libraries.[29]

Before 1977, the State of California (exclusive of the State Library) was little involved in intra-state library activities. The California Library Services Act of 1977 initiated funds for cooperative library activities and made it state policy that:

> The Legislature finds and declares that it is in the interest of the people of the State to insure that all people have free and convenient access to all library resources and services that might enrich their lives, regardless of where they live or of the tax base of their own government.[30]

While this Act provided for library cooperation, it provided no direct State aid for day-to-day maintenance of public libraries. After Proposition 13, public libraries in California began to receive about 12% of their budgets in State dollars, via State bail-out monies to local governments.[31] As mentioned earlier, direct state aid was formalized, beginning July 1, 1983, via SB 358. The tax revolt sent funding for California's 168 public libraries plummeting. Whether local officials are library supporters or not, they work with a municipal or county budget which is about 75 to 80% mandated. In the discretionary areas, cutting libraries has usually produced minimal political flak.

In June of 1982, Mayor Dianne Feinstein hoped to shut down several branches of the San Francisco Public Library. Massive protests from the neighborhoods affected miraculously produced funds ($270,000) to be used to keep those branches open. Mayor Feinstein, in her words, was "overwhelmed" by the outpouring of support for libraries.[32] This kind of activity can be repeated in each and every California library community. The San Francisco example demonstrates that library fortunes can be improved by politicizing, by using the system. Special techniques need to be used, and library supporters must understand what can be done, and how to do it, at the different levels of government.

Political Action: A Plan

The situation appears bleak: cut-backs, retrenchment, confusion and gloom. Nonetheless, within the crisis, there are seeds of hope. Delineated below is a brief sketch of how libraries might be turned around using the political system itself.

Public librarians and library supporters must study the political machine in California in order to learn how its energies may be directed toward the library cause. Some of the issues in need of scrutiny are: philosophical underpinnings of policy-making (distribution of social equity); campaign techniques (especially tax override proposals); potential political allies; the unique character of state and local government in California, and so on.

One of the most interesting claims often made by librarians is that U.S. citizens have a "right to information", and that this right is integral to the proper functioning of our democracy. This idea is made clear in the following quote:

> Free access to ideas and information, a prerequisite to the existence of a responsible citizenship, is as fundamental to America as are the principles of freedom, equality, and individual rights. This access is also fundamental to our social, political, and cultural systems.[33]

Fortunately, this idea supports the current thinking about social equity in the provision of services by public agencies. Librarians can take note that:

> The last decade is rich in examples of political events and policy disputes which have revived interest in the public value of equity. . . . Who gets what? Who benefits? Who pays? These questions are the essence of practical politics.[34]

Viewed in the light of California's Serrano-Priest decision, receiving information and materials from a public library could be construed as a service that, if provided insufficiently or not at all, is of such public significance that the disparity implies some kind of stigma, deprivation, or harm.[35] Libraries need, as noted earlier, a strong mix of intergovernmental support:

> Equity in the sense of offsetting imbalances between service needs and revenue capacity frequently constitutes the basis for intergovernmental fiscal relations.[36]

This expert also suggests that the thinking in public administration began to move, in the 1960s, beyond the narrow idea of productivity and efficiency to include ideas of equitable service provision as well. For libraries which traditionally "produce" a non-marketable, non-quantifiable matrix of services, this augurs well:

> In the late sixties, Frederickson, as an advocate of the new public administration, extolled the norm of social equity as an ethical precept for public servants; thus, he challenged the traditional values of efficiency and neutral competency.[37]

In the post-Proposition 13 world, proper political campaign techniques loom as the *quid pro quo* of success at the ballot box. A tax override campaign has special requirements: "a central philosophy behind the campaign: ignore the no-votes; get the yes-votes to the polls."[38] According to experts on the California Library Association's Government Relations Committee, yes-votes, on any issue, are more difficult to get than no-votes. . . and, in the course of the campaign, tend to become no's. Public opinion polls, therefore, should be taken before, during, and near the end of the public relations effort.[39] A tax override after Proposition 13 requires a 2/3d's vote of the people and, successful or not:

Overrides may provide instruction in politics and campaigning, and they may very well be a realistic test of librarians' public relations efforts.[40]

Michael Dillon, CLA's professional contract advocate, made the following points in a personal communication with this author:

1. The techniques of legislative advocacy for public versus private clients do not, generally, differ. Public agencies are at a disadvantage in that they usually do not make campaign contributions. This can be offset by larger numbers of constituents generating influence through letters, telegrams, etc.
2. Legislators need, more than anything, pertinent and reliable data relating to subject areas of legislation. Legislative advocacy involves supplying this to both friendly and unfriendly legislators, as both are needed to obtain the necessary majority of votes.
3. At this point, an alliance with powerful education lobbies would be counter-productive . . . the power structure of education is becoming more closely tied to the State, while libraries remain, so far, under exclusive local control. Also, education lobbies sometimes see library lobbies as going after portions of "their" money.
4. Master Plans—as in *California Libraries in the 80s*—do not generally have much political potential.
5. Librarians and library supporters have made significant progress in the political arena . . . especially since 1979. The single most important strategy is for librarians and library supporters to get to know legislators on a first name basis. Legislators like to be able to refer to their librarian as a friend, as a resource person. Legislators are always appreciative of new ideas, especially if they make the legislator look good. . . . One strategy is to make legislators honorary Friends of the Library.[41]

At the local level, public administrators in libraries must immerse themselves in the techniques of public relations and outreach. The public library needs allies in its struggle. Influential people in each community must become library supporters. Average citizens can become supporters by being asked for their opinions about library service . . . by being asked to participate in and to validate their local library's activities.

Granted, beyond a vague and mellow feeling about their local library, most people won't respond actively, and this caveat is an important one. The benign and mild opinion many have for libraries may not be politically potent:

this opinion comes very close to being politically irrelevant—and most politicians know that to be the case because the opinion is formed on virtually no information,

reflects human sympathy rather than policy assessment of any kind, and is of so low
an intensity that no political action would be expected to come of it.[42]

Robert Eyestone, the author of the above thoughts, has further advice
on how to turn benign support into active advocacy. He believes that
political action is most likely to have success if an issue's supporters: (1)
maintain modest expectations of governmental effectiveness and political
activism; (2) keep the battle goals incremental and do-able.[43] If a politician
can be made to see that a social wrong may be righted by his or her action,
then such issue campaigns may have success if the supporters have done
their "homework", for "a politician's main interest is to find a problem
for which there is a solution ready to hand."[44]

Those who will commit to active support will do so wholeheartedly.
Studies have shown that the typical public library patron is a middle-class,
well-educated person . . . most likely active in the community and in service groups.[45,46] This kind of library patron is often a power on the local
scene. Public librarians must form links of service and friendship with
other local groups. Local government is especially susceptible to this kind
of activity. Will Manley claims that:

> It's extremely hard to resist pressure when those applying it include your next-door
> neighbor . . . and a lot of people whom you see and work with every day. That is
> why, when there are difficult decisions to make, nine out of ten times, councillors
> or board members will vote in favor of the interest group that has applied the most
> pressure. The hardest thing to do in the world is to vote against the wishes of a large
> group of concerned citizens who are looking you right in the eye as you cast your
> yea or nay.[47]

It is important, too, for the public library to project itself as something
more concrete and appetizing than, "Think of all those books!, or "Libraries are just good for you!" How about, "Where is your kid going to
study on Saturdays if the library's closed?", or, "Cost you $75 to have
your car tuned-up, huh? You could have used an automotive manual at
the library for free!" Libraries provide services that serve gut level needs,
and people must be nudged into recognizing it. Public relations is a vital
component of any political activity:

> All public institutions have some form of public relations, whether they recognize it
> or not . . . libraries as institutions must make sure the desires and aspirations of the
> community permeate the library's decisions, and librarians must intensify their efforts
> to demonstrate to all citizens the basic human needs they can help meet, and convince
> that large body of non-users that libraries can become an important element of their
> 'survival kit' in an increasingly complex society. Being in tune with society will be
> a matter of survival, since today's users become tomorrow's legislators.[48]

One of the tools in a public relations effort, among many others, is library statistics . . . hard facts that enable the funding authorities to assess the specifics of library operation.

In the never-ending battle for obtaining funding as adequate as possible to community needs for library and information services and for justifying the library's budget requests to funding authorities, the absolutely necessary weapons are the statistics of library use.[49]

A problem with this approach is that many libraries with reduced budgets and hours of service show declining statistics of books bought and circulated, and patrons served.

Additionally, the unique characteristics of California politics require special techniques. Political "troops" in the library support "army" must come exclusively from the ranks of the average citizen, and not necessarily from political parties or machines. Why? California politics are so clean as to be almost emasculated in the sense of political party vitality, thanks to the Progressive movement of 70 years ago:

In many eastern seaboard states . . . party organizations tended to be comprised of state and local government employees whose jobs depended upon their party's staying in power. Progressives promoted the concept of civil service reform. This meant that the traditional work force of eastern party organizations, government employees, was virtually absent from California political parties.[50]

Often, rather than approaching the individual legislator or voter, library supporters may have to work through, and enlist the aid of professional public relations firms:

The weak party structure, the size of the State, the concomitant need to use mass media to reach voters . . . were factors that encouraged the development of professional public relations firms in California campaigns.[51]

People must be reached by the library message in their heart, stomach, pocket-books . . . not just their brains. Ralph Nader, super-guru of public interest groups has this to say about consumer-oriented causes:

I'll tell you what the real problem is. We ask people to think, instead of asking them to believe. And history has always gone to those who ask people to believe.[52]

Politicians want to stay in office, to keep right on legislating. Not only will they listen to those groups which they perceive as potentially helpful or harmful to them, but the tax revolt and Watergate have had another spin-off. Ed Salzman, an astute observer of California politics, says that: "The prevailing view is that a politician can only survive by following the public, not by leading it."[53]

Beset with hard times, people are flocking to libraries and to schools in record numbers. Let the politicos see that the tide of common feeling is shifting toward, not away from strengthened libraries. Hotlines and library newsletters can stream toward library troops when bills are pending that affect libraries. Library associations and support groups must link with labor, education, and senior-citizens' groups to broker their power together where appropriate. The support must be strong in the "policy" committees of the legislature and of Congress . . . it must be vociferous and overwhelming in the "money" committees. Executives like the Governor and the President must feel that their state or nationwide constituency gives strong libraries high priority. These same library support groups and associations must establish political action committees . . . using computerized mass mailings so that nickels and dimes flow by the truckload into library issue campaigns, and into the war chests of friendly legislators.

Conclusions

Public libraries in California have a legal right to exist. They received, in the past, benign support from users and non-users, alike. The actual fiscal support flowing to public libraries has been tiny in relation to other budget sectors of local government. This small portion of support has, since 1978, been substantially eroded. There has been an increase in funding to public libraries from non-local sources (state and federal governments), but even these are under attack by recession and Reaganomics. Public libraries, as are other agencies of local government, are being reevaluated by the tax payers, and are losing some of their traditional support.

Political action is proposed as a partial solution to this dilemma. Participants in this action must include the people and groups who interact in the public library sphere of operations: librarians and library supporters; professional library groups; library schools; the State Library; local, State, and the Federal governments. Librarians are not trained, traditionally, in politics. They can learn on the job, via association conferences and workshops, or via Public Administration programs. Experts such as Phyllis Dalton and others trace the success or failure of a library administrator directly to their skills in the political process. No longer are librarians and library supporters able to concentrate, politically, on local government to the exclusion of state and federal levels.

Cut-backs create their own built in paradoxes: efficiency, effectiveness and increased production are required by local officials, by tax payers, and by the library profession. Yet, because there are no tangible pay-offs, retrenchment tends to work against such activities.

Politics and administration are inseparable halves of the administrative whole. They both require distinct methods and orientations. Social equity, in the policy half, can be a powerful influence on decisions . . . though the idea, with its liberal connotations, is temporarily out of vogue.

Librarians and library supporters are becoming politicized. The California State Library, the Master Plan, the White House Conference . . . and, perhaps most of all, Proposition 13, have been important influences in this process. Several other ongoing processes have been pivotal: Focussing on politics as a separate and vital activity for library supporters; the introduction into the fray of libraries of all types together into a team effort. Finally, library supporters have worked to create an image in the mind of the average Californian: that the public library is an irreplaceable link in the chain of lifelong education and information service that holds our society together.

California politics are unique, and require special handling. Good public relations, perhaps supplied by professionals, are essential. Political success is only one objective in meeting the overall goal: enlightened operation and adequate funding for California public libraries.

FINANCE

Introduction

A survey of the literature on public library finance reveals a shrinkage of the role of local government in funding local public libraries. The importance of other sources of money to public libraries has been growing: state and federal governments; gifts and bequests; fund-raising projects; and fees. As other agencies and groups have an increasing role in funding public libraries, questions of accountability and influence are raised. As will be discussed later in this chapter, different mixes of funding can affect both the mission and the policies of a public library. The basic character of service provision is affected, as well.

How public libraries are and continue to be financed in California is of obvious importance to their survival and continued viability. This chapter will discuss how libraries both within California and around the country are dealing with the issue of finance. The discussion will focus on three levels of funding: local, state, and federal. Conclusions will be drawn as to desirable financial directions for California public libraries. It will be demonstrated that public libraries are funded not from a single source, as was the tradition in past years. Rather, monies from different agencies and jurisdictions swirl into public library budgets in a myriad of patterns, creating a marble cake effect of both funding and of influence.

Public Library Finance: Past and Present

Providing public library service, even while absorbing but a small portion of local budgets, is a big business. Total public library expenditures nationwide for 1978, were $1,467,891,000. Assuming 5% of the country's population was not in a public library service area, this works out to an expenditure of $6.70 per person.[1]

Government support of public libraries began in the second half of the 19th century, as library services came to be provided as a direct item of government budgets. The Boston Public Library was one of the first, founded in 1852 as a department of the city government.[2] Public libraries grew as our nation grew, aided at specific times by special circumstances: Andrew Carnegie, between 1886 and 1919, provided enough money to build over 1,500 library buildings in the United States.[3] In 1956, the federal government intervened through the Library Services Act (renamed in 1964 as the Library Services and Construction Act). This Act made funds available to build libraries in any area without facilities so that, today, almost 95% of the population lives in areas served by public libraries.[4] Malcolm Getz, in the source just cited, notes the following:

> In many ways, it is useful to think of the institutions providing public library service as an industry, similar to other industries dominated by nonprofit service oriented institutions. . . . On the other hand, of course, the public library industry is different from other service industries. Most public libraries are financed primarily by local property taxes, and make significant services available to all comers without charge.[5]

Many scholars, doing research in a variety of disciplines, have noted with alarm the precariousness of the property tax as a revenue source to local government. William Summers supplies the following quote:

> Unlike many other developed countries around the planet, the United States has not developed a state or a national system of support of public libraries. As a unit of local government, the local public library has been dependent almost exclusively on local tax sources. In large part, this has meant the property tax. A modern library program is costly. At its most evolved stage, an adequately-funded library program is beyond the resources of all but the largest or most affluent communities. This implies that, for most jurisdictions, the property tax is an inadequate funding mechanism for the public library.[6]

Another expert, from the field of municipal finance, Glenn Fisher, claims that there is much evidence that public confidence in government is eroding and that the fiscal crisis in many areas is more political than economic. He notes that the property tax has consistently been voted the least popular tax in opinion polls. Interestingly, he observes that an important advantage of the property tax is that it permits local government to raise a great deal of money and to retain a considerable degree of fiscal independence.[7]

As a consequence of this dependence upon the property tax, "the fiscal health of libraries is a reflection of the fiscal health of local governments."[8] Budget cut-backs in cities around the country, due to tax reduction initiatives and declining property tax bases, have hurt public libraries. A study by the National Commission on Libraries and Information Science revealed that on a nation-wide basis, over 81% of the public library budget came from local revenue sources. This problem is compounded when localities are forced to fund mandated programs, thus leaving them with fewer discretionary funds to meet other important needs.[9] In the same article, Frank Goudy discovered this trend: In FY 1966, local library outlays were .836 of one percent of total direct general expenditures allocated to all government functions. By FY 1980, these figures had slipped to .7 of one percent.[10]

As local funding capability has been reduced to a certain extent, the State and the federal governments have stepped in, as indicated in Table 1.

Thomas Ballard has some interesting thoughts that link public library support with economic prosperity. Following the ideas of William Baumol, a Princeton economist, Ballard suggests that productivity potentials dictate the fortunes of public library support. Namely, the service sector being labor intensive means that productivity increases are much more difficult to develop than in the production sector.[11] With the onset of economic difficulties, public indifference toward public sector spending has grown. Without large productivity gains, there can no longer be a swiftly rising standard of living; non-essential services/expenditures are viewed by the public with increased cynicism. From these economic arguments, and from a study of our change from a producing to a service oriented economy, Ballard concludes that "the problems of public library funding are relatively long term."[12]

Public Library Finance: A Local Perspective

There are many ironies surrounding the current era of retrenchment in public libraries. Among a few are these facts. Of all the governmental levels serving people, the local level may well be the most cost-effective and the one which is most responsive to local concerns. Yet, of all governmental levels, the local level is often the one most constricted and restricted in its possible range of activities and, most importantly, in its tax base possibilities. In California, taxing powers of local government are strictly regulated by the state government. These local fiscal powers were hamstrung even further by the mandates of Proposition 13. At least at the local level, people seem to be demanding that their local mix of services be maintained . . . that the policeman and fireman remain on

Table 1.   Public Library Funding Sources

	1978	1979	1980
Local sources	89%	76%	73%
State sources	n.a.	10%	12%
Federal sources	.06%	.08%	.08%

Source: California State Library. *Survey of California Public Libraries 1978–1980: Before and After Prop. 13.* (Sacramento: The Library, November, 1980), p. 2.

duty, that their streets be repaired, that their library be open evenings and on Saturday. Yet, in many opinion polls, respondents still claim that their taxes are too high, that there is fat yet to be trimmed.

One item of interest that will be discussed further in the fourth chapter (which covers techniques of cut-back management) may be mentioned briefly here. In past years, there has been much interest in the management literature on the value of alternative budgeting schemes. These schemes include: program, performance, and zero-based budgets. This author was intrigued that nowhere in the library literature are these budget types mentioned as being important or as being utilized to improve the effectiveness of budgets as planning and management tools.

One suggestion as to why innovative budgeting schemes have not been successful nor subject to widespread use comes from Laurence Lynn, Jr. Lynn notes that program, performance, and zero-based budgeting (ZBB) systems tend to ignore two crucial factors in the bureaucratic process: many if not most programs are value-loaded and subject to political forces and the quality and quantity of information required. To quote Lynn:

> ZBB required quantum increases in the quality and quantity of information required for decision making, but it made no provisions for the ways that this knowledge was to be generated. [13]
>
> (This procedure) vastly overestimates man's limited ability to calculate and grossly underestimates the importance of political and technological constraints. [14]

Laurence Lynn observes that, in a few select cases, management commitment and perception enabled ZBB and program or performance budget systems to increase information flows and refine overall objectives within a particular agency. These systems broke-down as overall evaluative tools for agency performance. [15] Lynn is of the opinion that, except in special cases, innovative budget systems ignore important political and informational factors and are not part of the solution to improving bureaucratic performance. [16]

The response of public libraries to hard times in this country has taken both reactive and proactive directions. A few interesting examples of both types of activities will be listed.

An article entitled "Library Funding" in the January 15, 1983 issue of *Library Journal* attempts to provide an overview and a prediction for library funding nationwide. Kansas libraries were better off in 1982 due to statewide property valuation increases. The San Francisco Public Library, following a study by Lowell Martin, attempted to reorganize its branches and the resultant public outcry helped to win generous new funding. Prosperous Houston allotted its library a 34% budget boost. Voters ordered library increases or continued support in Ohio, Oklahoma, Florida, and Alabama.[17] In Shirley, New York:

> The Amway organization, which is known for arch conservatism and opposition to government spending . . . urged the many and far-flung members of its sales organization to give their support and their votes to public libraries seeking funding.[18]

The other side of the library coin reveals a more sobering message: New York's Buffalo and Erie County Library lost 40 staff members. The Paterson, New Jersey Library and its seven branches were closed at year's end for over two weeks due to lack of funds. The Seattle Public Library's restricted budget forced it to turn away as many as 1,300 reference telephone calls a day.[19] Of 11 members of the North State Cooperative Library System in California polled in early 1983, only three were open to the public on Saturdays. Before Proposition 13, all were open.[20] Public libraries are simultaneously trying to cut expenses and to raise revenues. Some techniques currently being tried by public libraries to reduce expenses and/or increase productivity include the following: better administration; resource sharing; automating library procedures; using volunteers, part-timers, and substitutes; and energy conservation measures.[21]

Fundraising by public libraries in the past year has been carried out in both traditional and bizarre veins: some libraries have institutionalized the annual book sale by establishing their own book stores for library discards, gifts, and other wares.[22]

Other semi-traditional yet innovative techniques appear in an article in the *Unabashed Librarian*. The Salt Lake County Library System recently appointed a professional fund raiser—reclassifying an existing staff member for these duties. He plans to look for larger numbers of dollars from fewer people, utilizing marketing research, and a multi-media presentation. The Arlington Heights, Illinois, library has increased fines to 20 cents per day. The Cleveland, Ohio, Public Library stopped sending overdue notices altogether, and continued to receive the same amount of overdue revenues over a six month trial period.[23]

The Harrodsburg, Kentucky library (Mercer County Public) recently sponsored a basketball game between a library team and a local merchants team, utilizing celebrities from the much admired basketball team from the University of Kentucky in the fund raising efforts. The game netted over $2,000 in donations.[24]

Other fund raising events by public libraries cover the gamut of possibilities: a celebrity book auction; a celebrity shoe auction; a belly dancing competition; chain letters, a pennies-from-heaven project (whereby local banks matched and donated to the library all pennies turned in to them).[25]

Three other important ideas that deserve attention in library finance are: foundation grants, marketing techniques, and public relations. Librarian Donna Dunlop is employed by the Foundation Center in New York City. The Center was incorporated in 1956 and is a national clearinghouse on information for grants. She quotes Nelson Rosenbaum, president of the Center for Responsive Governance, as speculating that in response to governmental retrenchment and current economic conditions, non-profit organizations would be subject to a ten to fifteen percent death rate. Dunlop further notes that private foundations give, yearly, approximately $2.8 billion, with libraries historically attracting less than 3% of that figure.[26]

Adapting private sector marketing techniques to library service provision can also turn budget downswings around. According to Daniel Carroll:

> Budget crises, as we all recognize, are not relieved by comparing income to expenses and blaming marketing. Rather, shortfalls are relieved by developing new or improved services that in turn generate greater user activity. This activity, if encouraged and sustained, will invariably beget the financial support that makes for successful libraries.[27]

An extensive study by Patricia Berger supported the idea that public relations efforts correlated positively to higher budget allocations. The key elements of such a program, according to her findings, were: having a part or full-time specialist in public relations on the staff; and careful groundwork that would include research, planning, and evaluation.[28]

Some libraries have adopted fees for services to combat declining revenues. Though most public libraries have long used some types of fees— for example charging for photo-copies, lost library cards, overdue books— two examples of recent trends are illuminating. In 1981, the Denver Public Library suffered massive cuts in its budget. Studies of patron demographics showed that many of the Denver PL's users came from outside of the city. The library decided to impose steep nonresident fees ($10 for a daily pass, $100 for an individual yearly pass, $200 for a family card, $350 for a corporate card).[29] The imposition of fees caused ripples of concern far beyond the environs of Denver. According to John Berry, Editor of *Library Journal*, the decision forced both citizens and politicians in neighboring jurisdictions and at the state level to assess the importance of library service.[30] After months of the fee system, a unique, short-term solution was worked out: a complex plan whereby neighboring counties and the State of Colorado would appropriate funds to allow the DPL to reopen statewide reference services, and allow reciprocal borrowing to citizens from neighboring metropolitan counties.[31]

The Huntington Beach, California Library has been experimenting with a fee system since 1981. The library and its Director answer to the Director of the Community Services Department. Vincent Morehouse, the Community Services Director, had reduced costs in the city's harbor and beaches department by transferring costs of maintaining the public beaches from the taxpayers to the users. The city council asked him to do something similar with the library system.[32] Morehouse, who was likened to Attila the Hun by librarians who knew his reputation, saw his challenge as "how can this city maintain and provide a first-class level of service for the citizens at a reasonable cost?" Morehouse explained that his purpose was to make the library reasonably self-supporting. In 1983, Morehouse expected the library to earn about $245,000 or about 11% of its $2.1 million annual budget.[33] Morehouse believes that anything beyond basic services should be paid for by the user. What he considers basic may be subject to interpretation. For example, the library attempted to charge admission to children for library story hour. After public reaction, the story hour remains free.[34] Another of Morehouse's ideas is to have the library's ninety thousand patrons charged a $10 deposit for library cards. Critics claim that this idea would make it that much harder for the city's poor to use the library. Morehouse responds:

> We're not saying you have to have a library card to use the facilities. I'm sure you could devise a system that allows a person to be investigated. If he really, truly qualifies, fine . . . but, "there's no free lunch".[35]

Other experts in public finance, both within and without the library field, support the concept of expanded use of fees for tax-supported, public services. Malcolm Getz claims that: "Most public libraries can make more aggressive use of fees to improve the quality of services."[36] Scholars in municipal finance propose that: "cities must seek the lowest, safe, and just levels of services" and, "further, that governments and their subunits must identify core services and offer the public a choice on whether they want to pay extra for peripheral services."[37]

Since we have noted earlier that most libraries have always charged a fee for certain activities, the key question becomes: if a fee is charged, how should it be done so that the fee be not inimical to the public library's stated purpose of egalitarian service? Nancy Van House, in her book on public library user fees, makes some interesting observations: Time allocation theory proposes that all library users have an economic or sociological value to their time. Further, this cost affects how and when they use the library. The existence, lack of, and nature of fees have a direct bearing on the time it takes to exploit a library's resources and consequently affects whether people choose to use the library or not.[38] Van House, while not necessarily recommending that all public libraries initiate fees, makes the following points: Imposing or rejecting the idea of library fees is a major policy decision that must be based on a variety of considerations.[39] Critics of public library user fees have concentrated on the inhibiting effects of fees on use, while ignoring the correlary situation: exclusively free service inhibits the depth and range of library service as well.[40] Finally, fees are not advisable for basic and traditional library service; fees can be justified for services that are innovative and that reduce the time-cost of the potential user.[41]

Library finance and political activity by librarians and library supporters are very much related. Will Manley comments that public libraries will be able to obtain more favorable climates for their budgets if they integrate their activities with those of local government. He recommends at least two courses of action. First, public library directors should attend and participate in municipal and county conferences.[42] Second, where appropriate, public libraries should establish branches specifically designed to serve as local government information centers . . . possibly even locating them in city halls or county court houses.[43]

One avenue always open to librarians desiring improved funding is the tax initiative. Since 1978, the author is aware of only one successful tax initiative in California: the struggle of the Berkeley Public Library to raise a local library tax levy. Such initiatives require approval of the voters by a two-thirds margin. Other realities, according to the California Library Association's Government Relations Committee, make the concept even more tricky: It is difficult to get a two-thirds consensus on any issue, regardless of content. A "yes" vote is much more difficult to get than a "no" vote. Voters do not seem to prefer single-service tax increases.[44] Perhaps the answer lies in promoting coalition style tax elections, in conjunction with other local service agencies—education, police, fire, etc.

Public Library Finance: A State Perspective

As noted earlier in this paper, the role of the State in funding California public libraries is increasing. The increasing State presence in local public library finance brings with it new ramifications, some of which will be discussed below. Statewide, counties receive 34% of their support from the state, sustaining, in part, the two out of three county dollars spent on state-mandated programs in public assistance and public protection.[45] As noted earlier, in 1980, the State provided 12% of public library budgets.

Nationwide, public library budgets and state aid to public libraries are not improving. Twenty states and one territory passed legislation in 1981 providing fiscal increases either for public libraries or for state library agencies. In 1982, this figure slipped to 19 states.[46] In California, the Legislative Analyst's Office has recommended drastic changes in the California Library Services Act (CLSA), and in the way the Library Services and Construction Act (LSCA) is used to fund cooperative library systems.[47]

Some good news, perhaps, for public libraries is the establishment of a partnership between Governor Deukmejian and local governments—represented by groups such as the County Supervisors' Association and the League of Cities. The "New Partnership Task Force on State and Local Government" hopes to provide local government with, among other things, a stable source of funding and a reduced number of unfunded state mandates.[48]

The main source of state activity in helping to finance California public library activity is through the California Library Services Act. CLSA was signed by Governor Brown in October 1977, at a level of $5,300,000. The funds are administered by a 13 member board, appointed by the Governor. The provisions of the Act allow for state monies to be spent in five major areas: direct loan and interlibrary loan; development of a statewide library data base; communications and delivery; reference services; and the maintenance of system-level advisory boards.[49] A very important role of the Act is to subsidize the sharing of resources among all California libraries. In 1980/81, over nine million items were loaned under the provisions of the Act. Ironically, the very popularity of the Act has led to a short-fall in Act monies. State Librarian Gary Strong comments, "If we do not find some remedy to this funding situation, we will very likely see libraries close their resources to those outside the local taxing jurisdictions."[50]

One of the driving forces in California librarianship in recent years has been the desire to provide library users with a uniform fabric of service, regardless of where they live. Following this line of reasoning, any user's library is bound to provide a limited matrix of services. Cooperative library systems began to develop in California in the late 1960s. The goal underlying this process was to provide a coordinating agency for inter-library cooperation.

As can be seen from Table 2, in the example of the FY 1982 budget for the North State Cooperative Library System, most of the System activities closely follow the provisions of CLSA. The FY 1982 NSCLS budget is supported in large part by state (CLSA) monies (69%); the remaining 31% derives from federal (LSCA) monies.[51]

Table 2. NSCLS Funding Sources, 1982

Program or Project	1981–82 Budget	% of Total	Explanation
S. L. A. P.	$ 3,565	(0.9)	Funded through CLSA Program for SLAP equipment purchase
Reference:	63,882	(15.4)	Funded by a CLSA Allocation
Delivery and Communication	94,673	(22.9)	Funded by a CLSA Allocation
System Advisory Board:	9,452	(2.3)	Funded by a CLSA Allocation
Inter-Library Loan Program	114,195	(27.5)	Funded by CLSA Reimbursements pooled by Member Libraries and System Information Centers for print and nonprint resource sharing
System Administration: California	67,095	(16.2)	Funded through LSCA because this component of Calif. Library Services Act was not funded.
Tri-System Delivery and Access Network:	45,300	(10.9)	Funded by an LSCA Grant to promote interlibrary cooperation and resource sharing.
System Level Access Project:	11,600	(2.8)	Funded through an LSCA Grant to enable System to compare and experiment with OCLC and RLIN
Statewide Finding List Proj.:	4,467	(1.1)	Funded through LSCA to promote resource sharing through a microfiche catalog of materials entered into a statewide data base of mono-graphs

Source: NSCLS Coordinator

The rationale underpinning the development and functions of California cooperative library systems has been that local public libraries either could not or would not—without state and federal incentives provided through these systems—cooperate to the benefit of their patrons.

A theory exists that if public libraries in California all evolve efficiently to the point where they are willing and able to share resources and information among themselves, the need for systems will disappear. Meanwhile, these sharing activities—as funded by the state and national governments—are very much influenced by fiscal and policy changes far from the local power base of public libraries.

Fiscal experts are now examining possible ways for local governments to continue to provide needed services in all service areas. Malcolm Getz notes that public library service is quite often subject to a "spillover" effect—that is, spillover occurs when services are used by persons other than local taxpayers.[52] Indeed, spillover is one of the purposes behind state and federal funding of cooperative library activities. Getz suggests that one approach to dealing with spillovers is to tie intergovernmental transfers to the level of spillovers.[53]

Getz goes on record as preferring the property tax as a stable source of public library funding, as one which allows the maximum degree of local voter accountability. He claims that the very existence of permanent, dependable, programmatic aid from the state may stifle incentives for change and responsiveness.[54] The evidence in California, at least in the form of CLSA monies, may not support this claim. Shifts in the mix of sources for local public library funds reflect in microcosm the new political trends of funding and power in the macrocosm. Mel Hing observes that:

> Something has to give. It could signal the beginning of the end for California's almost unique non-partisan form of local government. Or it could be the beginning of a new era of cooperation, rather than rivalry, between state government and the counties . . .[55]

Hing suggests that voters have "ordered elimination of the traditional means of dealing with money problems . . . (that) the time has come for a genuine cooperative relationship to replace the traditional adversary bickering".[56] Hing provides a travelogue of three possible paths for this relationship: greater control by the state of local government expenditures, with the Legislature annually setting guidelines or specific amounts for virtually all local expenditures; or, allowing crises to establish the allocation process, which is the trend since 1978; or, finally, a path of increased freedom, leading to reduced mandates, elimination of earmarked funds, and creation of revenues for local government on a continuing and stable basis.[57]

This author does not pretend to be able to look into the future. The present, however, indicates that public library service is now depending upon an increasing state role in local library budgets. At whatever level this role continues, state policy will intrude to that degree into local libraries.

Public Library Finance: A Federal Perspective

As noted earlier in this paper, the Federal role in funding public libraries began with the passage of the Library Services Act in 1956. Table 1 of this paper shows that the Federal role in local public library funding has been small, less than 1% of California public library budgets. The ways LSCA monies have helped public libraries have been important to a degree belying their small percentage of the total, as noted under Politics.

A review of the current literature on federal policy towards involvement in sub-national affairs reveals some interesting changes. The era of "new federalism" in which the federal government sought to intervene directly in state, regional, and local affairs may be past. The "new, new federalism" of the Reagan Administration could be described as a hands-off stance; a trend of fewer federal dollars going to sub-national units, while giving these units more discretion on how to spend the revenue. The position of President Reagan was to get the federal government out of educational policy and move the responsibilities back to state and local government "where it belongs".[58] So far, Congress has rejected this zero-funding approach.[59] In California, LSCA funds in the amount of several millions annually are distributed to the State's public and institutional libraries in the form of project awards, approved by the State Librarian with advice from the California State Advisory Council on Libraries. In order to receive LSCA grant funds, the project must address one or more of the following priorities:

1. Inadequate services;
2. Low income persons;
3. State institutions;
4. Physically handicapped;
5. Regional resource centers;
6. Interlibrary cooperation;
7. Services for older persons;
8. Limited English speaking.[60]

In FY 1981, the California State Library granted $4,529,077 to 33 individual projects and five multiple project awards under LSCA.[61] State Librarian Gary Strong noted in his FY 1981 annual report on LSCA:

> We must keep in mind that it is the citizen that benefits from these funds, not the institutions and agencies that administer the programs. Reauthorization of LSCA and continued funding is vital . . . for several reasons: helping public libraries respond to the changing information flow in our society, further establishing and improving services to minorities and the disadvantaged, and facilitation of resource sharing.[62]

Malcolm Getz, believes that federal help and leadership in local public library funding are important, but that the help itself is laden with pitfalls.

> Such grants are unlikely to be a way out . . . state and federal governments have even more difficulty in identifying the real social value of a service than local officials. Therefore, the band of discretionary authority is likely to be even greater than with local government . . . intergovernmental transfers cannot differentiate aid according to the local situation.[63]

A case in point on this item is the recent re-funding of LSCA Title II, for the first time since 1973. The Emergency Jobs Bill, HR 1718, pumped some $50 million into LSCA II, to create jobs in areas suffering from high levels of unemployment, and to build onto or renovate public libraries in need of such projects.[64] This author is the director of a county public library badly in need of expansion, located in an area whose unemployment rate approached 30% at the time HR 1718 passed. Upon investigation, it was revealed that the typical federal matching share of such grants is only 43%.[65] Thus, for a total projected building cost of $300,000, the financially-strapped county would have to provide over $170,000 of its own.

As LSCA is subject to squabbles over its funding each year, experts say that the following key elements in its authorizing legislation will be: (1) the degree to which state and local governments are free to determine how funds are to be spent, and (2) the inclusion or exclusion of maintenance of effort or matching requirements. These same experts believe that if there are no matching requirements, support for educational programs (including libraries) could drop over 50%, as federal dollars are substituted for local money.[66]

Malcolm Getz makes the following observation about public library funding:

> The sharp turns in library budgets hardly reflect sharp shifts in the use, value, or cost of library services. That is, the efficient level of library services does not change so markedly from year to year. Rather, the sharp turns may reflect the small size of libraries relative to total city budgets, the fact that the deterioration of library services does not pose an immediate threat to public health or safety, and the fact that political support for libraries may not coalesce until a crisis is at hand.[67]

Getz does believe a crisis is at hand, and suggests that continued and strengthened federal support is vital, in spite of its pitfalls. Noting the important role of public libraries in sustaining the cultural and scientific needs of American society, he opines that:

> A strong case can be made for federal support of the production of knowledge and culture. Leadership in these activities may not meet market tests, and public action is desirable. . . . A more agressive, sophisticated federal role is very important for the new technologies to meet their potential.[68]

Conclusion

Public libraries in California are an industry. They produce products which continue to be in high demand over the years. However, the customers of such products seem to be less and less willing to pay a fair price to get the products. Public cynicism about government and a changing, declining economy both have initiated a steep, downward spiral in public library funding. Unlike other governmental services, public library service is not protected by the strong shield of mandates of service. The amorphous, benign concern most citizens have for their local public library is scant protection against the knife of budget cuts.

California public libraries have traditionally been funded almost 100% by the local property tax. The roles of state and federal governments have been minor. Libraries have not had to explore alternative or off-beat paths to fund their operations. Since the late 1970s, all this has changed. Some experts believe this change will last a long time.

The property tax, since Proposition 13, is no longer a viable funding source. This tax is very much tied to the fiscal health of local government. As public libraries become more dependent upon intergovernmental transfers, the power and policy base for their operations shifts to Sacramento and Washington, D.C.

California public libraries, as have libraries across the country, have had to cut services and re-evaluate their service mix. Different and new funding mechanisms have been explored.

Some of the techniques tried at the local level have had mixed results. The absence of discussion in the literature of innovative budget techniques gives mute evidence of their value as a planning/policy tool. Attempts to gain money through unique (and often bizarre) fund-raising projects have yet to prove that they can supply an important or long-lasting percentage of day-to-day expenditures. The creation of national or regional foundation-grant clearing-houses may be a boon to public libraries. Application of appropriate marketing and public relations techniques has been shown to be closely related to library budget increases.

Libraries charging fees for basic or peripheral services are now more common than ever before. This issue, almost more than any other, is one that inspires extreme levels of anger and controversy among public librarians. Some public libraries have experienced budget improvements when they have integrated their activities more closely into the local governmental structure. However, local tax initiatives to raise library levies have not yet proven their worth. The unique two-thirds' requirement of Prop. 13 makes any such effort very difficult.

State aid to California public libraries is increasing, via CLSA and the Public Library Fund. As power follows money, so will state influence increase in local library affairs, if state aid increases.

The Federal role through LSCA has provided important monies to California public libraries over the years. The dollars have principally been funneled towards innovative, demonstration projects aimed at promoting increases in service to the underserved or at increases in library cooperation. In the process, libraries have been built where there were none before; improvements in basic public library service have occurred; and institutions across governmental jurisdictions have cooperated which otherwise might never have done so.

The very nature of state and federal aid, however, makes its benefit and future precarious. Much if not most of the aid is programmatic and temporary. Once the worth of a program is or is not demonstrated with these outside dollars, the project is either carried on with local money, or it dies. Secondly, state and federal grant requirements may or may not be a good reflection of local needs. Finally, the levels of state and federal aid are subject to political currents at a great distance from any given local jurisdiction.

Most of the actors involved in the public library funding drama seem to prefer a locally-funded public library. This scheme provides incentive for change and accountability, a strong match with local needs, and a more dependable future for local public library service.

PERSONNEL

Introduction

Public libraries—and, indeed, all public agencies—have been experiencing double trouble of reduced budgets due to tax revolts and a malaise caused by suspicion and mistrust of government in general. Demagogues in and out of government like to claim that if there is a problem, less government will fix it. This attitude lowers morale in the ranks of public employees and also erodes the popular concept of dependable job security as a major characteristic of government employment.

While government service is no longer as attractive or secure, other changes are radically affecting people who work in public libraries and other areas of the public sector. Accountability and productivity are being closely scrutinized. Automation and technology are changing library procedures and jobs in radical and unpredictable ways.

Library managers exploring new ideas in personnel administration are evaluating the efficacy of traditional managerial hierarchies. Separations of personnel into line and staff, professional and clerical, supervisor and subordinate are blurring and evolving into mixtures based upon expertise and competencies rather than on formal job descriptions or educational background. As the computer becomes more ubiquitous, knowledge is available to management as well as rank and file. Experts predict that this universal access to information within the library may cause the traditional pyramidal shape of personnel structure to flatten substantially.

This chapter will not attempt an in-depth study of personnel practices in public libraries. Rather, an attempt will be made to outline some of the problems and possibilities related to producing more effective and efficient library service by working with library employees in enlightened ways. All discussion will be overshadowed by the premise that the present era of retrenchment requires a fresh look at how people lead and should be led in the public library.

Library Personnel Issues: A Statement of the Problem

A study of the literature related to personnel in any field points out the unique importance of people in an organization; no matter what areas are considered related to success of the organization, the level of effectiveness with which people carry out their work is probably the single most critical factor. A manager may be inspiring and dynamic, but if he or she does not have the skills to bring out the best in the employees, then all is for naught.

Lawrence J. White observes that the public library has been viewed by the American people as a cornerstone in the development of our nation:

> That faith is definitely a part of American culture. And yet, there also has been a sense of uneasiness about the functions and role of the public library, a sense of foregone potential of the institution, a sense that it is failing to live up to the expectations that it serve as a major educational and information force in American society.[1]

How a public library responds to this sort of indictment depends upon the reactions of the people that staff it. New methods of leading and being led may be indicated, as described by Barbara Conroy in a recent article on staff development:

> At best, personnel administration is not the most stable or integrated library function. Now, faced with these challenges, it may become even more ambiguous and less effective. Its focus on the human element is vital, acknowledging that element's importance in what will become an increasingly technological world. So, personnel administration will also need to change with the times to stay viable, assuring that needs of people are not submerged by needs of technology.[2]

We noted earlier that as prices rise, and incomes and profits stabilize, people will be looking to organizations to increase their productivity and the effectiveness with which they carry out their tasks. These kinds of gains will probably be more easily effected in areas of the economy able to take advantage of new technologies. Sectors of the economy which are heavily labor intensive, such as libraries, may encounter difficulty: how can library workers become more productive?

Productivity in libraries is a concept affected by a variety of forces: morale, leadership, personnel theories, job security, etc. In an era of retrenchment, much is required of people while their morale, incentives, and job security may be on a downward slide. Morale and motivation are one of the first areas that need to be examined.

At the turn of the century, librarianship was recommended to women who felt a need to escape from the hustle and bustle of daily life to a safe and quiet island of tranquility. Library work, as was much of government service, was perhaps not the most remunerative, but it guaranteed, at the very least, job security. Several different currents are flowing together to change this idea.

California public libraries were among the first agencies in the country to face the uncertain future of reduced public sector job security:

> The significance of the California experiences with mass lay-offs is that public em-
> ployees may have no greater job protection than those in the private sector. While
> private employment is subject to economic cycles, public employment is at the mercy
> of the political climate and the taxpayers' acceptance of ever-increasing taxes. The
> result may very well be an increase in competition for government jobs and uncertainty
> in holding such jobs.[3]

Externally, then, library jobs are less secure than they were. Internal factors are also working to reduce the library workforce, as noted by Lawrence J. White: "The implication . . . is that libraries could probably increase usage by devoting more of their budgets to purchasing materials and devoting less to other things, primarily personnel."[4] Malcolm Getz studied library budgets and labor costs, and concluded:

> If a library chooses to provide as much service value as possible within a given budget,
> it will substitute less expensive for more expensive activities. In particular, those
> libraries that face higher labor costs may be expected to adjust the mix of services
> so as to economize on the use of labor.[5]

The public revolt against government and its effect on libraries is a national trend not limited to California:

> Initiatives and referenda designed to dimish tax collections came before the voters
> in 16 states in the general election of 1978. Tax or spending limits were endorsed by
> the voters in 11 of those 16 states. Such an obvious mood cannot lead public employees
> toward a feeling of confidence or security in their jobs.[6]

Charles H. Levine, in a recent symposium on governmental cut-backs, made these observations about hard times and the public sector:

> The political vulnerability of public organizations is an internal property indicating a
> high level of fragility and precariousness which limits their capacity to resist budget
> decrements and demands to contract from their environment. Organizational atrophy
> is a common phenomenon in all organizations, but government organizations are par-
> ticularly vulnerable. . . .[7]

Levine describes ways in which declining resources can simultaneously be both a cause and a result of internal atrophy and declining performance.[8]

The public library, then, is faced with many changes and new demands: its funding base is being reduced, the public is demanding better performance and accountability, a revolution in technology is looming. It is clear that morale and productivity must be improved.

Library Personnel Issues: Some Suggested Solutions

It is argued in this chapter that enlightened personnel practices are one of the key elements to putting public libraries on a productive track in the current era of cut-back management. Before touching upon some of the different theories of improving personnel practices, such as Management By Objectives (MBO), Organizational Development, and so forth, a more basic look at organizational structure is required.

Thomas G. Spates, a former Vice-President of General Foods, defines personnel administration as:

> organizing and treating individuals at work so that they will get the greatest possible realization of their intrinsic abilities, thus attaining maximum efficiency for themselves and their group, and thereby giving to the enterprise of which they are a part its determining competitive advantage and its optimum results.[9]

The character of personnel administration in any organization is closely linked to the unique structure of that organization. Thus, we first need to ponder how organizations function, and how this affects the people who work in them.

Some experts believe that typical organizational structure, with its traditional hierarchical patterns, is antithetical to client-oriented performance and to employee needs. One of the more radical thinkers, Frederick C. Thayer, maintains that all organizations are dysfunctional. He sees this pathology as arising from hierarchy within the organization and competition among organizations. Further, he believes that conflict and consensus-building can lead to increased efficiency and productivity only if they are free of one person's domination (i.e. "the boss").[10] Another critic of organization is Guy Benveniste, who notes that the biggest stumbling-block to healthy organizational evolution is middle and upper management; they don't want their subordinates giving them advice . . . they don't want a client coming in to tell them how to deliver a service.[11]

John Rizzo proposes, perhaps less radically, that some organizations can be inherently dysfunctional when they emphasize internal control over client needs, which creates goal displacement and drains energy away from objectives.[12] The consensus of these scholars seems to be that pyramidal management structure is obsolete, for reasons of efficiency, effectiveness, and—last but not least—equity to both employees and clients.

Technology is supposedly creating conditions within the modern organization which, of themselves, will require that flatter, more participative organizations will soon be the norm. This trend will become even more salient in times of retrenchment:

> In a dynamic and volatile environment, contingency management creates a flexible, organic form of structure which relies more on expertise and problem orientation rather than on hierarchy or formal role relationships . . . data show that organizations that cling to formalized hierarchy when their environment becomes dynamic do poorly in the marketplace. Those that shift to organic forms tend to prosper.[13]

Flexibility and willingness to adapt to new demands upon the organization are seen as vital. Carlton Rochell, Dean of Libraries at New York University, predicts that:

> in the future, libraries will inevitably choose flatter, more participatory organization to function well in a fast-moving technological environment. Such arrangements are flexible and enable a quick response to change that is virtually impossible in traditional hierarchies.[14]

Laurence E. Lynn, Jr. also believes in the new and organic form of leadership: "The problem of leaders in these complex organizations 'is to create and use multiple centers and multiple styles of leadership' within a general framework of purpose that guides the separate parts."[15] Lynn continues by noting from the "humanist" school of management that the key to improving performance in an organization is not concentrating solely on changing employee behavior, but rather looking at the managerial approach or "style" as the single factor which will most strongly promote or undermine cooperation and effective performance.[16]

The arguments above describe how traditional organizational structures are, due to technological changes and the exigencies of retrenchment, no longer adequately serving their clients or their employees. One of the most important components in this discussion is the question of employee productivity: How can it be improved? What are the variables that affect employee productivity?

Library agencies are basically office environments. Eric Matt Stout claims that: "Office systems are especially underproductive . . . office productivity is creeping up 20 times slower than industrial productivity. The office has stagnated, despite automation."[17] He believes the human factor in productivity—as compared to management and technology—has been sorely neglected.[18] Stout goes on to enumerate a "shopping list" of the theories of the most prominent thinkers on employee motivation and productivity: Abraham Maslow, Rensis Likert, David McGregor, and Chris Argyris. The gist of the arguments of all these theorists is that human needs must be respected in the workplace to maximize productivity. Employees need to be able to identify with organizational goals, work in a safe environment, and feel that their opinions are respected by management.

The humanist orientation, however, can be a deceptive one; a "happy" employee is not necessarily a productive one. Rewarding productive behavior is more important than simply trying to keep the employees happy. Rewards lead to increased performance as well as increased satisfaction. Increased satisfaction does not, necessarily, lead to increased performance.[19] One of the obstructions in the public sector to this scheme is that one of the most typical rewards in the private sector—the *ad hoc* pay raise or the pay bonus—is almost unknown. Warren Bennis notes that enlightened personnel management can suffer in uncertain times:

> In turbulent times, we not only lose consensus over basic values, but disparate views are ridgidly polarized into a myriad fragments and splinters."[20]

Bennis also believes that people—managers and employees—can be brought together: "What I think most people in institutions really want—and what status, money, and power serve as currency for—is affection, acceptance, a belief in their growth, and esteem."[21]

The discussion of personnel administration in this chapter will now shift to a brief examination of some of the most popular management theories discussed in the literature: Organizational Development, Management by Objectives, and Participatory Management. All of these strategies have their positive and negative points, and their relevancies for public libraries in times of stress. Increased productivity and organizational effectiveness may well be tricky goals to achieve, as indicated by this skeptic:

> While there is clearly room for improved management at the local government level, large savings (relative to projected deficits) from increased productivity in the public sector are not a realistic expectation. Service level cuts are the most likely route, but levels must be cut deeply to realize any savings, due to constantly escalating costs (personnel wages and benefits, inflation, etc.).[22]

Some thoughts, on productivity, of one of the preeminent management gurus, Peter F. Drucker, are illuminating to the discussion at hand:

> Productivity is the source of all economic value.[23]

> Productivity, after a century of increase in all resources is subject, now, to stagnation and decline.[24]

> To reverse the trend in productivities is thus a major managerial task. It is the single most important contribution managers of major institutions, whether business or public service institutions, could make toward calming the turbulence.[25]

Whatever particular personnel management theory is examined, education and changing of attitudes stand out as paramount. One library scholar claims that the library profession stands at a crossroads, and faces challenges and opportunities which the profession has never before experienced and may never come again.[26] This expert calls for a continuous program of education, in which "The purpose of the learning program must be to strengthen the cooperative's capacity to achieve its goals."[27] In fact, the components of many discussions of so-called continuing education programs, sound suspiciously similar to what is called Organizational Development.

Organizational Development (OD) involves a variety of enrichment and lubricating components whose purpose is to promote flexibility and productivity within an organization. What is actually being developed, within an organization, according to this scheme?

Guy Benveniste states that OD "is concerned with the well-being of people inside the organization", and that it has "a strong commitment to systematic, rational thinking designed to adapt work situations to human dimensions."[28] OD is devoted to giving a greater management voice to workers in the organization, and to clients and the community at large.[29]

A central idea of OD is feedback: First the awareness of one's self and one's role in the organization must be increased. Then, the success of OD depends upon the ability of staff and management to communicate freely and honestly in an upwards and downwards fashion.[30] OD is concerned with uncertainty and is a response to it, so that organizations may be capable of responding to rapid change.[31] Thus, OD would seem to be a good candidate for improving productivity and organizational effectiveness in times of turbulence and retrenchment.

OD processes include team building and linking, continuing education and enrichment, job rotation, and other concepts. Barbara Conroy believes that:

> At no other time has the ability to learn been so crucial to those who work in libraries. At no other time has a systematic approach to staff development been so important to preserve human resources as they integrate technological resources to achieve the vital role of the library in new, more effective ways.[32]

Byron Cooper claims that any library that intends to be dynamic and maintain a motivated staff must institute a program of in-service training which is tailored to in-house objectives.[33]

Job rotation and purposeful blurring of professional versus non-professional concerns have occurred or been indicated in a variety of settings. The Long Beach, California Public Library rotates the responsibility of Director among their three top-ranking librarians.[34] Library managers must act in concert towards organizational goals, so that professionals act as managers of a team, and not as a group with disparate goals.[35] This sort of agenda is a two-way process, because it is possible only when the subordinate sees the relationship as consistent with personal and organizational goals, is able to comply with the professional's demands, and when: "the subordinate in an organization literally grants authority to the superior."[36]

Some of the training sessions related to OD harken to the "touchy-feely" school of personal interrelating that flourished in the 1960s. Some people do not respond to this sort of soul-baring in front of their peers. Even more importantly, as we will see with Management By Objectives (MBO), middle and upper management are typically the prime barriers to this sort of program.[37]

Two management styles arise out of turbulent times, both with their own adherents: one group says that stress and declining resources combined with increasing client demands urge for a centralized, more autocratic management structure. The other group leans in the direction of theories like Organizational Development. OD is really all about decentralization of power: this implies that there will be errors of articulation, greater uncertainty, and fear of punishment. This process can be healthy, but only if management is committed to the process.[38]

A logical extension of OD is the process whereby organizational purposes, goals, and objectives are explicitly stated, scrutinized, and acted upon. Why does the organization exist? Where is it going? How is it going to get there? Who is going to help it get there? How do we know when we'll be getting there? These sorts of questions are typical of the theory of Management By Objectives. According to some experts, OD and MBO must go hand in hand if either strategy is to work to the organization's advantage.[39]

We will examine some of the characteristics, advantages, and disadvantages of MBO with focus on how it helps leaders and the led with the exigencies of retrenchment now and in the decades ahead.

Ellis Hillmar was quoted earlier as pointing out that OD and MBO are very closely linked together. Certainly from an intuitive viewpoint, managing an organization by developing clear goals and objectives for its performance would seem logical and highly important in perilous times. Hillmar notes, however, that: "most American organizations tend to use MBO for control or administration rather than organizational management", and, that: "When an organization begins to conceive of MBO as its management process rather than another control technique, the need for OD increases rapidly and dramatically."[40]

John Rizzo notes that change itself increases the need for employee development through enrichment and training; these tasks must blend effectively into a grand scheme of organizational development; and overall organizational needs analysis is the one approach that begins this process.[41] Another interesting focus to this discussion is who does the deciding on organizational goals and objectives? Will the process be democratic? Hill-mar observes an important change that tends to take place in organizations under stress:

> An important characteristic of this second generation MBO is the shift from individual to organizational results . . . there is much greater need for defining results to be achieved by the organization. This tends to create quite a different perception of what results really are.[42]

Byron Cooper believes that proper use of MBO requires that performance on objectives be geared to individual as well as organizational objectives. Employees must have an active role both in helping to develop the objectives and evaluating themselves on the proper implementation of strategies aimed at fulfilling those objectives.[43]

William Petru lays out what are, in his opinion, the steps to developing a productive Management By Objectives program: Both management and staff must commit themselves wholeheartedly to the specification and attainment of outcomes. Management and employees must be aware of overall goals of the organization. Both management and employees must participate in the development of objectives and alternative strategies for attaining those objectives. For proper evaluation to take place, the objectives must be concrete and set within a certain time-frame.[44] Petru lists some of the expected results of a good MBO program:

1. There will result a higher degree of organizational purpose.
2. Managerial motivation will increase.
3. Self-direction and control on the part of the staff will improve.
4. Among staff, and between staff and management, better cooperation and communication will result.[45]

MBO can be of great benefit to organizations, and especially to public libraries which typically have difficulty defining organizational goals and objectives. One library described in the literature claims that their program, using MBO, "is working beautifully". Each employee meets quarterly with his supervisor to develop "season projects" for the upcoming quarter. Work is monitored, encouragement and feedback given, and employees who satisfactorily complete their assignments are treated to a free breakfast at a staff meeting held at a local restaurant.[46] Since the slant of this chapter is on public libraries in times of stress, what might be some problems related to the use of MBO in this set of circumstances?

The first caveat about MBO comes from Laurence Lynn, who observes that crisis management in turbulent times often does not allow the time to spend on developing carefully delineated goals and objectives. MBO developed "in a hurry" or without all the pertinent details results in a process where objectives neither relate to each other nor develop as mutually reinforcing towards a common goal.[47]

Another in-depth study of MBO, this time carried-out in academic libraries, reveals some interesting problems: MBO may not be applicable to all ranges of employees; professional and managerial job classifications seem to be most appropriate. Traditional MBO, especially for rank and file employees, increases pressure on the individual and, using reward-punishment psychology, can be a destructive force rather than a productive one.[48]

An interesting aspect of this discussion, at least to the author, is the way MBO was described as helping the library to run in a "business-like" manner.[49] The academic library study mentioned above noted that:

> Librarians' initial reluctance to adopt management techniques used in business and industry finds some justification in the fact that libraries usually lack the extrinsic rewards which profit-oriented enterprises can offer.[50]

The authors of this study went on to observe that, at least in this experiment, MBO itself did not provide the hoped for intrinsic rewards.[51]

One would find it difficult to argue with the idea that any organization would be hurt by an attempt to delineate goals and objectives, and then to seek to perform in a manner that such ideals were attained. One key to the process may lie in how the process is developed, which leads to our next topic of participatory management for public libraries in times of uncertainty and cut-backs.

In this chapter, we have discussed some of the key issues and theories related to producing more effective and viable public libraries by developing better methods of leadership and followership. One might propose that the logical conclusion of such theories as Organizational Development and Management by Objectives is the concept known as Participatory Management. Many experts claim, as we will see in the following discussion, that an organization faced with stress, change, and stable or declining budgets can chart a path to survival only by radically democratizing the workplace.

Experts have differing opinions about why Participatory Management (PM) is good for organizations. William Reeves believes that libraries will be made more effective if the workplace is "professionalized". That is, library operations must be consonant with policies and orientations developed in the profession of librarianship. According to Reeves, "The success, however, of the professionalization of the workplace depends upon the collective orientation toward the ideal goals of librarianship".[52] This collective orientation would necessitate the involvement of both professional and non-professional library workers.

Donald Sager believes that libraries will be forced to develop into more democratic organizations. While he believes that this shift is inevitable, there will be complications. As libraries become more democratic, individual staff members will be asked to accept more responsibility. Some may not want it due to personal reasons or lack of aptitude. Others may resist unless the change is coupled with the opportunity for economic return or increased status.[53]

Terry Dean has some interesting things to say about PM. He believes that it can be viewed in at least three ways: (1) As a democratic management technique; (2) As an information soliciting device; (3) As a SOP to employees . . . creating the illusion that the employee is contributing to the decision-making process.[54] I will return to this last concept later in the discussion. Dean believes that there are at least six prerequisites to the success of PM:

1. A strong sense of leadership and creation of a psychological climate which fosters participation.
2. Sound planning.
3. PM must include vital areas of library operation as well as "cosmetic" areas.
4. "If it's not broke, don't fix it."
5. Equal access to all information must exist—no secrets!
6. While options on important decisions must be developed by everyone, the manager alone must make the final choice among the alternatives.[55]

Dean proposes that the expected results of PM will include: increased staff commitment and higher quality of decisions and strategies; better communication; and increased morale and sense of self-worth for employees. Dean cautions, however, that this "committee-style" of management depends very much upon intangibles such as interpersonal skills, trust, and goodwill.[56]

The success of an organization in times of stress may well depend upon building a committed, cohesive organization. But stress and change can inhibit this process as well. Warren Bennis offers the following opinion: expecting results from simple discussions about the crisis at hand will not necessarily lead to improvement. "Talking it out can work in times of shared values, but not in charged or polarized situations."[57]

We can observe a paradox: PM is recommended in stressful, changing environments. Yet, because of stress and change, it is difficult to implement. Donald Sager, the advocate of organizational democracy, notes that: "History will demonstrate that organizations in crisis usually centralize decision-making and policy determination. That is especially true in the public sector."[58]

The experts seem to agree that successful use of PM requires some specific changes to take place in the work environment. These changes involve both management and employees in some important ways. Bennis continues his discussion by commenting on the management of organizations in uncertain times:

> Creating and managing change requires at least three things: (1) Participation of the people involved in the change; (2) Trust in the people who are the basic proponents of the change; and (3) Clarity about the change.[59]

Several things are required of the manager in this respect. The manager must become a leader who: is caring and responsible; has a sense of flexibility about people and organizations; possesses a willingness to share power; is very self-aware and conscious of his own weaknesses and strengths; is concerned with his own self-development and that of others; and possesses the gift of a strong sense of humor.[60] Michael Maccoby is the author of the above concepts, and describes what he believes to be the characteristics of the modern manager in struggle, change, and stress:

> They don't try to control everyone. They involve subordinates in planning and evaluation of work . . . spending time in meetings so that the whole team shares an understanding of goals, values, priorities, and strategies. They spend more time up front developing consensus, but they spend less time reacting to mistakes and misunderstandings. They are skilled at leading meetings and turning off people who ramble or tend to dominate.[61]

The manager of an organization must initiate the process of PM for it to be successful. The manager, as stated before, must be aware of both his own strengths and weaknesses and those of others, while remaining in tune with the total library program.[62] The manager must realize that participatory management requires intimate knowledge of the skills, duties, strengths and weaknesses of each and every employee. Why is this so?

Frederick Thayer points out that organizations experimenting with the participatory style require development of interlocking, interdependent, overlapping, work/task teams.[63] Thayer also believes that this scheme is often politically unrealistic because:

> organizations are often inherently dysfunctional; the manipulation of goals and objectives usually affects only the workers and middle management . . . not the elite managers who are, more often than not, disoriented and repelled by the idea of employee participation in organizational policy setting.[64]

Participatory management challenges, in a fundamental way, the traditional methods and structures of organizations. The employee must take on new responsibilities and risks for PM to work effectively. Thayer goes on to note that employees involved in PM need to acquire skills in two vital areas: the substantive issues affecting the organization, and the dynamics of directed and successful group interaction.[65]

Interestingly, technology plays a key role in this drama. We have spoken before how some experts believe that technological evolution in libraries will create flatter, more participative management structures. The following quote from S. Michael Malinconico, proposes that if managers and employees work together in mutual trust and segment all jobs into their most basic components, technology will allow a new era of participation and productivity in the workplace:

> Technology compensates for the limitations of average workers and reduces dependence on the unique abilities of scarce, exceptional workers. To accomplish this, however, it is necessary to reduce jobs to their component parts and prescribe that they be performed in an unvarying manner. To a great extent, technology makes jobs interchangeable, making it relatively easy to transfer or replace workers who do not perform as expected. The result is a model in which the frailties of human workers are handled by the installation of more equipment that reduces dependence on those workers and their limitations.[66]

Earlier in this chapter, the observations of one scholar revealed that managers can implement PM for a variety of reasons, only some of which are ultimately productive. Nick Moore, writing in the *Canadian Library Journal,* observes that in many cases, PM has not fulfilled its promise:

> I think it is true to say that the experiments with participative management have not met with the hoped for success. . . . It was introduced in an attempt to improve job satisfaction and therefore rather than to improve productivity rather than to improve management of the organization. . . . As a result of the poor response to participative management, there is a tendency to move back to more hierarchical systems with clear lines of responsibility. They may not be as democratic, it is argued, but they are at least efficient and economical of staff time.[67]

Both managers and employees may be reluctant to take on the risks PM poses, even when the substantial rewards of PM can be forecast. Managers should make it clear that rewards for all concerned are possible, and train their employees to be competitive and resourceful.[68] Managers must realize that the traditional division between those who create policy and those who carry it out will blur:

> As organizations become more dynamic and participative, the line between the two is almost totally fragmented . . . an invalid assumption is that daily implementation of programs cannot or usually does not alter or establish policy.[69]

Warren Bennis realizes that true PM is rare, and the restructuring of an organization to using PM effectively must come from above.[70] He claims:

no really basic, radical restructuring of an institution by consensus has ever taken place. This sort of situation requires someone in power to say, 'This will take place.' Why? Because people have a terrible time restructuring themselves when they fear that their status, their power, their esteem are going to be lowered.[71]

Further, Bennis notes that the art (rather than science) of managing is vital in this respect: "It is not so much the articulation of goals . . . that creates a new practice. It's the imagery that creates the understanding, the compelling moral necessity that the new way is right."[72]

Guy Benveniste, in his book, *Bureaucracy*, neatly sums up some of the major pros and cons to PM in the following points. Participation is costly in terms of the time and work involved in the sharing of power. Participation does not necessarily reduce conflict and, indeed, can provide a vehicle for destructive attacks on the organization. Also, much PM is perceived as ersatz and, thus, as a hoax and waste of time and effort.[73] In a time of uncertainty, organizations tend to centralize decision-making. PM implies the creation of smaller units of decision-making . . . and the greater the degree to which this is so, the more decisions that have to be made in a decentralized way.[74]

On the plus side, however, PM creates a vehicle for healthy change that otherwise would not exist. Internal and external conflicts are reduced by giving a "voice" to those who were previously mute. Decisions, while taking longer to make, are often so much on-target in the implementation phase that fewer mistakes are made and fine-tuning can be kept to a minimum.[75] Even pseudo-participation can be helpful because it demystifies the organization and provides official, approved ways for communication to move upwards and downwards throughout the organization.[76]

Conclusion

The research cited in this section makes it abundantly clear that increased productivity and better targetting of services to the clientele is the task for the organization. All else is so much fluff. Equally clear is the fact that traditional methods of centralized management will no longer do.

The apparent paradox of turbulent, uncertain times requiring a return to the old ways when other scholars are recommending the opposite is a sort of fog that can be burned-off, according to this author, by the following observations: Yes, uncertain times create a tendency to centralize decision-making and reduce democratizing trends. Yes, it is recognized that organizations in this country—both public and private—are being outstripped by their counterparts in foreign countries in a frightening manner. Eric Matt Stout noted in this chapter that office environments (read: public libraries) are stagnating and dying from managerial neglect of the human component in the workplace. Thus, what tends to happen in a cut-back environment, a return to the old, hierarchical patterns, is not what should be occurring if the modern organization is to be turned around toward a healthy and productive future.

The management scholars consulted for this chapter point out, almost unanimously, that the conditions we are now seeing; turbulence, stress, declining resources, and the exploding use of technology, demand an emphasis on organic, flexible, participatory organizations. The burden of this message falls, at least initially, on the manager. What are the characteristics required of the manager of the future? How does this manager interact with a constantly shifting and threatening environment? These points will be discussed in detail in the next section.

LEADERSHIP

Introduction

The reader of this paper will have gleaned several viewpoints from the previous three sections: society at large is changing in some important ways that juxtapose declining resources and productivity with increased demands for accountability and service excellence. Libraries are institutions squarely caught up in this dynamic. The topics covered so far— politics, finance, and personnel—delineate three critical areas where the manager of a public library in stressful times must concentrate his energies and attentions.

This section on the intricacies of leadership in cut-back management is, in certain ways, a conclusion to the three topics covered previously. In other important ways, however, it presents an overarching whole or gestalt, which is much more than the sum of the three parts. The portrait that will be painted of the library manager of the present and future is that of the manager as "artist". The cut-back manager has at his or her disposal a pallette loaded with paints of different hues and textures. These paints will be derived from such disparate fields as politics, public administration, psychology, sociology, forecasting, and librarianship. The paints will be blended by a person whose vision is caring and artistic, not calculating and scientific.

The most formidable challenge to effective management in hard times is probably that so much must be done with so few resources and the pay-off, more often than not, is more heartache, frustration, and uncertainty. The problem, in many ways, seems to defy a solution. The simplistic prescription of: "Do what you do best, do it better, and do it for less money!'' will not be of much help to public library managers. However, if the problem is looked at closely, certain directions for positive action do present themselves.

Background

One of the most interesting ironies about the public library in the United States today is the paradox of increasing demand and declining resources. "Americans are giving their public libraries a workout," is how a journalist recently characterized her reaction to a study measuring increases in public library activity over the past 40 years.[1] The study referred to, by Herbert Goldhor, shows that loan of library materials shot up 160 percent from 1941 to 1982 while population nationwide increased only 70 percent.[2] Goldhor believes that a change of attitude on the part of librarians plays an important role in this trend:

> I think librarians are more user-friendly, to use the computer term. They're setting more convenient hours and giving better service. And they're building more balanced collections, giving people less of what librarians think they ought to have and more of what people really want.[3]

In another report on the same study, the author noted that Goldhor found that, in real dollars, library expenditures have only increased four percent over the past ten years, while circulation has climbed 22 percent.[4] Thus, libraries are used more heavily than ever before, and funding has not kept up with this activity.

The public library is caught in a high stakes game whose rules are changing constantly. Another author, Richard De Gennaro, describes his view of some of the competition libraries will be facing in the years ahead:

> Libraries have a near monopoly on one of the most important but unprofitable pieces of the information business—that of selecting, acquiring, preserving, organizing, and providing free access to the retrospective records of our civilization. That is both their strength and weakness. For-profit information companies will be offering an increasing number and range of information services, but it is unlikely that any of them will ever find it profitable to acquire and maintain comprehensive collections.[5]

Thus, the role of the public library will no doubt grow more important in providing free access to information. But will this role be sustained by the governing bodies of which these libraries are a part? Some statistics on the kinds of libraries used by most of our citizens will provide some instructive facts. The typical public library is characterized thusly:

1. 82 percent of the public libraries in the United States serve populations under 25,000.

2. 66 percent of these libraries serve populations of 10,000 or below.
3. The libraries studied in this survey were open an average of only 37 hours per week, with the range from a low of 13 to a high of 58 hours per week.
4. During hours open, 6.85 staff members per library were available to serve the public. Well over half of these were volunteers. On the average, there were only .68 (24 percent of total staff) professional staff per library.[6]

The author of this study, Bernard Vavrek, notes that: "To assert that there is a gap in the availability of trained staff in the rural public library is an understatement of no small magnitude."[7]

Thus, the public library is faced with a crisis of great proportions. They have weathered hard times before and survived, as one librarian compares the current era to that of the Great Depression:

> Librarians should not regard these as the worst of times. . . . We should recognize instead that we are in a period of professional stress, an era dominated by a sense of crisis, but it is a time combining tension and anticipation. . . . The potential is great for a new practice of librarianship. . .[8]

A further challenge by an expert skeptic is thrown at public libraries not at the potential of public libraries, but at how they have run their operations in the past:

> On close examination, the case for a public library that provides services to users at zero cost is not a strong one. The strongest arguments are for public library services to children and students; the educational benefits of these services appear to provide adequate justification. The case is much weaker for adult services. Actual use patterns will not support educational or income-distribution arguments. The positive externalities from adult use are not substantial or pervasive. The institution does not meet the standard criteria of a public good. There would be no need to fear monopolistic exploitation by the private sector if the public library did not exist. In the end, one can only fall back on the notion that library use is a good thing and on the library community's assurances of just how good a thing it is. This notion is not a solid foundation for a public institution.[9]

The author goes on to discuss the future of public libraries if they continue in a mode of "business as usual":

> the library may not be able to continue to muddle along; the combination of slower national economic growth and changing electronics and telecommunications technology could create a severe crisis for many public libraries by the mid- to late-1980s.[10]

Clearly, there is a crisis at hand, and one that demands action. It has been argued that the action required involves new attitudes and skills.

Much of the burden of the task falls upon the shoulders of innovative library managers and leaders. These leaders need help from many areas, one of the most important of which is incisive and up to date research and models for behavior. A recent conference on library management in hard times had 750 participants whose top priorities were that libraries need stronger advocacy of more active leadership, and a replacement of post-crisis management with a pre-crisis style.[11] The need for this kind of research is heightened when, among a list of twenty projects of top priority mentioned in a recent study of library research activities, the issue of cutback management was not explicitly mentioned at all.[12]

The Director of the District of Columbia Public Library, Hardy R. Franklin, made the following observation in a 1981 article:

> Among the suggestions I received for a speech during the ALA conference in New York was one to develop a 'general model for managing cutbacks.' I told them that I do not believe that such a general model is possible at this time, especially in light of the fact that our own libraries are so different, and that the problems created and affected by cutbacks are so many and so varied that they seem to defy any attempt at generalization in proposing and discussing any universal models for managing cutbacks.[13]

It will be argued that, at least for public libraries, there *is* a model which the library leader can use to chart new directions for his institution. This leader might be described, in a humorous way, as a sort of "super-person". In reality, though, this person will be portrayed as an ordinary human who does things in extraordinary ways. He or she has a vision, and is able to communicate it to others. He or she actively seeks information, guidance, and help from three vital sectors: (1) the public; (2) the library staff; (3) the leadership talents and skills latent in the manager himself.

Public Input As A Management Tool

It might seem redundant to express the thought that public library managers must manage according to the explicit and implicit needs of their customers—the public. This is a basic dictum of librarianship. However, many experts in the field complain that the traditional public library has not fulfilled this mission and that, indeed, much of the apathy and cynicism of the taxpayers and library users relate to this mismatching of service and need. This section will attempt to explore some of the salient ideas related to needs of the public and library management. Some recommended solutions and guidelines for this activity will also be discussed.

Satisfying the public is of critical importance, as one expert notes: "Being in tune with society will be a matter of survival since today's users become tomorrow's legislators".[14] Many library scholars believe that library managers are both ignoring or misunderstanding the needs of their public and making unwise decisions about allocation of scarce resources.

If library materials—providing the things people want when they want them—are seen as best serving the public, then Kenneth Shearer has observed an ominous trend:

> materials expenditures have sunk dramatically. . . . Materials are being squeezed between salary requirements and expenditures on new services, technologies, and cooperative networks aimed at a relatively small segment of the public. It is doubtful that these trends can continue without widespread dissatisfaction with the timeliness and variety of materials available for reference, browsing, and information at the library.[15]

Charles Robinson, of the Baltimore Public Library, is a leading exponent of "demand" theory—in prosaic terms, "give 'em what they want!" He also claims that library dollars are being spent for fancy, technological services that the user neither wants nor recognizes the importance of.[16]

In a recent study, Patricia Berger emphasized the importance of the style and substance of the interaction between the library as service provider and the public as service user:

> Whether or not libraries receive adequate support is strongly influenced by the kinds of relations they have with their public—their total public, including non-reading and non-library using groups. . . . If libraries expect to get their fair share of the tax dollar, they must follow the example of business and industry, of analyzing and evaluating the opinions and needs of their total public, not just the "higher levels of the socio-economic class structure.[17]

There is an inherent paradox to these arguments that libraries must only do what they perceive as the needs of their total public. What if those needs are ephemeral? Which "public" should be listened to? Patricia Berger asserts above that library managers must consider the needs of *all* the public, not just the well-educated upper middle class who typify the average public library patron. How are needs of non-readers or non-users to be assessed? What weight is to be given the input of different kinds of people?

Some of the problems to this line of thought become apparent in an examination of some data from a recent Illinois survey of library users:

> The overwhelming majority of public library users in Illinois give the library an extremely high rating . . . sixty nine percent (of users) saw no need for improvements or additional services . . . ninety three percent (of non-users) saw no need for improvements or additional services.[18]

An interesting irony of the cut-back era, at least to this author, is that bureaucrats and politicians seem to be intent on following the public's

shifting opinions in great detail and, perhaps, slavishly. Is this attention
to the expressed needs of the public enough of the stuff library managers
will need to manage? To repeat a point made under Politics, Ed Salzman
notes that:

> The prevailing view is that a politician can only survive by following the public, not
> be leading it. . . . Now, there are few politicians on the scene with the time or in-
> clination to build something for future generations.[19]

Part of the mystery surrounding this process may be attributed to the
confusion between the two related concepts of "need" and "demand".
Lawrence White believes that there is a constant tension, unlikely to disappear, between differing philosophies of librarianship: to serve the "value
theory" (raising people's consciousness by supplying material of high social significance), or to serve the "demand theory" (that which people
seem to want, and generally of a less weighty or intellectual nature). This
controversy can also be seen in the differing wants and needs of social
classes: the middle class, educated patron (typical user); and the poor
(one of the public library's supposed prime clientele but not, in reality,
very well represented in the library).[20]

The problems evident in the Illinois survey already mentioned include
this dilemma: that a needs survey seems to indicate that users and non-
users seem blithely happy about their library and have no idea whatever
as to how its services might be improved. Lawrence White contrasts the
subtle difference between need and demand, and points the way to our
next topic of marketing:

> Needs . . . do not provide a satisfactory basis for library decision-making. In the
> end, it is expressed user demands, not needs that may or may not be perceived by
> librarians, that determine the actual use of the public library. And, it is these actual
> uses that ultimately must guide choices.[21]

Enlightened marketing techniques—raved about and disparaged by equally
vocal groups of librarians—may provide an answer for translating user
demands into effective and efficient service programs.

If we agree, for the moment, that the following librarians, when they
use the word "need" also mean "demand", then we can see that library
experts concur that the public must be listened to for library managers to
do their job correctly. JoAn Segal believes that library managers must
learn ever more about the characteristics of their public, by using techniques for identifying markets and market segments, and for tailoring one's
product or service to that market or segment.[22] Richard De Gennaro claims
that librarians need to examine their ideas about what the real needs of
the users are, and what it takes to satisfy them. Somehow, these needs

are to act as guidelines for building selectivity among various services and to create "lean, quality collections from the mass of printed and other materials that are gushing forth from the world's publishers."[23]

Though this author is a bit suspicious about scholars who assert that for-profit practices may be transplanted with perfect congruency to the not for-profit sector, Harold Jenkins' point is well taken:

> the successful library director should see the operation of his library as a business. Operating as a business, he realizes that the continued existence and value of his library is dependent upon his organizational ability to satisfy the needs of his library customers.[24]

The purpose of enlightened marketing techniques, to this author, would be translating intelligently expressed user demand into service orientation. The idea, as explained below, is to break your community into segments, use leadership, community skills, and capabilities wisely, and reorient the image and priorities of any given library to its community.

Daniel Carroll proposes the following idea about libraries and marketing:

> Marketing and public relations are not in any sense charged with restructuring a library, but they are charged with divining and creating the image required by the ambitions of that library.[25]

The correct application of marketing techniques to a library setting will supposedly systematize public demand into parameters for service provision by that library. The difference between selling a product and marketing one is pivotal: If we librarians have done our work well in creating a truly useful product, one that is really based on the intellectual needs of the community, the need to 'sell' the library and its product may become unnecessary. As Peter Drucker said it, "The aim of marketing is to make selling superfluous".[26]

Alan R. Andreasen published some of the most interesting research on marketing for libraries in 1980. Some of his more important ideas are discussed below. A selling orientation implies an internal orientation (one which poses the question, "what do we have to sell, and how may we make it attractive to the public?"). A marketing orientation implies an external view (one which asks "what is it that the public demands and how may we orient ourselves to provide it?"). In a selling bias, consumers are often viewed as impediments to sales! In a marketing bias, consumers help to create the products which, subsequently, sell themselves.[27]

Andreasen notes that marketing, if used wisely, has the built-in components to be able to help the organization shift priorities as conditions change:

A true modern marketing orientation is only rarely found in public service organizations
. . . the only place that marketing planning should begin is with an understanding of
consumer needs, wants, and their present perception of the organization and its offerings. This understanding then determines the current offerings of the institution
as well as the nature of its communications programs. It also provides the impetus
to change these offerings and programs as the market changes.[28]

Andreasen's marketing plan for libraries involves, among other things,
market segmentation, multivariate analysis, and focus groups. The focus
group concept is especially intriguing; it involves bringing together representative members of one or more segments of a target population in
small groups to discuss the research topic at hand under the guidance of
a trained leader.[29]

Building quality input from focus group members may well be the key
to translating vague "need" into potent "demand". This idea also touches
upon the fact that key people in the community and the library management
may provide the ingredients for properly aligning the library program with
its community. Pauline Wilson discusses this idea from the perspective
of community elites:

The most active citizens in a community seeking social change are a communications
elite similar to the public library's public. These individuals gather their data from
all media and depend strongly on interpersonal communications among themselves.[30]

Interestingly, the public library does not seem to be depended upon by these people
to a great extent, for their information needs.[31]

Perhaps most importantly, what needs to be established is the linkage between the
library and the community group.[32]

Perhaps the elites in all target segments could provide the linkages that
Mr. Andreasen and Ms. Wilson are alluding to. It is critical, from the
previous discussion, that public demands be ferreted out by marketing
techniques using, among others, the ideas of market segmentation and
delving into those markets using target group "elites" to supply the needed
data for library decisions. Two other vital components of this equation
remain to be scrutinized: Library staff interaction in this process, and the
library leader or manager. Someone must bring it all together in a coordinated and directed fashion. The public will not be capable of this and
the staff will most likely not be able to make the overarching decisions
needed. The overall fine-tuning of the library marketing program must be
carried out by the library manager:

The individual department or unit . . . is too far away from the market for its performance to be related to market success. . . . Marketing and market price cannot
perform their 'social role' of supplying objective performance tests for managerial
ability.[33]

The data that marketing techniques supply must be coordinated and managed in such a fashion that they provide direction on the decisions the manager must make. Employees staffing "the individual department or unit" can help this process in some important ways.

Staff Input As A Management Tool

To set the stage for the discussion, once again we need to highlight two of the important ironies of cut-back management. First, retrenchment requires positive change in a drastically reduced time frame. In other words, key decisions need to be made, based on a new and uncertain set of ground rules, and there is often no time to plan the decisions or to plot their consequences. In addition, unlike the fat times, the lean times imply that many of the decisions and changes made will be painful ones: programs are eliminated, staffing levels reduced, incentives such as pay and job security can melt away, and so on.

A public library facing cut-backs is often bewitched by a fiscal double-whammy. Funding for the library is reduced at the local level because of demands by the voters for tax relief and tax cuts. At the same time, on a state and national level, grants to local governments decrease with tragic predictability.[34] These reductions cause public employee staffing levels and compensation levels to decline more rapidly in stressed areas than in the nation at large.[35]

How does a manager discover ways to use his staff as a tool for streamlining and revitalizing the public library in such uncertain and threatening circumstances? Some possible answers will be offered below.

In a recent *Wall Street Journal* article, one manager stressed what might be clear to most managers, but which is often forgotten in hard times, when fear causes the tendrils of decentralized management to shrivel into the rigid and wooden style of centralized, autocratic management. This author noted that:

> Managers often think of themselves as systems specialists or problem solvers or functional experts. They lose sight of the common sense practicality of getting others committed to doing things for them willingly. The essence of good management is letting people know what you expect, inspecting what is done, and supporting those things that are done well. Average people can easily double or triple their output without even exerting themselves. If managers would begin thinking in terms of doing things for their people, instead of to them, we would see productivity increases off the scales.[36]

Inspiring and stimulating library employees to send the productivity increases "off the scales" is a key aspect of the art of leadership. Somehow, some way, the manager must structure his actions so that the seams and stitches disappear, and so that the final garment is seen as something which the staff itself feels was created by them alone. Warren Bennis, quoted by Michael Malinconico, notes that: "The change effort should be perceived as being as self-motivated and voluntary as possible. . . . This can be done by providing as much true volition as possible."[37]

Warren Bennis, along with other experts of leadership, stresses the concept that information gathered from the staff—in good times as well as bad—provides the answers to many a management dilemma. Writing over one hundred years ago, Charles Ami Cutter had these words on the value of the staff to a library:

> It is a more glorious thing to organize and administer a great library, but full as good results may be got even in very small collections of books by a sort of spade husbandry. . . . Our chief librarian is not more successful in the conduct of the whole than his subordinates are in the cultivation each of his own little plot. On the one hand their knowledge of the shelves, volume by volume, on the other their personal intercourse with the students enable them to give every book to that reader to whom it will do most good—as a skillful book-seller suits the tastes of his patrons—and to answer every inquiry with the best work the library has on that matter, as the doctor prescribes the right medicines for his patient. No one man could do this for our half million volumes and our chief librarian's ability, for all his enormous acquaintance with literature, is best shown in his selection of the men who do it for him.[38]

Besides the commitment of management to participatory styles of leadership, there is at least one other critical element to the idea of using staff wisely: getting the information that they have about their perceptions of the organization out of their heads and onto the table.

Public librarians, ever struggling for better ways to gauge the effectiveness of their efforts, are now implementing the Public Library Planning Process, developed by one of the divisions of the American Library Association, the Public Library Association. In a recent article discussing the advantages of this process, the author concluded that of all the surveys and data collected, "the library benefited the most from the staff survey, since lines of communication were opened between library management and library staff."[39]

Warren Bennis refines this idea by examining the role of a special kind of staff member. As indicated below, the input supplied by these persons can be, all at once: vastly illuminating, destabilizing to the status quo, and of a transitory nature since this type of person tends not to "hang around long":

> Every organization has people who, while often on the periphery of the structure, are very much in direct contact with clients and the latest developments in both theory and practice. These 'gatekeepers' should be listened to and recognized.[40]
>
> They act as variance sensors and problem identifiers. As a result, they are under

continual tension, and in danger of being fired for telling the boss what he thinks 'ain't necessarily so'.[41]

We have seen how vital it is to involve staff in the information gathering and planning that must accompany library management decisions. The twin challenges of change and retrenchment make this process all the more imperative. The final portion of this section will examine some of the components of the library manager as leader, as artist. Quite unlike some management texts which depend upon models of decision-making, rigid theories, and sweeping pronouncements, this discussion will be more fluid, tentative, and introspective. Effective leaders perform in a mystical, ill-defined arena. Everyone may be able to recognize a successful leader from an unsuccessful one, but how he or she does it is another matter.

Management As Art: Leadership In The Public Library

This last section concentrates upon the manager himself. What are some of the typical characteristics of the ideal library leader? What are the inner and outer resources he or she may draw upon? How does one go about allocating scarce resources among a welter of conflicting constituencies, existing programs, and possible future programs? Two central areas will be explored in some detail: (1) what are the desirable characteristics in a library leader and why they are of critical importance; and (2) what are some of the strategies these leaders will use in guiding their libraries through stressful times.

One factor that would affect the quality of library leadership is the training future library leaders receive in library school and the continuing education they take advantage of throughout their careers. Chris Albertson notes a trend for employers of library directors to be increasingly concerned with choosing candidates who have professional degrees beyond the standard Master's in Library Science, usually a Master's degree in either Business or Public Administration.[42] Lawrence White opines that the library literature which purports to fulfill part of the continuing education requirements often falls short:

> The standard library journals that public librarians are likely to read . . . have not served the library community well with respect to decision making. They have reflected and reinforced the public library community's focus on needs, aspirations, and inputs; only rarely have they encouraged librarians to think about trade-offs and the need to allocate scarce resources.[43]

White goes on to say, perhaps cruelly, that in the face of turbulent change and increasing technological delivery of information to the social classes who can afford it, public libraries may be in for a surprise:

In the absence of an appropriate response, the public library could well become an even less important source of information and of reading material than it already is. These technological advances will, of course, first affect affluent and then middle class households. One ironic but possible result is that the public library will eventually be left largely with the clientele it would like to believe it is servicing and one that would provide a better rationale for the library's public subsidy—low-income individuals. But the institution will be a shrunken version of its former self.[44]

It is clear that public libraries are in danger as never before. It may be that one of the reasons extraordinary times require above-par leaders is the high degree of conflict and confusion surrounding the issues:

It is the paradox of our times that precisely when the trust and credibility of our leaders are at their lowest . . . we most need people who can lead.[45]

Another management expert points out the difficulty of attracting superior managers to jobs in contracting organizations because, quite simply, the rewards are much greater in expanding organizations.[46]

The subtle distinction between the qualities of managing versus those of leading provides a few clues about the desirable attributes of public library directors in the years ahead. Warren Bennis claims that "Leadership and management are distinct entities."[47] and, "The manager carries out policy—the leader creates it."[48]

The distinctive idea about the difference between managers and leaders is especially important when new, non-incremental decisions must be made. Safe and traditional ways of doing things may not be applicable when the rules of the game change drastically and daily. Attempting to define what are the attributes desirable in a cut-back library leader can be a slippery issue. Laurence Lynn observes that what counts above all other formal structures, policy mechanisms, and so on, is the array of personal qualities possessed by key officials, plus their ability to work together. Lynn believes, further, that devising a group of reliable and identifiable leadership traits is an elusive goal.[49] Lynn goes on to say that the manager who does best when deadlines are pressing and information is lacking can be described as:

intuitive and preceptive, reacting with impatience to carefully structured, systematic staff work, appearing to shoot from the hip, quickly and restlessly tossing out ideas and proposals, and making up their minds in a seemingly unsystematic way.[50]

Continuing this thought is the library scholar Richard De Gennaro who, along with Peter Drucker, emphasizes the superiority of doing the right things over doing things right. Facts, data, and models of management behavior can often obscure the proper direction a manager must take:

In the hands of ordinary managers (most of us), the quantitative systems can produce misleading and wrong solutions, while the behavioral systems can be used to manipulate and exploit people. The real danger with both types of systems is that they offer mechanistic formulas for dealing with complex realities. They keep us from managing in practical, realistic, and common sense ways.[51]

De Gennaro continues with some further thoughts of Peter Drucker that take us away from the incremental, mechanical activities of a manager into the almost mystical and esoteric world of the leader:

Peter Drucker says that the most important qualities a manager must possess are integrity of character, courage, and vision. These are not qualities a manager can acquire. Managers bring them to the job, and if they don't bring them, it will not take long for their people to discover it and they will not forgive the manager for it.[52]

It is appropriate, then, to examine some of the thoughts of authors who have attempted to get closer to a definition of what makes a successful leader. Michael Maccoby believes that some requisite attributes of the leader are: intelligence, ambition, will, optimism, and persuasive communication skills.[53] The good leader, in his words, typically takes time away from mundane tasks to question and re-evaluate the mission of the organization and views this work as a sort of disciplined play.[54]

Since no leader may lead without devoted followers, this fact places extreme importance on those who can, somehow, predictably elicit the commitment of their staff:

Some have argued that leadership is primarily a question of the exposition and pursuit of human values. Thus, a prime distinguishing feature of leadership is the degree to which the leader senses and identifies relevant and salient values and mobilizes forces toward goals that reflect those values.[55]

Another facet of leadership behavior views power as unlimited and proceeds to define effective leadership as increasing the feelings of power and self-control of followers.[56]

Charismatic leaders increase the sense of power and influence of their followers . . . this characteristic is thought to be rare.[57]

Warren Bennis and others believe that there is a progression through which a leader stimulates successful organizational behavior. The first step is introspection and self-development: "Leadership is as much an art as a science, and the key tool is the person himself, his ability to learn what his strengths and skills are, and to develop them to the hilt."[58] The leader must develop a "vision" and be able to communicate this vision to others in a manner that is attractive, understandable, and leads to action that is more of an "undertow" that pulls them along rather than a wave which pushes.[59] This process must increase the self-regard of the participants and be perceived as persistent and constant.[60] To repeat, we describe this process in a way far removed from mechanistic models:

> It is not so much that articulation of goals creates a new practice. . . . It's the imagery that creates the understanding, the compelling moral necessity that the new way is right.[61]

It is clear that people will follow a dynamic leader's vision if they understand it and are attracted by it. Even so, the relative degree of success engendered by such a process is dependent more than anything else upon the courage and will of the leader. Harold Jenkins proposes that:

> a major key to success in all management situations is found in the behavior of the chief executive.[62]
>
> The key to the character of these extraordinary individuals can be found in the concept of winning, where winning is defined as overcoming obstacles to achievement of the organization's ultimate goals.[63]

This thought is reinforced by the writings of Hugh Atkinson, who claims that libraries are entering a completely new era of management: "We are moving from a management style that tells people what to do to one which discusses what they have done. . . . That evaluative, encouraging, and discussing role can be just as powerful as the old directive role. In my view, it is the fundamental change in management."[64] Mr. Atkinson goes on to discuss the pressing changes libraries face and describes what he believes to be the key factor in this process:

> The way we achieve positive change cannot be passive. The primary ingredient of change, directed change rather than imposed change, is the sheer will of the library administrator and the library staff. . . . Once the process of change has started, it is imperative that one not give up the will to succeed. Only an extraordinarily strong commitment will overcome the many, many reasons for not going forward.[65]

At this point, where we have described the dynamic and artistic role played by the library leader, we should shift to the final focus of this chapter: what are some of the leadership tools which will help the library leader and staff to make the right decisions? What might seem at casual glance to be beyond careful analysis does indeed lend itself to reasoned scrutiny and plot some directions for organizational success in perilous times.

The recent era of declining fiscal and moral support for many governmental agencies has caused, among other things, a fundamental re-thinking of the way those agencies are carrying on their activities. Services may no longer be added to the public library framework willy nilly; the public library cannot be all things to all people now, if it ever was in the past.

Malcolm Getz puts the problem succinctly when he notes that: "The problem of evaluating policies is more difficult when the objectives conflict."[66] When resources—human, temporal, fiscal—are finite and must be distributed among policies and programs whose objectives compete greedily for these resources, tough decisions must be made. How?

The linch pin that keeps the program rolling is nothing more nor less than attitude; the mental orientation of the library leader and staff will make or break any attempt at successful cut-back management. The key attitude seems to be this: Be proactive. Let your mind wander over interesting alternatives which break with the past and present in possibly productive ways. In this unsettling and perhaps frightening "opening-up" of opportunities, there are some guidelines that will help keep the effort on track. Some of these guidelines will now be discussed.

Peter Drucker offers his opinion about how a shift of attitude is required by the revitalized "direct democracy" movements, which are especially typified with California and even more so with Proposition 13 and its aftermath:

> The shift from pluralistic consensus oriented politics to single-issue 'nullifying' politics has created new influences on successful management. The manager must no longer depend on the political process to be the integrating force; he himself has to become the integrator.[67]

John Rizzo makes a similar comment and relates it directly to libraries:

> Data suggest that librarians are often insufficiently proactive in service definition and provision. Rather, they tend to concentrate on resource acquisition and already existing functions. Thus, the argument is that unless libraries work to become more effective in providing needed service and becoming more indispensable in this regard, they will be increasingly vulnerable to withdrawals of support.[68]

It is clear that more flexible attitudes and proactive stances are required of the "new" public library managers. Are there any other ideas which could help the manager gain direction in this struggle? Luckily, some of the most perceptive library experts have considered these issues. Some of their thoughts are examined below.

Mary Jo Detweiler, one of the first library directors to implement the newly-developed Public Library Planning process, found that the success of the process for her library hinged upon a clear understanding of library purpose more than anything else. Planning was only an "after the fact" tool in this effort. She quoted the famous study on public libraries carried-out by Bernard Berelson in 1949: "The library's problem is a problem of optimum allocation of resources. . . . Since it cannot be all things to all men, it must decide what things it will be to whom."[69]

Lowell Martin sees some clear problems for public libraries if they are to survive the next few years and remain important to the community. He puts the blame squarely on the library leader:

> The policy reactions by library administrators have been paradoxical. Lacking funds to adequately serve those who come to it, the public library has been reaching out to attract non-users. Lacking the materials that people seek, it has cut back on the book funds while holding on to staff.[70]

For Martin, a continuation of the status quo is out of the question, and he gives his opinion on the proper direction in the last sentence:

> Why would a continuation of present policies, of cutting service across the board, bring those lost users back? Why would adding more functions—each on a partial basis—build new clientele? The results of this scenario are trim, cut, dilute, and try to survive—a rearguard action in defense of a wide territory. The keynote of the other alternative is concentrate and strengthen.[71]

In the above quote, we have two of the watchwords of library management in the 1980s: concentrate and strengthen. Concentrate and strengthen those services which best fulfill a double criterion of: what is it that the public most desires of us that we also do best? Certainly, what is kept and what is discarded in a particular public library serving a particular community will be different in each setting. The job of the public library leader is to sort out this enigma for his own agency.

The first step would be putting into motion a constant program of evaluation about the library's mission . . . which will change with time. Planning is the next stage and has some peculiar requirements, especially in an era of cut-backs and uncertainty. Michael Malinconico observes that:

> Planning should . . . identify those points in a program of change where a reasonable probability exists that unexpected and significantly different events, which could materially affect the outcome of a venture, can occur. When these sensitive points have been identified, contingency plans for dealing with them can be developed. . . . Because every strategy must operate in the future and the future is always subject to uncertainty, the need for contingency strategies cannot be overlooked.[72]

It is eminently clear, at least to this writer, that a flexible style of management—one that is open and adaptive to new possibilities—is the only one that will allow the opportunities to arise out of the ashes of disaster created by retrenchment and cut-backs. If we cast our thoughts back to 1959 and Charles Lindblom's classic on "muddling through," we see an ironic twist. Lindblom defined two distinct kinds of management styles: (1) muddling through, which is the style of most public managers . . . poking-along, making incremental decisions, not rocking the boat, adjusting practice with political policy as needed; and (2) the root and branch method where all information is known about all alternatives and the best one is chosen by the ever-astute manager.[73]

What this writer is suggesting is that cut-back management means that all the information on all the alternatives will never be available. Rather, the appropriate direction is one of enlightened muddling-through. The enlightenment concept implies that the manager's attitude and careful use of guide-lines allows the seemingly unsystematic and undirected muddling to produce an organic and successful organization. Hardy Franklin believes that this task has a good chance of success:

> The very nature of fiscal turmoil, which continually brings new problems to solve, cutting down on both money and manpower available, develops a constructively critical frame of mind and requires constant not occasional reevaluating of any step taken. In a climate in which nothing can be taken for granted, the criteria of evaluation themselves tend to become simplified and easier to apply.[74]

Along with the concept discussed earlier, of the organic (as opposed to rigid) organization, we see an indication for organic leadership:

> Situational approaches to leadership refuse to over-simplify the world; rather they complicate it. They ask the leader to study the situation and diagnose it accurately. The leader must have or develop a repertoire of alternative styles to draw upon . . . for those who are willing to practice and learn new attitudes and skills, the pay-offs can be high.[75]

Even though the library leader of tomorrow might be muddling along, he or she is doing so—not in incremental hops—but in quantum jumps that defy the rigidity of the past.[76] This manager is working to create a climate of "candor and openness where we embrace error rather than aim for the safe, low-risk goals that get eventual pay-offs and rewards."[77]

The library leader of the future must be concerned, as never before, with examining the performance of his agency based not upon inputs but outputs. These outputs reflect the articulation not of needs and aspirations but of demands.[78] Simultaneously, however, the perceptive library leader must realize that "co-producing" the library's service matrix by religiously following the "public choice" style may lead to dead-ends. If a minimum of library service, for example, is devised as the least which people will accept and "extra" services are subject to fees and restrictions, then the traditional concept of free and egalitarian public library service may become both empirically and ethically bankrupt.[79] Additionally, listening too closely to the public can be dangerous, as well. According to Joseph Jezukewicz, community analysis will only reveal programs for eliminating or cutting (in his words "suitable hollow linkages"). Community analysis will not necessarily reveal valid direction for service enhancement.[80]

Warren Bennis also supports this idea which is especially appropriate for the cut-back style of management: "In the case of controversial decisions (i.e. cut-backs, radical changes), complete and thorough public scrutiny—public observation of the process—can impede the process itself."[81]

By way of conclusion, the following comments are offered: This section has emphasized several aspects of cutback management: the background to the challenge; potential help to the library leader from staff and public; and the heavy dependence on the skills and "artistic talent" of the leader himself. While many directions and parameters to the process have been discussed, the exact role of the dynamic leader remains, necessarily, mysterious. It is art; not science. It is a qualitative approach which more easily demonstrates the fact of its success rather than the specific mechanisms that led to success.

SUMMARY AND CONCLUSIONS

The writer of this essay has attempted to present a structured approach to the intricacies of managing a public library in an era of stable or declining resources. The structure involved drew upon some of the latest research in two fields of scholarship: public administration and public librarianship. The approach to the problem was characterized by an eclectic selection of theory and practical examples which were all, it is hoped, geared to a practical application of solutions to everyday concerns.

Most libraries, and especially public libraries, are only one constituent group of a wide array of public sector organizations. Their public nature makes them subject to many strong, and often competing, currents of policy formation, economic and technological change, and expectations from the public.

A public library is an entity which fulfills a spectrum of societal roles which are themselves often confusing, amorphous, and difficult to measure. As in any other organization, a few of the day-to-day management decisions are value-free and subject to discrete measures of correctness and appropriateness. This writer suggested, however, that the bulk of the decisions and choices in a public library are value-loaded policy matters which do not lend themselves to evaluation or measurement on a concrete scale of correct or appropriate behavior.

For these reasons, the concept of "politics" becomes very important to the public library manager. He or she is managing a political agency in an environment increasingly characterized by constraints and pressures which require a proactive, astute orientation. The writer places the concept of politics in quotation marks above to emphasize the specific connotation of the term as used in this paper. The public library manager defines politics as simply working with people. The public library manager works with people—the public, staff, colleagues, and decision-makers at all levels of government—to promote adequate service to the library user. As a result of this activity, the agency itself is made more effective, more efficient, and more accountable.

In California, political action by library supporters and librarians has allowed tremendous gains in the years since 1978. Local support for adequate library service has coalesced, and this grass-roots movement has had great impact on all governmental levels. One might wonder, if Proposition 13 had never happened, would public library supporters in California have developed this level of political expertise?

The concept of political action (or lack of it) is intimately related to public library finance. Local funds and control now are blended with dollars and policy influence from both state and national governments. It is unlikely that we will ever see a return to a situation where the local public library is funded and controlled at only that level.

While many different and innovative schemes of library finance were discussed in this essay—ranging from celebrity shoe sales to categorical grants—this writer believes that continued tax-based support of the public library is essential. If the democratic purpose of the public library is to be realized, now and in the future, then the government must fund it in such a way that both basic and sophisticated services—free to the user— are provided. This writer asserts that the fact that public libraries are able to garner funding support from local, state, and national governments is an admirable example of the commitment of those governments to local library service. However, one should always maintain this perspective: in the long run, it is local government which, through adequate financing and control, will provide library service most appropriate for the needs of the public library user.

It is most likely that the group which will provide the key influence for public library evolution now and in the years ahead will be comprised of the people who work in them: library management and staff. Library management and staff are partners in a dynamic and interactive relationship. The best leader in the world cannot take a step forward if the support and commitment of the employees are lacking.

It was noted in the previous section that the library leader needs guidance and information from both the public at large and from library staff. Both these groups supply direction and perspective which complement—rather than interfere with—the training, expertise, and professional orientation of the library manager. The concerned user, and the gate-keeper employee described by Warren Bennis, can be ignored by the library leader only to the peril of all concerned.

It was demonstrated in this paper that change and innovation are, in the best of times, difficult to manage in a public agency. When rewards and hope seem only dim memories, change and innovation seem intractable goals in an uncertain and fearsome world. While the library leader does not stand alone in this struggle—joined as they are by concerned members of the public and library staff—the burden of the effort does indeed rest upon the shoulders of the person at the top.

The library leader must possess an intimidating array of positive personal characteristics: courage, flexibility, vision, interpersonal skills, humor, and a single-minded commitment to winning. The library leader must have a proactive, not reactive, orientation to the job, to the library, and to life. This writer also believes that, in no way, should these personal characteristics be construed as sex-specific (i.e. only a "man" can do it). Without this influence at the top, the cohesiveness and direction needed to pull the public library through retrenchment will be lacking. The public library as we know it would be, then—if not dead—moribund.

There are several constraints on the process as described in this essay. The average taxpayer may withdraw his support (fiscal and moral) even further from the public sector. Libraries already on a restricted diet of money and public involvement would literally starve to death. Thus the one agency in our society that, in a professional and disinterested capacity, provides our citizens with the data that capture our past, present, and future would be lost.

As the wonders of technology unfold, both the quantity and quality of information available to the public will increase. There will be a shift to home delivery of information. Will people still come into the public library for service? Will the institution itself (centered around a building and a physical collection of materials) be of less importance than it is now? There may well arise a group of public librarians who are not tied to any one library. The role of providing public access to public information, however, will probably increase in importance. The public librarians will be there to provide it.

Much emphasis has been placed in this paper on the characteristics of a "new" breed of public librarians. These new librarians will be comfortable in the political arena, adept at fund-raising and budgeting, and expert at inspiring and motivating their staff. They will also possess a dynamism and vision, which will be less obvious in the way these and other qualities interact, than in the positive results obtained.

There are also several constraints to the development of this new leadership. Government service is no longer as attractive, secure, or remunerative as it once was. Will dedicated and talented people choose public service as a career? Librarianship is a special subset of government in that benefits and respect have been much lower than that accorded public professionals in other fields. Library schools, to date, have not concentrated on the vicissitudes of successfully managing a public agency. New directions for library school education are now being charted by these schools in cooperation with practicing librarians, library scholars, and professional library associations. There is reason for optimism because of these efforts.

There is another constraint which must be mentioned. Librarians are, in many cases, subject to the sorts of bureaucratic blind spots mentioned by Guy Benveniste and Frederick Thayer. Librarians can be overly concerned about their own "turf". Librarians managing institutions of various types, such as public, school, academic, and special, are sometimes suspicious and uncooperative with each other. While the importance of increasing user-input to library management decisions has been stressed as vital in this paper, many librarians shrink from the prospect of having members of the public or colleagues in other libraries "mess" with their library.

There is a further danger, in these times of change and stress, of simply becoming confused and incapacitated. The library literature burgeons with testimonials by experts. These experts will, alternately, support or oppose different fundamental philosophies on library issues, such as automation, inter-library loan, book selection policy, user-involvement, and so on. There is a danger that library management in such times might become a slave to fads and the idea that whatever is "new" must be good.

The library leader must, upon careful consideration and data-gathering from his own staff and community, take the long view. Purpose and goals must be established. Objectives and alternative action plans must be developed. Ongoing activities must be constantly evaluated and scrutinized for their efficacy in fulfilling the basic purpose and goals of the library. In such a scenario, the public library will continue to provide for the information needs of the public for many years to come.

NOTES

Politics

1. Dalton, Phyllis I., "The Library and the Political Processes," in *Local Public Library Administration*, Ed. Ellen Altman, (Chicago: American Library Association, 1980), p. 31.
2. Summers, William F., "Finance and Budget," in Altman, p. 132.
3. California State Library. *Survey of California Public Libraries, 1978–80, Before and After Proposition 13*. (Sacramento: The Library, 1980), p. 5.
4. California State Library, p. 33.
5. "It's Back to Block Grants in Reagan's Proposed Budget," *American Libraries*, 12(April, 1981):173.
6. Dalton, p. 31.

7. Sertic, Kenneth, "Rural Public Libraries and the Planning Process," *Public Libraries,* 21, no. 1(Spring, 1982):20.

8. Weatherford, John W., *"Money: Hidden Costs of Collective* Bargaining," *American Libraries,* 9(May, 1978):273.

9. Dalton, p. 36.

10. "It's Back to Block Grants in Reagan's Proposed Budget," p. 173.

11. Levine, Charles H., "Organizational Decline and Cutback Management," *Public Administration Review* (July/August, 1978):316.

12. Sertic, p. 20.

13. Landau, Martin, *Political Theory and Political Science Studies in the Methodology of Political Inquiry,* (New York: Macmillan, 1972), p. 198.

14. *Ibid.,* p. 199.

15. Dye, Thomas R., *Understanding Public Policy.* 4th ed. (Englewood Cliffs, N.J.: Prentice-Hall, 1981), p. 1.

16. California State Library. *California Libraries in the 80s: Strategies for Service.* (Sacramento: The Library, 1982), p. 9.

17. "Now More Than Ever: Defending Federal Aid for Public Libraries," *Public Libraries,* 20, no. 3 (Fall, 1981):70.

18. Interview with Grace Gilman, Shasta County Librarian, May 15, 1982.

19. California State Library. *California Libraries In The 80s . . .,* p. 11.

20. Norton, Alice, "Public Relations—Its Meaning and Benefits," in Altman, p. 51.

21. California State Library. *Draft Mission Statement.* (Sacramento: The Library), p. 3. (unpublished document).

22. Interview with Gary E. Strong, California State Librarian, September 8, 1982.

23. Hall, Frances, "The Proposed National Library and the Information Services Act to Replace LSCA," *Public Libraries,* 20, no. 2 (Summer, 1981):60.

24. California State Library. *California Libraries in the 80s . . ., p. 12.*

25. *Ibid.,* p. 19.

26. *Ibid.,* p. 20.

27. Interview with James H. Kirks, North State Cooperative Library System Coordinator, December 10, 1981.

28. Bell, Charles G. and Charles M. Price, *California Government Today: Politics of Reform,* (Homewood, Illinois: Dorsey Press, 1980), p. 65.

29. Martinez, Delia, "Now More Than Ever: Defending Federal Aid for Public Libraries," *Public Libraries,* 20, no. 3 (Fall 1981):71.

30. Text of SB 792, 1977, excerpt.

31. California State Library. *Survey of California Public Libraries After Prop. 13 . . .,* p. 5.

32. "Backing Down on the Library," *San Francisco Chronicle,* June 7, 1982, p. 38.

33. Public Library Association. Public Library Principles Task Force. "The Public Library: Democracy's Resource, A Draft Statement of Principles, *Public Libraries,* 20, no. 4 (Winter, 1981):112.

34. Merget, Astrid E., "Achieving Equity in an Era of Fiscal Constraint," in *Cities Under Stress, The Fiscal Crisis of Urban America.* Ed. Robert W. Burchell and David Listokin (New Brunswick, N.J.: Rutgers Univ. Press, 1981), pp. 404, 406.

35. *Ibid.,* p. 413.

36. *Ibid.,* p. 421.

37. *Ibid.,* p. 423.

38. Schuyler, Michael, "Overcoming the Retrenchment Blues—Overriding the 106% Tax Limitation Rules in Washington State," *Public Libraries,* 20, no. 1 (Spring, 1981):14.

39. California Library Association. Government Relations Committee. "Making the Public Library Tax Connection" Proceedings of a Workshop presented at the annual CLA

Conference, December, 1981, San Francisco, CA. (from notes by the Author, from an oral presentation).
40. Schuyler, p. 15.
41. Interview with Michael F. Dillon, California Library Association Legislative Advocate, October 28, 1982.
42. Eyestone, Robert, *From Social Issues To Public Policy*, (New York, NY: John Wiley & Sons, 1978), p. 76.
43. *Ibid.*, p. 184.
44. *Ibid.*, p. 172.
45. "Illinois Surveys Users and Non-Users," *The Unabashed Librarian*, no. 29 (1978), pp. 25–28.
46. D'Elia, George, "A Procedure for Identifying and Surveying Potential Users of Public Libraries," *Library Research*, 2 (Fall, 1980):239–244.
47. Manley, Will, "Facing the Public," *Wilson Library Bulletin* (May, 1982):685.
48. Proeschel, Diana C., "Public Relations in the 1990's," *Public Libraries*, 20, no. 1 (Spring, 1981):23.
49. Franklin, Hardy R., "Hurdling Handicaps—Services in Spite of Dwindling Funds," *Public Libraries*, 20, no. 1 (Spring, 1981):9.
50. Bell, p. 163.
51. *Ibid.*, p. 173.
52. Nader, Ralph, (Interview), *New York Times Magazine*, January 18, 1976, p. 52.
53. Salzman, Ed, "The Meager Remains of California Political Leadership," in *California Government and Politics Annual*, 1981–82. Ed. Thomas R. Hoeber, and others (Sacramento: California Journal Press 1981), p. 68.

Finance

1. Scilken, M. H., "Per Pupil/Student Expenditures," *The Unabashed Librarian*, no. 42(1980):25.
2. Getz, Malcolm, *Public Libraries: An Economic View*, (Baltimore: Johns Hopkins University Press, 1980), p. 3.
3. *Ibid.*
4. *Ibid.*, p. 4.
5. *Ibid.*, p. 2.
6. Summers, William F., "Finance and Budget," in *Local Public Library Administration*, Ed. Ellen Altman, (Chicago: American Library Association, 1980), p. 133.
7. Fisher, Glenn W., "What Is The Ideal Revenue Balance? A—Political View," in *Cities Under Stress: The Fiscal Crisis of Urban America*. Eds. Robert W. Burchell and David Listokin, (New Brunswick, NJ: Rutgers University. Center for Urban Research, 1981), p. 454.
8. Getz, p. 12.
9. Goudy, Frank W., "Funding Local Public Libraries: FY 1966 to FY 1980," *Public Libraries*, 21(Summer, 1982):52.
10. *Ibid.*
11. Ballard, Thomas, "Public Library Finance: An Economic Forecast," *Wilson Library Bulletin*, 57, no. 6, (February, 1983):471.
12. *Ibid.*, p. 474.
13. Lynn, Laurence E., Jr., *Managing the Public's Business: The Job of the Government Executive*. (New York: Basic Books, 1981), p. 83.
14. *Ibid.*, p. 82.
15. *Ibid.*, p. 84.

16. *Ibid.*
17. "Library Funding," p. 96.
18. *Ibid.*
19. *Ibid.*
20. Interview with the North State Cooperative Library System Council, January 14, 1983.
21. "Library Funding," *Library Journal* 108, no.2 (January 15, 1983): 96.
22. *Ibid.*
23. Library Finance," *The Unabashed Librarian*, no. 42 (1980):6.
24. "Hoops for Books Nets Big Points for Library," *American Libraries*, 14, no. 1 (January, 1983):8.
25. "Library Funding," p. 96.
26. Dunlop, Donna, "Library Partner in an Austere Economy: The Foundation Center," *Wilson Library Bulletin*, 57, no. 2 (October, 1982):133.
27. Carroll, Daniel, "Library Marketing: Old and New Truths," *Wilson Library Bulletin*, 57, no. 3 (November, 1982):215.
28. Berger, Patricia, "An Investigation of the Relationship Between Public Relations Activities and Budget Allocation in Public Libraries," *Information Processing & Management*, 15, no. 4 (1979), p. 187.
29. Berry, John, "Denver's Deliverance—Lessons for All," *Library Journal*, 107, no. 19 (November 1, 1982):2029.
30. *Ibid.*
31. *Ibid.*
32. Newman, Donald, "Vincent Morehouse—He Means Business," *Wilson Library Bulletin*, 57, no. 6 (February, 1983):486.
33. *Ibid.*, p. 487.
34. *Ibid.*
35. *Ibid.*
36. Getz, p. 170.
37. "Community Services: The Action Plan Charts a New Course," *Western City*, (November, 1981):9.
38. Van House, Nancy A., *Public Library User Fees: The Use and Finance of Public Libraries*. (Westport, CT: Greenwood Press, 1983), p. 73.
39. *Ibid.*
40. *Ibid.*, p. 120.
41. *Ibid.*, p. 126.
42. Manley, Will, "Facing the Public," *Wilson Library Bulletin*, 57, no. 4 (December, 1982):322.
43. Manley, Will, "Facing the Public," *Wilson Library Bulletin*, 57, no. 3 (November, 1982):228.
44. California Library Association. Government Relations Committee. "Making the Public Library Tax Connection" (Workshop at annual CLA Conference, December, 1981, from notes of the author).
45. Brownlow, Peggy, Ed. "Controller's Report of County Transactions," *County Supervisors Association of California Legislative Bulletin*, no. 13 (April 11, 1983):5.
46. Chodos, Laura, "Results of the White House Conference and Public Libraries—the 1982 Survey," *Public Libraries*, 21(Winter, 1982):132.
47. Analyst Reports on Governor's Budget, *California State Library Newsletter*, no 27 (March, 1983):1.
48. Brownlow, Peggy, Ed. "Governor Sets Task Force to Restore Local Power, Resources," *County Supervisors Association of California Legislative Bulletin*, no. 12 (March 28, 1983):1.

49. "Highlights of Activities: California State Library, 1980–81," (Sacramento: The Library, 1982):2.

50. "Transaction-based Reimbursement Shortfall Still Certain," *California State Library Newsletter,* no. 15 (March, 1982):3.

51. Kirks, James H., December 10, 1981.

52. Getz, p. 151.

53. *Ibid.,* p. 152.

54. *Ibid.,* p. 159.

55. Hing, Mel, "A Local-government View of the Moment of Fiscal Truth," in *California Government and Politics Annual,* 1981–82, p. 111.

56. *Ibid.*

57. *Ibid.*

58. "It's Back to Block Grants in Reagan's Proposed Budget," *American Libraries,* 12(April, 1981):173.

59. "Congress Rejects Reagan Plan to Zero Library Programs," *American Libraries,* 13(July, 1982):445.

60. California State Library. Library Development Services Bureau. *Library Services and Construction Act Approved Projects for California, Fiscal Year 1981–82.* (Sacramento: The Library, 1981), p. 2.

61. *Ibid.,* p. 1.

62. *Ibid.*

63. Getz, p. 174.

64. "$50 Million for LSCA II," *ALA Washington Newsletter,* 35, no. 3 (April 5, 1983):1.

65. Interview with J. Michael Stein, International Systems, Inc., Consultant, April 25, 1983.

66. "It's Back to Block Grants in Reagan's Proposed Budget," p. 173.

67. Getz, p. 144.

68. *Ibid.,* p. 13.

Personnel

1. White, Lawrence J., *The Public Library in the 1980's: The Problem of Choice.* (Lexington, Mass: D.C. Heath & Co., 1983), p. 1.

2. Conroy, Barbara, "The Human Element: Staff Development in the Electronic Library," *Drexel Library Quarterly,* 17(Fall, 1981):95.

3. Levenson, Rosaline, *Job Security in Public Employment: A Vanishing Myth.* (Chico, CA: California State University, 1979), p. 35.

4. White, p. 89.

5. Getz, p. 37.

6. O'Reilly, Robert C., and Marjorie I. O'Reilly, *Librarians and Labor Relations: Employment Under Union Contracts.* (Westport, CT: Greenwood Press, 1981), p. 167.

7. Levine, p. 319.

8. *Ibid.*

9. Cooper, Byron, "Personnel Procedures and Practices," in *Local Public Library Administration.* Ed. Ellen Altman (Chicago, Ill: American Library Assn., 1980), p. 109.

10. Thayer, Frederick C., *An End to Hierarchy! An End To Competition! Organizing The Politics and Economics of Survival.* (New York, NY: New Viewpoints, 1973), p. 6.

11. Benveniste, Guy, *Bureaucracy.* (San Francisco, CA: Boyd & Fraser, 1977), p. 127.

12. Rizzo, John R., *Management for Librarians: Fundamentals and Issues.* (Westport, Conn: Greenwood Press, 1980), p. 120.

13. *Ibid.,* p. 122.

14. "Cooperative Management Replaces Hierarchies In Online Age," *American Libraries*, 14, no. 7 (July/August, 1983):478.

15. Lynn, p. 162.

16. *Ibid.*, p. 91.

17. Stout, Eric Matt, "The Human Factor in Productivity . . . The Next Frontier In The Office," *Journal of Micrographics*, 14 (April, 1981):25.

18. *Ibid.*, p. 26.

19. Greene, Charles N., "The Satisfaction-Performance Controversy," in *Public Personnel Management: Readings in Contexts and Strategies*. Ed. Donald E. Klinger (Palo Alto, CA: Mayfield Publishing Co., 1981), p. 221.

20. Bennis, Warren G. *The Unconscious Conspiracy: Why Leaders Can't Lead*. (New York, NY: Amacom, 1976), p. 153.

21. *Ibid.*, p. 99.

22. Bahl, Roy W., and Larry Schroeder, "Fiscal Adjustments in Declining States," in Burchell, p. 325.

23. Drucker, Peter F., *Managing in Turbulent Times*. (New York, NY: Harper & Row, 1980), p. 16.

24. *Ibid.*, p. 18.

25. *Ibid.*, p. 19.

26. Charles, Sharon A., "Developing Human Resources in Public Library Systems," *Wisconsin Library Bulletin*, 77(Winter, 1981):137.

27. *Ibid.*

28. Benveniste, p. 125.

29. *Ibid.*

30. Cooper, p. 123.

31. Benveniste, p. 133.

32. Conroy, p. 106.

33. Cooper, p. 122.

34. "Long Beach, Calif. Library Has Job Rotation At The Top," *Library Journal*, 108, no. 5 (March 1, 1983):440.

35. Rizzo, p. 67.

36. *Ibid.*, p. 103.

37. Benveniste, p. 127.

38. *Ibid.*, p. 40.

39. Hillmar, Ellis D., "Where OD and MBO Meet," in Klingner, p. 107.

40. *Ibid.*, p. 107.

41. Rizzo, p. 261.

42. Hillmar, p. 107.

43. Cooper, p. 123.

44. Petru, William C., "Management By Objectives," in *Library Management in Review*, Ed. Alice Bruemmer and Others (New York, NY: Special Library Assn. SLA Management Division, 1981), p. 2.

45. *Ibid.*, p. 3.

46. McMorran, Charles E., "Season Projects At The Boone-Madison Public Library," *West Virginia Libraries*, 35(Spring, 1982):15.

47. Lynn, p. 175.

48. Lewis, Martha, "Management By Objectives: Review, Application, & Relationships With Job Satisfaction & Performance," *Journal of Academic Librarianship*, 5(January, 1980):330.

49. McMorran, p. 15.

50. Lewis, p. 333.

51. *Ibid.*

52. Reeves, William J., *Librarians As Professionals: The Occupation's Impact on Library Work Arrangements* (Lexington, MA: Lexington Books, 1980), p. 141.
53. Sager, Donald J., *Participatory Management in Libraries* (Metuchen, NJ: Scarecrow Press, 1982), p. 173.
54. Dean, Terry, "Participatory Management," in Bruemmer, Alice, et al., p. 5.
55. *Ibid.*, p. 6.
56. *Ibid.*, p. 7.
57. Bennis, p. 13.
58. Sager, p. 176.
59. Bennis, p. 86.
60. Maccoby, Michael, *The Leader: A New Face For American Management* (New York, NY: Simon & Schuster, 1981), p. 221.
61. *Ibid.*, p. 223.
62. Jenkins, Harold R., *Management Of A Public Library* (Greenwich, CT: JAI Press, 1980), p. 200.
63. Thayer, p. 21.
64. *Ibid.*, p. 30.
65. *Ibid.*, p. 139.
66. Malinconico, S. Michael, "People And Machines: Changing Relationships," *Library Journal*, 108, no. 21 (December 1, 1983):2222.
67. Moore, Nick E., "Staff Planning In A Time of Recession," *Canadian Library Journal*, 36(December, 1979):336.
68. Deutsch, James I., "Where The 'Unemployable' Do The Impossible," *American Libraries*, 12, no. 10 (November, 1981):609.
69. Rizzo, p. 15.
70. Bennis, p. 89.
71. *Ibid.*, p. 87.
72. *Ibid.*, p. 93.
73. Benveniste, p. 139.
74. *Ibid.*
75. *Ibid.*, p. 138.
76. *Ibid.*

Leadership

1. Mouat, Lucia, "More Americans Are Curling Up With A Good Library Book," *The Christian Science Monitor*, 75, no. 184, (August 15, 1983), p. 4.
2. *Ibid.*
3. *Ibid.*
4. "Fat Circ Figures No Fluke, Goldhor Survey Figures Show," *Library Journal*, 108, no. 6 (Sept. 15, 1983):1750.
5. De Gennaro, Richard, "Libraries, Technology, and The Information Marketplace," *Library Journal*, 107, no. 11, (June 1, 1982):1050.
6. Vavrek, Bernard, "A Struggle For Survival: Reference Services In The Small Public Library," *Library Journal*, 108, no. 10 (May 15, 1983):966.
7. *Ibid.*
8. Pankake, Marcia, "New Growth In A 'No Growth' Era: Librarianship in Hard Times," *Library Journal*, 107, no. 20, (Nov. 15, 1982):2143.
9. White, p. 137.
10. *Ibid.*, p. 155.

11. Casey, Genevieve M., "The Management of Retrenchment," *Public Libraries*, 18, no. 2 (Summer, 1979):30.

12. Sager, Donald J., "Public Library Research Needs: An Agenda," *Public Libraries*, 21, no. 3 (Fall, 1982):111.

13. Franklin, p. 9.

14. Proeschel, p. 23.

15. Shearer, Kenneth, "Public Library Trends In 1982," *Public Libraries*, 22, no. 2 (Summer, 1983):49.

16. Robinson, Charles W., "Libraries And The Community," *Public Libraries*, 22, no. 1 (Spring, 1983):11.

17. Berger, p. 180.

18. Illinois Surveys Users and Non-users," *The Unabashed Librarian*, 29(1978):26.

19. Salzman, p. 68.

20. White, p. 72.

21. *Ibid.*, p. 83.

22. Segal, JoAn S., "Managing The Cooperative Network," *Library Journal*, 108, no. 20 (November 15, 1983):2134.

23. De Gennaro, Richard, "Theory Vs. Practice In Library Management," *Library Journal*, 108, no. 13 (July, 1983):1321.

24. Jenkins, p. 7.

25. Carroll, p. 215.

26. Jenkins, p. 209.

27. Andreasen, Alan R., "Advancing Library Marketing," *Journal of Library Administration*, 1, no. 3 (Fall, 1980):18.

28. *Ibid.*, p. 19.

29. *Ibid.*, p. 28.

30. Wilson, Pauline, *A Community Elite And The Public Library: The Uses Of Information In Leadership.* (Westport, CT: Greenwood Press, 1977), p. 145.

31. *Ibid.*, p. 147.

32. *Ibid.*, p. 148.

33. Lynn, p. 107.

34. Bahl, Roy W., in Burchell, Robert W., and Listokin, David, p. 323.

35. *Ibid.*, p. 320.

36. Falvey, Jack, "Try Saying Thank You," *Library Administrator's Digest*, 18, no. 4 (April, 1983):27.

37. Malinconico, S. Michael, "Listening To The Resistance," *Library Journal*, 108, no. 4 (Feb. 15, 1983):354.

38. Cutter, Charles Ami, "A Library Science Fiction Classic: The Buffalo Public Library In 1983," *Public Libraries*, 21, no. 4 (Winter, 1983):133.

39. Sertic, p. 20.

40. Bennis, p. 63.

41. *Ibid.*, p. 137.

42. Albertson, Chris, "Advancing By Degrees: Should Public Library Administrators Have MBAs? MPAs? Or None Of The Above?" *American Libraries*, 14, no. 1 (January, 1983):25.

43. White, p. 92.

44. *Ibid.*, p. 157.

45. Bennis, p. 157.

46. Cyert, Richard M., "The Management Of Universities Of Constant Or Decreasing Size," *Public Administration Review* (July/August, 1978):345.

47. Bennis, p. 27.

48. *Ibid.*, p. 29.

49. Lynn, p. 173.
50. *Ibid.*, p. 174.
51. De Gennaro (Theory vs. Practice . . .), p. 1320.
52. *Ibid.*
53. Maccoby, p. 220.
54. *Ibid.*, p. 222.
55. Rizzo, p. 13.
56. *Ibid.*, p. 14.
57. *Ibid.*, p. 300.
58. Bennis, p. 134.
59. McDonough, Robert, "Leadership Is For Everyone" (From notes taken by the Author at Mr. McDonough's presentation to the California Library Assn.'s Annual Conference in Los Angeles, on Dec. 12, 1982).
60. *Ibid.*
61. Bennis, p. 93.
62. Jenkins, p. 4.
63. *Ibid.*, p. 5.
64. Atkinson, Hugh C., "Strategies For Change: Part II," *Library Journal*, 109, no. 5 (March 15, 1984):556.
65. *Ibid.*, p. 557.
66. Getz, p. 145.
67. Drucker, p. 221.
68. Rizzo, p. 68.
69. Detweiler, Mary Jo, "Planning—More Than Process," *Library Journal*, 108, no. 1 (January 1, 1983):26.
70. Martin, Lowell A., "The Public Library—Middle-age Crisis Or Old Age?" *Library Journal*, 108, no. 1 (January 1, 1983):21.
71. *Ibid.*, p. 22.
72. Malinconico, S. Michael, "Planning For Failure," *Library Journal*, 108, no. 8 (April 15, 1983):798.
73. Lindblom, Charles E., "The Science of 'Muddling Through'," *Public Administration Review*, 19(Spring, 1959):79.
74. Franklin, p. 10.
75. Rizzo, p. 318.
76. Glassberg, Andrew, "Organizational Responses To Municipal Budget Decreases," *Public Administration Review* (July/August, 1978):328.
77. Bennis, p. 95.
78. Robinson, p. 10.
79. Biller, Robert P. "Leadership Tactics For Retrenchment," *Public Administration Review* (November/December, 1980):608.
80. Jezukewicz, Joseph, "Austerity Management: Planning Good Library Programs," (Taken from notes by the Author at an oral presentation at the annual Calif. Library Assn. conference in Oakland, CA: Dec. 4, 1983).
81. Bennis, p. 119.

REFERENCES

Albertson, Chris. "Advancing By Degrees: Should Public Library Administrators Have MBAs? MPAs? or None Of The Above?" *American Libraries* 14, no.1 (January, 1983):25–26.

"Analyst Reports On Governor's Budget." *California State Library Newsletter* 27(March, 1983):1.

Andreasen, Alan R. "Advancing Library Marketing." *Journal of Library Administration* 1, no.3 (Fall, 1980):17–32.

Atkinson, Hugh C. "Strategies For Change: Part II." *Library Journal* 109, no.5 (March 15, 1984):556–557.

"Backing Down On The Library." *San Francisco Chronicle,* June 7, 1982, 38.

Bahl, Roy W., and Schroeder, Larry. "Fiscal Adjustments In Declining States." In *Cities Under Stress: The Fiscal Crisis of Urban America,* pp. 301–329. Edited by Robert W. Burchell and David Listokin. New Brunswick, N.J.: Rutgers University Press, 1981.

Ballard, Thomas. "Public Library Finance: An Economic Forecast." *Wilson Library Bulletin* 57, no.6 (February, 1983):471–474.

Bell, Charles G., and Price, Charles M. *California Government Today: Politics Of Reform.* Homewood, Ill.: Dorsey Press, 1980.

Bennis, Warren G. *The Unconscious Conspiracy: Why Leaders Can't Lead.* New York, NY: AMACOM, 1976.

Benveniste, Guy. *Bureaucracy.* San Francisco, CA: Boyd & Fraser, 1977.

Berger, Patricia. "An Investigation Of The Relationship Between Public Relations Activities and Budget Allocation In Public Libraries." *Information Processing & Management* 15, no.4 (1979):179–193.

Berry, John. "Denver's Deliverance—Lessons For All." *Library Journal* 107, no.19 (November 1, 1982):2029.

Biller, Robert P. "Leadership Tactics For Retrenchment." *Public Administration Review* (November/December, 1980):604–612.

Brownlow, Peggy, Ed. "Controller's Report Of County Transactions." *County Supervisors Association Of Calif. Legislative Bulletin* 13(April 11, 1983):5.

Brownlow, Peggy, Ed. "Governor Sets Task Force To Restore Local Power, Resources." *County Supervisors Assn. of California Legislative Bulletin* 12(March 28, 1983):1.

California Library Association. Government Relations Committee. "Making The Public Library Tax Connection." Proceedings of a Workshop Presented at the Annual CLA Conference, December, 1981, San Francisco, CA. (from notes by the Author, from an oral presentation).

California State Library. *California Libraries In The 80s: Strategies For Service.* Sacramento: The Library, 1982.

California State Library. *Draft Mission Statement.* Sacramento: The Library (unpublished document).

California State Library. *Highlights Of Activities: California State Library, 1980–81.* Sacramento: The Library, 1982.

California State Library. Library Development Services Bureau. *Library Services And Construction Act Approved Projects For California, Fiscal Year 1981–82.* Sacramento: The Library, 1981.

California State Library. *Survey of California Public Libraries, 1978–1980, Before and After Proposition 13.* Sacramento: The Library, 1980.

Carroll, Daniel. "Library Marketing: Old And New Truths." *Wilson Library Bulletin* 57, no.3 (November, 1982):212–216.

Casey, Genevieve M. "The Management Of Retrenchment." *Public Libraries* 18, no.2 (Summer, 1979):29–30.

Charles, Sharon A. "Developing Human Resources In Public Library Systems." *Wisconsin Library Bulletin* 77(Winter, 1981):137–139.

Chodos, Laura. "Results Of The White House Conference And Public Libraries—The 1982 Survey." *Public Libraries* 21(Winter, 1982):136–137.

"Community Services: The Action Plan Charts A New Course." *Western City* (November, 1981):6–9.

"Congress Rejects Reagan Plan To Zero Library Programs." *American Libraries* 13 (July, 1982):445.

Conroy, Barbara. "The Human Element: Staff Development In The Electronic Library." *Drexel Library Quarterly 17(Fall, 1981):91–107.*

Cooper, Byron. *"Personnel Procedures And Practices."* In *Local Public Library Administration,* pp. 109–129. Edited by Ellen Altman. Chicago: American Library Association, 1980.

"Cooperative Management Replaces Hierarchies In Online Age." *American Libraries* 14, no.7 (July/August, 1983):478–480.

Cutter, Charles Ami. "A Library Science Fiction Classic: The Buffalo Public Library In 1983." *Public Libraries* 21, no.4 (Winter, 1982):131–135.

Cyert, Richard M. "The Management Of Universities Of Constant Or Decreasing Size." *Public Administration Review* (July/August, 1978):344–349.

Dalton, Phyllis I. "The Library And The Political Processes." In *Local Public Library Administration,* pp. 29–37. Edited by Ellen Altman. Chicago: American Library Assn., 1980.

Dean, Terry. "Participatory Management" In *Library Management In Review,* pp. 5–6. Edited by Alice Bruemmer and others. New York, NY: Special Libraries Assn. SLA Management Division, 1981.

De Gennaro, Richard. "Libraries, Technology, And The Information Marketplace." *Library Journal* 107, no.11 (June 1, 1982):1045–1054.

De Gennaro, Richard. "Theory Vs. Practice In Library Management." *Library Journal* 108, no.13 (July, 1983):1318–1321.

D'Elia, George. "A Procedure For Identifying And Surveying Potential Users of Public Libraries." *Library Research* 2(Fall, 1980):239–244.

Detweiler, Mary Jo. "Planning—More Than Process." *Library Journal* 108, no.1 (June 1, 1983):23–26.

Deutsch, James I. "Where The 'Unemployable' Do The Impossible." *American Libraries* 12, no.10 (November, 1981):608–610.

Dillon, Michael F. California Library Association Legislative Advocate. Interview, 28 October 1982.

Drucker, Peter F. *Managing In Turbulent Times.* New York, NY: Harper & Row, 1980.

Dunlop, Donna. "Library Partner In An Austere Economy: The Foundation Center." *Wilson Library Bulletin* 57, no.2 (October, 1982):133–138.

Dye, Thomas R. *Understanding Public Policy.* Englewood Cliffs, NJ: Prentice-Hall, 1981.

Eyestone, Robert. *From Social Issues To Public Policy.* New York, NY: John Wiley & Sons, 1978.

Falvey, Jack. "Try Saying Thank You." *Library Administrator's Digest* 18, no.4 (April, 1983):27.

"Fat Circ Figures No Fluke, Goldhor Survey Figures Show." *Library Journal* 108, no.6 (Sept. 15, 1983):1750.

"$50 Million For LSCA II." *ALA Washington Newsletter* 3 (April 5, 1983):1.

Fisher, Glenn W. "What Is The Ideal Revenue Balance?—A Political View." In *Cities Under Stress: The Fiscal Crisis of Urban America,* pp. 439–459. Edited by Robert W. Burchell and David Listokin. New Brunswick, NJ: Rutgers University Press, 1981.

Franklin, Hardy R. "Hurdling Handicaps—Services In Spite Of Dwindling Funds." *Public Libraries* 20, no.1 (Spring, 1981):6–11.

Getz, Malcolm. *Public Libraries: An Economic View.* Baltimore: Johns Hopkins University Press, 1980.

Gilman, Grace. Shasta County Librarian. Interview, May 1982.

Glassberg, Andrew. "Organizational Responses To Municipal Budget Decreases." *Public Administration Review* (July/August, 1978):325–332.

Goudy, Frank W. "Funding Local Public Libraries: FY 1966 to FY 1980." *Public Libraries* 21(Summer, 1982):52–54.

Greene, Charles N. "The Satisfaction-Performance Controversy." In *Public Personnel Management: Readings In Contexts And Strategies*, pp. 218–230. Edited by Donald E. Klingner. Palo Alto, CA: Mayfield Publishing Co., 1981.

Hall, Francis. "The Proposed National Library And Information Services Act To Replace LSCA." *Public Libraries* 20, no.2 (Summer, 1981):60–61.

Hillmar, Ellis D. "Where OD And MBO Meet." In *Public Personnel Management: Readings In Contexts And Strategies*, pp. 105–111. Edited by Donald E. Klingner. Palo Alto, CA: Mayfield Publishing Co., 1981.

Hing, Mel. "A Local-government View Of The Moment Of Fiscal Truth." In *California Government And Politics Annual, 1981–82*, pp. 111–112. Edited Thomas R. Hoeber and others. Sacramento: California Journal Press, 1981.

"Hoops For Books Nets Big Points For Library." *American Libraries* 14, no.1 (January, 1983):8.

"It's Back To Block Grants In Reagan's Proposed Budget." *American Libraries* 12 (April, 1981):173.

"Illinois Surveys Users And Non-Users." *The Unabashed Librarian* 29(1978):25–28.

Jenkins, Harold R. *Management Of A Public Library*. Greenwich, CT: JAI Press, 1980.

Jezukewicz, Joseph. "Austerity Management: Planning Good Library Programs." (Taken from notes by the Author at an oral presentation at the annual California Library Assn. conference in Oakland, CA, on Dec. 4, 1983).

Kirks, James. North State Cooperative Library System Coordinator. Interview, 10 December 1981.

Landau, Martin. *Political Theory And Political Science: Studies In The Methodology Of Political Inquiry*. New York, NY: Macmillan, 1972.

Levenson, Rosaline. *Job Security In Public Employment: A Vanishing Myth*. Chico, CA: California State University, 1979.

Levine, Charles H. "Organizational Decline And Cutback Management." *Public Administration Review* (July/August, 1978):316–325.

Lewis, Martha. "Management By Objectives: Review, Application, & Relationships With Job Satisfaction & Performance." *Journal of Academic Librarianship* 5(January, 1980):329–334.

"Library Finance." *The Unabashed Librarian* 42(1980):6.

"Library Funding." *Library Journal* 108, no.2 (January 15, 1983):94–96.

Lindblom, Charles E. "The Science Of 'Muddling Through'." *Public Administration Review* 19 (Spring, 1959):79–88.

"Long Beach, Calif. Library Has Job Rotation At The Top." *Library Journal* 108, no.5 (March 1, 1983):440.

Lynn, Laurence E., Jr. *Managing The Public's Business: The Job Of The Government Executive*. New York, NY: Basic Books, 1981.

Maccoby, Michael. *The Leader: A New Face For American Management*. New York, NY: Simon & Schuster, 1981.

Malinconico, S. Michael. "Listening To The Resistance." *Library Journal* 108, no.4 (Feb. 15, 1983):353–355.

Malinconico, S. Michael. "People And Machines: Changing Relationships." *Library Journal* 108, no.21 (December 1, 1983):2222–2224.

Malinconico, S. Michael. "Planning For Failure." *Library Journal* 108, no.8 (April 15, 1983):798–800.

Manley, Will. "Facing The Public." *Wilson Library Bulletin* (May, 1982):684–685.

Manley, Will. "Facing The Public." *Wilson Library Bulletin* 57, no.3 (November, 1982):228–229.

Manley, Will. "Facing The Public." *Wilson Library Bulletin* 57, no.4 (December, 1982):322–323.

Martin, Lowell A. "The Public Library—Middle-age Crisis Or Old Age?" *Library Journal* 108, no.1 (Jan. 1, 1983):18–22.

McDonough, Robert. "Leadership Is For Everyone." (From notes taken by the Author at Mr. McDonough's presentation to the California Library Assn.'s Annual Conference in Los Angeles, on Dec. 12, 1982).

McMorran, Charles E. "Season Projects At The Boone-Madison Public Library." *West Virginia Libraries* 35(Spring, 1982):15–17.

Merget, Astrid E. "Achieving Equity In An Era Of Fiscal Constraint." In *Cities Under Stress, The Fiscal Crisis of Urban America*, pp. 401–436. Edited by Robert W. Burchell and David Listokin. New Brunswick, NJ: Rutgers University Press, 1981.

Moore, Nick E. "Staff Planning In A Time Of Recession." *Canadian Library Journal* 36(December, 1979):335–337.

Mouat, Lucia. "More Americans Are Curling Up With A Good Library Book." *The Christian Science Monitor* 75, no. 184, August 15, 1983, 4.

Nader, Ralph. "Interview." *New York Times Magazine*, January 18, 1976, 51–54.

Newman, Donald. "Vincent Morehouse—He Means Business." *Wilson Library Bulletin* 57, no.6 (February, 1983):485–489.

North State Cooperative Library System Council. Interview, 14 January 1983.

Norton, Alice. "Public Relations—Its Meaning and Benefits." In *Local Public Library Administration*, pp. 47–60. Edited by Ellen Altman. Chicago: American Library Association, 1980.

"Now More Than Ever: Defending Federal Aid For Public Libraries." *Public Libraries* 20, no.3 (Fall, 1981):69–73.

O'Reilly, Robert C., and O'Reilly, Marjorie I. *Librarians and Labor Relations: Employment Under Union Contracts* Westport, CT: Greenwood Press, 1981.

Pankake, Marcia. "New Growth In A 'No Growth' Era: Librarianship In Hard Times." *Library Journal* 107, no.20 (Nov. 15, 1982):2142–2143.

Petru, William C. "Management By Objectives." In *Library Management In Review*, pp. 1–4. Edited by Alice Bruemmer and others. New York, NY: Special Libraries Association. SLA Management Division, 1981.

Proeschel, Diana C. "Public Relations In The 1990's." *Public Libraries* 20, no.1 (Spring, 1981):22–23.

Public Library Association. Public Library Principles Task Force. "The Public Library: Democracy's Resource, A Draft Statement of Principles." *Public Libraries* 20, no.4 (Winter, 1981):112.

Reeves, William J. *Librarians As Professionals: The Occupation's Impact on Library Work Arrangements*. Lexington, Mass: Lexington Books, 1980.

Rizzo, John R. *Management For Librarians: Fundamentals And Issues*. Westport, CT: Greenwood Press, 1980.

Robinson, Charles W. "Libraries And The Community." *Public Libraries* 22, no.1 (Spring, 1983):7–13.

Sager, Donald J. *Participatory Management In Libraries*. Metuchen, NJ: Scarecrow Press, 1982.

Sager, Donald J. "Public Library Research Needs: An Agenda." *Public Libraries* 21, no.3 (Fall, 1982):111.

Salzman, Ed. "The Meager Remains of California Political Leadership." In *California Government and Politics Annual, 1981–82*, pp. 67–68. Edited by Thomas R. Hoeber, and others. Sacramento: California Journal Press, 1981.

Schuyler, Michael. "Overcoming The Retrenchment Blues—Overriding The 106% Tax Limitation Rules In Washington State." *Public Libraries* 20, no.1 (Spring, 1981):19–20.

Scilken, M.H. "Per Pupil/Student Expenditures." *The Unabashed Librarian* 42(1980):25.

Segal, JoAn S. "Managing The Cooperative Network." *Library Journal* 108, no.20 (Nov. 15, 1983):2133–2135.

Sertic, Kenneth. "Rural Public Libraries and The Planning Process." *Public Libraries* 21, no.1 (Spring, 1982):19–20.

Shearer, Kenneth. "Public Library Trends In 1982." *Public Libraries* 22, no.2 (Summer, 1983):49–52.

Stein, J. Michael. International Systems, Inc., Consultant. Interview, 25 April, 1983.

Stout, Eric Matt. "The Human Factor In Productivity . . . The Next Frontier In The Office." *Journal of Micrographics* 14(April, 1981):25–34.

Strong, Gary E. California State Librarian. Interview, 8 September 1982.

Summers, F. William. "Finance And Budget." In *Local Public Library Administration* pp. 130–140. Edited by Ellen Altman. Chicago: American Library Association, 1980.

Thayer, Frederick C. *An End To Hierarchy! An End To Competition! Organizing The Politics And Economics Of Survival*. New York, NY: New Viewpoints, 1973.

"Transaction-based Reinbursement Shortfall Still Certain." *California State Library Newsletter* 15(March, 1982):3.

Van House, Nancy A. *Public Library User Fees: The Use and Finance of Public Libraries*. Westport, CT: Greenwood Press, 1983.

Vavrek, Bernard. "A Struggle For Survival: Reference Services In The Small Public Library." *Library Journal* 108, no.10 (May 15, 1983):966–969.

Weatherford, John W. "Money: Hidden Costs of Collective Bargaining." *American Libraries* 9(May, 1978):271–274.

White, Lawrence J. *The Public Library in the 1980s: The Problems of Choice*. Lexington, Mass: D.C. Heath & Co., 1983.

Wilson, Pauline. *A Community Elite and the Public Library*. Westport, CT: Greenwood Press, 1977.

LIBRARY RESOURCE SHARING IN MASSACHUSETTS:

TRADITIONAL AND TECHNOLOGICAL EFFORTS

Robert E. Dugan and MaryAnn Tricarico

INTRODUCTION

It is paradoxical that in a state in which local autonomy is indigenous, traditional and technological cooperatives thrive. Libraries in Massachusetts have united to form resource sharing alliances for functional purposes to improve access to information for their clientele and to cope with limited resources, such as funding, space and personnel.

The history of resource sharing in Massachusetts dates back to the beginning of this century. New cooperatives are forming continuously as the individual library realizes its inability to be self-sufficient and its need

Advances in Library Administration and Organization
Volume 6, pages 79–116
Copyright © 1986 by JAI Press Inc.
All rights of reproduction in any form reserved.
ISBN: 0-89232-724-3

to go beyond the local collection to satisfy information requests. Many libraries are joining existing cooperatives or developing new ones to take advantage of the efficiency and effectiveness offered by the application of automated technology.

Since automation is playing a major role in the resource sharing efforts in the state, a statewide automation plan has been developed which sets forth a conceptual framework within which all types of libraries can use computer technology to improve their resource sharing activities. Network clusters, in which two or more libraries share an automated circulation control system to create shared bibliographic and item records, form one of the focal points for Massachusetts networking. Understanding how these clusters were formed and how they govern themselves is a study of how resource sharing cooperatives develop, expand, and evolve.

While resource sharing efforts, particularly the network clusters, are successful in their stated missions, the cooperatives could increase their effectiveness if members would review their attitudes concerning the cooperative and its relationship to the library. Lastly, there is a need to develop qualitative evaluative measures that supplement the numerous quantitative measures applied.

BASIS FOR RESOURCE SHARING IN MASSACHUSETTS

People need information contributing to survival and success in living. They have always needed it, but now, in a complex society, the need is growing. Life information needs range from survival such as in general life maintenance (food, clothing, jobs, housing, personal care and safety, social and emotional integration) to self-enrichment and growth (recreation and leisure, education, and self-actualization).[1]

Recognizing the citizens' need for diverse types of information the Massachusetts Board of Library Commissioners, the state agency possessing the statutory authority and responsibility for the total library enterprise in the Commonwealth, has as an overall goal:

> To provide every resident of Massachusetts with equal opportunity to access that part of the total information resource which will satisfy the individual's educational, occupational, cultural, and recreational needs and interests, regardless of the individual's location, socio-economic status, possible physical disability, or level of intellectual achievement.

Libraries strive toward self-sufficiency to meet the demands from users that materials be available on-site and immediately. However, self-sufficiency is limited by financial, physical, and professional factors. Financial issues impede building comprehensive local collections; physical and architectual limitations restrict collection expansion; and circumscribed abilities in developing and evaluating information resources hinder collection growth.[2]

Moreover, the traditional, book-oriented library can no longer meet the information needs of its patrons. The distribution of knowledge and information relevant to all aspects of an individual's life span requires the ability to find the location of the information in a timely manner both within and beyond the local library collection. It further requires the receipt of the right amount of information in the most efficient mode possible once the individual's need is determined.[3]

Meeting residents' information needs when considering the limitations to self-sufficiency reflects the need for resource sharing. Therefore, the Board of Library Commissioners developed a resource sharing objective to:

Increase citizens' access to Massachusetts information resources by sharing resources as broadly and effectively as possible.

Librarians today acknowledge the impossibility of maintaining comprehensive collections and of providing totally comprehensive services to their users based solely upon their own resources.[4] Balancing the need to maximize the availability of materials and services and to minimize operational expenses, libraries can provide their users with access to resources beyond the local collection through resource sharing arrangements with other libraries.

In its simplest definition, a library cooperative is a mechanism which facilitates the sharing of resources among libraries for the mutual benefit of their clienteles. A library cooperative exists when two or more libraries engage in a common pattern of information exchange, through communications, for some functionally interdependent purpose.[5] Library networks are more formally organized than resource sharing cooperatives and dependent upon an established system of communication. Activities of a cooperative or network can be summarized briefly as:

1. shared access to collections (through expanded interlibrary loan and borrowing privileges);
2. coordinated collection development to avoid unnecessary duplication of materials;
3. shared access to bibliographic data; and
4. continuing education and development of technical expertise of staff members.[6]

Furthermore, the sharing of collections among libraries of a single type cannot meet the needs of the total community because users need varied information from more than one type of collection. The argument in favor of multitype library networks (i.e. cooperatives of two or more types of libraries) over single-type networks is convincing. Among the many benefits derived from participating in multitype networks are:

1. access to information about bibliographic resources in other types of libraries;
2. increased access and increased confidence in the availability of resources held in other types of collections in the network which enables libraries to gain increased flexibility in the spending of their book and journal funds;
3. access to highly specialized and general collections to broaden locally-held resources;
4. the capability of sharing services such as cataloging and ordering of materials; and
5. increased access to human resources, such as subject specialists, general information specialists, and school librarians who have the opportunity to train future users of libraries and information services.[7]

Consequently, resource sharing among various libraries will broaden the scope of resources from which to meet the users' needs.

A library's decision to cooperate in a resource sharing effort should be based on two criteria. First, potential members must acknowledge that they have common interests and could achieve higher levels of service and efficiency by working cooperatively. Second, potential members must be willing to commit the necessary financial and philosophical support on a continuing basis.[8]

Past and recent activities in Massachusetts illustrate an evolving shift in perception on the part of librarians from "collection-oriented, self-sufficiency" toward the need for expanding beyond the scope of the local collection and acquiring access to a wider range of materials through cooperative efforts. These efforts have been undertaken to meet the needs of both user and librarian.

MASSACHUSETTS APPROACH TO RESOURCE SHARING

As stated above, people have a need for all types of information located in all types of sources in all types of libraries. Libraries cannot be self-sufficient because they lack the financial resources and/or the physical space to acquire and store all the materials needed by their patrons to meet their needs. There is increased access to information for library users when libraries agree to cooperate with each other to share resources. Resource sharing cooperatives and networks increase the effectiveness of locally-based efforts and provide libraries with a means to meet user and library needs.

Cooperative arrangements between libraries in Massachusetts have long existed. In 1911, the Massachusetts Free Public Library Commission (predecessor to the Board of Library Commissioners) paid a $50 subscription fee on behalf of ten rural towns for library privileges at the Berkshire Athenaem in Pittsfield. In that same year, a committee was formed to explore ways in which larger libraries might be of assistance to smaller libraries.

While limited cooperative efforts were undertaken in the ensuing decades, the first official cooperative was the Hampshire Inter-Library Center, a collective of what later became the Five College Corporation. Five Colleges is an educational association which binds Amherst College, Hampshire College, Mount Holyoke College, Smith College, and the University of Massachusetts at Amherst together in a mutually beneficial relationship. Cooperation among the schools is as old as the institutions themselves, but the present network of library cooperative programs dates from the 1950s. In 1951, the first formal collectively supported project was created called the Hampshire Inter-Library Center (HILC). This was a joint repository for rare and little-used periodicals, serials, and monographs impractical for any one institution to acquire, but nevertheless, desirable for research. In the 1960s, the colleges formalized their arrangements with financial commitments to develop and support additional cooperative projects.

The New England Library Information Network (NELINET) was originally created in the 1950s as a program of the New England Board of Higher Education, an interstate agency responsible for expanding educational opportunities and services to the residents of the six New England states. NELINET's mission in the 1960s was to facilitate the sharing of information resources by developing and operating a computerized bibliographic network. Early membership included the state university library systems and other major academic libraries in the six-state region. In 1972, NELINET established its affiliation with OCLC when one member, Dartmouth College, initiated online shared cataloging via a dedicated telephone line to Ohio. In 1978, NELINET separated from the New England Board of Higher Education and became an independently corporated network, governed by elected representatives of the voting member institutions.

Although other cooperative efforts were underway, it was the passage of the 1960 state legislation establishing the Regional Public Library Systems that formally marked the beginnings of large scale cooperation and shared services in Massachusetts libraries. This act authorized the Board of Library Commissioners to establish a comprehensive statewide program of public library services supported by state funds appropriated on a per capita basis. Between 1962 and 1967, three geographic regional systems were established to support local public libraries with interlibrary loans, reference and research services, audio-visual material and equipment lending, centralized purchasing of supplies, bookmobile services, deposit collections, and various consultant assistance.

These regional systems were established to guarantee all residents equality of access to library resources and to improved services by interlibrary cooperation. For a coordinated enterprise of this type to be successful, formal arrangements between members were required. Accordingly, each community in the Commonwealth is represented on a regional advisory council with members electing officers and delegates to serve on the Executive Committee and the various standing committees.

Within the three regions, libraries, usually in close proximity, have continuously formed cooperatives to provide user and library services. For example, the following multitype groups: the Cooperating Libraries of Greater Springfield, Worcester Area Cooperating Libraries, Southeastern Massachusetts Cooperating Libraries, and the Boston Library Consortium have developed union lists of serials. In addition, all but the Springfield libraries have walk-in reciprocal borrowing among members and interlibrary loan using the consortium's motor delivery service. Two of the groups offer staff development programming.

Other Massachusetts cooperatives offer similar services. The Essex County Cooperating Libraries, another multitype consortia, has union lists for serials and business and art reference materials. It has also received grants for establishing legal reference collections and rotating collections of large print books. Based in Boston, the Fenway Library Consortium maintains a directory of the services of its academic, special and public library members, and walk-in interlibrary loan for users to facilitate access to the members' collections. Members of the Wellesley-Lexington Area Cooperating Libraries have a union list of serials, accept telephone interlibrary loan requests from its multitype members, and provide free photocopying. Merrimack Inter-Library Cooperative members receive group discounts for joint purchases of reference materials, and share the union list of serials project with the Essex County group.

Dozens of other library cooperatives exist throughout the state. While several include members of more than one type of library, many cooperatives are single type and share specialized resources among themselves, such as the hospital consortia.

THE COMPUTER'S ROLE IN NETWORKING

From the preceding discussion, it is clear that libraries formed alliances to cost-effectively share resources beyond their local collections in order to respond to user needs for materials and services. These cooperative relationships have traditionally been established along functional lines. Early collaborative efforts through the regional public library systems and through the numerous library consortia focused on the production of union catalogs and the sharing of resources through reciprocal arrangements to satisfy the needs of user groups. Union lists of serials, cooperative cataloging projects, book purchasing collectives, children's book reviewing committees, rotating collections of specialized materials (i.e., art prints, large-type books, books-on-tape) and topical bibliographies characterized the type of shared library activities undertaken.

Members of these informal cooperatives realized the advantages of cooperating with neighboring libraries. Collectively, they could obtain added resources for their users and broader professional assistance for their libraries than would be available independently. Yet they could continue to maintain their individuality. Local practices, policies and budgets would remain unaffected by cooperative associations.

The combination of rising costs, evolving technologies, and the urgent need to deal with the rapidly increasing flow of published information provided a major incentive for libraries to seek new ways and means for acquiring, processing, and accessing the vast wealths of recorded data. Libraries began to explore the application of automated technologies to their cooperative activities, since computers provide the necessary processing capabilities required for effective and efficient retrieval in terms of response time, storage capacity, and the necessary linkage and switching between components.[9] Problems of information access are alleviated and the speed in receiving information is improved by computer and telecommunications technologies.

Besides utilizing a computer's processing power to increase the scope and space of access, the benefits of an individual library's participation in computer-based library networking are related to reductions in unit of cost which result from economies of scale. However, many libraries are too small to take advantage of economies of scale and too poor to invest in advanced technologies by themselves. Therefore, libraries need to pool their resources by forming and participating in networks and sharing in the development and use of sophisticated online computer technology. This cooperation would permit rapid and effective resource sharing rather than having individual libraries undertake the full burden of development and operational costs alone.[10]

Therefore, the computer's role in networking for resource sharing is one of mediation between the need to control expenses and the need to expand services in light of ever-increasing demands from the users.[11] While cooperatives provide a mechanism for resource sharing, applying automated technologies to a resource sharing cooperative's processes and functions will increase the network's efficiency and cost-effectiveness.

DEVELOPMENT OF THE STATE'S AUTOMATION PLAN

Several library cooperatives and networks in Massachusetts began applying automation to their resource sharing efforts, while others began to plan. Many of these cooperatives approached the Board of Library Commissioners for project funding to incorporate technology into their operations. The Board, anticipating the potentials of automation, felt a plan was needed to provide guidance and structure for the cooperative efforts because:

- Sharing resources between all types of libraries would broaden the scope of resources from which to meet users' needs.
- Barriers to resource sharing exist, but can be reduced or eliminated by designing a network that not only increases access and sharing, but also allows for necessary local flexibility.
- A viable structure will increase the ability of libraries to locate and deliver needed materials to users.
- Existing cooperatives are currently pursuing their own independent course. Guidance and coordination, particularly in the application of bibliographic and communication standards, are essential or so much variation will develop that it will become increasingly difficult for the cooperatives to interact with each other.
- The Massachusetts Legislature, a potential source of funding for aspects of the network, would need a plan prior to considering funding.

Planning efforts for resource sharing began as early as 1975. Unfortunately, the first statewide conference on interlibrary cooperation was unsuccessful in developing a plan because participants disagreed with the conference facilitator's summary report.

In 1977, the Statewide Advisory Council on Libraries (SACL) began to revise the Massachusetts Long Range Program to include library cooperation. A "Statewide and Regional Impact Program" was initiated after a survey to develop a plan:

which provides a united front for libraries in planning priorities, policies, and programs for all types of resource sharing and for seeking the funding/legislation necessary to implement them while balancing all library interests. The development of this plan shall be the major goal of this five-year program.

The development of a resource sharing plan within the five-year period targeted in 1977 was not fulfilled. However, the Statewide Advisory Council on Libraries revised the purpose of the Statewide and Regional Impact Program throughout the five years, from developing a resource sharing plan in 1977 to studying automated resource sharing in 1980 to designating, as a priority in 1981, the use of automation in developing resource sharing databases. The intent of the proposed plan was clearly evident; the text was missing.

Massachusetts State government became noticeably more concerned with the sharing of library resources through networking when Policy Report #13 appeared in the Senate's FY1982 budget narrative. A discussion of library resources available in the public higher education institutions, the report supported the development of a comprehensive, machine-readable database of holdings of library materials in the State's college and university system to stimulate resource sharing. A retrospective conversion process utilizing the bibliographic resources of OCLC was recommended as the most viable, cost-effective method of constructing the holdings database.

The Board of Library Commissioners prepared a position paper in response to Policy Report #13. Building holdings databases was a cost-effective approach to resource sharing, but the concept should be broadened to include libraries of all types instead of the single-type (public academic libraries) advocated in the Report. Not only would the more comprehensive database intensify the economies of scale phenomenon, but it would increase the scope of the total information resource accessible to all residents of the Commonwealth.

In October 1981, staff members of the Board of Library Commissioners (BLC) met with representatives of the Massachusetts Conference of Chief Librarians of Public Higher Education Institutions (MCCLPHEI) to discuss the implications of Policy Report #13. A BLC/MCCLPHEI Automation Planning Committee was charged to design "a mechanism for the planned development of a computer-linked network of economically and politically viable systems to provide resource sharing among all types of libraries."

Committee members decided that Massachusetts librarians needed to be surveyed to learn their perceptions of priorities and needs related to resource sharing. In late 1981 and early 1982 the needs of public, academic, and special libraries and library consortia were assessed and prioritized using a modified Delphi technique employing a two-stage questionnaire. Eight high priority areas were identified:

RANK	MEAN	NEED
1	8.09	Union list of serials on a statewide/regional/local basis
2	7.60	On-line catalogs for resource sharing (interlibrary loan capability)
3	7.54	Support of capital costs for library participation in networks
4	7.26	Development of a statewide plan for library automation
5	7.12	Automated circulation systems on a statewide/regional/local basis
6	7.00	Development of networks and interfaces among networks
7	6.94	Access to bibliographic utilities
8	6.78	Training/workshops on automation

The rankings indicated a desire to share resources by participating in cooperative activities and networks. Circulation systems were suggested as a major tool of resource sharing with interfaces and communications between systems constituting a network.

When Committee members met again in February 1982 to discuss the survey findings, it was decided to include representatives from public, private academic, and special libraries. After several meetings of the expanded Committee between March and July 1982 which accomplished very little, members agreed in mid-August to develop a plan based upon telecommunication links between existing and future automated circulation systems, creating a resource sharing network. In addition, the plan would specify a mechanism responsible for evaluating the network and making recommendations for changes. A smaller working group composed of library representatives from all types of libraries was considered the most appropriate vehicle for developing the plan.

The new working group, renamed the Automation Planning Committee (APC), convened in October 1982, charged with planning a multitype resource sharing network. The APC met regularly from late 1982 through mid-1983 developing drafts which were reviewed by the Committee members and the Statewide Advisory Council on Libraries (SACL). A final draft was sent to 200 librarians and organizational representatives throughout the state for comment. In August, 1983, the Board of Library Commissioners approved a plan from the APC and the SACL for the establishment of a statewide automated resource sharing network for libraries. The planning document, *Automated Resource Sharing in Massachusetts: A Plan,* sets forth a conceptual framework within which public, academic, school, and special libraries can use computer technology to improve their resource sharing efforts.

ASPECTS OF THE AUTOMATION PLAN

Purpose and Principles

The purpose of the network in Massachusetts is to voluntarily coordinate, facilitate, and improve access to the information resources of libraries in the state. Objectives include providing cooperative development and maintenance of common bibliographic and holdings databases, developing and operating systems for cooperative use of cataloging data, cooperative acquisitions and other forms of resource sharing, and developing and implementing procedures for document request and delivery. The network is not to interfere with the prerogatives of existing library boards. The network participant will continue to enjoy autonomy without diminution of authority since the powers of the network, expressed mainly through governance agreements, relate only to the activities and programs of the network itself. Its primary concern is increasing access to resources.

To reflect the needs of the user and the library in this automated resource sharing effort, "principles" considered as basic attributes were employed in developing the network:

1. Each individual has the right to access the information that meets his or her needs.
2. All network services should be provided at a level of operation as close to the user as possible. A local library should be the user's most efficient and appropriate service center. Therefore, network services should be provided through libraries as often as possible. The network must support local libraries; not compete with them.
3. The objectives of the resource sharing network should be realized without harm to the missions of participating libraries, although their methods of operation invariably must be adjusted. All libraries have a responsibility to collect the materials needed regularly by their own constituents. Resource sharing is a supplement for local acquisition, not a substitute.
4. It is essential that the network enable individual libraries to maximize the gains of resource sharing while allowing for local flexibility; network members must understand and recognize existing individual constraints.
5. The resource sharing network should be built upon existing cooperative systems and existing library strengths. New resource

sharing systems, built upon strong individual library collections and services, should evolve where existing cooperatives are no longer effective. The network should not compete with existing arrangements, but rather improve, redirect, and extend those already existing, and offer alternative approaches which will prove more valuable and useful.

6. Networking is not free. Besides equipment and material costs, staff time is necessary to provide shared services. Therefore, each participant must be able to balance benefits with investment. This balance need not be measured solely in the traditional interlibrary loan concept of net borrowing versus net lending of materials. Attention also must be given to the increased benefits of improved access to more resources. A cost-benefit analysis is an appropriate methodology to study the benefits of network investment.

7. The financial and fiscal basis of the continued operation of network components must depend upon local rather than federal, state, and private funding sources. Local funding sources include assessed membership fees, cost recovery/reimbursement fees, and allocations from the institutions. Governmental and private grants and intermittent local fund raising are unreliable as a financial base since they are more apt to change annually.

8. Resource sharing efforts must not be limited to within the State. When and where economically, technically, and politically feasible and desirable, the State's resource sharing network and its related services should overcome geo-political boundaries, broadening access into the total information resources of the region and the nation.

Based upon the need for resource sharing and considering automated technology, the plan's Mission Statement is to:

Develop cost-effective methods of resource sharing that will increase access to the information resources needed by Massachusetts residents by promoting cooperative efforts among libraries of various types and by reducing barriers to networking.

Considering the mission statement of automated resource sharing networking and the aforementioned principles to be utilized in designing a network, the library network concept for Massachusetts is based upon the linking by telecommunications of independent cooperative systems of libraries, each with a center that not only coordinates the internal activities of the system, but also serves as the cooperative's link with the center of other systems. Cooperatives locate needed material (documents and/or bibliographic citations), ascertain availability status (if technologically feasible) and place requests for the desired items. Material is delivered in the most efficient manner available. The network is hierarchical in that cooperative centers communicate with other centers in a planned outward and upward process. For users, this resource sharing network, with its local basis and hierarchical expansion process, can provide access to the full scope of information resources to meet their needs.

Network Activities

Two major activities of the network in Massachusetts relating to automated resource sharing were conceptualized and established related to the goals of increased access and cost-effectiveness:

1. Develop and link bibliographic databases to provide greater access opportunities to resources by developing access points into the information resource, and by developing telecommunication linkages between access points.
2. Develop document requests and delivery procedures.

The first major activity of the network is to develop and link bibliographic databases, and to provide greater access to resources by developing more access points into the information resources represented by these machine-readable records. One basis of automated resource sharing is the ability to create machine-readable records containing information, and the capability of others to access the database file.

Database files are accessed for resource sharing by three services:[12]

1. *Search services:* database files which provide the searcher with bibliographic citations and/or abstracts of resources indexed in the database, or full document text, such as articles, transportation schedules, or current news stories
2. *Cataloging/ILL services:* database files of shared machine-readable bibliographic records which are created and/or modified by libraries during the cataloging process and which indicate library ownership; these files may be searched for interlibrary loan purposes
3. *Circulation/ILL services:* database files of machine-readable bibliographic records which not only indicate ownership, but also current availability (on the shelf and available for loan, in circulation, or on the shelf for reference use) to the requester

Increasing the number of libraries of all types participating in these services will increase the number of access points into the information resources, thus facilitating the sharing of resources between libraries for the benefit of the user.

The plan provides two distinct means to increase the number of access points. Resource sharing is greatly facilitated by utilizing online circulation control systems. Therefore, one of the means to increase access points is to expand participation in online circulation/ILL control systems where it is technically and economically feasible, and develop new systems where they are needed.

In Massachusetts, automated circulation control systems are referred to as either "stand-alone" systems or network "clusters". A stand-alone is operated for the benefit of only one library while a network cluster has two or more libraries sharing central site hardware, software and the resulting bibliographic and specific item databases.

One of the most powerful automated resource sharing tools is a network cluster. Its many benefits include:

1. Increased access and speed of retrieval: It is possible for an individual to search the holdings of several libraries very quickly, determine the item's physical location, and immediately know its availability status (on the shelf, in circulation, on reserve, etc.). Location and availability information save personnel time and costs and reduce turnaround time for document request and delivery because requests are forwarded only to libraries known to own the item, and more likely forwarded only to those libraries with the item immediately available.

2. Cooperative collection development and maintenance: Duplication of low priority materials can be reduced; collection development by subject can be assigned to members; user demand and patterns of borrowing statistics can be generated for analysis; and individual library responsibilities for maintaining unique resources can be decided.

3. Simplifying the distribution of lending loads: This enables the system to become a more equitable proposition for the lending libraries.

Because of the importance of circulation/ILL clusters in facilitating resource sharing, the Plan calls for expanding existing clusters in size and scope to include more libraries as participants when and where it is feasible, considering hardware, software, and other factors. Building on existing clusters broadens the database files by increasing the number of resources accessible for sharing and also increasing the number of access points into the shared database file. Furthermore, expanding existing clusters saves costs by requiring only marginal increases in network systems while distributing the operational cost burden among more participants. When it is not feasible to include more participants in existing clusters, new, shared, online circulation clusters should be encouraged and developed. State and federal funds administered through the Board of Library Commissioners would be allocated for establishing and/or expanding the central site hardware and software of network clusters.

Access to information should be available to all users and libraries by a local library within a reasonable distance of the user. A second means to increase the number of access points into the information resources of the state's libraries called Information Network Centers (INCs) considers that many public, academic, special, and school libraries do not currently participate in a circulation/ILL cluster and may not be able to in the near future for a variety of reasons. Also, these libraries may lack the means to access search and cataloging/ILL services for resource sharing purposes.

INCs, which are also funded with state and federal funds administered through the Board of Library Commissioners, are a cooperative effort of two or more local libraries (of the same or different types) in which one library houses the appropriate equipment and serves as the access point for the public and for other librarians that are members of the INC. The primary responsibility of an INC will be to provide access into sources of information for resource sharing:

1. *Search services:* INCs will be capable of accessing information retrieval systems for bibliographical citations, abstracts, and full document text.

2. *Cataloging/ILL services:* INCs will create machine-readable records of the acquisitions of the member libraries by using an appropriate cataloging service. These records, which provide the physical location (ownership) of holdings, must then be placed in an automated system so that they can be accessed for resource sharing by other access points. In this way, materials in INC libraries are made available for interlibrary loan to other libraries, thereby expanding the State's resource sharing efforts.

3. *Circulation/ILL services:* INCs will have the capability of dial-up access to those clusters participating in the network for location information and, if possible, availability status.

Another aspect of the first major activity is to develop telecommunications linkages between access points. The automated resource sharing network for Massachusetts is based upon telecommunications links between access points (such as between shared circulation/ILL control systems, and between clusters and Information Network Centers) capable of providing both physical location and availability status information for the holdings of cluster members. Developing the technology to link similar and disparate circulation/ILL control systems using telecommunications enables a library in one cluster to search the holdings of another cluster, thereby expanding resource sharing capabilities.

The second major network activity concerns document request and delivery procedures. As access into the information resources of the Commonwealth improves, the need arises for more efficient and effective methodologies to request documents for loan and to ensure their delivery increases.

The automated resource sharing network in Massachusetts will be necessarily hierarchical. Technically, access points can only search one database file at a time, and cooperative arrangements between clusters, and between INCs and clusters, will help structure the searching and routing patterns into a hierarchical network. Linking circulation/ILL control systems with other clusters, and INCs with clusters, will result in more horizontal patterns of lending and borrowing between libraries, replacing the present pattern of upward, vertical borrowing.[13] Such a hierarchy will allow larger and special libraries to function as last recourse centers and to give more attention to those requests which they are best equipped to handle.[14]

Using electronic means to identify the holdings and to transmit the request increases the success rate and is more efficient. Whenever possible, the request should be placed in machine-readable form online in realtime rather than in a batch mode so that processing can begin immediately.[15]

Although access points will be able to locate a resource, ascertain its availability, and request its delivery online, the delivery mode for the near future will be painfully slow. Electronic document delivery is technically feasible, available—and expensive. The document delivery mode chosen to fill a request should utilize the fastest, most cost-effective and reliable means available. The choice of technology to implement delivery is a function of several factors—distance, response time necessary, size of item, and cost of service.[16]

Therefore, the basis of the network is the development, continuation, and linking of physical access points into the information resources of the state's libraries. In its simplest form, an access point (circulation cluster or Information Network Center) locates which library owns the desired item. Requesting and receiving the item may occur at the access point or through the user's local library. Not all libraries will be access points; however, most libraries will either become an access point or share an access point with other libraries. In the network framework, the access points utilize automated means to locate materials, ascertain availability status if possible, and request the items. Delivery will become more automated as more machine-readable formats become more available. Access, rather than ownership, has become the dominant concern; and automated, rather than manual communication mechanisms, has become the accepted standard. The point is that the network's purpose is to increase access to information resources and to reduce the cost of computerized technology by sharing resources and expenses. The network is not to become a bank of computers.

Network Advisory Committee

The Board of Library Commissioners is responsible for the planning and implementation of activities related to the network. Many recommendations concerning the network such as priorities, use of federal funds for network projects, revising the automated resource sharing plan and others will come from the Statewide Advisory Council on Libraries. However, both the Board and the Council are concerned with matters of a broad nature and are not, on the whole, network participants. When approving the plan, the Board established the Network Advisory Committee (NAC) as a forum for the discussion of issues related to resource sharing and networking.

The Network Advisory Committee, whose membership includes representatives of automated and non-automated libraries and consortia throughout the state, assists the Board on a continuing basis providing advice and submitting reports concerning the activities and aspects of the network and the plan. The NAC also assists the Board in implementing network activities and by providing evaluations of network objectives through its operation.

Evaluation of the Network

For evaluation purposes, the Massachusetts network must have a positive impact on users in terms of access to more materials. The network should also enable an individual library to provide a corresponding level of service at less cost, increased service at commensurate cost, or much more service at less cost than if the services were undertaken individually.[17] The effectiveness of resource sharing depends upon the availability of appropriate communications, technology, and delivery systems.[18] To be minimally effective, a library network must:

1. provide library service to at least as many users via the network as were served by each individual library prior to the network;
2. fulfill at least as many requests for library materials via the network as were met by each individual library prior to the network;
3. provide bibliographic access to library resources at least as rapidly as conventional location devices such as local card catalogs;
4. offer access to a larger collection of materials than is available at any one of the libraries in the network;
5. provide delivery of materials borrowed via the network within a specified amount of time (determined by members) in a majority of network loans.[19]

EXAMPLES OF AUTOMATED RESOURCE SHARING—
THE NETWORK CLUSTERS

The historic development of automated resource sharing in Massachusetts based upon a shared circulation/ILL control system spans a very brief period. It began with the common belief that collective automation would be an economical means of providing expanded access and services to library users.

In 1980, the first network in Massachusetts designed specifically for automated resource sharing based upon the network cluster concept was established. Partially funded with federal Library Services and Construction Act (L.S.C.A.) appropriations administered through the Board of Library Commissioners, NOBLE (North of Boston Library Exchange) united libraries in an automated circulation/ILL control system. Since the creation of NOBLE, L.S.C.A. funds have made possible the planning, development, and expansion of six other network clusters in Massachusetts:

- Central/Western Massachusetts Automated Resource Sharing (C/W MARS), 1982;
- Merrimack Valley Library Consortium (MVLC), 1983;
- Minuteman Library Network (MLN), 1984;
- University of Lowell Collaborative (ULowell), 1985;
- Old Colony Library Network (OCLN), 1985; and
- Automated Bristol Library Exchange (ABLE); 1985

In addition, the Five College Corporation, through the Hampshire Interlibrary Cooperative, has established a cluster without L.S.C.A. funding.

The reasons provided by members for establishing clusters were remarkably similar: to acquire, process, access, and disseminate the vast quantities of available information which was over-burdening the human, financial, and technical capabilities of the libraries. To expand access to information, a method of sharing resources utilizing technology was needed. Computer-based networking offered a viable mediation for the dilemma of access, ownership and cost containment. Still, the cost of technology was beyond the reach of the medium and small library. Economically, a cooperative organization was required to distribute the high cost of automation.

Each of these network clusters pursued its own course of development, aided by state guidelines when available. The members established organizational entities to accommodate their technologically-oriented foundation, sought federal funds for initial costs, determined financial obligations and fiscal responsibilities needed to sustain the network, and defined the administrative and operational functions of the organizations.

As with the earlier cooperative efforts, automated resource sharing clusters formed along functional lines. Some of those functions include: union catalogs, automated circulation, bibliographic/subject searches, electronic interlibrary loan, statistical data reports, public access catalogs, and communication linkages to database files of other networks.

Such functions are designed to provide greater access to library resources and greater efficiency in the identification and delivery of these materials. A shared database of current, accurate, and complete holdings information facilitates local access, improves collection management, and broadens the base of total resources. Using automation, local efficiency improves for each member library.

The following section discusses the developmental process, the organizational structure, and the operational activities of the Massachusetts clusters, presented chronologically.

NOBLE

NOBLE (North of Boston Library Exchange) represents the first joint effort of Massachusetts libraries from unaffiliated political and fiscal jurisdictions to unite in a cooperative automation venture.

The unpretentious origin of automated resource sharing in Massachusetts began in 1979 with the purchase of a computerized circulation system for the newly-renovated Peabody Institute Library. When Peabody acquired a CLSI LIBS 100 unit to support its main library and two branches, the potential for developing this local system into a shared automated database for inter-library loans and reciprocal borrowing was quickly apparent since successful cluster operations using the same technology were functioning in Illinois and Connecticut. Towards that end, neighboring libraries were surveyed for their potential interest in converting Peabody's local system into a shared database. Four libraries responded positively. After a joint meeting with the trustees of the respective libraries, a $115,000 L.S.C.A. grant proposal was filed to cover the cost of expanding the storage capacity of Peabody's system. Once funding was insured, the participating libraries purchased their own terminals, leased telecommunications lines, and directed their data entry operations.

The consortium was governed by a network management committee, composed of the directors of the five libraries. Decisions were by majority vote, except those decisions requiring expenditure of funds. Here, a unanimous vote of the five was required. The governing body's only official was a chairman.

Each library signed an agreement to participate in the automated circulation and bibliographic system. The libraries agreed that Peabody owned the system and that the members would independently purchase and maintain their own equipment. Maintenance on the central console was calculated as follows: Peabody would pay an amount equal to the maintenance of its original unit, while all members would equally divide the maintenance cost for the upgraded console.

Individual financial obligations, the agreement concluded, were contingent upon the availability of local funds, and the obligation of each member was subject to the remaining members having sufficient funds to fulfill their commitment to the network. The agreement, the first of its kind in Massachusetts, placed the onus of support upon Peabody. The rationale was that if Peabody supported a stand-alone system, as originally planned, it would be incurring the full cost independently. Moreover, since Peabody's collection was limited, it needed access to other collections to serve its local clientele, but it was also offering others the opportunity to automate. Resource sharing would, thus, be mutually beneficial. Furthermore, since no other automated network existed in Massachusetts, local authorities were, needless to say, skeptical about the concept as well as the practice. The liberal wording of the agreement was to encourage membership and to ease the financial worries of municipal officials. Cooperating with other towns to share books was a long-accepted practice, but expending local money collectively on an ambiguous technological notion was unprecedented.

Once the project had received L.S.C.A. funding, librarians and trustees met with town officials to secure local financial support. By the summer of 1980, each library had convinced its fiscal authorities of the project's validity, and by August of the following year, the first remote library went online. Automated networking had begun.

Later that year, a grant proposal was written to further expand the network to support an additional cluster of libraries. In 1982, the Board of Library Commissioners approved $99,600 in L.S.C.A. funding to upgrade Peabody's central console unit to enable four more libraries to participate in the resource sharing project. This group now became known as the North of Boston Library Exchange, or simply, NOBLE.

The admission of new members created a need to formalize the organizational structure. The original management committee met informally to discuss local implementation problems and general policy questions while a second committee, made up of technical service librarians, met bimonthly to develop details of data entry. The four new members joined the original group at the management and technical meetings.

Concurrent with this phase of NOBLE's development was an additional expansion project. The Board of Library Commissioners sought admission to the network for a group of regional academic and special libraries. The additional processor required to accommodate them was obtained with L.S.C.A. funds and installed at the campus of a community college. The result was a bipolar network consisting of NOBLE Public and NOBLE Academic with a separate console for each branch connected by CLSI's Datalink technology. Datalink is a method, via dial-up telephone access, of linking disparate automated systems.

With a network this complex, a defined organizational structure was essential. A governance committee was appointed to study the issue and to draft organizational bylaws.

The resulting document stated that the purpose of the organization was to provide increased access to information through a computerized, shared bibliographic database and circulation control system. Participants, who constitute the Users' Council, would be financially responsible for the annual costs of the central processing unit and would enter and share their bibliographic records. The Users' Council, consisting of the directors of the participating libraries, authorizes the annual budget and schedule of fees, establishes priorities for the network, determines policies, implements programs, approves membership applications, and designates special committees. Its officers are a President, a Secretary, and a Treasurer. Network personnel is provided by the central site library staff.

All members share in the total expenses of the system while individual libraries pay their local maintenance and telecommunications charges. NOBLE Public and NOBLE Academic are, however, financially independent, each with its own budget and schedule of fees. New members joining the network are assessed an entry fee which is applied towards the purchase of additional processors and disk drives to accommodate network expansion. For the members of NOBLE, the concept of networking was approached as a solution to the problem of expanding resource sharing capabilities and providing for effective collection management. Automation, however, proved to be a centralizing force in which commonalities and disparities between autonomous libraries needed to be recognized. When a loose confederation of libraries expanded into a complex organization, informal relationships yielded to formalized structures. As a result. NOBLE's pioneering initiatives have provided the genesis for the development of computer networking throughout Massachusetts.

As NOBLE was developing, groups of libraries in the Central and Western parts of the state were designing a network which would geographically encompass two-thirds of Massachusetts.

C/W MARS

From the early beginnings of what was eventually to become C/W MARS (Central/Western Massachusetts Automated Resource Sharing), participants realized that the development of any automated system would require a high level of cooperation, coordination, and planning. The joint automation project undertaken by the Central and Western Massachusetts Regional Public Library Systems started from separate inquiries into the feasibility of using automated systems to expand resource sharing, to make more productive use of staff time, and to control operational costs.

In 1977, thirteen libraries in Western Massachusetts, in conjunction with the Regional System, began analyzing their needs and exploring the potentials of automation. The sharing of resources, particularly interlibrary loans, was a key interest for the libraries and for the Regional System. Participants recognized the considerable collection strengths in the area libraries and the benefits that could be accrued by sharing materials as opposed to duplicating them. Concurrently, several groups of libraries in the Central Region also began exploring automation as a means of resource sharing.

In 1980, the two regions wrote an L.S.C.A. proposal to hire an automation consultant. Because the consultant's model for system development focused on group involvement and the development of local expertise, the project coordinators had responsibility for the overall implementation of the system, and for gathering information, reviewing data, and making recommendations. The librarians, with the consultant's aid, prepared planning documents for the procurement and implementation of an automated system for the two regions, and drafted precise plans for funding, site selection and preparation, vendor selection, contract negotiation, and installation. From these documents, a grant proposal was written seeking funds for a shared system. In September, 1981, the Board of Library Commissioners approved the proposal and awarded funding of over $671,000. The project would establish a shared automation system geographically covering two-thirds of Massachusetts and including public, academic, and special libraries.

Evaluation task forces gathered information on various systems and prepared a report of recommendations, criticisms, and concerns. Dataphase Systems, Inc. was the choice of the evaluation teams. By September, 1982, a contract was signed with the vendor, a central site selected, a system manager hired, and twenty-eight public, academic, and special libraries had contracted to join the C/W MARS network.

Governing a network that covers two-thirds of the state and includes multitype libraries from disparate fiscal and political jurisdictions was a major undertaking. The Western Region, a non-profit corporation, agreed to represent the members until C/W MARS incorporated. A legal framework, necessary for the individual libraries to participate, affirmed that the cities and towns would appropriate money to their local libraries to pay the Western Region for network services.

The network agreement declared that C/W MARS was a cooperative library network providing shared bibliographic records, circulation control, interlibrary loan, cataloging and acquisition services. Members, constituting the Users' Council, would pay a proportional share of the total operational costs, purchase local equipment, and enter bibliographic information into the database.

The contractual network agreement bound members to participate, but bylaws were needed to define how the organization was governed. In defining the organization's executive authority, the following issues concerned the network members: that there be geographic representation and a balance of powers to reflect the interests of the various types and sizes of member libraries, and that the largest public libraries not serve on the executive board concurrently. The resulting bylaws were designed to coalesce the divergent interests. In their conception, the bylaws were intended to encourage direct involvement by all members of the Users' Council, to involve the Central and Western Regional Administrators, and to allow for flexibility to accommodate details learned from experience. The bylaws described the purpose of the organization, defined membership criteria, and provided for the composition, powers, and responsibilities of the Executive Committee and its officers.

The Executive Committee composed of 11 members recommends the annual budget and fees, develops policies and programs, and advises the Network Manager. The officers of the Executive Committee are a President, and a Secretary, who is a Regional Administrator. A Network Manager is responsible for the daily administration, management, and supervision of the network.

Funding is a major issue in the management of C/W MARS. In determining fiscal requirements, two points were stressed. It was felt that the accident of geography should not affect the financial assessments of the members, and that an allocation for the differences in size of collections and number of transactions should be made. Typically, academic libraries require more storage space, while public libraries engage in more circulation transactions because academic libraries have larger collections, and the public libraries have greater circulation of materials. To reduce conflict and to recognize the differences in usage, storage, and geographic location, certain operational costs were shared equally, based on a set cost allocation formula. All central site costs (staffing, telecommunications, and rental of central facility) are to be shared equally at a base charge of $5400 per library. In addition, each library is charged a per unit storage rate of $.025 for the number of volumes in their collections; and a $.025 unit transaction rate for their annual circulation activity. New members are charged a higher initial-year base rate plus the unit rates.

In order to permit libraries too small to consider online membership the option to participate in C/W MARS, the regional microcomputer project was designed. Libraries may, at reduced prices, purchase a micro-computer, related software, and a modem for dial-up access to the C/W MARS database. The library is charged a C/W MARS fee and is required to enter its current holdings into the network database. It may query the database for interlibrary loans and send electronic message requests for items.

The organization of the network is one of division of responsibilities in which the Users' Council is the overall policy formulation body. It is administered by the Executive Committee which oversees the Network Manager and the central site computer operations staff. The Executive Committee also appoints special task forces to advise, recommend, and formulate policies and procedures for such areas as bibliographic data, circulation procedures, and interlibrary loan policies. These groups advise the User's Council on the technical aspects of system operations.

In designing its network, the goal of C/W MARS was to establish an organization to increase the effectiveness of library services to the public through an efficient use of resources. The resources were human as well as financial and material. The investment in people, and the group effort that resulted, provided the cohesive element to link the network into a cooperative whole.

In the western part of Massachusetts, the Five Colleges Corporation was exploring ways to build upon twenty-five years of collaboration.

Five Colleges Corporation

As discussed earlier, the Five Colleges Corporation is an educational association which fosters cooperative activities between a cluster of neighboring academic institutions: Amherst College, Hampshire College, Mount Holyoke College, Smith College and the University of Massachusetts. The Hampshire Inter-Library Center, an administrative unit within the Corporation, is directed by the Librarians' Council. The Council consisting of the five library directors, comprises the management, planning, and policy-making body for the cooperative efforts. The libraries have cooperated on union serial lists, joint acquisitions, catalog card production, borrowing privileges, document delivery, and reference services. In 1980, the Librarians' Council recommended the introduction of an online automated system to link the five libraries. The Five Colleges Corporation approved the request and with financial support from private foundations, installed an automated system to create a unified database from the holdings of the five libraries.

In 1982, Five Colleges entered into an agreement with OCLC to implement this automated local library system. A minicomputer was installed at the University of Massachusetts and the five libraries entered their bibliographic holdings into the central database. The system is designed to support circulation, cataloging, public access, serials control, and administrative functions, and to be linked to the OCLC shared cataloging system.

Since Five Colleges has operated as an established consortium for twenty years, the installation of an automated system for the Hampshire Inter-Library Center posed no organizational changes for the parent corporation. The automation project was, thus, instituted within the pre-existing organizational structure.

When computerization was set as a priority, the consortium merely applied the telecommunications network to the existing cooperative arrangement. Funding for hardware acquisitions was provided by an initial grant; and retrospective conversion was achieved by local funds from each college. The ongoing operational costs for the network are divided annually into five equal portions. In addition, each library has independent agreements with OCLC for services and payments.

The Five Colleges Corporation library automation project was an integral part of long-established cooperative affiliations. New technology offered a chance to enhance an existing consortia effort. In another part of Massachusetts, networking was developing from a single library's efforts to lower its operating costs while making its collection more accessible.

Merrimack Valley Library Consortium

According to its bylaws, the Merrimack Valley Library Consortium (MVLC) was established "to improve user access to area library materials and resources through the coordinated development of an automated system." For the seventeen cities and towns represented in the consortium, the need to cooperate was instigated by economic reasons: inflation had affected the purchasing power of materials, and state-mandated budgetary restrictions had resulted in materials and staffing reductions for most Massachusetts communities.

MVLC evolved in several stages. The first stage began with the acquisition of an automated system for a single library. In 1981, the Memorial Hall Library in Andover, a regional center of the Eastern Massachusetts Regional Library System, investigated the available options for library automation and elected to lease a CLSI (C.L. Systems, Inc.) unit. With the lease arrangement, the vendor would continuously upgrade the system to provide for growth in terminal and storage capacity and for the addition of other libraries in a shared cluster configuration.

Since the contract assured reduced maintenance costs if other libraries joined in a cooperative cluster, Andover contacted neighboring libraries in its region concerning potential network partnership. Five libraries agreed to participate. The alliance of these libraries in January, 1982 marks the transition from a library's stand-alone system to the formation of the Merrimack Valley Library Consortium. This network was founded under CLSI's support unit concept which involved a one-time purchase of access to central hardware and software at a price below that of ownership. The computer would be housed on site and the library would be responsible for site preparation costs and yearly lease fees. Hardware, software, and storage upgrades, on the other hand, would be guaranteed as needed and provided without charge to the leasing library. The vendor would retain full ownership of the central unit, but the host library and each participant would purchase and maintain local equipment.

While this scheme was practical for the original development of the network, it did not represent a cost-effective method for growth and expansion. Were the consortium able to purchase the system with sufficient storage capacity, the payments which were being made to the vendor could, in turn, support the network itself. Over the years, the amount paid to CLSI would far exceed the cost of ownership. By charging its members port usage fees, rather than paying a vendor lease fees, the consortium would become financially self-sufficient. Towards that end, in 1983 MVLC applied for and received $135,500 in L.S.C.A. funding to purchase an upgraded CLSI system and additional libraries were able to join the cluster at this stage. All of the libraries had separately been seeking economical ways to automate independently. None were available. Resource sharing in a network environment proved to be the only cost-effective means of achieving this goal.

To qualify for full membership in MVLC, a library agrees to pay a yearly port fee, telecommunications charges from its location to the central site, and local equipment costs. The annual charges are the network's income to pay expenses and to provide for a capital funds account.

To encourage network growth, two other categories of membership have been established—intermediate and associate. For a set annual fee, the intermediate member is entitled to one inter-active port to enter holdings, search the database, and circulate materials online. This participant is a non-voting member of the network. Associate membership is a database subscription. The participant pays for the shared use of a port; a maximum of three libraries may share one port. The library may search the database and enter its own holdings. It cannot, however, circulate items online. The various membership categories allow libraries to begin conversion of their holdings and participate in resource sharing at an affordable rate.

Organizationally, MVLC is a non-profit corporation with a governing unit consisting of a Management Committee composed of the directors of the member libraries. Its officers are a Chairman, a Vice Chairman/Treasurer, and a Recording Secretary. The Chairman and the Recording

Secretary are elected annually. The Vice Chairman/Treasurer serves indefinitely and is the director of the central site library. The Management Committee is the network's administrative and policy making body. Within this group is a subcommittee, the Long Range Planning Committee, which recommends policies, fee schedules, and future objectives. In addition, a Technical Committee functions to decide all technical and operational questions. Personnel for network operations is provided by the central site library's technical services staff.

The development of the Merrimack Valley Library Consortium parallels that of NOBLE. An independently automated library recognized that it was more economical to encourage satellite participation than to operate alone, and nearby libraries, unable to afford their own computer systems, willingly responded to a network invitation. The result was a seventeen member cooperative.

The next group of libraries to form a network cluster evolved into the Minuteman Library Network.

Minuteman Library Network

The Minuteman Library Network (MLN), a multitype consortium composed of twenty public and academic libraries, was created specifically as a resource sharing network to provide improved library service through the use of current technology in library communications and information systems.

In December of 1981, a small group of library directors considered the possibility of a shared automation system. Six months later, the first formal meetings of interested librarians were held and fourteen communities north and west of Boston agreed to participate in designing a network.

Since the possibility of each library automating separately was financially prohibitive and the ability to join an existing cluster was geographically impractical, the group looked towards several stand-alone systems. Two towns expressed interest. One of them ultimately became the central site for the consortium.

Prior to network affiliation, the various city and town libraries represented a diverse mixture of formal and informal associations. The types of resource sharing efforts common among the group included the establishment of medical information networks, the preparation of union listings, the development of special rotating collections, the cooperative purchasing of legal materials, and the formation of professional staff committees. The cooperative tradition was firmly rooted. However, to facilitate their present resource sharing pattern, to provide for a union catalog, and to allow for expansion to other communities thereby broadening the database for potential resources required an automated system. In 1983, the group was awarded an L.S.C.A. grant of $440,000 to establish such a system.

In planning the network, libraries from the participating communities formed three committees: specifications, conversion, and governance. The specifications group queried vendors and established the required system capabilities for resource sharing; the conversion committee presented recommendations for methods of converting bibliographic and patron records into machine readable format; and the governance committee designed the policy-making and administrative unit of the network. Bylaws, written by the governance group, defined membership, officers, and committee categories.

Membership, the bylaws state, is open to those libraries who agree to purchase and maintain local equipment and to share in central site system costs. They pay annual dues and appoint one representative per library as the voting member. The officers of the organization, a President, a Vice President, a Secretary, and a Treasurer, and four members at large comprise the Executive Committee which functions as the Board of Directors for the network.

A network agreement, which all libraries sign, affirms that the members will share in the costs of operating the system. The income to support the network is established by a formula in which 25% of the annual costs are shared equally by all members and 75% are prorated according to the number of terminals owned by each participating member.

In 1984, MLN was expanded to include four additional public libraries and two academic libraries. A $443,000 L.S.C.A. proposal was awarded to allow these libraries to join Minuteman by expanding the computer hardware configuration at the central site to increase port and storage capacity. This expansion project then coalesced contiguous towns into one cohesive network for bibliographic access and resource sharing.

In addition to the online resource sharing functions available, MLN participates with three public libraries in an Information Network Center (INC). The INC members, using a microcomputer, can access MLN's database for bibliographic searches and for interlibrary loans using an MLN dial-up port.

Collective automation as a cost effective means of providing expanded services to library users was the basis for the formation of the Minuteman Library Network. The well-established patterns of association in the nonautomated environment played a vital role in shaping the nature and direction of their cooperative venture.

Other Network Clusters

The librarians which were to follow the early network developers had functioning examples to guide them in their automation planning. No single model, however, would fit the needs of every incipient consortium, but these newer groups were able to amplify, improve, redirect, and extend the patterns of cooperation currently operating in Massachusetts. The newest networks Old Colony Library Network (OCLN), Automated Bristol Library Exchange (ABLE) and the University of Lowell Collaborative evolved from an array of unaffiliated libraries into organized consortia.

In January, 1985, the Old Colony Library Network submitted an L.S.C.A. proposal to the Board of Library Commissioners for $400,000 to acquire central site hardware and software. Ten months previously, a group of Massachusetts South Shore communities united with the mission of developing cost effective methods of resource sharing to increase information access.

For several years, libraries in the region had discussed the need for automation. In early 1984, an organizational meeting was held for interested librarians to participate in developing a plan for a shared automation system. The purpose of the meeting was to form an organization which would officially represent them. This organization could then be the recipient of federal L.S.C.A. funds. At their first meeting, they voted to form an organization, to define its purpose, to elect officers, and to appoint committees to study governance, resources, conversion methods, and circulation and interlibrary loan policies. Within six months, the network's bylaws were completed and its organizational structure designed. The bylaws, patterned after those of Minuteman, stated that membership was open to all who would agree to make their general circulating books and periodicals available for direct or interlibrary loan, and would agree to pay annual membership fees. Currently, sixteen libraries are members.

Officers of the network are a President, a Vice President, a Secretary, and a Treasurer. An Executive Committee serving as the organization's board of directors consists of the elected officers and five other members. The Executive Committee manages the affairs of the organization, recommends the annual budget, develops programs and services, and establishes committees as needed.

The budget for the network provides for the purchase of central site equipment, personnel, telecommunications, rental of facility, and equipment maintenance. Initial funding was $400,000 from the L.S.C.A. grant and $100,000 from the Eastern Regional Library System. Yearly expenses will be paid by the members. Participating libraries will obtain and support their own local equipment, but telecommunications charges will be handled centrally with individual assessments based on a proportional formula.

Committees, which have been established to address system issues, are attempting, wherever possible, to institute uniform lending periods and common and consistent patterns of operation within the entire network. In addition to the committees, network personnel include a coordinator, a supervisor of computer operations, and computer operators.

In less than a year, the entire concept of a network organization was developed: members were identified, objectives established, a governing structure created, a central headquarters located, working committees enacted, operational policies and procedures developed, budgetary and staffing issues addressed, and functions and activities specified.

Certainly, OCLN has had the decided advantage of being one of the most recent networks to develop in Massachusetts. The organizational and governance issues that C/W MARS and NOBLE, as network precursors, struggled to resolve, were readily (and rapidly) solvable problems for the designers of the Old Colony Library Network. The model established earlier helped pave the way for this consortium.

Another newly created network, the University of Lowell Collaborative, emphasizes resource sharing in the health community. This group evolved through the cooperative efforts of the University of Massachusetts Medical Center, the Northeast Consortium for Health Information (NECHI), the Northeast Consortium of Colleges and Universities (NECCUM), the Central Massachusetts Consortium for Health-Related Libraries, and the University of Lowell.

These varied libraries united to share their resources and offer enhanced services to the health community. Through dial-up ports into the University of Lowell system, the members can locate resources and determine item availability status from a database of some 200,000 monograph, serial, and audiovisual records.

In 1979, the University of Lowell began utilizing an integrated library system (Data Phase ALIS II) for in-house cataloging and circulation functions, and by 1981, an online public access catalog became available for the library users.

In 1980, a federal Area Health Education Center grant funded a three year program to enter the records of five health libraries into the University of Lowell bibliographic database. The University of Lowell Library provided the computer storage space, while the grant provided terminals, modems, and personnel for data entry for the five libraries. This effort was later broadened to include all members of the Northeast Consortium for Health Information (NECHI).

In 1985, the University of Lowell Collaborative received an L.S.C.A. Title III grant of $193,000 to purchase hardware to upgrade the existing central site at Lowell. The upgrade enabled additional libraries to convert their holdings into the automated union catalog, to provide public access and automated circulation functions, and to facilitate their interlibrary loan program. The grant formally united the University of Lowell, NECHI, and the Northeast Consortium of Colleges and Universities (NECCUM) in an automated resource sharing network.

Students, practicing health professionals, patients, and others served by the NECCUM, NECHI, and University of Lowell libraries had limited access to the information resources required for their educational, professional, or personal health needs. Joining in an automated network gave them access to the bibliographic records of fififty-three academic, hospital, and special libraries.

Unlike the other automated resource sharing networks in Massachusetts, the University of Lowell Collaborative has united established consortia rather than individual libraries into a collaborative association. The primary objective of this group is to serve as an interlibrary loan tool. The combined online union catalog is an access service for locating needed resources and for electronically arranging interlibrary loans. Since many of the participants are small health libraries, the Collaborative also assists in the coordination of holdings for special collections and periodicals.

The network exists not as an organizational unit, as do the other Massachusetts networks, rather it exists to provide resource sharing functions. There are no bylaws, network agreements, contractual arrangements, committees, officers, or administrative units. Each participant is governed by the provisions of its local consortium. Each consortium conducts its own meetings and a University of Lowell staff member meets with them to report on progress, problems, and new information, and to address their concerns and special needs.

The University of Lowell Library maintains the central site facility and provides the staff—a systems librarian, computer room operator, and a project director. Participants obtain and maintain their own equipment and pay local personnel and telecommunications charges. There is no shared network budget.

With the upgraded system, the University of Lowell will pay for the maintenance of the equipment for the first year. After that, the members will be assessed a percentage of the maintenance cost based upon their use of the system, whether it is for storage of records, public access catalogs, interlibrary loans, or circulation of materials.

The University of Lowell Collaborative differs markedly from the other Massachusetts networks. It is united by type of library—academic and medical, with informal arrangements, rather than contractual agreements, constituting the organizational structure. Since the Collaborative is composed of numerous small libraries, the network addresses individual needs within the shared system and determines the members' financial commitment based on their level of usage. Access to a union catalog and the provision of electronic interlibrary loans, rather than the use of automated circulation functions, are the prime activities of the Collaborative.

The newest member to Massachusetts networking is ABLE, the Automated Bristol Library Exchange. ABLE was founded in 1984 by five southeastern Massachusetts public libraries. Their purpose is to share resources, cooperatively manage collections, and provide joint services. The five communities geographically constitute a cohesive service area in which neighboring libraries have traditionally encouraged their patrons to use the facilities of the adjacent towns to locate needed informational resources. Likewise, the institutions have professionally cooperated on acquisitions, on book binding projects and on rotating collections of books.

In 1981, the town of Seekonk undertook a project to build a new library. With the opening of the new building, a renewed interest for library services developed in the town resulting in a rapid increase in library usage and in materials circulation. It soon became apparent that the manual system for library operations was outmoded. An investigation proved that, while installing an automated system was the next logical step, the cost was prohibitive. Therefore, the concept of developing a shared system was explored. A quantitative needs assessment survey of both users and non-users was conducted in the projected target area. The results showed that users were dissatisfied with the size of their individual library collections and with the lengthy response time for requested materials. Another response indicated that the majority of users were unwilling to wait more than ten days for a requested book, and instead would travel elsewhere to locate it. The surveyed subjects believed that the library's holdings were inadequate in size and scope to readily meet their needs. A major conclusion from the survey showed that many citizens disregarded the library as a primary source for their personal information needs or for information on local agencies and community events. Usually, an informal network of friends, associates, local merchants took precedence over the library.

A shared library system was selected as the solution to the problems identified in the survey. Automation would increase the number of volumes available to citizens without affecting local book budgets; it would determine availability of items more easily; it would accommodate remote access to the libraries by patrons from their homes, thus allowing the homebound and the handicapped to request information and materials; it would reduce the waiting time for requested items by electronically accessing holdings and availability information of other library collections; it would provide a community information and referral database; and it would allow for cooperative collection development among the libraries. With these objectives identified, the group was, in 1985, awarded a $281,000 L.S.C.A. grant to implement a shared system.

ABLE, which is still undergoing its developmental stage, has thus far designed its organizational framework, addressed financial commitments, commenced bibliographic conversion, and analyzed system specifications from potential vendors.

The goal of the Automated Bristol Library Exchange, and indeed the goal of each network in Massachusetts, is to provide every citizen with the opportunity to access information resources that will satisfy the individual's educational, cultural, occupational, and recreational needs and interests regardless of his own personal debilities or the limitations of his individual library.

OBSERVATIONS ABOUT AUTOMATED RESOURCE SHARING IN MASSACHUSETTS

The network clusters appear to be successful in providing a means for resource sharing in Massachusetts. Over the past five years, the number of libraries participating in shared automated circulation/ILL control systems has increased from five to nearly 150. Almost twelve million volumes are included in the cluster databases. While the state and federal funds administered through the Board of Library Commissioners for network cluster development since 1980 exceeds four million dollars, it is estimated that the member libraries have locally expended nearly half that amount for bibliographic conversion, necessary hardware, telecommunications, and operational costs. Other resource sharing projects using automated technology, especially those developing union list of serials, have been equally successful.

It is difficult to state the reasons for the success of automated resource sharing in the state. Many libraries which traditionally were non-participants in formal resource sharing efforts are becoming members of cooperatives because they have learned from their neighbors of the increased effectiveness and efficiency available with automated technologies. Another factor may be the governance agreements which thoroughly protect the local library's investment in the cooperative insuring that the cooperative will not "consume" the individual. Equally important is that most governance agreements encourage the member to participate in the management of the cooperative to the degree that the local library's situation (political, economical, staffing, etc.) will allow. Involvement of the local library in the network as a whole is provided through their cooperative's participation on the Network Advisory Committee.

Many participants, however, believe that using federal and state funds to increase the opportunity for local libraries to function as an access point into informational resources through the establishment and expansion of the central site (hardware and software), or the development of resource tools such as an online union list of serials, makes it possible for the local library to take advantage of resource sharing efforts. Therefore, one of the primary reasons for the success of automated resource sharing in the

Commonwealth is related to economies of scale through the "carrot" approach to funding.

Although automated resource sharing appears to be successful in Massachusetts, the effort could be improved. To increase their resource sharing effectiveness, the cooperatives must evolve beyond their present structures and apply qualitative evaluative methodologies to assess activities beyond quantitative descriptions.

Essentially, three phases of development can be traced concerning resource sharing efforts in Massachusetts libraries—the library joins a cooperative or assists in forming a cooperative, the cooperative provides services, and the cooperative examines the means used to provide services.

In this first phase, a library identifies a need—such as access to additional resources beyond their collections or to cataloging services and then seeks others with similar needs, usually of the same type and in the same geographical area. If mutually beneficial, the library will join an existing cooperative, or if none is available, initiate the formation of a resource sharing unit for specific functional or process purposes, the justification of which is based primarily upon an anticipated increase in efficiency and effectiveness, usually through economies of scale.

The cooperative's governance agreement necessarily emphasizes the individuality of the library. The notion of individuality of an institution in Massachusetts is based upon "local autonomy" dating back to pre-revolutionary times. In this concept, the local unit of government, or the institution, must feel that it controls its own destiny at all times. As applied to cooperative efforts, the library may fear losing its identity if it becomes part of a larger resource sharing enterprise even though it realizes that it cannot succeed alone. Further, the library must be able to exert its influence on the cooperative at all times through the governance structure, and perceive to possess the ability to leave the cooperative if it should feel threatened by encroachment into its independent operations. These attitudes concerning local autonomy have served as a barrier to establishing or expanding library resource sharing efforts.

During the second phase, the cooperative develops and implements procedures to conduct functional or process activities in which means to increase efficiency and effectiveness are applied. Members reap benefits from the functions or processes conducted by the cooperative on behalf of the individual libraries.

In phase three, the cooperative re-examines methods of operations and seeks to improve its efficiency and effectiveness by applying new procedures or technologies. The cooperative may also be redefining its mission and conducting long range planning in this phase. There may be a change in the governance structure which would provide the cooperative with the necessary flexibility to adapt new methodologies, but still maintain the individuality of the local library.

For many resource sharing cooperatives, evolution stops at the second or third phase. The cooperative provides efficient service that the individual library could not provide itself. However, although application of new procedures or technologies has improved the efficiency of the cooperative and the economies of scale may be realized, effectiveness may not be maximized. In most instances, effectiveness in Massachusetts library resource sharing cooperatives would be improved if member libraries would view the interests of the cooperative first, apart from the individual library. Thereupon, the next logical phase, phase four, would be the realization by cooperative members that effectiveness can be achieved through the development of cooperative-wide policies. These policies may affect the specific functions or processes of the individual libraries, but would result in improved benefits for all cooperative members.

For example, implementation of cooperative-wide collection development policies and procedures would increase the effectiveness of circulation/ILL clusters. Cluster members take advantage of economies of scale by sharing the necessary centralized hardware and software. Efficiency is based upon the automated technology applied. Knowing which library owns the desired item, and whether or not it is available for loan is central to meeting the needs of the patron.

But the needs of the patron could be further met if cluster members adopted comprehensive collection development policies. Rather than seeing its own collection as singular and the collections of other cluster members as supplementary, the library would view the collections of all members as a united whole. What is the point in every library in the cluster buying a book that may have few circulations when the cooperative could buy fewer copies of the items and use the "remaining" funds to acquire additional titles? For instance, rather than all twenty libraries buying a newly-available book on birds, why not develop and institute a cooperative policy in which ten copies of the book are purchased and available cluster-wide? The funds saved from the ten copies not purchased could be used to purchase ten other titles which would not otherwise have been acquired.

System-wide collection development policies would not affect the library's purchasing of materials basic for its patrons, but would, instead, be used to develop specified collection strengths throughout the cooperative. Therefore, no conflict exists between cooperative collection development policies and the local library's need to acquire material for its primary patrons. In fact, the principle can be used by the cooperative as a guide for developing collections, taking advantage of user needs to assist the cooperative in planning which library will develop collection strengths in particular areas.

Unfortunately, phase four may be years away as local autonomy in Massachusetts will certainly pose as a barrier to implementing collection development policies. Specifically, how would collection development policies be explained to municipal officials, institutional managers, trustees, and the public, among others? Libraries may want (insist upon) compensation from the cooperative for acquiring materials they would not usually purchase. Furthermore, current cooperative governance agreements, and the Commonwealth's automated resource sharing plan, perpetuate and enforce the individuality of the library. If phase four is an evolutionary step that many cooperatives will need to consider to improve their effectiveness, attitudes about local [library] autonomy, cooperative governance agreements and the state's automated resource sharing plan must be re-appraised.

A common difficulty faced by librarians is the absence of a relative standard by which to assess network operations and performance. As we have seen, each of the Massachusetts cooperatives evolved in its own unique fashion to achieve its goal of providing more effective library service by utilizing automated technology. Additional efforts are now required to develop the components of both a quantitative and a qualitative evaluation process to measure whether the resource sharing network meets its performance criteria.

Evaluation is the systematic appraisal of an operation to judge the extent to which objectives are being reached. While its major purpose is to improve program effectiveness, the concept of evaluation is intertwined with planning. The goal of library management as well as network management is to increase the efficiency and effectiveness of the total library operation. To do this, it is necessary to understand the present situation, analyze its successes or failures, allow for corrective action, and then plan for future needs. Since there are no fixed benchmarks for determining an exact organizational pattern, the evaluation rests on comparisons with other similar types of organizations. The ability to compare the network's operations with other networks is aligned with the ability to make sound decisions.

The evaluative methodology for examining a network should encompass a systems analysis approach, i.e., describing the cooperative in detail, quantifying its component parts, establishing objective criteria for measuring its performance, analyzing the data by comparisons with other cooperatives, and reviewing the results to refine, modify, and ultimately implement the final design.

Network performance is defined in terms of quantifying services to users: the probability of satisfying a user's request, the average waiting time to satisfy that request, the resources required, and the costs involved.

Qualitatively, the ultimate goal of the network is to increase services to users. The functional processes the network carries out are intended to accomplish desired results for the beneficiaries of these activities. In short, the purpose of an evaluation is to enable the cooperative to operate better in the future by identifying areas needing improved performance and by planning for remedial actions. As the network and its activities mature, additional research is needed to design a detailed evaluative module with standardized methods for measuring the effects and benefits of resource sharing. Has the effort and resources applied justified the results?

NOTES

1. National Commission on Libraries and Information Science. *Library and Information Service Needs of the Nation*. Washington, D.C.: Government Printing Office, 1974. pp. 254, 268.

2. Chaplin, Richard E. "Limits of Local Self-Sufficiency." *Proceedings of the Conference on Interlibrary Communications and Information Networks*. Edited by Joseph Becker. Chicago: American Library Association, 1971. pp. 57–8

3. Swartz, Roderick G. "The Multitype Library Cooperative Response to User Needs." *Multitype Library Cooperation*. Edited by Beth A. Hamilton and William B. Ernst, Jr. New York: R. R. Bowker Co., 1977. p. 15.

4. Wilcox, Alice. "Academic Library Participation in a Resource Sharing Network." *Library Acquisitions: Practice and Theory*, II 3/4 (1978). p. 168.

5. Becker, Joseph. "Network Functions: Reactions." *The Structure and Governance of Library Networks*. Edited by Allen Kent and Thomas J. Galvin. New York: Marcel Dekker, Inc., 1979. p. 88.

6. Casey, Genevieve M. "Cooperation, Networking, and the Larger Unit in the Public Library." *The Library Quarterly*, XLVIII (October, 1978). p. 460.

7. Roman, Mary Ann, and Day, Heather. "The Role of the Special Library in Networking." p. 301. and; DeGennaro, Richard. "The Role of the Academic Library in Networking." p. 306. *Networks for Networkers: Critical Issues in Cooperative Library Development*. Edited by Barbara Evans Markuson and Blanche Woolls. New York: Neal-Schuman Publishers, Inc., 1980.

Sorenson, Richard. "The Place of School Libraries/Media Centers in Library Networks." *Library Acquisitions: Practice and Theory*, II 3/4 (1978). pp. 310–13.

8. Patrick, Ruth J. *Guidelines for Library Cooperation: Development of Academic Library Consortia*. Santa Monica, CA: Systems Development Corporation, 1972. p. 47.

9. Williams, James G. "Performance Criteria and Evaluation for a Library Resource Sharing Network." *Library Resource Sharing*. Edited by Allen Kent and Thomas J. Galvin. New York: Marcel Dekker, Inc., 1977. p. 228.

10. Drake, Miriam A. "The Economics of Library Networks." p. 225. and; DeGennaro, Richard. "The Role of the Academic Library in Networking." p. 306. *Networks for Networkers: Critical Issues in Cooperative Library Development*. Edited by Barbara Evans Markuson and Blanche Woolls. New York: Neal-Schuman Publishers, Inc., 1980.

11. Kesner, Richard M. "The Computer and the Library Environment: The Case for Microcomputers". *Journal of Library Administration*, III (Summer, 1982). p. 40.

12. Epstein, Hank. "The Technology of Library and Information Networks." *American Society for Information Science Journal*, XXXI (November, 1980). p. 425.

13. Galvin, Thomas J. "Library Networks—Trends and Issues in Evaluation and Governance." *Illinois Libraries*, LXII (April, 1980). p. 291.

14. Ernst, William B., Jr. "Potential for Growth in Multitype Library Cooperation." *Multitype Library Cooperation*. Edited by Beth A. Hamilton and William B. Ernst, Jr. New York: R. R. Bowker Co., 1977. p. 180.

15. Williams, James G., and Flynn, Roger. "Network Typology: Functions of Existing Networks." *The Structure and Governance of Library Networks*. Edited by Allen Kent and Thomas J. Galvin. New York: Marcel Dekker, Inc., 1979. p. 75.

16. *Ibid.*

17. Kent, Allen. "Directions for the Future." *Library Resource Sharing*. Edited by Allen Kent and Thomas J. Galvin. New York: Marcel Dekker, Inc., 1979. p. 323.

18. Kent, Allen. "The Goals of Resource Sharing in Libraries." *Library Resource Sharing*. Edited by Allen Kent and Thomas J. Galvin. New York: Marcel Dekker, Inc., 1979. p. 27.

19. Montgomery, K. Leon. "Library Resource Sharing Networks—Problems Needing Attention." *Library Resource Sharing*. Edited by Allen Kent and Thomas J. Galvin. New York: Marcel Dekker, Inc., 1979. p. 137.

REFERENCES

Dugan, Robert. *Automated Resource Sharing in Massachusetts: A Plan*. Boston, MA: Massachusetts Board of Library Commissioners, 1983.

Paranya, Kate. "C/W MARS: Automated Resource Sharing in Massachusetts." *Technicalities*, vol. 3, no. 5, May 1983, pp. 6–8.

Peterson, Lorna M. *Glancing Backward: Twenty-five Years of Cooperation*. [Amherst, MA]: Five Colleges, Inc., 1984.

Tricarico, MaryAnn. *Development of Automated Resource Sharing Networks in Massachusetts*. Doctoral Field Study. Boston, MA: Graduate School of Library and Information Science, Simmons College, 1985.

ON THE NATURE OF INFORMATION SYSTEMS

Charles B. Osburn

INTRODUCTION

The notion of an information society has attracted much popular attention to the importance of information and its proper management. In just the past two years, the phrase "information management" has achieved unprecedented frequency. Computers pervade industry, business, education, and government, a situation which has both stimulated and been stimulated by the new image of information. Jargon and genuinely new technical terminology relevant to information management crop up at a very rapid rate, leading the casual observer to surmise that the essential functions and concepts of information management are brand new. Meanwhile, new positions in almost any kind of organized activity are being identified as some kind of information position, whose purpose it is to address in a formal and organized way an information management responsibility.

Advances in Library Administration and Organization
Volume 6, pages 117–140
Copyright © 1986 by JAI Press Inc.
All rights of reproduction in any form reserved.
ISBN: 0-89232-724-3

But certainly, the use of information is not an invention of the latter twentieth century; it just is getting better press. Nor are the essential concepts and functions of information management new; they only are described in a new vocabulary that is, unfortunately, both imprecise and restrictive as a communications medium. Now we are finally seeing that libraries have been engaged in information management for a long time, but are like the Bourgeois Gentilhomme, who has only recently gained the awareness that what he speaks is prose. More significantly, still, we are beginning to understand better that the library institution traditionally has also been engaged in the broader aspects of information, which include, above all, communication, knowledge, and learning. Other information agencies seem not to have come to grips yet with these more complex human implications of information management.

The inherent relevance of librarianship to information management is becoming more evident to agencies outside the traditional library sphere as they are brought into working contact with libraries. And as the essential characteristics shared among information management functions dispersed among a wide range of society's agencies begin to emerge, they are causing information to be recognized as a phenomenon, rather than just as a commodity. Through trial, error, and comparison, we are all learning that there is a common denominator of concepts, principles, and functions underlying the wide variety of information management as it is manifested throughout society.

Why is this so? What has molded this underlying structure and what continues to influence and sustain it? The answers to these simple questions should be translatable into a theoretical framework or basis for the management of all library and information services. This paper attempts to advance a tentative answer to such questions.

SOME PROPOSITIONS

Information systems are intellectual artifacts, fashioned of necessity by society and protected and advanced by society through an evolving process of trial, selection, and adaptation, because information is as essential as organic nourishment to the survival and evolution of the human species. Information systems are created as means to select, organize, preserve, and transmit information through a hierarchy of cognitive processes. The aggregate of these systems, generated through a purposeful evolutionary process, constitutes the distinction between humans and other animals and renders social beings of humankind. An information system will either be adapted to the changing needs of society or will be abandoned if it performs a function no longer needed or fails to perform one that is needed.

In any case, information systems of various kinds will continue to flourish as long as the species survives, and the duration of survival may be highly dependent upon the quality of information systems fashioned by humanity.

This set of propositions is probably as unprovable and irrefutable as any other theory in the social sciences, yet it may provide a useful perspective from which to view the social phenomena called information systems. Consequently, the purpose of this paper is not to prove the theory, but to demonstrate that such a theory offers a specifically significant and coherent synthesis of theory in a number of disciplines, especially biology, psychology, anthropology, sociology, and philosophy, when perceived through the common feature of information.

THE ROLE OF THEORY

Given the above statements about the importance of information, it would seem that a great deal surely must be known about this phenomenon, especially among the ranks of those engaged in library and information services. It is true that each year the relevant indexing services cite tens of thousands of contributions to the literature of library and information work, still it is equally true that there seems to be little advancement of our understanding of the foundation concepts of the field. We remain uncertain about whether it is two distinct disciplines and even about whether it is a legitimate discipline at all. Is it proper to use the word "science" in referring to this field that produces so must introspection and observation that are unguided by theory? Others can debate and perhaps even definitively answer the latter question. Like other professions, the information professions are caught up in the press of business and the immediate concerns of finding efficient ways to provide a service. The literature of the field, whether it is called information science or library science, reflects a highly pragmatic attitude and often a mechanistic view of information, for it is characterized predominantly by empirical studies and by the exposition of methodology.

There can be little question that we need an accumulation of facts achieved through the reporting of observation because, over time, this serves as a monitor of activity. But the sheer accumulation of facts can be the opiate of a profession; we can be lulled into a smug sense of satisfaction by the appearance of a scientific approach and, what is worse, we run the very clear risk of constantly narrowing our focus on small parts of the phenomenon of information, neglecting their relation to the whole. The information profession has reached a plateau beyond which little progress is likely to be made by further reporting of empirical evidence. For example, Bertalanffy points out that the history of science shows that progress depends upon the establishment of theoretical constructs, and that. "Idealizations never completely realized in nature . . . form the basis of physical theory."[1] The primary function of theory is to create order in what would otherwise be a chaos of natural phenomena. Order is fundamental to the cognitive process. Theory establishes relationship among otherwise isolated phenomena; it provides a structure for further questioning and a basis for new ideas that can advance understanding. Consequently, theory has a predictive power. F.S.C. Northrop observes that a science that restricts itself to directly observable entities and relations automatically loses predictive power, and that "The strongest relation of necessary connection between any two factors, such as the present and future states of a system, is logical implication . . ."[2] Finally, theory, not sheer empirical data, is the basis upon which action is taken.

In spite of the efforts of the social sciences, particularly during the past forty years, to emulate the physical sciences, they are different. The social sciences are not necessarily less scientific, but different by virtue of much greater complexity. Both areas begin by addressing a problem, which Northrop observes takes two forms in the social sciences: "What is the character of social institutions?" and "How ought social institutions to be?"[3] These are questions of both fact and value, not just of fact, and they are directly pertinent to the information profession. If information systems are more than mechanistic entities—and too often we do treat them only as such—then our first step toward understanding relevant phenomena is to perceive them as social agencies, working within society, which is a collective of social beings, not of mechanisms. This means understanding the most subtle processes of society that result in action and change. "Any conception of what is 'strictly speaking' empirical or observable that excludes this dimension of human life . . . is emasculated and epistemologically unwarranted."[4]

THEORY AND PRACTICE

This brings us to the question of theory and practice, or, as the issue is characterized more commonly: the debate about theory versus practice. The opposition of these fundamental aspects of human behavior is especially unfortunate in the professions, where a capacity to meet increasingly more complex, social needs is derived from the constructive dialectic of theory and practice. Bernstein observes the relationship of the theory—practice distinction to several other categorical distinctions—the distinction between empirical and normative theory; between descriptive and prescriptive discourse, and between fact and value—and notes that these dichotomies are persistently called into question.[5] Certainly theory and practice have always been integral parts of one process, but the necessity of consciously adapting this notion to daily thinking may be of unprecedented importance now that activities and knowledge in many areas of life are becoming more evidently intermeshed. Dahrendorf advises, therefore, "that neither the theorist nor the practitioner can avoid reasoning about them in a single context and with equal intensity."[6]

Perhaps the unfortunate split between theory and practice in the information profession (which, however, may not exhibit this tendency to a greater extent than any other profession) is responsible for the ambiguity in which the profession, and many of its individual members, sees itself. There seems to be little consensus about what the job is, why it is, and about its range of responsibilities. There is a great sense of individual security that can be derived from viewing a job or a whole profession very narrowly and very mechanically. Similarly, a great deal of managerial security can be found in the withdrawal from personal judgment, allowing decisions to be made almost automatically, on the weight of empirical evidence only. This approach to decisions is certainly faulty, but it also has the insidious effect of strengthening the narrow view of the profession, as though it were a self-contained entity rather than a socially integrated system with a long history and a profound purpose. In this regard, the information profession, perhaps more than any other, is both humanistic and social scientific. It is humanistic insofar as its purpose in the long term is to maintain continuity useful to the attainment of the goals of humanity. It is a social science because of its methodology and because when it functions well it does so as a self-aware social sub-system.

BACK TO BASICS

There has been a debilitating confusion of theory and methodology in the information profession during the past fifteen years or so. It is really the ways of doing things that have been given the greatest attention by the profession, second only to observation of specific functions and phenomena. Methodology, it would appear, has become an end in itself. How to do it has become more important than why it should be done, except that methodology almost seems to have become its own justification. This trend is not unique in the information field, to be sure, particularly among the social sciences where methodology has achieved the status of expressing the essence of some fields. But the emphasis on methodology coupled with an emphasis on the recording of empirical data—each evidently feeding the other—weakens the power of the discipline to advance its base understanding of itself and its base corpus of knowledge from which further questioning and testing can develop. Although the collection of data and the refinement of methodology are certainly integral functions of the advancement of knowledge, this extreme emphasis has become a diversion from the more fundamental function of constructing theoretical systems, which can then generate substantive need of new data and improved methodology, and which can advance understanding.

In the guise of theory, much of the literature relevant to the information profession consists of theories for doing, or of management theory, which often really amounts to methodology. The profession can benefit from theories for doing, but even more at this time, it can benefit from theories for understanding the nature of information and its place in the universe. In this instance, the notion of "getting back to basics" means constructing a theoretical framework that will be conducive to insights into the nature of information services, one that can suggest an attitude, one that can guide the collection of empirical evidence and the formulation of methodology.

INFORMATION

There are enough definitions of information available that yet another appropriate one need not be invented for the purpose of this paper. Nonetheless, the definition of so elusive a concept as information in the present context is not simple. First, information is a hierarchical phenomenon, which at one level may be treated as a commodity, while at another level has to do with knowledge and tradition. Along the framework of this hierarchy is a continuum of various levels of choice, whose realization in decision or action can be considered a manifestation of information. There is an analogous and related hierarchy of information that applies to society, just as it does to individuals, but it is superimposed over greater periods of time, involving even more complex processes than aggregate individual behaviors. It is the cumulation of selected information elements moving upward in the structure of the information hierarchy within individuals that generates the structure and substance of the hierarchy of societal information. The reasons, the processes, and the outcomes of information from all levels of both hierarchies thus have some degree of influence on each higher level, thereby culminating in what Kenneth Boulding[7] refers to as the social transcript and what Edward Shils[8] describes as tradition.

Boulding characterizes the human knowledge structure as an image, or one's view of the world, with all the subtle implications that notion suggests. It is the image upon which behavior depends. The image includes a sense of time, of relationships, of cause and effect, continuity and repetition, and a high degree of self-consciousness and self-awareness. It has a reflective nature that leads to rational behavior, for the response of humans, "is not to an immediate stimulus, but to an image of the future, filtered through an elaborate value system."[9] The image makes society and society remakes the image, and so on. Boulding observes that in this process "an enormous part of the activity of each society is concerned with the transmission and protection of its public [collective] image."[10] He also draws an analogy between the learning process and the mutation-selection process of biological evolution, which is of interest to later sections of this paper.[11]

With an emphasis on the concept of information, Pratt has used Boulding's notion of image to arrive at an explicit definition of information, which will be applied throughout this paper. Basically, this is the process of giving new form to the image.[12] Such a definition may not be much different from that derived by McGarry from several sources, which is that "information is any context that reduces uncertainty or the number of possibilities in a situation; and on the social and biological plane of human activity, all our behaviour patterns are geared to the reduction of uncertainty."[13] However, the notion of image characterizing the human knowledge structure as elaborated by Boulding is essential to the development of theory in this paper.

Viewed in this way, information has a most pervasive influence on the individual, on organization, on society and culture. It influences specific individual actions and attitudes as well as evolutionary change. Katz and Kahn conclude that the exchange of information and the transmission of meaning form "the very essence of a social system or an organization."[14] More recently, Holzner and Marx have emphasized that the issues of knowledge use "have connections to subtle cultural and psychological processes, like those encountered in the forming and changing of conceptions of identity and cultural movements."[15] Information ranges from elements of data and the most basic sensory perception to the collective societal perception of itself. The senses of time and relationship that are essential to the human image find their highest form of expression in the social transcript. This is guaranteed in some form by the self-consciousness of humankind, which finds its most influential expression in tradition. "The connection which binds a society to its past can never die out completely; it is inherent in the nature of society, it cannot be created by government fiat or by a 'movement' of citizens that aims at specific legislation."[16] From the selection and survival of information through the characteristics of image and to the natural force of tradition a purpose is in evidence. That purpose, that teleological element, must be a requirement of the survival of the human species.

EVOLUTION

Expressed in many different ways by biologists, psychologists, philosophers, and others, there is general agreement that the chief distinction— at least the most significant one—between humans and other forms of life on earth has to do with the capacity to engage in certain cognitive processes of a "high level." Other forms of life either cannot engage at all in these processes or cannot do so at anywhere near the same degree as humans. It is difficult, in contemplating this fact, not to relate it to the theory of evolution in nature and what it might suggest about the role of information.

In his synthesis of the theory of evolution, Julian Huxley declares that, "The last step yet taken in evolutionary progress . . . is the degree of intelligence which involves true speech and conceptual thought; and it is found exclusively in man. . . . Conceptual thought is not merely found exclusively in man; it could not have been evolved on earth except in man."[17] This suggests that an historical pattern of intellectual evolution can be discerned as part of the biological evolution of human beings. Boulding makes this more explicit in noting that knowledge is the field within which evolution takes place, and that, "Changes in knowledge are the basic source of all other changes, even though changes in knowledge themselves depend on other changes."[18] It is Boulding who furnished the basis of the definition of information used in this paper, which, in essence, defines information as the element that stimulates the human cognitive processes at the social level as an integral part of the structures, patterns, and forces of natural evolution.

In general terms, evolution is a gradual process of change. In the Darwinian sense, it is genetic change of organisms from one generation to the next, affecting population. This is the biological theory that has been the subject of great debate since it was first fully elaborated for public consumption in 1859. Since then, the theory has been extended to many other areas of life in attempts to explain and give order to them. Stephen Toulmin has analyzed a number of these efforts and the general influence of the theory advanced by Charles Darwin.[19]

Cultural evolution is a change in culturally transmitted artifacts, behavior, institutions, or concepts from one generation to another. The extension by analogy of organic evolution to cultural evolution seems logical and tempting, even though plagued with problems. It at least presents a perspective on social change that can be very useful in understanding that phenomenon. For example, Talcott Parsons holds that "social science cannot be complete without the careful study of dimensions that can properly be called 'evolutionary.' "[20] The aspect of sociology involving cognition that has been studied more than any other is science, especially the notion of the growth of knowledge and its close relationship to scholarly communication. In his much debated and highly influential exposition of theory about the role and processes of theory in science, Thomas S. Kuhn[21] is clearly influenced by the fundamental concepts of evolution. Kuhn postulates that the actions of scientists in all mature fields are directed by a paradigm in which most of science takes place in the intervals between points of breakthrough, referring to those long periods of science as "normal science." The scientific revolution is prepared when the beliefs and assumptions governing normal science are challenged by questions and evidence they cannot accommodate. The critical period comes when the effort is made to advance a new theory that will accommodate those questions and the new evidence. With information marshalled in a convincing way, the new scientific theory then supplants the old one, thus beginning again a period of normal science that functions according to the newly accepted beliefs and assumptions. This is not a single cycle, but an evolutionary process. Kuhn's use of the word "revolution" can be misleading in this context. No doubt, in substance the new theory may be perceived as revolutionary, but the way it comes about is no more revolutionary, in the sense of suddenness, than the process by which the last straw breaks the camel's back.

Although Kuhn was not specifically demonstrating an analogy between genetic evolution and the evolution of science in his monumental exposition of theory, he has spoken of scientific theory as showing descendancy through an evolutionary process of selection and adaptation, noting that its movement is "unidirectional and irreversible. One scientific theory is not as good as another for doing what scientists normally do."[22] This raises another point to be addressed later in this paper, which is the question of direction or purpose. For the time being, however, it can be noted that even though cultural evolution, whose example in this case has been the advance of scientific thought, does exhibit characteristics closely analogous to those of genetic evolution, the former derives its energy from human rationality and the latter does not. This distinguishing feature may or may not have anything to do with value, but it has everything to do with purpose and direction.

Before examining this and other concepts that are embodied in either genetic or cultural evolution, it may be useful to note that there is somewhat of a composite of these two essential interpretations of human evolution. Treated separately here because the theory is not yet fully accepted even though it appears to be gaining in wide acceptance, is the theory of gene-culture coevolution. As described by Edward O. Wilson and Charles J. Lumsden, gene-culture coevolution occurs when genetic and cultural evolution are coupled in a reciprocally interacting manner: specifically, in their terms, it is "any change in gene frequencies that alters culturgen frequencies in such a way that the culturgen changes alter the gene frequencies as well."[23] A "culturgen" is the basic unit of inheritance in cultural evolution, "a relatively homogeneous set of artifacts, behaviors, or mentifacts (mental constructs having little or no direct correspondence to reality) that either shares without exception one or more attribute states selected for their functional importance or at least shares a consistently recurrent range of such attribute states within a given polythetic set."[24] Gene-culture translation is the transformation of individual cognition and choices of culturgens into cultural patterns.

To the extent that this theory is developed further and is tested successfully, it will bridge the gap that has separated organic and cultural evolutionary theory; a gap that has frustrated scientists and philosophers for well over a century. The originators of the theory of gene-culture coevolution believe that the connection was not made convincingly heretofore by sociobiologists because they did not take into proper account either the human mind or the diversity of cultures: "Thus in the great circuit that runs from the DNA blueprint through all the steps of epigenesis to culture and back again, the central piece—the development of the human mind—has been largely ignored."[25]

Fundamental to any account of evolution is the theory of natural selection and adaptation, which raises the issue of purpose and direction: Are evolutionary changes made through purposeful selection and adaptation, and is this done according to some master plan? Long before the promulgation of a theory of evolution, the philosophers of antiquity developed what we can call the mystical theory, which simply was a belief in some kind of generalized cosmic order of things in the universe. Then followed the religious theory of events, changes, and evolution, claiming these to be of providential design in the form of God's divine plan. The humanist theory, focusing on cultural evolution, opposes this idea and credits human foresight and ingenuity for the development of social progress in all forms. In all cases the idea of progress is tied to the evolution of humans, whether organically or culturally, through the processes of natural selection and adaptation. The homeostatic theory, combining physical and systems theory to explain social change, stresses that social systems regulate themselves to maintain equilibrium, within an acceptable range of variance, through the principle of "feedback." The maintenance of stability could in this case, be considered the purpose of change. With regard to the theory of homeostasis, however Toulmin points out that it is, in fact, a theory of stasis, not of change, at least not of long-term change, and therefore could not account for any but the short-term adaptations of social institutions to defend themselves at any given time.[26]

The effort to draw a very tight analogy between organic and cultural evolution, to make one reflective in every way of the other, has perhaps obscured some of the processes that belong only to one or the other area. Julian Huxley's assessment of natural selection, that, "It does not ensure progress, or maximum advantage, or any other ideal state of affairs,"[27] may not apply at all to the function of selection in cultural evolution, which is a related, possibly even mutually dependent, but different process. Similarly, while efforts in the social sciences to mimic the physical sciences doubtless have in most ways strengthened the social sciences, they may be misleading or impeding in others. Progress, a value, is movement toward fulfillment of purpose. Humans, as highly self-aware beings, are rational beings, therefore endowed with purposeful thought. The human processing of information is goal oriented. This distinction has not been fully taken into account in the study of selection and adaptation processes of cultural evolution.

True natural selection is characterized by the seeming randomness of selection. It follows a process of selection, leading to either adaptation or disappearance, and, in the case of adaptation, eventually leading to selection, beginning the cycle again. Huxley warns against the adoption of the methods of natural selection in social and cultural development, advising that it would, however, be most advantageous to study them with the aim of discovering how to modify and control them and of learning what to avoid. He advises that, "Not only is natural selection not the instrument of a God's sublime purpose; it is not even the best mechanism for achieving evolutionary progress."[28]

The selection that motivates cultural evolution is a more generalized version of the development of scientific thought, for it is characterized by a gradual trial and error process in a social context, and by a purpose. Harmonizing the interplay of the environment and the socio-psychological needs of rational beings seems to be the purpose of cultural evolution. Boulding describes this great difference between organic and cultural evolution quite succinctly in observing that, "whereas prehuman organisms occupy niches and expand to fill them, the human organism is a niche-expander creating the niches into which it will expand."[29]

These "niches" are expanded and created, following a course of trial and error, through the "diversification and selective perpetuation of thought"[30] and behavior that have proved successful in assisting humanity to adapt to the changing conditions of its relationship to the environment. This evolutionary process results in a complex hierarchy of interdependent social behaviors, including individual cognition, organization, institution, and the social transcript. It has been argued—convincingly to many authorities—that all evolution is a knowledge process, even in its biological aspects.[31]

At least in the adaptability of society and its evolution toward greater refinement and diversification, the knowledge process is in evidence. Relating cultural evolution to biological evolution, Bronowski draws a fine but important distinction in observing that any animal species survives by adaptability, rather than by adaptation. In that context he notes that it is the human brain that is to be credited with the progressive success of the evolution of society, for "the brain is not an adaptation, but a wonderfully complex store of adaptability."[32] Individual mental evolution and cultural evolution are importantly and integrally connected by means of the process of information, which stimulates selection and adaptation. Information is the energy that drives the regenerating processes of cultural evolution and therefore constitutes a subsystem of that inclusive system. It is itself a social system.

THE SYSTEM CONCEPT

The concept of system as applied to information is not yet uniformly or even widely acknowledged in the information profession, although the usefulness of this approach apparently is rapidly gaining acceptance. Interestingly, if not ironically, attention to the application of concepts embodied in systems theory to information seems to have taken hold first as the result of efforts to design electronic information management tools in the image of individual human behavior, rather than as the result of an interest in information first and foremost as a social phenomenon. The former, of course, is a subsystem manifestation of the latter.

Systems theory is described in depth elsewhere,[33] so it will be treated only cursorily here. Developed to explain certain phenomena in the physical sciences, systems theory was later adopted by behavioral scientists in order to view organizational and societal processes through a conceptual framework that would account for a great deal of complexity and dynamism. This is just the kind of conceptual framework needed to order our thoughts about information in society.

The processes of information constitute a social system, which has the properties of an open, natural, system. Such a system is conceived as an integrated whole, comprising many interrelated components that are constantly in motion, responding to energy infused from outside the system (input) and generating energy beyond the system (output). Depending upon the nature of the system, output can be just about anything from a single idea to a condominium complex. Changes in any of the interrelated components will affect other components in the system to some degree, depending upon the nature and magnitude of change and on the relationship of the components. As a whole, the system possesses properties that are different from and greater than the sum of its components.

Open, natural systems are conceived to exist in a concentric hierarchy, those below or incorporated by a given system being subsystems, and those above or incorporating the given system being supersystems. It is with these surrounding systems that the exchange of energy, or input and output, takes place. Input into the system is informative in character about the environment of the system as well as about the system's own functioning relative to the environment, and the reception of input is selective. The pattern of energy exchange tends to be cyclic. One of the great advantages of the systems view is that highly complex phenomena may still be observed in discrete but meaningful units, for "We can enter the hierarchy of systems at any convenient point,"[34] without having to know all about the subsystems and supersystems.

Dynamism and change are essential characteristics of these systems, for they must maintain whatever variables may be required for survival in their environment, which is to say, to satisfy the energy needs of the supersystem. "Inert equilibrium is a sure sign of decay."[35] Constant interaction with the subsystems and the supersystem is the response to this requirement for survival. A key concept in systems theory is that of the entropic process, whereby energy used within the system reduces energy available within the system. A system that runs out of energy ceases to exist; one that has the likely potential to do so is called a "closed" system, while one that has the likely potential to replace used energy is an "open" system, the kind under discussion in this paper. This, of course, is what is meant by survival of the system. The process of survival for an open system, therefore, is the acquisition of negative entropy. "Negative entropy" is not really the circumlocution it appears to be, since it highlights the natural inclination of all systems: the development of entropy. One way a system engages in this process is through the acquisition of energy from subsystems and the supersystem, as described earlier. With the counterbalancing influx and outflow of energy the system maintains a steady state, but this does not mean that its properties, functions, and goals always stand the same.

On the contrary, in the process of counterbalancing entropy, natural, open systems "develop toward states of a higher order, differentiation and organization."[36] They transform the energy available to them "evolving new structures and new functions, they create themselves in time."[37] As they grow in size they develop new, and more complex functions, with more specialized functions superseding diffuse global patterns.[38] Thus, new mechanisms for the import and export of informative energy are created. The trial and error process in the adaptation toward new and more complex functions produces both useful and useless output, "the criterion of usefulness being established by the suprasystem."[39] The ultimate goal of the system is to satisfy that criterion of the supersystem. With a focus on information as the primary force in the evolution of society, the application of the concept of a natural, open system endowed with the attributes just outlined can afford the advantage of a new perspective both on the dynamics of information and on societal change.

INFORMATION, MIND AND SOCIETY

Although this paper emphasizes the role of information in society, it is impossible not to address also the function of information in the individual mind. The extrapolation from the human being to humanity is difficult because there is no incremental progression joining them in hierarchy; only a quantum leap. Again, in this case it is far more useful not to view society as a collection of beings, but rather as a system in relation to sub- and supersystems and collateral systems.

As a system, the mind is greater than the sum of its interactive components; it expands, modifies, and even creates new informative energy from its sources of energy, chief among which are genetic transmission, experience, and cultural norms. Therefore, the informative energy it emits (its output) always has the potential to influence change in the environment, including changes in tradition, social norms of behavior, and perhaps even genetic structure.[40] The system functions within the cultural supersystem in a cyclical, evolutionary manner. Analogous to the cultural supersystem, the purpose of the mind is to maintain an equilibrium between the psychological needs of the individual as a social, rational being and the complex changes of its environment. This is carried on through a process of trial and error and selection from within the storehouse of adaptability that is the mind. Adaptability, the ability to create and expand niches rather than just to adapt to existing ones, is the result of a purposeful dialectic between the genetic structure of the mind and the other inputs it receives from the environment. It is particularly this internal dialectic that makes the mind a system that is irreducible to the sum of its parts.

Stimuli in the mind leading through this process, which results in what Boulding refers to as the image, is information. With the purpose of achieving its own system goal, the mind receives input in the context of its own conditioning, modifies it accordingly to create reality or a new image, and initiates behavior, which is expressed as output toward its environment or input into the supersystem: society and the culture that defines it. "The mind once arisen is, indeed, limited by biological conditions but it gradually comes to control them by a purposeful handling of the environment and in so doing modifies the conditions of its own survival."[41]

The functioning of information in society can be understood properly only in the context of the way society evolves through time. Cultural evolution is a process analogous to the patterning of an open system dependent on the exchange of informative energy, and especially dependent for its dynamism on information. The receipt, selection, variation, and retention of information in the individual mind is visualized by Campbell as follows:

There is a nested hierarchy of knowledge processes, the lower (more advanced, less fundamental) of which substitute for the more fundamental, operating as shortcuts. In each process, at each level, there is a variation—and selective—retention mechanism. The short-cutting, substitute mechanisms are themselves the products of a blend-mutation-and-selective-retention process, and as such have no "entailed" status as vicarious knowledge processes. Further, they probe reality still less directly and still more presumptively. At each level there must be a mechanism for (1) variation, (2) selection among variations, and (3) preservation and/or propagation of variations.[42]

It is through this hierarchy of processes that information is used or rejected or even modified upward through the hierarchy to become a concept or belief and thus a new framework for processing further information. At that generalized and higher level, the sociologist-philosopher Robert K. Merton held information to be crucial to the pattern of structural choice behavior in his social analysis. The social patterning of information influences even the rates of socially significant choices, "by influencing the sanctions attached to choices, by influencing the perceived alternatives between which people choose, and by influencing the rate of success of the alternative chosen."[43] Boulding calls the social system's stock of knowledge and values "the genetic structure of all social construction."[44] He relates the process of choice more simply to the image of the future, or rather to competing images of the future, for in his view it is largely the strong sense of future that separates humans from other animals. He emphasizes the importance of the image of the past informing the image of the future, pointing out that from the record, which consists of artifacts as well as images, new images are created constantly and subjected to selection as knowledge is transmitted from one mind to another and from generation to generation. For Boulding, the changing, adapting, ever more complex image of the future is the teleological element of the knowledge process. Very much in the manner of open systems, generally, this system has a purpose whether it is derived from internally developed norms or from norms imposed from outside the system.[45]

The progressive projection of the image eventually results in the forming of the collective, social image, which is the net of accepted tradition, beliefs, and norms of the cultural, or the supersystem of the mind. This process can be viewed as a paradigm functioning much in the same way that Kuhn describes scientific development, both being information processes. Using this description of science as a model from which to work analogously toward a better understanding of social change, Imershein concludes that, "The development of a new paradigm in response to the anomalies and crises can be seen, in part, as the result of a shift in metaphysics or background assumption, or as a change in the beliefs about 'how the world works'."[46] As in the evolution of science, society changes through a rational process, because its adaptations through selection from among the choices, whether presented as inputs into the mind from the environment or created by the mind, are guided by purpose.

This rationality is characteristic of the mind. The question then arises whether a higher level of rationality in adaptation would result from a more conscious, systematic use of information by society, thus greatly accelerating cultural evolution. Given the increasing rate at which society presents itself with alternative images of the future, and the steadily higher level of consciousness at the macro level of alternative global futures, it is not far-fetched to imagine such an evolutionary change as "nature's way of maintaining itself in stable equilibrium."[47] Kochen, whose words in this context have just been cited, believes that society is on the brink of a shift in the growth of organizational focus toward adaptivity by bringing accumulated knowledge to bear on the vital functions of communities. Out of this evolutionary change, he sees the emergence of new forms of social organizations that will be analogous to the mind.

Whether or not Kochen is correct in this assessment of the status of cultural evolution remains to be seen. Whether the mind is a product of society, or society a product of the mind has been a well debated issue for quite a long while. At least, however, it is clear that the dynamics of information constitute the functional link between mind and society so that there is a mutual influence between society and knowledge. The social creations called information systems, in a variety of manifestations, have evolved because humans are highly self-conscious, rational beings while, conversely, those beings instinctively create such systems for their purposes. This whole, made up of many hierarchical and complex processes, forms the structure of a self-generating, open system that evolves in a cyclical manner. If, as current research suggests, the processes of learning, valuation, and decision are mechanisms for the coevolution of genes with culture, then the essentialness of information to society runs even deeper. Should further research show this theory to be lacking, there still seems to remain quite ample justification of Bronowski's judgment that, "Knowledge is our destiny. Self-knowledge, at last bringing together the experience of the acts and the explanations of science, waits ahead of us. . . . We are a scientific civilisation: that means, a civilisation in which knowledge and its integrity are crucial."[48]

INFORMATION SYSTEMS

Information systems function in size and complexity ranging at least from the system that informs the genetic structure to the great libraries and bibliographic systems of the world. They can be both mind-created and mind-creative, and they organize all kinds of information processes according to the broad definition of information determined earler in this paper. The stimulus to the information process, which is conceived to function as a system, can be characterized as a record. The choice of focus on a record either as an individual unit or as a file or collection of units is determined by the perspective taken of it from within the hierarchy of systems. For example, an analysis of the management of a library as a system would treat the library as a collection of records, while an analysis of the transmission of culture through time could treat the library as a record. Similarly, in the design of an abstracting system, the product would be considered a collection of records, whereas it could be a record of the discipline from the perspective of intellectual history.

In this paper, emphasis is placed on those information systems that fall within a limited, yet unspecifiable range within the complex hierarchy of these systems. That range, whose boundaries are not always clear, is defined by those information systems that are created and maintained by society through its subsystem organizations. It is important not to ignore the fact that the information systems under discussion do constitute only a range in the hierarchy—not its totality, because a general understanding of the patterned context of information as a pervasive process is basic to the potential to gain insight into the nature of information systems. It is a question of adopting the most useful perspective from which to observe or modify a given information system. Therefore, it also is a question of an awareness of the deep structure (to borrow a concept useful in linguistics) that subtly influences the surface structure. In that light, the following brief description of an information system can be used. Borko concludes that "an information system consists of a collection of recorded information, custodians who organize and maintain the collection, a retrieval procedure, and the users who refer to the information to satisfy a variety of needs."[49] The study of the interrelationships of information systems within the hierarchy, in terms of theory, observation, and development, is called, in the United States, information science.

It is quite likely that the discussion of information and information systems can lead to a confounding of information and communication. Vickery observes that there are basically four types of communication that intended to inform, to instruct, to motivate or persuade, and to amuse or entertain.[50] He identifies the first mentioned—to inform—as the substance of information science. However, this function, when selected from among the four functions of communication, seems too limiting given the range of the hierarchy of information systems. Another perspective, drawn from the purpose of the system, needs to be brought to bear. A consideration of the definition of information as the process whereby the mind's image is changed, with the record as the basic element in stimulating that change consistent with system movement toward fulfillment of purpose, suggests that information may include all of the various kinds of communication, but each one only to the extent that it contributes significantly to a change in the image relevant to system goals. Therefore, the concepts of informing and information have a particular meaning when applied to information systems. Information builds on its contextual past and contains the potential of new insight into the future by reducing complexity and uncertainty.

The individual image of the future, when functioning in the aggregate as a social phenomenon, places great demand upon the information systems designed by organizational subsystems of society. For in that framework a predictive capacity is expected and is of necessity an inherent attribute of any such system. Kent finds four images of the future which cannot be projected with certainty yet which must guide the development of systems in this range of the hierarchy. These are the images of what society will be like, what words will mean, how people will act, and how people will view events.[51] It should be noted that Kent does not cite these as images of the future, but rather as assumptions that cannot be avoided in the design of a system. Nonetheless, assumptions determining the design and maintenance of information systems are, in fact, images of the past projected through new records to create images of the future and, what is more important, new structures for image making in the future.

"Just as language not only expresses thought but also is a shaper of ideas,"[52] the patterning and classification of records both reflect society's image of reality and, conversely, help order society's image of relationships and possible new relationships. The structuring of records through information systems helps to organize records to form or modify images that result in behavior, artifacts, new records, new images, and new image structures. Such a concept of information systems lends support to Heilprin's comment that "The conclusion is inescapable that the record is essentially a tool for making artifacts."[53] Furthermore, as suggested earlier, the structuring of records through society's hierarchy of information systems is a conscious behavior that greatly facilitates the sharing of images on a large scale, thereby expediting the process of institutional adaptation.[54] In a continuation of the evolutionary cycle, institutional adaptation generates informative energy upward into the greater system (society), and also downward, filtering and channeling it through the hierarchy of information systems.

This sketchy model of the functioning of information systems in society helps to define the concept of "environment," at least insofar as information is concerned. Use of the concept of environment, however it may be used in reference to information, clearly represents a major advance in progress toward understanding information phenomena and in guiding the design and maintenance of information systems. But too often, it seems that the word environment is used very loosely, loosely enough that the full value of the concept is not realized because its meaning is not shared commonly among writers in the information profession. More precision in definition would help. Environment need not be considered the anomalous totality constituted by everything other than the specific information function under study. For the environment is structured by systems that have some degree of independent dynamic pattern, while interacting with others, also endowed with some degree of dependency.

Boulding points out the significance of value in assessing the roles and relationships of "environmental" systems. His chief concern in considering environment is to emphasize that any evaluation of world environment can be meaningful only from the point of view of human values, observing that, "We are not talking about the nonhuman part of the system and evaluating it by its own values, because it does not have any."[55] In information systems, as defined in this chapter, the fabric of value that connects systems throughout their hierarchy is precisely the rational goal of human survival; a goal that often is rendered obscure through countless iterations of the evolutionary cycle to ever higher levels and greater complexity of individual system functions.

EVOLUTION AND SYSTEM DESIGN

The concept of evolution, when applied to information systems, does not denote a passive mode on the part of society and its organizations. Yet, the fact that libraries, traditionally viewed as very passive institutions, have survived disruptive, chaotic, anti-intellectual upheavals quite regularly for hundreds of generations—even flourishing and developing—leads one to suspect the opposite. The issue is raised pointedly in the axiom advanced by Swanson: "To the extent that a system is designed, implemented, or managed, its freedom to evolve is diminished."[56] The substance of this argument, however, is not the denigration of systems design and management. It is, rather, that their most advantageous design will enhance rather than inhibit the natural evolutionary processes at work throughout the hierarchy of information systems.

This approach to the design and management of that particular information system called the "library" evidently has been largely responsible for the evolution of that category of agencies into a major social institution. In the discipline of "institution building," which establishes a perspective on planned and guided social change, the achievement of institution status is considered the pinnacle of success for an organization; it is a goal achieved when the organization and its innovations are accepted and supported by its environment. In terms of design and management, it is useful to note that in the process of developing toward this status, the environment accommodates institutional innovation.[57] The institution survives because it is accepted and supported by the society to which it is responsive, but it also fulfills a proactive function depended upon by society for further adaptation. This process is further stimulated by the dialectical nature of organizational cycles.[58] Consequently, social systems create their own reality (image) as much as their reality is influenced by the super-system.

In the context of a hierarchy of evolutionary processes, the purpose of information systems is to organize an enormously diverse spectrum of information for individual and societal purposes. This is an increasingly essential function in an increasingly mercurial environment wherein selectivity, as the pivotal determiner, is increasingly elusive. "Without structure, without spacing, without specification, there is a babel of tongues, but there is no meaning."[59] The realization of the concept of purposeful selectivity depends upon information systems. Critical to the success of the system, then, is its ability to anticipate the characteristics and nature of the environmental dynamics, and to adjust in a manner and with the timeliness that best serves the supersystem purposes. In recognition of the evolutionary mode of the hierarchy of information systems, the design and management of such systems would most usefully be translated into attitudes, perspectives, processes, and structures for gathering intelligence about surrounding systems and for appropriate adaptation.

If it is true that humanity is evolving toward an information age, that is because, as suggested earlier, society has attained a new level of consciousness about its cognitive processes and the role of information. Perhaps this is the equivalent to what Boulding considers the creation of a new niche. It is at least a question of a profound change in societal sophistication about how it evolves and adapts to survive. To state it simply enough, it is not just that information has become more important to society or that it involves more people, but rather that society is more keenly aware of itself.

Indeed, it could be that humanity is nearing the point of evaluating its development on the basis of "the growth of knowledge of nature and of insight into human needs, value and potentialities, and by the extent to which this knowledge and insight are used in the direction of human affairs."[60] This is probably what a "scientific" society does. At least, it is clear that society's subsystem organizations and institutions are developing quite deliberately along these lines, and it is useful to bear in mind that they not only are responsive to society, but are also its major agents for change and models for conceptualization. For example, in the analysis of the successful development of an organization into an institution, emphasis is placed on the systematic gathering and control of information about the environment in order to arrive at rational decisions anticipating both dangers and opportunities for further development.[61] Similarly, in the broader social sense, recent research even indicates that so-called "common sense," defined as comprising substantive capsules of folk knowledge, is becoming "supplemented by a means-oriented attitude to accessing information that is known to be socially stored."[62] There seems to be a more widely shared faith in information and knowledge, or a greater awareness by society of itself.

The evolution of culture toward a noticeably higher level of awareness that information is society's image of the future as well as of the past; that it is the stimulus to behavior and the tool for creating artifacts; that it is the essence of survival, calls for renewed assessment of the library as an information system. It is almost a cultural paradox that just as this major evolutionary change seems to be occurring, the most consistently protected social institution for the collection, preservation, organization, and dissemination of information spanning the hierarchy of information is judged by many to have outlived its usefulness. Such a judgment ignores the continuity guarded by the processes of social evolution. Such a judgment, therefore, also ignores the evolutionary progress of the library as the quintessential information system. The library has evolved and will continue to do so, adapting, creating innovation, adding functions, modifying functions, and discontinuing functions in the manner of an open system. The library as a place and as a set of technologies will change visibly, to be sure, in the coming decades, but as a functioning concept essential to human progress, change will come considerably more gradually. This is the time to be strengthening the continued development of the library, not undermining it.

But it is equally true that at this critical juncture in evolutionary time, the design of information systems such that they can seize the momentum and turn it to full social advantage is unusally important. Leadership in designing these systems has many requirements, which range from constant adjustment of internal subsystems to maintaining significant linkages with the supersystem, and all of this in an atmosphere of uncertainty and ambiguity. The knowledge base from which the design and management of information systems can most profitably proceed is to be found in the mirroring spheres of information science, which are the sociology of knowledge and social epistemology. Essentially, this is the study of the reciprocal actions of information, the individual, and society. Although this entails entry into a very extensive list of disciplines, the common thread of unity is information. The application of this core knowledge to the specific tasks manifested by the mission of the profession at any given time involves still another, but rapidly changing, set of disciplines. Among these would be record creation, file maintenance, classification, abstracting and indexing, date processing, or other subjects as appropriate to the chosen specialty within the information profession at a given time.

SUMMARY

The importance of context for design can hardly be overstated, yet it seems that with the daily demands of operation, insufficient attention is accorded to context, rendering design and plans shortsighted and narrowly focused.

In this paper, the context of the information profession has been described as the cognitive processes of individuals and society and how they evolve through a hierarchy of systems, whose interactive dynamism is generated and modified by information. The design and management of any system out of context is anathema, but the design and management of an information system in the absence of that context is doubly so—an irony. The information profession, in the main, tends toward that direction, however, which no doubt explains the stagnation of its theory and the emphasis on its operations to the detriment of attainment of goals and fulfillment of mission.

In presenting a context, this paper has outlined reasons for the adoption of models analogous to those found in nature (evolution and systems), working together with the focus of information. Such a methodology is quite common in the social sciences. Where this superimposition of models is found to be appropriate, it can afford useful insights and perspectives and suggest new hypotheses; where it is found wanting, it may at least provoke new lines of inquiry.

NOTES AND REFERENCES

1. Ludwig von Bertalanffy, *A Systems View of Man*, edited by Paul A. LaViolette (Boulder: Westview Press, 1981), p. 121.

2. F.S.C. Northrop, *The Logic of the Sciences and the Humanities* (New York: Macmillan, 1949), p. 115.

3. Ibid., p. 255.

4. Richard J. Bernstein, *The Restructuring of Social and Political Theory* (New York: Harcourt Brace Jovanovich, 1976), p. 230.

5. Ibid., p. 173.

6. Ralf Dahrendorf, *Essays in the Theory of Society* (Stanford: Stanford University Press, 1968), p. 272.

7. Kenneth E. Boulding, *The Image. Knowledge in Life and Society* (Ann Arbor: University to Michigan Press, 1956).

8. Edward Shils, *Tradition* (Chicago: University of Chicago Press, 1981).

9. Boulding, pp. 25–26.

10. Ibid., p. 64.

11. Ibid., p. 133.

12. Allan D. Pratt, *The Information of the Image* (Norwood, NJ: Ablex, 1982), especially pp. 35–41.

13. Keith J. McGarry, *Communication, Knowledge and the Librarian* (London: Bingley, 1975), p. 22.

14. Daniel Katz and Robert L. Kahn, *The Social Psychology of Organizations* (New York: Wiley, 1966), p. 224.

15. Burkart Holzner and John H. Marx, *Knowledge Application. The Knowledge System in Society* (Boston: Allyn and Bacon, 1979), p. 326.

16. Shils, p. 328.

17. Julian Huxley, *Evolution. The Modern Synthesis* (London: Allen and Unwin, 1942), p. 571.

18. Boulding, p. 224.

19. Stephen Toulmin, *Human Understanding* (Princeton: Princeton University Press, 1972), pp. 319–356.

20. Talcott Parsons, The Present Status of 'Structural-Functional' Theory in Sociology," in *The Idea of Social Structure*. Papers in Honor of Robert K. Merton, edited by Lewis A. Coser (New York: Harcourt Brace Jovanovich, 1975), p. 74–75.

21. Thomas S. Kuhn, *The Structure of Scientific Revolutions*. 2d ed. (Chicago: University of Chicago Press, 1970).

22. Thomas S. Kuhn, "Reflections on My Critics," in *Criticism and the Growth of Knowledge*, edited by Imre Lakatos and Alan Musgrave (Cambridge: Cambridge University Press, 1970), p. 264.

23. Charles J. Lumsden and Edward O. Wilson, *Genes, Mind, and Culture. The Coevolutionary Process* (Cambridge: Harvard University Press, 1981), p. 372.

24. Ibid., p. 368.

25. Ibid., p. ix.

26. Stephen Toulmin, "Evolution, Adaptation, and Understanding," in *Scientific Inquiry and the Social Sciences. A Volume in Honor of Donald T. Campbell*, edited by Marilynn B. Brewer and Barry E. Collins (San Francisco: Jossey-Bass, 1981), p. 31.

27. Huxley, p. 485.

28. Ibid.

29. Kenneth E. Boulding, *Ecodynamics: A New Theory of Social Evolution* (Beverly Hills: Sage Publications, 1978), p. 136.

30. Toulmin, "Evolution. . . ," p. 33.

31. For example, Donald T. Campbell, "Evolutionary Epistemology," in *The Philosophy of Karl Popper*, edited by Paul Arthur Schilpp (LaSalle, IL: Open Court, 1974), pp. 413–463.

32. Jacob Bronowski, "Introduction," in *Darwinism and the Study of Society. A Centenary Symposium*, edited by Michael Banton (London: Tavistock Publications, 1961), p. xiv.

33. Cf. Bertalanffy. See also Ervin Laszlo, *The Systems View of the World. The Natural Philosophy of the New Developments in the Sciences*. (New York: Braziller, 1972).

34. F. Kenneth Berrien, *General and Social Systems* (New Brunswick: Rutgers University Press, 1968), p. 18.

35. Laszlo, p. 46.

36. Ludwig von Bertalanffy, *A Systems View of Man*, edited d by Paul A. LaViolette (Boulder: Westview Press, 1981), p. 113.

37. Laszlo, p. 47.

38. Berrien, p. 53, and Katz and Kahn, p. 25.

39. Berrien, p. 71.

40. Cf. Lumsden and Wilson.

41. Morris Ginsberg, "Social Evolution," in *Darwinism and the Study of Society. A Centenary Symposium*, edited by Michael Banton (London: Tavistock Publications, 1961), p. 103.

42. Donald T. Campbell, "Natural Selection as an Epistemological Model," in *A Handbook of Method in Cultural Anthropology*, edited by Raoul Naroll and Ronald Cohen (New York: Columbia University Press, 1973), p. 55.

43. Arthur L. Stinchcombe, "Merton's Theory of Structures," in *The Idea of Social Structure. Papers in Honor of Robert K. Merton*, edited by Lewis A. Coser (New York: Harcourt Brace Jovanovich, 1975), p. 23.

44. Boulding, *Ecodynamics*, p. 219.

45. These two potential generators of goals in a system are distinguished by Richard Mattessich, "The Systems Approach: Its Variety of Aspects," *Journal of the American Society for Information Science* 33(November 1982):388.

46.   Allen W. Imershein, "The Epistemological Bases of Social Order: Toward Ethnoparadigm Analysis," in *Sociological Methodology 1977*, edited by David R. Heise (San Francisco: Jossey-Bass, 1977), p. 38.

47.   Manfred Kochen, "Evolution of Brainlike Social Organs," in *Information for Action. From Knowledge to Wisdom*, edited by Manfred Kochen (New York: Academic Press, 1975), p. 2.

48.   Jacob Bronowski, *The Ascent of Man* (Boston: Little, Brown, 1973), p. 437.

49.   Harold Borko, "The Conceptual Foundations of Information Systems," in *The Foundations of Access to Knowledge. A Symposium*, edited by Edward B. Montgomery (Syracuse: Syracuse University Press, 1968), p. 67.

50.   Brian C. Vickery, "The Nature of Information Science." in *Toward a Theory of Librarianship. Papers in Honor of Jesse Hauk Shera* (Metuchen, N.J.: Scarecrow Press, 1973), p. 150.

51.   Allen Kent, "Unsolvable Problems in Information Science," in *Information Science: Search for Identity*, edited by Anthony Debons (New York: Marcel Dekker, 1974), pp. 299–311.

52.   Benjamin Lee Whorf, *Language, Thought and Society: Selected Writings of Benjamin Lee Whorf*, edited by John B. Carroll (New York: Wiley, 1956), p. 212. See also Edward Sapir. "The Status of Linguistics as a Science," in *Selected Works of Edward Sapir in Language, Culture and Personality*, edited by David G. Mandelbaum (Berkeley: University of California Press, 1958), esp. p. 162.

53.   Laurence B. Heilprin, "The Library Community at a Technological and Philosophical Crossroads: Necessary and Sufficient Conditions for Survival." *Journal of the American Society for Information Science* 32 (November 1980): 390.

54.   Cf. Stinchcombe. Similar to this interpretation is a theory presented in some detail by Gary W. Strong, "Adaptive Systems: The Study of Information, Pattern, and Behavior," *Journal of the American Society for Information Science* 33(November 1982):400–406.

55.   Boulding, *Ecodynamics*, p. 31.

56.   Don R. Swanson, "Evolution, Libraries, and National Information Policy," *Library Quarterly* 50 (January 1980): 91.

57.   Milton J. Esman, "The Elements of Institution Building," in *Institution Building and Development. From Concepts to Application*, edited by Joseph W. Eaton (Beverly Hills: Sage Publications, 1972), pp. 21–39.

58.   See Noel M. Tichy, "Problem Cycles in Organizations and the Management of Change," in *The Organizational Life Cycle, Issues in the Creation, Transformation, and Decline of Organizations*, edited by John R. Kimberly and Robert H. Miles (San Francisco: Jossey-Bass, 1980), p. 171.

59.   Katz and Kahn, p. 226.

60.   Ginsberg, p. 121.

61.   Esman, p. 31.

62.   Holzner and Marx, p. 25.

FISCAL PLANNING IN ACADEMIC LIBRARIES:
THE ROLE OF THE AUTOMATED ACQUISITIONS SYSTEM

Carol E. Chamberlain

INTRODUCTION

The literature abounds with testimonials on how libraries cope with stringent budgets and the loss of purchasing power in this era of austerity.[1] Despite the abundance of guidance, the resource budget planning process in many academic libraries remains difficult and overwhelmingly complex. As Brownrigg states, "managers look at their budgets through a rear view mirror; and projecting their actual budgets into the future becomes an exercise in divination."[2]

Management information systems, or, in more recent terminology,

Advances in Library Administration and Organization
Volume 6, pages 141–152
Copyright © 1986 by JAI Press Inc.
All rights of reproduction in any form reserved.
ISBN: 0-89232-724-3

"decision support systems," are thought to be the solution to library resource problems. Yet the large scale application of these automated management systems has not occurred in libraries, largely due to the emphasis
on automation of technical service operations (cataloging and acquisitions)
and user services (circulation and online public access catalogs).[3] Microcomputers with software packages for specific accounting applications
have replaced ledgers and calculators in some libraries, but the need for
sophisticated mechanisms for resource control persists today in many academic library environments.

Effective library resource planning requires a thorough knowledge of
library expenditures, of academic programs and collection goals, and of
the external economic factors affecting library budgets. Librarians have
come to terms with the economic forces that have plagued college and
university libraries since the 1970s. They have survived the crises that
brought about severe restrictions on book purchases and massive serial
cancellation projects, and have realized that now even more than in the
past, it is essential to seek creative approaches to financial management.[4]
One approach is to look at the operations and services that provide support
for material purchases. What management information is available from
the automated system that a library may already possess? How can that
information assist the budget planning process? The automated acquisitions
system is an excellent example of such a support mechanism. An acquisitions system can be utilized to perform statistical analyses of expenditure
data, to provide support for collection assessment and for fund allocations,
and to project future costs based on economic trends.

THE ACQUISITIONS SYSTEM—DESIGN AND CONTEXT

Automated acquisitions systems vary widely in terms of how they are
designed (stand-alone versus designed as part of an integrated system)
and the context in which they are used (replicating manual ordering and
receiving routines versus supporting a wide range of functions from placement of online order requests from bibliographers to maintaining online
audit trails). Generally, they perform a set of operational tasks to support
the selection, ordering, monitoring and receiving of library materials.[5]
While acquisitions professionals agree that fund accounting and management information controls are important components of an acquisitions
system, these functions traditionally have been seen as secondary to the
need for online order and in-process records, largely because of the emphasis placed on eliminating manual files and on reducing labor-intensive
file maintenance.[6] However, with the relative sophistication of today's
integrated library systems, these short-comings have been addressed; ac-

quisitions systems do support a full range of services including control of accounting activities and a variety of management information.[7] A closer look at these two functions will set the stage for exploring how they can help the budget planner.

Fund Control Function

The fund accounting portion of an acquisitions system provides for control of the library's materials budgets by recording and monitoring the allocations, expenditures and balances of each budget category. The organization of a library's budget categories is typically based on its funding sources, i.e., endowments, state and federal support, institutional support, and on broad subject designations which reflect the academic curriculum (e.g., humanities, social sciences, science and technology). Further breakdowns may reflect specific subject areas (art, literature, history, engineering, etc.) and specific library collections (government documents, reference, rare books, etc.).

Links between the accounts data and other acquisitions data may provide controls such as the system-activated encumbrance of the appropriate fund when orders are placed, disencumbrance and expenditure when items are received and when invoices are processed. Links between the library's accounting system and campus-wide, university-wide or state-wide accounting systems may facilitate efficient communication and adherence to standardized accounting procedures. Other control mechanisms may include: setting limits on fund balances and blocking the placement of an order if the balance of the designated fund reaches that limit; having various security levels for access to and manipulation of accounting data; the ability to access data by broad academic group (e.g., college of liberal arts), academic department (e.g., languages) and by various subject disciplines; maintaining currency conversion tables online; and producing reports of account status and transactions.

Management Information Function

The management information function typically includes statistical analyses of acquisitions and accounting data to support budget assessment, collection development, acquisitions performance measurements and supplier performance measurements.[8] Data can be batch processed and produced in the form of reports[9] (budget reports, reports of new acquisitions, outstanding order reports, reports by supplier indicating average discounts and fulfillment rates, etc.), or data can be accessed online for up-to-date status information on funds, on outstanding orders and receipts in process.[10] Reports may be produced on demand or at set intervals (quarterly, year-to-date, end of fiscal year) and may provide comparative data from previous years. Information may include: average prices of books, serials and other materials by designated subject categories; amount of the budget committed for continuing orders; materials acquired through purchase, from approval programs, as gifts or on exchange; materials purchased from individual gift donations; and projected expenditures based on items received, average prices and average inflation rates.

Electronic links between the acquisitions system and external commercial databases can provide additional sources of management information. For example, online access to the R. R. Bowker databases can provide evidence of new publishing trends and of the availability of material. Access to library suppliers' online inventories and ordering systems which enable acquisitions personnel to transmit orders electronically to those suppliers which are most likely to fulfill the orders quickly and cost efficiently, can be a helpful device in determining how many outstanding orders are likely to be fulfilled (and money actually spent) by the close of the fiscal year. Access to the holdings of other institutions as well as access to their collection development guidelines (through bibliographic utilities such as OCLC and RLIN or through regional networks) may provide the stimulus for resource sharing and cooperative acquisition decisions.

Integrated systems provide links between acquisitions and other support systems internal to the library such as circulation or interlibrary loan systems. Circulation rates, the number of reserve requests for items and interlibrary loan statistics may indicate collection weaknesses and may greatly influence the kinds and quantities of materials acquired.

How can the fund accounting and management support functions described be successfully exploited to enhance the budget planning process? Let us examine the factors affecting library material budgets and how the automated acquisitions process can work to address this concern. Some of the applications described are operational in many acquisitions systems. Others are largely theoretical in nature and may not be in general use today, but most probably will be in the future.

INTERNAL ASSESSMENTS

Among the factors affecting library resource budgets are those relating to the internal acquisitions operation—the characteristics of materials purchased and the methods used to purchase them. An assessment of these factors may yield evidence of trends in the kinds of materials acquired for an individual library. It also may signal ways purchase arrangements can be changed to enhance the library's purchasing power. An automated acquisitions system can assist in the process by providing an analysis of historical data on acquisitions, showing how the data relates to publishing patterns, and by supplying data on payment policies and methods.

Expenditures and Publishing Patterns

Martin asserts that the allocation of resources for library purchases is typically based upon looking backward at previous years' budgets.[11] This approach has much merit, because by examining historical data, one can identify patterns of spending over several years. An acquisitions system which includes in its records data elements for price, subject (derived from cataloging classification), fund account and acquisition type (e.g., firm order, subscription, materials received through approval programs) and which is capable of linking this data to accounting transactions can perform analyses to derive:

- year-to-year comparisons of costs for materials by subject
- average prices of materials purchased by defined categories
- the number of publications acquired by subject area
- the number of publications acquired by format (e.g., books, journals, microforms, computer software) within subject area
- the cost of continuing commitments such as subscriptions and approval programs
- year-to-year comparisons of allocations among subject areas and among books, serials, binding, etc.

For example, the pattern of spending within a specific subject area such as physics may indicate that over the past several years, the library has suffered a loss of purchasing power—average prices increased, more money was spent and fewer books were bought to show for it. It may also show that there is a decreasing emphasis on acquiring books in the physics field and an increasing emphasis on serials (fewer books purchased, fewer books received through approval plans and an increase in the number of subscriptions). In contrast, patterns of spending in the humanities area may indicate little or no relative decline of purchasing power and no shift in emphasis from books to serials.

Knowing how money has been allocated and how it has been spent provides the foundation for future budget decisions. But what about the relationship of these expenditures to external factors? How can we know if the library's spending patterns actually reflect the needs of the academic curriculum and trends in scholarly publishing, or if they are a product of benign neglect—the lack of adequate monitoring controls and unleashed buying habits? The use of industry statistics on publishing output (e.g., from Bowker, Book Industry Study Group and from academic booksellers) and the various published materials price indexes for books and serials can be a means toward identifying whether spending patterns are a legitimate response to external conditions. These statistics could be input into the library's accounting portion of the acquisitions system and matched against corresponding library account transactions. Resulting data could then be interpreted within the library's appropriate collection development guidelines.

The value of establishing accurate spending patterns lies in achieving an awareness of *why* money was spent in certain ways in the past. It prepares the budget planner with essential background and a firm base of knowledge with which to make better decisions.[12]

Payment Methods

An examination of payment methods is another important component of internal cost assessment. Many libraries purchase the same kinds of materials from the same suppliers over and over again throughout the fiscal year. A library which is making many small payments for single items purchased may be incurring substantial additional service charges and hidden charges reflected in lower discounts (not to mention the hidden or absorbed costs of issuing a large number of individual checks). An acquisitions system can track the number of invoice transactions with a given supplier within a specified period of time and provide a listing of payments and charges for review. An evaluation of such a listing may reveal that it would be more cost-efficient to set up a deposit account with a supplier and make one large payment covering anticipated purchases for an entire year. The system would then monitor deposit account balances throughout the year and by means of a regular reporting mechanism, signal when balances are low. The system could produce year-to-year comparisons of activity useful in planning annual allocations and payments.

Likewise, the knowledge of cost-efficient payment methods can be an effective tool for negotiation with suppliers. Many suppliers offer substantial savings for libraries which make "early" payments for materials, such as the pre-payment of subscriptions several months before the subscription agency must issue its payment to the publishers. The terms of early payment (e.g., percentage of discount or credit earned on various prepaid dollar amounts) could be entered into the fund accounting portion of the acquisitions system and dollar savings calculated yearly. The acquisitions system can additionally provide a measure of control over actual expenditures after prepayment credits are applied. It also can supply data on potential dollar savings based on projected expenditures with a given supplier which the librarian can use in negotiation of future discounts.

ACADEMIC PROGRAMS AND COLLECTION GOALS

The strengths and weaknesses of a library collection reflect the historical development of the institution in its academic mission.[13] The same can be said of the budget allocation process, as the level of funding given to support collection development in various subject areas reflects the teaching and research needs of academic programs. Program needs change over time, as new areas of research open up and as new discoveries are made (witness the advances in computer technology in the last two decades). Library collection goals and levels of support are likewise constantly evolving in order to strengthen support of new academic programs and reduce support of other programs. How can an acquisitions system play a role in responding to these changing conditions? First, acquisitions systems can support electronic links to external databases and second, they can support online profiles of collection policies, acquisition policies, and budget allocation formulas for each academic program or discipline.

System Linkages

Links with commercial databases can be particularly useful when the library must assign funds for materials in support of new academic programs. In addition to providing ordering information, access to databases such as *Books in Print* or publisher inventories of books and serials can help determine how much literature exists in a given field (at least in the United States) and how much it could cost the library to acquire it. Links to regional networks could provide access to other libraries' holdings in a given discipline so that the library could determine the prospects for resource sharing within a region as an alternative to purchasing some materials. All of this information can aid the librarian in establishing reasonable fund allocations for new subject areas instead of blindly assigning an arbitrary figure and hoping that it will be enough to support necessary purchases, but without allocating too large a budget to spend within a given fiscal year.

Electronic linkages may support short-term budget planning in other ways. Subject bibliographers can access external databases for lists of new editions of works to be published and for online reviews of books, serials, software and other materials they may wish to select for purchase in the future. Because the information is in machine-readable form, it could be downloaded to a bibliographer's personal computer or workstation in the home or office and eventually become a selection request file. These online files can become part of an automated selection profile containing requests for purchase in all subject areas. System linkages to administrative academic records maintained at the college or university level may also provide support for collection librarians and selectors. Data on enrollment, research grants and projects, and data on faculty productivity in specified academic programs could be downloaded into the selection profiles. Profiles would be created and maintained by the collection development librarians and supported as a component of the library's integrated system.

Online Integrated Profiles

One difficulty inherent in the budgeting process for materials is the fact that usually the budget planner does not have sufficient information to predict with much measure of accuracy what will be selected for purchase in a given subject discipline, what will be ordered and received (or what will be ordered and *not* received) and what will be received unexpectedly within a given fiscal year. Combine this with a lack of quick, easy access to data on academic programs, and it is a wonder that budget allocations have any basis in reality!

One of the greatest potential management functions of an acquisitions system is to serve as a mechanism for controlling and accessing this wealth of information. It can be done by designing profiles[14] to derive and utilize data on academic programs, on acquisitions transactions and on selection guidelines. The academic profile could consist of program descriptions and the elements typically used in allocation formulas such as number of faculty, student enrollment, number of courses, degrees granted, etc. The acquisitions profile, derived from the acquisitions and accounting database, could include payments and transactions of the previous year (or several years) in terms of allocations, fund account balances and the rate at which funds were expended during the fiscal year, orders received, fulfillment rate, average prices, items received on approval programs, and comparison figures from the publishing industry. The selection profile could consist of the data from an individual selector's online file and could include requests for special purchases including expensive sets or collections, requests for items based on analyses of circulation and interlibrary loan statistics, selection guidelines, collection policies, and a statement of critical collection needs. The profiles could be integrated to allow the library manager to retrieve relevant data from all three files in response to a specific search for a subject discipline, academic department, library fund account, etc.

By accessing these files, decisions relating to budget allocation would be greatly facilitated. For example, the budget planner could review the characteristics of an academic program in engineering, note the growth of research and course work in robotics, compare the previous year's acquisitions and expenditures in that discipline, and review purchase requests and collection needs to support robotics. These factors could be weighed against publishing output and average prices in the subject area. An informed decision could then be made on the level of financial support for robotics for the next year (or for the next two or three years). In addition to making annual budget allocations, the financial planner would be prepared to respond effectively to exceptional situations, such as receiving a windfall of money at the end of the fiscal year and knowing how to spend it to meet critical collection needs, or losing money that has already been allocated and knowing where to reduce allocations to incur the least negative effect. This kind of management information could be provided online as needed or produced as profile reports at certain intervals, such as the end of the fiscal year.

ECONOMIC FACTORS AND FORECASTING

So far this examination of the automated acquisitions system has focused on some short-term strategies to establish accurate spending patterns and to support the allocation of funds. What about predicting long-term needs? Other important factors affecting the budget planning process are worldwide economic conditions, such as inflation rates and fluctuations in the strength of the dollar overseas, that dictate the amount of books and journals that a library can afford to buy and the kinds of materials ultimately purchased. It is difficult to predict how economic indicators will actually affect the library's purchasing power in the long run, but one way is to look at the statistical data generated internally as a byproduct of the acquisitions process. This data, along with national and international economic indicators, can be used to formulate long-term budget plans.

Figuring Costs

If the fund accounting and management information functions of an acquisitions system can monitor expenditures and report fund balances based on the account and invoice data entered into acquisitions records, they can also manipulate price data to determine:

- the rate of inflation of the cost of books, serials and binding
- postal rate increases or decreases for shipping and handling
- discounts given or added charges applied by the library's suppliers (bookdealers and subscription agents)
- the cost of foreign purchases based on currency conversions to U.S. dollars, including bank charges paid by the library.

Once these cost figures have been established, it is possible to produce these data on a yearly basis for comparison purposes. If the inflation rate

150   CAROL E. CHAMBERLAIN

for serials and binding costs is significantly more than the inflation rate for books, then the budget allocations for books, serials and binding should reflect that difference. If they do not, allocations could be adjusted gradually over a three- to five-year time period until they are in line with costs. If postal rate increases are announced by the government, or if the library is considering alternative mailing services (UPS or express mail services), these probable costs could be input into the accounting portion of the database and be compared to present costs.

Discounts and added service charges applied to book and serial purchases by library suppliers may fluctuate with the economy, usually in conjunction with publishers' costs for paper, printing and manufacturing. An acquisitions system which computes discounts and charges for each of its suppliers as part of measuring vendor performance, could also be used to evaluate changes in discount schedules and service fees as announced by the suppliers and to determine the effect of these changes in terms of library costs. The cost of foreign publications may also fluctuate largely due to the strength of the dollar abroad. When exchange rates show substantial changes, an analysis of the data on purchases from foreign countries could indicate whether the library is benefiting from favorable rates, or if the library is paying more to acquire from foreign suppliers and should consider U.S. sources for some materials.

Modeling

For long-term planning, it is possible to anticipate future costs by constructing a model, assigning values to each of the four variables and comparing this model to present costs. To illustrate, consider the following scenario: in 1990 inflation rates double for book prices and triple for serial prices over 1985 levels; postal charges which the library must pay for shipments increase a third over 1985 levels; discounts offered by the library's suppliers erode due to publisher print run restrictions and sales policies; and foreign currency exchange rates rise in response to the weakened dollar overseas. How will these factors affect the library's budget? By assigning appropriate numerical values to the categories and comparing them to 1985 levels, the system can illustrate possible expenses in 1990.

This is just an example of how the powerful capabilities of an acquisitions system can be exploited. Modeling can also be used to simulate the possible outcome of budget allocation cutbacks or huge budget increases.[15] If a library's major funding source does not allocate enough additional money to cover the increasing costs of ongoing commitments, will the library have enough in reserve funds to make up the difference? In contrast, if the library receives a substantial increase, will it be able to spend the money within the fiscal year? Since it is generally not known in advance exactly how much money will be provided for library purchases, it is important to analyze data for possible outcomes so that plans for action (how to cut costs, how to spend additional money) can be developed.

CONCLUSION

An automated acquisitions system can assist budget planning by providing historical financial data, external system linkages, online profiles and forecasting mechanisms. However, it is not by any measure a panacea which eliminates the librarian's responsibility for effective management of library resources. It cannot ensure that money for materials has been spent properly. How many times have librarians been forced to decide between buying an expensive multi-volume set or serials subscription which would support faculty research, and buying several less expensive materials to support the teaching of undergraduates? How many times has the price of an item caused one to lose sight of the need? Attempting to achieve a balanced collection within severe budget limitations requires an exercise in sound judgment and an ability to weigh the needs of teaching and research against the benefits of selective purchase decisions.

An acquisitions system also cannot automatically control or manage other aspects of the library's budget such as operating costs (salaries, supplies, equipment, building maintenance, etc.); aspects which could be supported by a sophisticated management information system (MIS).[16] However, when such systems become widely available (and affordable) to academic libraries, they could be integrated with the acquisitions system in order to access and transfer acquisitions data from one system to the other's management files. It behooves any library considering a MIS to plan for this eventual integration of acquisitions data before implementation.

The potential exists for the acquisitions system to play a greater role in management planning in the future. The evolution of technology is having a significant impact on publishing and indicates a growing emphasis on producing and managing information in electronic formats. The traditional acquisitions process may soon become more a process of negotiating contracts with suppliers for access to information resources rather than purchase of actual items.[17] This will require even greater skills and expertise to successfully manage complex contractual arrangements. The library financial manager will need the data and analytical support that the acquisitions system can provide to meet the challenges of the next decade.

NOTES AND REFERENCES

1.   John F. Harvey and Peter Spyers-Duran. *Austerity Management in Academic Libraries* (Metuchen, NJ: Scarecrow Press, 1984).

2.   Edwin B. Brownrigg. "An Online General Ledger System." *Library Automation as a Source of Management Information* (Urbana-Champaign: University of Illinois Graduate School of Library and Information Science, 1983), p. 160.

3.   *Library Systems Evaluation Guide.* Volume 5, Management Services (Powell, OH: James E. Rush Associates, 1984).

4.   Joseph Z. Nitecki. "Creative Management in Austerity." *Austerity Management in Academic Libraries* (Metuchen, NJ: Scarecrow Press, 1984), pp. 43–61.

5.   Richard Boss. *Automating Library Acquisitions: Issues and Outlook* (White Plains, NY: Knowledge Industry Publications, 1982).

6.   Association of Research Libraries. SPEC Kit 44, *Automated Acquisitions* (Washington, D.C.: ARL, 1978).

7.   *Library Systems Evaluation Guide.* Volume 4, Acquisitions (Powell, OH: James E. Rush Associates, 1984).

8.   J. Michael Bruer. "Management Information Aspects of Automated Acquisitions Systems." *Library Resources and Technical Services,* Fall 1980, pp. 339–342.

9.   Janet Uden. "Financial Reporting and Vendor Performance: A Case Study." *Journal of Library Automation,* 13:3, Sept. 1980, pp. 185–195.

10.   Brian Aveney and Luba Heinemann. "Acquisitions and Collection Development Automation: Future Directions." *Library Hi Tech,* Summer 1983, p. 51.

11.   Murray S. Martin. *Budgetary Control in Academic Libraries* (Greenwich, CT: JAI Press, 1978), p. 114.

12.   Ann E. Prentice. *Financial Planning for Libraries* (Metuchen, NJ: Scarecrow Press, 1983).

13.   Association of Research Libraries. SPEC Kit 31, *Allocation of Resources in Academic Libraries* (Washington, D.C.: ARL, 1977).

14.   Murray S. Martin. *Budgetary Control in Academic Libraries* (Greenwich, CT: JAI Press, 1978), p. 57.

15.   Michael Bommer. "Decision Models, Performance Measures and the Budgeting Process." *Library Budgeting: Critical Challenges for the Future* (Ann Arbor, MI: Pierian Press, 1977), p. 58.

16.   Betty Jo Mitchell. *ALMS: A Budget Based Library Management System* (Greenwich, CT: JAI Press, 1983).

17.   *Library Systems Evaluation Guide.* Volume 4, Acquisitions, p. 90.

TAKING THE LIBRARY TO FRESHMEN STUDENTS VIA THE FRESHMAN SEMINAR CONCEPT

John N. Gardner, Debra Decker and

Francine G. McNairy

INTRODUCTION

A movement is taking place in American higher education to change the way colleges and universities treat, welcome, assimilate, support, and most importantly, inform their freshman students in this new dawning age of information. That movement is something which has come to be known as the "freshman year experience" phenomena and it portends significantly increased opportunities for library administrators and faculty librarians on college and university campuses to have even greater access

Advances in Library Administration and Organization
Volume 6, pages 153–171
Copyright © 1986 by JAI Press Inc.
All rights of reproduction in any form reserved.
ISBN: 0-89232-724-3

to each year's entering freshman class in order to enhance their library utilization and information retrieval skills.

The purposes of this article will be to elaborate on this freshman year experience enhancement movement and to focus particularly on a vehicle for teaching library utilization skills to freshmen through what has become known as the freshman seminar or freshman orientation course concept. The article will focus on two particular applications of these concepts at two universities: The University of South Carolina and Clarion University of Pennsylvania. These are two prototypes of what now hundreds of institutions are practicing to successfully expand the traditional college orientation process to include extensive involvement of freshmen in libraries.

An incontrovertible fact and reality is that we live in an information society. Harlan Cleveland in the July/August 1985 issue of *Change Magazine* wrote that by the end of the century, approximately two thirds of all work will be information work and he asks "if information is now our crucial resource, what does this portend for citizenship and the education of citizens?"[1] It may also be asked what additional steps must library administrators and faculty librarians take to meet the needs of all entering college students for enhanced information retrieval skills, not only those students who chose to enter information producing and distributing industries. This article will suggest one model for greatly expanding the role and therefore the influence of libraries on developing academic consciousness and skills of entering college and university students.

It can be said that the 1984–85 academic year was the year of the report. Following the publication of *A Nation at Risk* in April of 1983, the next academic year saw the release of a number of reports which included scathing indictments of the current condition of undergraduate education in America. These reports were produced by such prestigious organizations as The National Institute for Education *(Involvement in Learning)*, The National Endowment for the Humanities *(To Reclaim A Legacy)*, and The Association of American Colleges *(Integrity in The College Curriculum)*. Many of the recommendations of these reports are relevant to the work of library administrators and faculty librarians, and a number of the recommendations have also fueled a parallel movement in American higher education which is suggesting that much greater attention must be placed on the freshman and sophomore years. It is being argued that a new kind of "front loading" is in order with a shift of resources, attention and effort from the esoteric specialities in the upper division to teaching the fundamentals of the college curriculum in the first and second years of the collegiate experience. This parallel movement is now being found not only in the United States but in countries like Canada, Great Britain, and Australia to enhance the first year of the college and university experience, and has come to be known in American higher education as "The Fresh-man Year Experience".

This term was coined and promoted by organizers of the University of South Carolina's first National Conference on the Freshman Year Experience which was hosted in February 1983 as an immediate outgrowth of a conference held the previous year entitled A National Conference on the Freshman Seminar/Freshman Orientation Concept. Some words about the evolution of this movement and its relationship to library administrators and academic librarians participating in a new vehicle for meeting freshman students' information needs is in order here.

Since 1972, the University of South Carolina at Columbia has had in place a unique course for freshmen entitled University 101, The Student in the University. The University 101 course (which will be described at greater length below) is one of a genre entitled The Freshman Seminar or Freshman Orientation Course (a brief history of the evolution of this type of course will also be presented below). As the decade of the seventies wore on, the University of South Carolina received literally hundreds of calls and letters from colleagues throughout the country and Canada requesting information on how to develop a freshman seminar/freshman orientation course which would, hopefully, enhance freshman retention. It became apparent to the leadership of this course at the University of South Carolina by the early 1980s that there were now enough individuals in the profession administering and teaching such courses and/or interested in eventually administering and teaching such courses that perhaps a meeting could be held with those of such common interests to share what they have learned and need to learn to more effectively promote freshman persistence. Thus, in February 1982, 175 educators came to the University of South Carolina at Columbia campus to discuss the history, organization, administration, politics and content of freshman seminars/freshman orientation courses. Participants at this conference gave conference organizers extensive feedback that not only should such meetings be continued, but that the focus should be expanded to consider instead the much broader questions involved in the entire freshman year and related efforts in addition to freshman seminar/freshman orientation courses to enhance the freshman year. In the following year of 1983, the first National Conference on the Freshman Year Experience was hosted. Of particular note to library administrators and faculty librarians is that the hosting of this conference in 1985 was provided not only by the University of South Carolina's University 101 program and Division of Continuing Education, but by that University's College of Library and Information Science signifying the vital stake that academic librarians have in meeting the information needs of entering college students. By 1985, interest and awareness of the freshman year as a cornerstone of the college experience had grown to mammoth proportions as evidenced by the 700 participants who attended that most recent Conference on the Freshman Year Experience. They came from across the United States, from Canada, England, Scotland, and Northern Ireland and they presented and heard more than 130 programs and exchanged ideas for strengthening and broadening freshman programs in public and private institutions at senior and junior colleges on large and small campuses including meeting increased freshman needs for critical information through enhanced library orientation programs.

A strong bias emanating from the kinds of educators that have participated in such conference activities is that the freshman year experience can only be enhanced by developing a partnership of faculty, academic administrators, student personnel administrators and library administrators and their faculty. In turn, this will model a partnership for the improvement of the freshman year and for the host of support services that are necessary to accomplish the successful assimilation of college freshmen. This Freshman Year Experience movement which now is having such considerable impact on academic librarians has its roots in a number of factors including:

1.   Altruism—there are still many in the profession of academe who genuinely care for the freshman for the sake of caring.

2.   Financial exigencies: the decline of traditional age enrollments, increasing competition for the available pool of students, concerns for job security, have all produced an equation which has led more leaders and more institutions to care more about freshmen.

3.   Increased attention is being paid to the poor quality of high school graduates and hence the greater need to remedy these deficiencies in the first year of the college experience. The President's National Commission on Excellence in Education in 1983–84 was particularly successful in focusing attention on this factor.

4.   The professoriate in American higher education is aging and hence there is increasing need for faculty development. Many of the Freshman Year Experience enhancement programs have strong faculty development components. The fact that the faculty are now advancing in years also means that more of them are tenured and full professors and hence can now politically afford to take more risks on behalf of freshmen.

5.   The decline of enrollment in the liberal arts and Education has had particular impact on the affected faculty who are looking for new markets, ventures and enrollments, for example, such as those that seem abundantly available in freshman seminar courses.

6.   Increased attention is being paid nationally to the rights of all consumers, and freshmen are being now treated more as consumers who need to be taught their options, rights, obligations, privileges and responsibilities (if only to prevent institutions from being litigated for failing to meet the

rights of their consumers). A natural vehicle for providing this kind of instruction is the freshman seminar at which much of that information can and is being provided through libraries.

7. A revival of sorts is taking place as a result of some scholarly academic revivalists, such prophets as Lee Noel, formerly of The American College Testing Service; John Whiteley of the University of California at Irvine; Alexander Astin, University of California, Los Angeles; and John Gardner of the University of South Carolina.

8. Because the competition for students has been increasing, more attention and focus has been directed towards their needs. There is now more study of students and more efforts to attempt to better understand them.

9. Declining revenues have led some institutions to reduce freshman enrollment by raising standards and, therefore, the overall quality of the freshman class at many institutions has increased. Concomitantly, institutions want that much more to keep the freshman they have worked that much harder to recruit. Such recruiting is also very expensive.

10. A number of states are under federal desegregation compliance agreements and it is now a matter of the law that institutions must do a better job of understanding, recruiting, and retaining certain types of students.

11. There has been a dramatic change in the nature of a "freshman". Now more are nontraditional, older, wiser, working, married, assertive, part-time, demanding, and less like much of the professoriate when they were freshmen.

All of the above factors have led to a variety of types of efforts being made to improve the freshman year. These efforts include such approaches as:

1. The reform/modification of the entire undergraduate experience with special attention being paid to the curriculum. Critics and cynics, however, allege that merely tinkering with the specific courses that freshmen must take may not change the way we go about teaching freshmen and providing them with the information and content which they so desperately need.

2. The enhancement of academic advisement.

3. Freshman seminar/freshman orientation courses.

4. Efforts to train faculty to perform academic advising and other special support tasks for freshmen, which are duties that clearly faculty were not trained to perform in graduate school.

5. Efforts to implement a reward system for caring about freshmen and for doing a better job teaching and advising them (through such mech-

anisms as released time, extra compensation, tenure and promotion credit, merit pay credit, etc.)

6.   Greater efforts to put more faculty into the classroom teaching freshmen (as opposed to graduate students) and more of the best teaching faculty.

7.   Improved orientation through the concept of what is now called extended or continuing orientation. It has been realized by most colleges that their traditional mechanisms for introducing students to higher education, that of the one day or one week summer orientation program, no longer suffice to meet the students complex needs for information. As the *New York Times* has said in its January 1984 Winter Supplement on Education, "Orientation is no longer a three day run."[2]

8.   The improvement of undergraduate housing so as to promote what had become known as living/learning environments and to ameliorate what are in many cases extremely depressing institutional ambiances as found in residence halls.

9.   Providing expanded extracurricular and co-curricular activities so as to heighten the investment of time, involvement, and interest by students in the life of the institution.

10.   Peer counseling and peer advising programs—realizing that much of what students report that they learn the most from in college are those activities involving extensive interaction with their peers.

11.   Special administrative units for freshmen such as freshman centers, freshman advising units, etc.

12.   Career counseling for freshmen, especially focusing on the needs of undecided students.

13.   Tutoring and study skills programs provided either by faculty, professional tutors and study skills specialists on peers.

14.   Early warning intervention systems to identify early in any given semester students who are yielding signs of potential problems and referring these students for special kinds of counseling and support.

15.   So-called "mentoring" programs to encourage and teach faculty to practice mentoring behaviors so that students will develop special bonding relationships with them and thus be more likely to persist.

16.   Special programs for unique populations of students: the mature, nontraditional, minority, commuter, international, etc.

17.   Special programs for parents of freshmen which are particularly important for the first generation college students for whom the college experience is as much of an education for their parents as it is for the students. To support the parents is often critical for the eventual success of the student, if only because so many of these students continue to reside with their parents.

18. Efforts to improve instruction in uniquely freshman disciplines (such as English composition).

19. To prove library orientation and information retrieval skills acquisition programs.

Now what are the commonalities in these freshman year experience type programs? First of all, they all represent a deliberately designed attempt to provide a rite of passage in which students are supported, welcomed, celebrated, and ultimately (hopefully), assimilated. These programs are analogous to the kind of "basic training" that has been provided by the U.S. armed forces for decades and most of America's major corporations for an equal amount of time. Secondly, these types of programs reveal a great concern about freshmen *per se* in which there is a deliberate process or mechanism developed which attempts to guarantee a mentor ("significant other") for each freshman, i.e. some caring adult employee of the institution.

The Freshman Year Experience is also something that institutions are marketing in advance when they attempt to sell the institution. Subsequently, the freshman year experience is a deliberate series of experiences which are provided for the students after they have arrived during the time when they are making that second critical decision as to whether or not to stay or leave the institution they chose originally. In marketing terms, this is the concept of the "second sale" in which institutions are trying to help students overcome "buyers' remorse" and instead make a commitment to remain at the institution. This kind of intervention and reselling of the institution appears to be particularly important during the first six weeks or so of the first semester of the freshman year; the time frame when the majority of students who decide to drop out during or after the freshman year appear to make this decision.

Freshman Year Experience programs are campus wide in inception, organization, support, and execution and generally have become a top priority of institutional leaders, decision makers, and opinion setters such as senior administration and faculty. The Freshman Year Experience programs involve a partnership of faculty, academic administrators, student personnel administrators, library administrators, and faculty librarians. Such programs recognize the total developmental tasks of freshmen: academic, vocational, personal, social.

Freshman Year Experience programs recognize that not all freshmen are the same and that they have a variety of special needs for orientation due the heterogeneity of their backgrounds. The Freshman Year Experience concept is based on the recognition that the freshman year is the foundation on which the rest of the college experience is based and that there needs to be a shift of attention and resources from the last to the first two years. This movement also has required acknowledging that concern for freshmen and the achievement of professional status need not necessarily be incompatible. In turn, this requires either the modification or the rejection of the graduate school model whereby status is measured in terms of one's direct distance from freshmen. Institutions with strong Freshman Year Experience programs in place have had to make an effort to develop a reward system to positively sanction those who care for freshmen and to make a concomitant commitment to put some of their best people forward on behalf of freshmen.

The Freshman Year Experience efforts are manifested by their deliberateness, their effort to make things happen by design, not by accident or spontaneity, i.e. those things that must happen if students are more likely to be successful. The Freshman Year Experience movement also includes a deliberate effort to provide role models for impressionable entering students which will hopefully be worthy of emulation, based on the notion that even though students may protest to the contrary, they are really hungry for people they can respect—heroes, if you will.

One example of the Freshman Year Experience enhancement movement which shall be a primary focus of this article is the freshman seminar/freshman orientation course concept. A freshman seminar is a new, yet not so new, discipline, a course for and about freshmen (women and persons). The course includes the concepts of studying the student, having the student study himself/herself, other freshmen, studying the institution, and studying higher education. The freshman seminar concept is neither new nor novel, yet its increased attention and proliferation makes it appear new and novel. That it is a growing national phenomena is indisputable as is evidenced by the 1984 American Council on Education Survey, *Campus Trends,* of 2,623 institutions which were asked whether or not they offered a course in "coping with college"; 77.8% of the institutions surveyed indicated that they did offer courses in coping with college.[3] This would suggest that this practice is no longer the exception but rather something approaching the rule. This growing national phenomena is especially due to the financial exigencies of the times as well as some of the reasons suggested previously in this article for increasing interest on behalf of freshmen.

Freshman seminar courses are for one, two, or three semester hours credit or the equivalent quarter hours. There are also non-credit courses. They are taught by faculty, student affairs professionals, faculty and student teams, and academic administrators, and librarians. Some are taught by faculty on overloads for money. Some are taught by faculty as part of their regular load. Some are taught by faculty as an overload for no money. Some of the courses are elective and some required. Some are pass/fail graded and some letter graded. Many institutions train faculty to teach these courses (the University of South Carolina and Clarion University being two such universities). Some institutions combine orientation and academic advisement in these courses in which the instructor of the seminar also becomes the student's academic advisor. Some of these seminars focus on special writing, analytical thinking skills, problem solving skills, and some of these courses have particular topical academic areas reflecting the expertise and interest of the faculty member teaching the seminar.

The first freshman orientation course began in New England at Boston University in 1888, followed by Iowa State in 1900 because both of these institutions recognized the need before the turn of the century for providing special guidance for entering college students. More recently in 1959, under the leadership of the noted American scholar, David Riesman, Harvard's contemporary freshman seminar was founded. The first orientation course for credit, however, was offered at Reed College in Portland, Oregon in 1911. The course was described as "the development of higher education, the purpose of college, the college curriculum, individual plan of study, the thought factors of study, and a variety of other topics relating to college life including health, college spirit, student government, intercollegiate activities, fraternities and sororities and college religion." The course was taught for a year for two hours per week, and men and women were taught separately. As early as 1911, the Carnegie Foundation suggested that colleges and universities "do something to help freshmen find themselves." Amherst College responded by initiating a freshman seminar in 1913 and Brown initiated one in 1915 entitled "Orientation Lectures", a course which gave advice and information about the University and counsel concerning "the freshman's personal habits and methods of reading and study."[4]

The freshman seminar at the University of South Carolina entitled University 101, the Student in the University, began in 1972. It was founded in reaction to the massive student riots which racked that institution in 1970 and was an effort to try and change student attitudes towards the University to make them more positive and less hostile. It was also an effort to institute a significant retention vehicle to combat the decline of traditional age high school graduates which would begin in the year 1981. Since its founding, over 16,000 students have taken the University 101 course on the Columbia campus, the flagship campus of the University of South Carolina nine campus System, and thousands of other students have taken the course on the other eight campuses. University 101 is a program for both students and faculty/staff. The course includes a three credit hour freshman seminar, elective, pass/fail graded course. In the fall of 1984, the largest percentage of the freshman class ever to take this course did so—45.8%—even though that class was the best qualified academically in the University's modern history. University 101 also includes a mandatory 5 day/40 hour faculty training workshop; a prerequisite for all those faculty, staff, and librarians who teach the course.

Some of the goals of the University 101 course are to promote retention as a byproduct of accomplishing the rest of the following:

1. An extended orientation . . . what colleges and universities call "continuing orientation".
2. Introduction to higher education as a discipline *per se.*
3. The teaching of survival skills.
4. Improving attitude towards faculty and the teaching/learning process.
5. Providing a support group and a sense of community.
6. Providing a mentor/significant other.
7. Teaching and requiring the use of the institution's support services.
8. Making friends.
9. Providing career counseling and assistance in making decisions about majors, especially for undecided students.
10. Getting involved in the life at the University outside the classroom.
11. Improving compliance with desegregation mandates by promoting persistence of minority students.
12. Making freshmen feel significant.
13. Generating enthusiasm for the institution.
14. Exploring the cultural life of the University.
15. Making students more informed consumers of the opportunities and requirements of their education in their institution.

This introduction to higher education in the format of a freshman seminar course at the University of South Carolina includes extensive involvement in the University's nine campus libraries. Library orientation is provided by a variety of approaches including the mandatory library orientation component in all the freshman English courses, as well as separate library orientation efforts provided by the University 101 faculty. The University 101 course has also enjoyed strong support from the University's College of Library and Information Science in which virtually all of that unit's faculty have been participants as instructors in the University 101 program. In most of the University 101 classes, students are given a "silent library tour" (so as not to disturb library patrons), in addition to the formal library orientation program sponsored by the University's Thomas Cooper Library which is non-experiential in nature. Students report it is not sufficient to get students in a library; they must be made to use it and use it in a way which appears useful to them. Thus, an exercise has been developed by Professor Charles Curran of the USC's College of Library and Information Science to get freshmen students using their library.[5] In brief, this exercise asks each freshman student to conceive of any imaginable topic which they would like to know more about for any reason whatsoever. It is most important that the students chose a topic which is of genuine interest to them which they will regard as being practical, useful, interesting and stimulating. The exercise requires that the students work through the following source materials:

1. General encyclopedias
2. Subject encyclopedias
3. Library of Congress List of Subject Headings
4. *Reader's Guide*
5. Subject indexes
6. Abstracts
7. *Editorials on File*
8. *New York Times Index*

As the students progress from the general to to the specific references, they are asked to ascertain how much more data becomes available to them about their topic. They are encouraged throughout this process to assertively but politely make use of reference librarians who they are encouraged to see as a helpful and supportive individuals even though they may look "busy" when initially approached in the library. Students are asked not only to note in what volumes and on what pages information is to be found on their topics in each of these possible types of sources, but more importantly, they are asked to explain why and how this information will help them discuss the topic in class and/or write a paper on the topic. What is critical here is not only showing them where the information can be found, but requiring them to make a judgment about its utility. In turn, this enables them to learn that certain types of information found in libraries are more or less helpful than others in terms of ultimately being informed about whatever it is they seek to be informed about.

Thus, through a freshman seminar course at the University of South Carolina, almost half of the freshman class is being given library orientation in addition to that which they receive in the traditional English library orientation course programs. This has the effect of reinforcing the orientation process, giving them additional practice and skill, further reducing anxiety, and further contributing to the development of good library habits early in the college experience. It also provides one further opportunity for demonstration early in the college curriculum that virtually all disciplines at freshman levels require library support, which demonstrates that learning about those things which students most want to learn can be facilitated through the successful use of libraries.

Let us now examine an alternative yet similar model in the place of a freshman seminar course at another university. Unlike the University of South Carolina, Clarion University of Pennsylvania is not a large state supported research urban university, but instead a medium-size, rural, state university which still has a very strong teaching orientation. Located in Clarion, Pennsylvania, a rural county seat approximately 100 miles northeast of Pittsburgh, Clarion University has 6,000 students and a freshman seminar course and faculty development program entitled "Project Flourish". Consideration of this model will provide additional illustration and amplification of a partnership of a freshman seminar course and a university library to meet the developing information needs of freshman students.

Begun in 1978 as an educational experiment, Project Flourish was adapted from the University 101 model at the University of South Carolina. Project Flourish is a two-faceted program including a faculty development workshop and a three-credit freshman seminar course (G.S. 110: The Student in the University). The impetus for such a program came as a result of a programmatic attempt to address two components of student attrition, i.e., the enhancement of the quality of faculty-student relationships and faculty-faculty relationships. The faculty development component begins with a four-day workshop where administrators and faculty from numerous disciplines and departmental lines, including the University Library, have an opportunity to meet, interact, exchange expertise and develop and/or strengthen their teaching skills. Since its inception, over one hundred and twenty seven faculty members and administrators out of Clarion's approximate three hundred and twenty complement have been trained in one of the seven workshops conducted. The success of the workshop is due to participants' willingness to address the following objectives:

1. The examination of new teaching techniques which enable participants to function more effectively in small groups with students;
2. The development of a faculty support group from colleagues drawn from across the campus;
3. The sensitization of faculty to the academic psychological, social, financial, and vocational needs of students, particularly freshmen;
4. The identification of the talent, expertise, and resourcefulness of Clarion University of Pennsylvania faculty/administrators; and
5. The integration of faculty and professional staff in a joint undertaking which is both academic and humanistic in its approach.

Participation in the workshop is a prerequisite for teaching the course, G.S. 110.

A critical aspect of the faculty development workshop is a component on the library as a resource which affords an opportunity for workshop participants to become more knowledgeable about library services and personnel. Key services that are presented to participants are as follows:

1. Librarians who function as subject specialists—they relate to specific departments and provide library informational technical assistance;
2. Faculty borrowing privileges and procedures;
3. Reserve material procedures;
4. Bibliographic instruction which could support faculty members' classes or professional development; and
5. On-line search and inter-library loan procedures for faculty.

Inclusion of this focus on the library and the helping roles of librarians is an essential part of the workshop. This emphasis is based on the belief that faculty who understand and utilize the library will encourage their students to do likewise.

The student development component of Project Flourish is the freshman course, G.S. 110: The Student in the University G.S. 110 (similarly to University 101 at the University of South Carolina) is designed to:

1. Enable the freshman student to explore and understand himself/herself as a developing adult interacting in a higher educational environment;
2. Identify and/or utilize campus and community resources that will enhance his/her academic program;
3. Develop strategies to facilitate the learning process; and
4. Apply those strategies in a practical manner in order to build upon a resource base for academic skill transference.

Specific behavioral objectives of G.S. 110 are as follows:

A. Objectives of Higher Education
    1. History of Higher Education:
        Thestudent will state the implications that the history of higher education has for him/her.
    2. Current and Future Status of Clarion University of Pennsylvania:
        Thestudent will state his/her rights and responsibilities in the role of a student at the University.
B. Survival Skills
    1. Resources—Structure of the University:
        Thestudent will identify and then explain how he/she can utilize

the campus resources such as advisement, counseling, tutorial services, health services, academic services, and the library.
2. Procedures:
Thestudent will identify and explain how he/she can utilize appropriate procedures and regulations such as drop-add, financial aid, residence hall, pre-registration, and others to be specified in the course outline.
3. Study Skills Overview:
Thestudent will examine various procedures and then develop or choose his/her own skills for:
   a. managing time
   b. improving memory
   c. taking notes
   d. improving concentration
   e. taking exams
   f. reading textbooks
4. Professors' Expectations Overview:
Thestudent will examine various procedures and then develop or choose his/her own for assessing and coping with professors' course expectations, teaching styles, and examination formats.
5. The class itself:
Thestudent will demonstrate the following skills:
   a. note taking
   b. anticipating examination questions
   c. class participation
   d. oral presentations
C. Verbal Communication
   1. Interpersonal/Small Group Communication:
   Thestudent will demonstrate the following skills in communication with peers, faculty, and administrators:
      a. listening
      b. effective use of silence
      c. reflection
      d. clarification
      e. summarization
   2. Assertiveness:
   Thestudent will demonstrate that he/she can maintain self-control, state the other person's point of view, and state possible consequences of his/her behavior.
D. Goal Setting
   1. Values Clarification:
   Afterexploring his/her values concerning education, society, and career, the student will share them clearly and concisely.

2. Career Education:
   After responding to measures of (a) interest, (b) temperment, and (c) abilities and after reviewing academic and career options, the student will state his/her goals and procedures for obtaining them clearly, concisely, and realistically.
3. Decision Making: Given a problematic situation such as one listed below*, the student will do the following:
   a. identify the problem
   b. analyze the problem
   c. develop alternatives
   d. evaluate alternatives and choose one
   e. test the alternative chosen
   f. evaluate the efficacy of the decision

*(a) test anxiety, (b) depression, (c) timidity, (d) lack of motivation, (e) deficiency in basic skills, (f) personality conflicts between faculty and student, (g) negative living conditions, (h) peer pressure, and (i) parental pressure

One special adaptation of the G.S. 110 course is the Honor's Section which is designed for freshmen who have a combined SAT score of 1000 or better. The Honor's Section addresses the same objectives delineated above. In addition, however, it incorporates the following:

1. Becoming cognizant of national and international issues;
2. Developing critical thinking skills in social, political, and economical issues;
3. Developing an understanding of the "Third World" and its impact on the United States, as well as the world; and
4. Developing an appreciation of the roles of men and women in an age of technology.

It has been found at Clarion University that high achieving students require the support system of faculty and peers even more than average students. G.S. 110 establishes a network for high achievers to identify, communicate, learn from each other, as well as to be challenged. These needs must be successfully addressed if retention of such students is to be enhanced.

Regardless of whether the course is taught as a regular or Honor's Section, G.S. 110 faculty interweave writing, speaking, critical thinking and library utilization assignments throughout the behavioral objectives. The interdisciplinary nature of the course has enabled faculty and administrators from both the Academic and Student Affairs Division to teach the course. Because Clarion University functions within the context of a collective bargaining agreement with the faculty, G.S. 110 faculty must be either released from their regular responsibilities or receive overload payment. Staffing the course therefore requires ongoing negotiations with college deans, program directors, and department chairs.

G.S. 110 is a three-credit course for freshmen which serves as an elective counting towards graduation, and is letter graded as are all other courses within the University. The course was first offered in the 1978 Fall semester on an experimental basis; 125 enrolled that semester. Since then, 1,910 freshmen have taken G.S. 110.

In order to evaluate the effectiveness of G.S. 110, a longitudinal study following the 1982–83 freshmen class has been conducted. This research on G.S. 110 has been performed by a faculty member in the Psychology Department who is independent of the Project Flourish Program. The data indicate the SAT scores for G.S. 110 total participants were significantly lower than the comparison group. However, when comparing actual G.P.A.'s for both groups at the end of the first and third semesters of completion, there was no significant difference, indicating that the G.S. 110 participants performed as well as nonparticipants despite the significant difference in SAT scores. The data also indicate that freshmen, G.S. 110 participants tend to be more aware of campus resources and more likely to utilize such resources.

The same findings are true for data SAT scores and academic performance of Black students who enrolled in the course in the Fall of 1983. In fact, after three semesters, black G.S. 110 student continued to perform better than those black students who elected not to take the course. Thus, Project Flourish, through its faculty and student development component, has become a valuable program within the University-wide retention program.

Students enter the contemporary University with a high "job" priority. Furthermore, for approximately twelve years, they have been passive receptacles of facts, ideas, and values. The freshman seminar, however, requires students to be active participants in the learning process. This active role is not only within the classroom, but is also reinforced in the University library. Clarion University Librarians (faculty) have been very supportive of Project Flourish, particularly G.S. 110. The Director of the Library and nine of the fourteen librarians have participated in the faculty development workshop and have thus developed a better understanding of the concerns and needs of first year students.

The library faculty contribute to Project Flourish in the following manner:

1.   One librarian teaches one section of G.S. 110 in both Fall and Spring semesters. She serves a dual role by serving as a direct link to the library as well as reinforcing the behavioral objectives of the course.

2.   Reference librarians provide comprehensive tours and bibliographic instruction to all G.S. 110 classes. These tours incorporate (a) resources available in the Instructional Materials Center, (b) procedures for charging out VAX computers, the listening room, typing room, and on-line searches, (c) materials that are available in the Reference Room, Periodical Section, card catalog, Reserve System and Main Circulation, and (d) resources that are provided on microfiche and microfilm.

3.   Reference librarians are also subject specialists who serve as resource persons for G.S. 110 students/classes assigned to complete research term papers. During the tours as described in Item #2 above, the subject specialists are introduced to freshmen so that students will know who to approach when seeking assistance in fulfilling assignments.

G.S. 110 library assignments vary according to the instructor. Specific models include (but are not limited to) the following:

1.   Some faculty members interweave their academic disciplines within the G.S. 110 course. In these instances, freshmen are expected to use the library as the major resource for writing a term paper. Faculty from the College of Education and Human Resources tend to encourage research on educational issues. Thus, students gain experience in utilizing the *Education Index* and Educational Resources Information Center (ERIC). On the other hand, faculty members from the social sciences direct their classes to the *Social Sciences Index, American Statistical Index*, and *Statistical Reference Index*.

2.   Another model that is used in G.S. 110 is the use of the library in strengthening problem solving skills. Examples include faculty members who require students to identify and read mystery novels and short stories from the library. Students, in turn, learn to compare particular authors' writing styles and problem solving methodologies. Subsequently, freshmen are able to incorporate stronger reading skills, and equally important, they integrate better problem-solving skills in their personal lives.

3.   As mentioned in the section on behavioral objectives of G.S. 110, all freshmen participate in a module on the "Meaning of Higher Education". Most faculty provide a bibliography of materials relating to the topic; some of the resources are on reserve while others are in the stacks. Students are assigned to locate and utilize the resources and then write their own essays on the meaning of higher education. The essays integrate the print and nonprint materials, as well as their personal reflections.

4.   A fourth approach to using the library focuses on the study skills' module. This theme relates to freshmen in G.S. 110 by identifying problematic areas in study skills, e.g., listening, concentration, note-taking, and test-taking. Students identify resources from the library that are de-

signed to help students strengthen those skills. It can be said that "a person knows something if he/she teaches it." Thus, not only must the students read the material, but they must teach that same content to the other students in the class. The teaching must incorporate an experiential format, as well as lecture. Thus, students learn specific information regarding study skills by teaching their peers.

Regardless of the faculty member's discipline or approach to teaching G.S. 110, all of the classes include an emphasis on library utilization. Such an emphasis requires freshmen to utilize the library resources that they have been introduced to during the tour. The assignments provide an opportunity for freshmen to become successful and informed library patrons. It also helps them to feel comfortable in approaching a librarian in order to complete an assignment and comfortable in the library. That relationship between the student and librarian becomes an ongoing one in that the freshmen will continue to seek out that librarian for a specific need in assignments for other classes. This is particularly important for our students from rural, as well as urban high schools who come to Clarion with a limited understanding of the value of a library and very limited skills in retrieving information in libraries.

The concept of the interdependent relationship between faculty and student development is ever present in Project Flourish. A catalyst within that relationship is the citadel of resources on the campus; the University Library. Its support of faculty and student development is critical to a healthy and informed learning process for the University community. It appears that the Project Flourish Workshop has given librarians a number of approaches for taking a more assertive role in helping freshmen become successful at Clarion University. A goal of higher education is to encourage a respect and enthusiasm for life-long learning, and the library facilities reinforce that goal by supporting faculty and student development.

In conclusion, it has been the experience of the authors who have participated in the development of freshman seminars at two universities that the library can be successfully taken to students via a freshman seminar course. Many associated benefits accrue for the institution and the academic library. Faculty librarians achieve a broader role and status in the instructional fabric of the institution by teaching freshman seminars. More faculty learn of the many helping services of the contemporary university library by the emphasis and attention given to the library in the faculty development workshop to prepare faculty to teach the freshman seminar course. Because of the library assignments given to freshmen students, entering college students receive an even more thorough and deliberate introduction to the academic library. The freshman seminar is an exploding phenomena in the reform of the freshman year experience in American higher education. These efforts cannot achieve their full potential to help students adapt to the demands of the information age without a full partnership with librarians, as faculty who teach freshman seminars and as information resources who render broad based support to freshmen not only in freshman seminar courses, but in all academic endeavors. Participation of librarians in such educational innovations as freshman seminar instruction is one more illustration that the library is the foundation for the undergraduate experience.

NOTES AND REFERENCES

1. "Educating for the Information Society"; Harlan Cleveland; *Change*, July/August, 1985, p. 13.

2. "A Nation at Risk: The Imperative for Educational Reform"; National Commission on Excellence in Education, April 1983.

"Involvement In Learning: Realizing the Potential of American Higher Education"; Study Group on the Conditions of Excellence in American Higher Education, National Institute of Education, October 1984.

" 'To Reclaim a Legacy': Text of Report on Humanities in Education"; William J. Bennett; *The Chronicle of Higher Education*, Vol. 29, No 14, November 28, 1984.

"Integrity In The College Curriculum"; Redefining the Meaning and Purpose of Baccalaureate Degree Association of American Colleges Committee; *The Chronicle of Higher Education*, Vol. 29, No. 22, February 13, 1985.

3. "Freshman Orientation: No Longer a Three-Day Run"; Sandra Friedland; *New York Times*, Winter Survey of Education, January 8, 1984, p. 11.

4. *Campus Trends*, 1984; Higher Education Panel Report #65; Elaine El-Khawas; American Council on Education, Washington, D.C., February, 1985, Table 1, Page 9.

5. "Early History of Freshman Orientation Courses"; unpublished paper by Virginia Gordon, Ohio State University; delivered at the February 1982 National Conference on the Freshman Seminar/Freshman Orientation Course Concept.

6. "Using the Library: A Ticket to Success", Charles Curran and Joe Lewis; in *College Is Only the Beginning*, John N. Gardner and A. Jerome Jewler; Wadsworth Publishing Company, 1985, Page 45–59.

CONCEPTIONALIZING LIBRARY OFFICE FUNCTIONS AS PREPARATION FOR AN AUTOMATED ENVIRONMENT

Edward D. Garten

INTRODUCTION

The decade of the 80s has been viewed as a time when extensive library automation became a reality. Clearly we are dealing with a major turning point in the way offices are conceived and operated. The technology making all this possible is the microprocessor. The new interface between humans and the power of computers has permitted major improvements and efficiencies to be brought into the office environment.

Increasingly, all types of libraries are recognizing the need for information on office automation as they seek to make decisions about the

Advances in Library Administration and Organization
Volume 6, pages 173–195
Copyright © 1986 by JAI Press Inc.
All rights of reproduction in any form reserved.
ISBN: 0-89232-724-3

future direction of their internal offices. This article was written as a brief introduction to office automation for library managers and as a general planning guide for the implementation of office automation systems.

Simply stated, a library office does not become automated by replacing the typewriter with a word processor or electronic typewriter. The incorporation of such equipment within a library office is, however, often the stimulus for further office automation. Our approach to the subject is such that it is assumed that those activities which occur in the central administrative suite of a library are not simply disorganized, random assemblages of unrelated tasks. Rather, a library office is a system of components that purposefully interact to accomplish concrete, directional, and support functions. Clearly, automated information systems in library administrative offices have much potential for substantially improving the interaction of what may at first appear to be discreet and often unrelated business and personnel functions.

Implementation of library office automation begins with a thoughtful examination of library administrative goals. One must ask such questions as: "What library office functions need to be done and are there better, more efficient ways of doing them?" "Are current work methods adequate?" Fundamentally, the perspective we share here views the library office as a place of business. Often, library managers have more of an understanding of what is occurring in the various departments of their libraries than they do of the processes that are occurring within their own administrative suites. The primary purposes of any library office are to realize a mission and to implement the functions which drive the rest of the library operations.

It has been observed that it is almost natural to deal with "the most tangible aspect of automation—the hardware".[1] When raising the issues surrounding office automation in the library, it is much more productive to concentrate on the central office service needs first. Certainly the only way in which an office automation effort will successfully realize benefits is through analyzing and defining office procedures that are involved in accomplishing an office's mission.[2]

The tangible pay-offs of a library office automation effort must be measured in business terms. Simply increasing the amount of information the central library office produces, or the rate at which that increased information is processed, does little to contribute to the quality of the office's real product or mission. Using a word processor, a microcomputer, or a totally integrated office system to revise a report or generate quantities of material, components of which may well go unread or unused, is valueless. Similarly, simply increasing the number of messages that a library manager receives at his or her workstation in a given day is counterproductive if the overall information content of each message is lessened.[3]

If your library is part of a larger entity such as a college, university, city or county government, it is wise to become acquainted early with those people who may already be engaged in various aspects of office automation. Cultivation of these people is both prudent and wise. As Joe Matthews and Joan Williams have so aptly noted:

> friends include: head of purchasing, data processing director, head of telephone communications, and legal counsel. Each of these people should be informed of the library's intention to install an automated library system in the future. In addition, you should determine the normal lead times they would require to provide assistance with the preparation of a Request for Proposal document, evaluation of vendor proposals, and preparation of system purchase and maintenance agreements. . . . If they are uncooperative at first, try chocolate chip cookies.[4]

The belief we share here is that library office automation is not simply a matter of technology; rather it is a matter of how technology is employed to reconceptualize/redefine the library office. Through placing the emphasis on library office procedures as a whole, and addressing individual tasks within that context, we bring the function and mission of the library into sharper focus. In short, we direct the automation effort where it is most needed. Hammer and Sirbu have committed in this regard:

> Focusing on an office procedure enables us to identify the framework for the office's activities and support them in a coherent and productive way; the alternative is haphazard automation of individual tasks without regard for the overall structure and operation of the office, which is as likely to have a negative impact on office productivity as it is a positive one. Any functioning system, even a manual one, is often highly tuned and sensitive to perturbation. It is necessary to take a holistic view of office work, and one that is moreover based on a thorough understanding of the particular needs and special characteristics of each office.[5]

Office automation systems are designed to improve the productivity of white collar workers. And as William Saffady has noted, since "the library workforce is overwhelmingly white collar in character and includes a significant office component, such systems are of potentially great importance."[6]

GETTING TO KNOW THE LIBRARY OFFICE

What do people do in library offices? Michael Hammer and Marvin Sirbu have noted that many of us have had the experience of attempting to explain to a small child exactly what it is we do in an office. The author's young son recently came into his father's library administrative suite after hours. He bounced first to a typewriter; then over to a telephone to pick it up and try to dial out; then gave a tug or two to the banks of file cabinets;

and than a twist to his dad's dictation machine. Explained little Noah, "Games, what great games daddy has and they are all different!" Hammer and Sirbu have gone on to note that:

> from a child's perspective, office work seems to be composed of simple tasks; reading, talking on the telephone, typing, shuffling papers, drinking coffee. Yet we know that these terms do not capture the essence of an office. The business of an office is about making payments, or scheduling production, or negotiating contracts. Tasks such as typing and filing are in an important way mere artifacts. If the business to be done in the office could be accomplished without these tasks, so much the better.[7]

Arriving at a clear-cut definition of the phrase "library office" is a difficult task. A whimsical librarian might be right in pointing out that a library "office" can constitute a few pencils, a pad of paper, and a few drawers in a desk devoted to "office" stuff. Other librarians might note that modern library offices are composed of word processors, typewriters, dictating machines, postal equipment, and perhaps even a microcomputer or an electronic mail network. Library managers have traditionally been portrayed as those who make decisions about running the day-to-day affairs of libraries. In this role, the library manager has been supported by a personal secretary or two, or perhaps an administrative assistant. This manager/secretaries team has been the basic organizational structure for most offices, including the library office. Leaders of various library units are typically brought together by the library administrator for coordinative purposes; however, each unit is typically allowed to plan, organize, staff, and control its own resources.

Because of the necessity for different library units to have some of the same information, duplicate copies of written messages are often made and stored in various units. As a result, unnecessary costs are often incurred. In addition, even larger costs are involved when needed information is retrieved. As more and more paper is processed, more and more secretarial employees often have been added to the employment rosters or, as is more often the case, more professional librarian time has been devoted to such activities. With people costs rising, librarians cannot afford to hire additional people to keep up with the increased volume of paper work. Instead, librarians must look toward some level of office automation as a means of increased productivity.

Traditionally, the ideas for a document (memo, letter, report) have been originated by the library manager and transmitted to his/her secretary by means of a longhand draft or dictation. The library administrator provided the input, while the secretary performed the role of processing the ideas, getting those ideas on paper, and preparing duplicate copies for others within the library and then sending out the original copies to the appropriate individuals. The perspective of the librarian concerning the processing of the information was to give the ideas to the secretary, then wait for a final copy. Most library managers have not concerned themselves with the various phases of the processing of information. Thus, the determination of the cost for handling information has not received much attention in the traditional library office environment.

The increase in the paperload experienced by many library offices has often resulted in a breakdown in the use of traditional manual systems for processing written information. Simply put, most library administrators have given little attention to the importance of the office functions in providing appropriate information for good decisions. Many of us hold deeply rooted prejudices when faced with the subject of automation of human-readable documents and office processes. Here, it would be a shame not to recite Kalthoff and Lee's insights into office behavioral patterns:

> Since it became a separate unit of information apart from the ledger book of a century ago, where all records were held in serial mode, the thing about the document is this habit we have of putting it into file folders—a device into which things flat and rectangular are placed, not necessarily legitimately.
>
> As the numbers began to proliferate, they soon found their way into file cabinets as both a storage and organizing device; and those into offices and work bays; and for those containing less current information, into halls, basements and warehouses. They continue to absorb floor space that ranges from $6 to $20 and even $30 per square foot per year for the former and $3 per square foot, and up, for the latter.
>
> The file folder functions as an open receptacle, but one clearly lacking a lid, and that is its greatest liability. The decision to file or toss is made millions of times every day. A combination of the office copier and the human propensity to follow the course of least resistance tends to skew that decision in the file direction—and often in triplicate. As a result, file folders thicken. They tend to grow promiscuously. They require increasing numbers of people to rummage their fat innards. And more people to track the people trying to get something of value out of the evergrowing banks of file cabinets that contain them.
>
> The system that has evolved around the file folder resists management. It has left us a generation of paper magpies who keep and keep and keep. It is a system that generates its own ultimate chaos. And chaos is what records management battles every day of its life. Although 5 percent is regarded as the average, in a well-run, hand-operated records system, chaos can be held to perhaps 3 percent, which means that at any moment 3 percent of the records the system is believed to contain are lost, misfiled, or have otherwise eluded control.
>
> It is a small wonder that the concept of the "paperless office" has enlivened the imagination of so many people in this paper culture of ours, which annually generated 25 percent more paper each year. Technology will be hard pressed to make a significant dent in this growth, let alone bring it to a screeching halt by the year 2000.[8]

Those people collectively identified as a library's administrative group occupy offices and perform functions which serve the library's collective information, communication, and decision-making center. A look at today's library office often reveals little more than the same library office one might find in 1960, if not in 1940: rows of bulk file cabinets (often filled with dog-eared, crumpled file folders), electric typewriters and access to a photocopier. Clearly, the technology to change this is available. Automated file storage and retrieval systems, optical scanners/readers, word processors, computerized communication and electronic mail systems, and higher speed printers are all available.

Much money is spent each year to provide necessary storage and processing for numerical summaries. Yet only a small portion of information in library offices consists of numbers; the large portion consists of words. Because of recent technological advances, business executives are beginning to concern themselves with improving the processing of words as well as data. Library administrators should do as much. The installation of automated equipment to process words as well as data will undoubtedly result in large savings as well as improved productivity. The goal of automating the library office is simply increased productivity, efficiency, and communication. Some common productivity gains that might be expected in libraries include the following:

- better use of staff
- increased effectiveness and efficiency
- increased performance
- increased quality of documentation and access to that documentation
- positive impact on library administrators

CONCEPTUALIZING THE AUTOMATED LIBRARY OFFICE

Because of the increased amount of money being spent on the processing of information in all offices, managers have begun to look for ways of gaining control of the ever-escalating spiral of office costs. One of the avenues available is the automation of previously manual functions and operations. Until the early 1960s the electric typewriter was the only major innovation for the improvement of office productivity. In the 1960s, IBM introduced the Selectric typewriter with a mag card/tape device. That equipment could store typed information electronically. Here was the start of automating office information processes. As many librarians will remember, the *pièce de resistance* during that period was the ownership of a mag typewriter.

The contemporary office in many businesses and industries consists of automated hardware—dictation equipment, word processing equipment, electronically and micrographically stored documents, electronic reprographic equipment, and telecommunications for transmitting messages from one point to another. As a result of the implementation of hardware, support personnel have become more specialized, new office procedures have been developed, and office productivity has increased. Office structures too, have been changed to meet the implementation of these new devices and techniques. For example, the library manager/secretaries' relationship or team may completely disappear as the basic pattern for completing office work. In an automated office environment, secretaries are often classified as administrative secretaries, depending on the types of activities performed. The administrative secretary is normally one who plays an assistant-to-the-library-administrator role and performs largely non-typing activities. Other secretaries may perform the production and dissemination roles for the office.

The availability of new electronic equipment has rapidly changed the face of the modern office. Through automation, the functions of the office (origination, production, expansion, storage/retrieval, and distribution) can be performed more efficiently. Reducing the indirect costs of maintaining the office and at the same time improving the productivity are two basic goals of most modern libraries. The automated library does hold a key for increased productivity. The nature of the automated office, however, will bring about many changes in the way library managers and support personnel interact. Although businesses are implementing automation at various levels of sophistication, the modern library automated office exists only in a few places at the present time. The fully automated paperless office remains a moving target.

In what ways will the automated office affect the library? Let's look at a systems approach to the processing of information for library offices. Library administrators have traditionally been thought of as those achieving stated objectives using the resources of the organization—people, procedures, hardware, and money. The primary objective of the library office is to create and/or manage information that is accurate, timely, and reasonably priced for executive decision making. Managing the office involves the four basic functions of any manager—planning, organizing, staffing and controlling. The manager of an automated office is faced with additional concerns that the traditional office manager does not have. Changes in procedures, equipment, and people are evident as one looks at an automated office—and, of course, additional investment is required.

A major objective of the central library office is to provide information for decision-making. Management functions must be performed in such a manner as to accomplish that objective. Information can be viewed as words, numbers, and graphics. This function involves developing a plan which identifies what needs to be done, when activities should take place, and who should perform the tasks. A plan for an automated office would specify the factors, forces, effects, and various relationships that are needed to provide the essential information on which managers will make decisions about business and control-related problems. Short-range goals as well as long-range goals would be included in such a plan. For an established library that has used a manual approach in performing the basic office functions, one needs to assess the needs of the paper-flow system in planning for the improvement of the office functions. Planning for automating the office functions is an attempt to improve the productivity of the office staff. Because of its high importance, word processing must be included in the plan for the management of information as a library-wide asset and must fit the overall library's directions and strategies.

The second basic function of management involves assigning the activities identified during planning to appropriate persons within the library. Within the office environment, tasks are grouped so that the output would contribute to the objective of the office—providing accurate, timely, reasonably priced information. The accomplishment of this objective in turn contributes to the overall success of the organization. Providing the right information at the right time for managerial decision making contributes to the overall success of the library.

The management fuction dealing with people is also commonly described under the notions of motivating, directing, actuating, and leading. The staffing function includes job analyses/descriptions, identification of qualified employees, recruitment, and training. In addition, staffing involves encouraging appropriate behavior on the part of the people by providing an atmosphere where people may satisfy their needs through work and the work environment. Higher productivity levels are generally associated with pleasant activities and surroundings rather than unpleasant activities and surroundings. Years ago, typing pools were created to increase the productivity of office workers. These early attempts to specialize typing tasks failed because of the unpleasant environment and the performance of often repetitive, boring tasks. In these early typing pools, workers were considered a cog in the production line rather than human beings needing worthwhile activities to perform in a pleasant atmosphere. The newer word processing centers we see today receive the respect of the office staff, thereby avoiding these pitfalls. Persons in charge of such centers must plan and organize the work to provide worth-while work in a pleasant atmosphere in order to improve productivity.

The fourth management function involves the constant gathering of information about performance, comparing the present performance to predetermined standards, and modifying activities—if needed—to meet the predetermined standards. Monitoring and refining the system is very important! If, for example, the office manager has implemented a plan for dictation by using a centralized dictation system and the system is not being used by the originators of messages, he will need to find out why the system is not being used even though it may have been determined to be the most cost effective with the least turn around time. An investigation might conclude that executives do not use the system simply because they are not comfortable with the dictation process or the dictation hardware. Action could then be taken to provide training sessions for all managers about the process of dictation; information should also be given on how to use the centralized system, and the managers should be made aware of the benefits and the relationship of the system to the overall goals of the organization. Monitoring and refining are ongoing processes.

Even though the managerial functions of planning, organizing, staffing and controlling may be viewed separately, these functions are inter-related—each depends on the other. The controlling functions, for example, can result in modifying the predetermined plans, organization structure, and/or the staffing arrangement to accomplish an objective more efficiently.

In managing information, the manager of an automated office uses four basic types of resources: people, procedures, hardware/software, and money. People use the hardware/software and procedures to produce, process, and distribute the recorded information so necessary for solid decisions. The skills possessed by the people and their understanding of the information system are critical to the manager.

In the office environment, procedures constitute the steps which need to be performed so that information is produced in an efficient and effective manner. Changing from a traditional office environment to one that is automated requires considerable changes in procedures for most libraries. Procedures for the users of the automated services are necessary. Hardware is the equipment with which skilled people are made productive; in the automated office, the software consists of the instructions for the automated hardware. The cost of the software is becoming an important concern for managers of the automated office. Money is used to purchase the needed services of people and hardware/software. In addition, library managers must quantify the benefits derived from implementing automation and prepare budgets which include these economic factors. The competent manager of the automated office plans, organizes, staffs, and controls the procedures, hardware/software, and people in an economical way to achieve the objective of providing information for decision making. The manager's role is one of making decisions about each of the functions and resources in accomplishing the predetermined office objectives. The office or information manager is directly concerned with improving the various functions to make them more effective and efficient. The implementation of automated hardware to improve productivity does result in drastic changes in the manual performance of office functions.

The input process in the automated library office consists of two functions—origination and capture. Origination starts with the formation of an idea in the mind of an originator who needs to transmit the idea to another person. The steps are the same whether the office is automated or not. The means of getting the idea recorded for transmission differ, however. For example, the most commonly used means of originator input is a costly longhand draft. Other means of input include dictation to a secretary or machine. In each case, a writer keyboard is used to capture or record the message. Traditionally, the typewriter keyboard has been used to capture keystrokes on paper; documents with major revisions must be retyped and reproofed. In the automated office, more sophisticated hardware utilizing a CRT and magnetic storage media are being used to capture the message. Since the keystrokes are captured on the magnetic media, only revisions need to be rekeyed and checked.

In addition to the keyboard input method, documents that have already been typed may be input by means of the optical character reader (OCR). Another means, though not widely used at present because of the cost and the complexity, is voice activitation; voice input is a promising input method of the future that will increase the speed of input over the keyboard method.

The library office is often very much like the factory production floor, with the exception that its product is information (decisions) rather than refrigerators, automobiles, television sets, or some other "hard" goods. Information is the raw material used to "manufacture" the product of the office which is a synthesis of raw input (information). The input information is stocked in various forms and formats. Some of these are:

- *Correspondence files*
- *Histories*—financial, performance, etc.
- *Computer output from management information systems*
- *Graphic libraries,* such as product catalogs
- *Manuals, specifications, instructional guides*
- *Engineering drawings and blueprints*

The reality, the list of the various raw input sources, is almost endless and is dependent on the specific mission and tasks of the office unit. It is impossible to generalize the necessary attributes of an efficient office information system since the term "office work" covers such a great variety of situations.

Traditional methods of input have become very costly and often can be improved through the use of automated equipment. With the ever-increasing volume of paper, finding ways of improving productivity is critical. Currently, the least costly method of input by the originator is through the use of machine dictation. To improve productivity, originators must be willing to change and develop communication and dictation skills. The increasing use of automated input hardware, such as word processing, can also affect the organization structure, people, and procedures. Staff members have to be prepared for the effects of change in order to increase the productivity of the office.

The process function includes document storage/retrieval and expansion. The process function differs greatly for the automated versus the traditional office setting. In the traditional office, messages are recorded on paper by means of carbon or photocopy with the original and copies being mailed to the appropriate people. A copy of the original is normally manually placed in a file cabinet for future reference.

In the automated office, the storage of the message often is on a magnetic medium such as tape or disk. Since the message is electronically stored, it can be manipulated in a variety of ways before being sent to the receiver. After a document has been input on the magnetic media, revisions can be made in the document; thus, only the revisions would need to be re-keyed saving considerable time over the traditional process of having to retype the entire document. Other editing and correcting features are possible with automated hardware as well as time-saving text and format-related fractures. The automatic insertion of a word or group of words within the body of a message merely by keying in the added word(s) can save considerable time and cost. Additionally, changing from single to double-spacing format with a few simple keystrokes allows a major format change with effort or time. If desired, the recorded message can be transferred to a microform file system for additional saving of computer space.

Retrieval of needed documents is enhanced through the use of electronically stored information. Documents stored electronically are normally coded in several different ways—for example, by name of addressee, subject of document, date, etc.—to make retrieval easier. In this fashion, a staff member who needs a document for decision making can bring up an appropriate indext on a CRT and retrieve the necessary document on the CRT screen without having to make a hard copy. Electronic storage uses random access memory (RAM) instead of sequential access recording. Information stored on a magnetic card or tape is stored sequentially. The stored information in this form becomes cumbersome to locate for rescue since one has to play through the entire card or tape until the desired information is located. Information stored on computers with RAM however, can be stored any place on the memory media. Each document is given an identification code when stored. Thus, any desired information can be selected without having to search through the entire memory. With the random access capability, a staff person can select any desired information in thousandths of a second rather than in minutes. The random access memory allows large amounts of stored information to be easily accessible for decision makers.

The storage/retrieval system may include complete storage of documents on a mainframe computer or a hybrid using a stored indexing system on the computer with the actual documents stored on some type of microform. The electronic storage of documents can drastically reduce the cost of files since the cost for space, furniture, and materials are lower. Instead of having to wait for someone to hunt for a document and perhaps never find it, the user for an electronic storage/retrieval system can have immediate access to the information within seconds. The valuable time can be saved for more productive activities. Documents currently stored under the traditional manual system are costly to store, costly to retrieve, and inaccessible to a variety of people at once without duplicating copies.

Using an electronic file involves identifying those documents that are placed in a general source (so that anyone who is authorized and needs the information may have access to the documents), and identifying those documents that need to be secure for various reasons. The electronic storage and retrieval system should include procedures such as the following: access codes; what information is to be stored; who is to have access to what information; security; etc. The use of electronic files greatly reduces the need for manual files that are found in traditional offices today. Offices of the future may have a total electronic file system.

Expansion refers to the process of making duplicate copies of a written message—called reprographics. In the old library, office carbon paper was used as the basic means of producing extra copies of an original. This was a time-consuming task, and the results were somewhat messy and/ or unclear. The use of photo-copier has practically eliminated the use of carbon paper as a means of making copies of the original message.

Photocopiers are also used in automated offices. Once messages have been captured on the magnetic media, however, the message can be stored and then transmitted electronically, thus, the need for additional copies would be eliminated. When messages are produced, stored, and transmitted electronically, the paperless office will have arrived. The electronic storage/retrieval system reduces the cost of the expansion function, and in fact, may eliminate or drastically reduce the need for the function.

The output function involves the complete document that is to be distributed or transmitted to the receiver. The final document may be produced in different ways. In the traditional office, the final output was the typed page that was finally approved by the originator. In case there were multiple recipients of the document, carbon copies or copy machines were used to produce the needed output; if many copies were needed, some process, such as offset printing, would be used to produce many copies at a reasonable cost. In the automated office, the out put can take different forms—hard copy or electronic impulses stored on the magnetic media. In the fully automated office, messages are transmitted over telephone lines or by satellite.

To complete the standard office functions, distribution of messages must be completed. In this function, the approved final document of the originator is sent to the recipient(s). In the traditional office, the U.S. mail and messenger services have been used for getting the completed documents to the desired recipient(s). In the automated office, hard copies may still be distributed by means of the U.S. mail and messenger service. However, the use of electronic storage also provides for the transmission of messages electronically. Both the sender and receiver must have electronic hardware capable of communicating. The communications capability of word processing hardware expands the document production capability tremendously. Electronic transmission of messages is gaining popularity as more and more CRT terminals are being added to more and more executives' desks. The facsimile process has also been used as a means of transmitting messages from one point to another. As electronic message transmission gains wider use, the distribution method used under the present manual system will undergo major changes for office personnel.

Many of the present developments in computer and communications technology are facilitating the trend to remote work activity. More significantly, the trend toward office automation will likely be the development of professional workstations: microcomputer-based systems which are tailored to particular professionals within an organization's administrative unit.[9] In time, library managers in their administrative capacity will simply not require the equipment, paper files, and supplies now seen in the typical library office. Such materials will be built-in to the work station. Clearly, the new office technology provides the potential to dramatically alter the locational definition of what we call administration in libraries. Even though we tend to view our entire libraries as information processing systems, we will most likely begin to view our administrative offices as micro-information processing centers. We will most likely be looking for an information processing system for our office rather than simply looking for a personal computer, a word processor, or various duplicators. These components will be regarded more as functions in the future and less as individual pieces of hardware.[10]

The future will see much traditional library office work centered in the work station. work stations will have high-resolution displays, mass-storage subsystems, memory, and numerous input/output parts. Such fully integrated work stations will provide for the storage, retrieval, and transfer of all forms of data, text, voice, and video information.[11]

A fully integrated library administrative office may be quite different than what we now envision. In many instances we may never hear again: "Take that report up to the front office." "Take these forms over to the administrative offices for processing." "Let's see if we can coordinate our meeting with the director's schedule." These and other questions may well be answered in the circulation department, technical services, media services, or government documents. The new library office will find that floors, walls, and distances are no longer obstacles to the distribution of documents and forms.

The problems associated with the task of integrating data and text are just beginning to become apparent. Many of the office systems which will be installed in businesses, libraries, schools, and hospitals between now and 1990 will be aimed at establishing an acceptable entry product for these various types of office requirements.

THE LIMITS OF OFFICE AUTOMATION

Hammer and Sirbu maintain that there is more than one conceptual model of how to go about assisting office work with modern computer and communication technology:

> For those with short memories, 'office automation' may appear to be a recent addition to the language. If one looks back at the literature that appeared in the late 1950s and early 1960s describing the migration of the computer from the research laboratory into business government, it is complete with discussions of the new 'office automation.' Certainly, we have gone a long way toward 'automating' the modern accounting and financial office. Yet in much of the current discussion of office automation, data processing is viewed as a foreign and unrelated technology. There is something perverse in a nomenclature that includes facsimile transmission as a form of electronic mail but not an on-line order entry system which eliminates considerably more correspondence; or counts word processing as office automation, but not the forms handling program which similarly reduces the typing workload. Certainly, data processing, as it is commonly understood, is a form of office automation.[12]

These comments are of interest for several reasons. They mention, in a capsule format, the most used computerized aids for performing clerical functions. It is typical in representing the confusion of office mechanization of clerical functions with the automation of the professional/managerial mission. Automation is defined (by *Webster's New Collegiate Dictionary*) as: "The technique of making a system operate automatically by mechanical or electronic devices that take the place of human organs of observation, effort, and decision."

In the factory production process, automation opportunities using computer-controlled machines are limited only by the availability of investment capital and some other considerations unrelated to the content of the work itself (labor contracts, cost-effectiveness, etc.). The managerial, administrative, and professional tasks performed in offices especially, however, offer few realistic opportunities for total automation.

The missions of functional office entities are often too complex for total computerization or real automation. This does not preclude, however, the effective use of computers and other electronic, electrical, or electro-mechanical appliances to support the white-collar worker by mechanizing the data collection and distribution necessary for the complex decision cycle. It is easy to be trapped into erroneous conclusions on the many different aspects of office work by oversimplifying the diverse missions and processes lumped together as "office work." The majority of people interested in technical or humanistic discussions regarding "the office" are white-collar (office) workers themselves. The mental image of office work is patterned after personal experience. Office work, unless carefully defined, is perceived differently by the chairperson of the corporate board than by the supervisor of the order-filling department or by the administrative assistant to the personnel manager.

Systems that support the knowledge worker in the office by supplying the raw input information for the decision process are called office information systems. Since the missions of functional office units vary and the tasks in fulfilling these missions can differ greatly, there is no single preferred approach to implementing the office information system. All of these systems have the dynamic nature of the data base in common. Many have to handle both human readable, noncomputer-generated information and computer-coded alphanumeric data. The actual mix of human-readable (analog) and machine-readable (digital) information may vary from system to system. Word processing systems and digital storage of documents are gaining in popularity, but it is generally recognized that for the foreseeable future, human-readable and machine-readable information will continue to occupy a high proportion of accessible recorded information. It is futile to dream for total automation of the substantive portion of library office work. Clearly, however, the most important part of what goes on in the library office concerns knowledge management and decision-making. What we can hope for, however, is that automated office systems will give the best possible support toward enhancing these human responsibilities.

ANALYSIS OF LIBRARY OFFICE FUNCTIONS

Before undertaking any library office automation, it is vital to gain an appreciation of what processes, activities, and functions actually are being undertaken by those individuals who occupy the administrative suite. This involves surveying the tasks currently being performed by the clerical staff, understanding the activities assumed by the library administrator(s) who are charged with the overall managerial functions associated with the library, and understanding the current use of workstations and the role these workstations play in the support of both clerical and professional staff.

While those activities charged to the administrative group may be assumed by as few as two (a director of the library and his/her secretary) in a small library setting, those same functions—granted albeit expanded— may be assumed by as many as six to ten individuals in a much larger context. Before initiating an office analysis, it is wise to conceptualize the activities that occur within offices. Chart 1 shows the results of analysis made within one library central office. The analysis was made of time spent involved with particular tasks by both administrative staff and clerical staff.

Clearly, it is apparent that a high proportion of clerical staff time was devoted to typing, proofing/editing, file handling and calculating, while the major amounts of administrative staff time was devoted to meetings, calculating activities, file handling, and reading and writing activities. In analyzing what actually goes on in the library office, however, one must dig a little deeper. Chart 2 suggests some of the major data gathering elements that should be considered in any analysis.

Also, in any office analysis, it is sometimes useful to conceptualize categories of library office products along with the products within these categories. Such an analysis is especially useful when one looks at form and file handling processes. Office automation product vendors often like to see the types of products that are produced within a given office. Chart 3, below, illustrates some of these products.

Finally, it is wise to have updated copies of position descriptions available (similar to ones illustrated in Charts 4 and 5) for use in the office analysis. Such descriptions, detailing duties and responsibilities of central library office staff, are also of value to consultants and to office automation

Chart 1. Typical Library Office Activity Analysis

Activity	Percent of time Spent in Activity Each Week	
	Administrative Staff	Clerical Staff
Meetings	25%	2%
Reading	10%	3%
Writing Original Material	10%	2%
Telephoning	5%	5%
In-Coming Mail Handling	1%	5%
Calculating/Analyzing	14%	10%
Travel	5%	0%
Searching for Information in the Office or Other Library Departments	5%	5%
Dictating	1%	0%
Proof Reading Copy	2%	10%
File Manipulation	10%	15%
Typing	5%	30%
Waiting for Others/Meetings, etc.	2%	2%
Photocopying	0%	3%
Editing	5%	8%
	100%	100%

Chart 2. Checklist of Library Office Processes

Activities	Tasks
• Record Keeping Processes	Filling out forms; posting information; tracking forms through the library or through the larger organization; updating budgetary and financial records; updating staff scholarship or continuing education records.
• Personnel Related Processes	Recording absences; processing time cards and sheets; arranging vacation schedules for staff; processing position transfers; processing leaves of absence; processing demotions, promotions, and terminations; appraisals of staff; salary file maintenance; skills update sheet maintenance.
• Calculating Processes	Performing mathematical calculations; creating charts and graphs using numerical data; analyzing statistical information; summarizing and distilling data.
• Mail Processes	Opening; dating; loging; preparation of route slips; delivery to central pick-up sites; addressing; stuffing bulk or mass letters.
• Supply Processes	Requisitioning; ordering; Supply Room Inventory.
• Research Processes	Searching for information; using files and periodicals in other parts of the library; abstracting and synthesizing material; creating reports and summaries.

vendors as they gain an appreciation of who does what and how within the library office environment.

Before a library office study is conducted, the library administrator should develop an itemized checklist of all the tasks that will be performed as part of the library office study effort. This list will include use of many of the charts suggested in this chapter and others which might be available from vendors and consultants, along with an overall timetable for the study which identifies initial and subsequent information requirements. Questionnaires, logs, and interview guides should be developed and available for the study early on.

In addition to questionnaires and interviews, certain tasks require the recording of data, either in self-recording logs or in logs in which the study team records its activities. Typical areas that should be studied within the library office through sampling logs include:

- Library distribution lists
- Typing jobs
- Incoming and Outgoing mail
- Print Shop Requests and Activities
- Telephone Use

Chart 3. Typical Library Office Products

Category	Product
• Forms	Personnel Action Forms: Time Cards; Purchase Requests; Maintenance Work Order Requests; Inspection and Acceptance Documents; Travel Requests; Inventory Transfer Forms; Print Shop Requests; Accident and Security Reports; Position and Job Descriptions.
• Correspondence	Letters; Messages and Quick Replies; Memoranda.
• Documents	Specifications; Blueprints; Procurement Plans; EEO Certification and Other Affirmative Action Documents; Change orders; Requests for Proposals; Sole source justifications; cost estimates; staff meeting agenda; configuration change status reports; action item lists; library administrative notices; model contracts; award contracts; annual call for bids or estimates; delivery orders; data management reports; library training plans; site survey reports; building environmental assessments; committee reports with attached documentation; warrantees; phase-in and phase-out plans.
• Reports	Travel; Management; Technical; Security Incidents; Personnel and Payroll; Fiscal; Weekly Library Activities; Training; In-House Project Status.

Chart 4.

Position
Administrative Assistant: Director's Office
Job Summary
   This non-exempt position serves as administrative assistant to the Director of Libraries.
Duties and Responsibilities
   A. Serves as administrative assistant to the Director. Administers clerical workload of the library office by reminding Director of deadlines, meetings, etc., by initiating preparation and completion of required reports, forms, and other paperwork. Coordinates workload of another secretarial position and several office part-time staff (student asssistants).
   A1. Serves as secretary to the University Library Committee. Take and type minutes and distribute to members. Compile requested materials and information about meetings.
   A2. Maintain ongoing record of equipment location in libraries and prepared annual equipment inventory report including transfer of equipment, discards, declaration of surplus property, etc. Reconcile discrepancies with Property Officer.
   A3. Forward information regarding procedural clerical changes to appropriate individuals and ensure that adjustments are made. Inform director of any unusual problems.
   A4. Complete questionnaires from University, State Board of Regents, and other universities an professional organizations concerning library budget, operations, policies, and procedures.
   A5. Compile data for interviewed applicants as received from department heads and administrators and ensure adherence to procedures.

A6. Submit job descriptions for professional positions to the appropriate places, e.g., journals, newspapers, etc. Clerical descriptions are developed by department heads. Maintain up-to-date job descriptions for all positions.

A7. Prepare arrangements for library-related meetings. Arrange rooms, etc.

A8. Preview Director's mail. Prepare routine responses where possible.

A9. Prepare application and final reports for grants.

A10. Maintain rosters for the Friends of the Library Foundation.

B. Administer clerical procedures related to all the library's budgets and accounts which are maintained in the central office.

B1. Assist Director with required paperwork for proposed and revised budget. Receive materials and guidelines from business office. Compile completed materials as received from Director. Review and ensure compliance. Edit and adjust as necessary and inform Director. Compile previous expenditure information and provide Director with data for decision-making regarding budget revision.

B2. Receive allotment advices and record appropriately. Receive donations from members of the Foundation, Memorial Library Fund, etc. Receipt and record and deposit.

B3. Prepare requisitions, IDT's and travel claims. Ensure adherence to purchasing procedures for non-collection items.

B4. Log invoices from vendors and distribute to acquisitions, collection management and development, bibliographic control, periodicals, gifts and exchange, and reference or government documents.

B5. Receive all copies of library purchase orders from acquisitions and match with appropriate invoice. Review invoice for proper totals, tax, postage, etc. Forward selected invoices to secretary for preparation of requisition and help if typing is necessary.

B6. Prepare requisition from appropriate prior year regular or prior year replacement accounts.

B7. Receive all invoices for non-collection items. Verify correct shipments and ensure requisition is prepared according to specifications. Adjust requisition as necessary. Ensure proper charging to accounts, proper postage, proper totals, elimination of tax, etc. Maintain paid invoice file and refer for questions regarding payment. Compose correspondence to vendors to correct billing or to correct shipping problems.

B8. Purchase all office supplies for library using own judgement and as requested by department heads. Oversee secretary's assistance.

B9. Prepare and maintain record of yearly contracts for purchased selected items including copiers, bindery service, SOLINET, service maintenance for office machines. Adjust as required. Make sure that bids are on materials or services we request. Consult with department heads as necessary.

B10. Resolve discrepancies and problems with Financial Aids Office regarding student employment. Reconcile expenditure reports. Maintain information of student assistant needs in various departments. Screen student workers and send them to the department which benefit both student and departments.

B11. Reconcile monthly expenditure report. Make adjustments as required. Work with business office personnel to resolve problems.

B12. Review all money transfers for required signatures and accurate paperwork. Initiate money transfer request and suggest possible sources.

B13. Assist Director with calculation of current estimate at the end of the fiscal year.

Chart 4. (Continued)

C. Assist as receptionist and secretary for Director's office with clerical work load as required.
    C1. Answer phone of library. Direct calls to appropriate department.
    C2. Type and compose correspondence, reports, etc.
    C3. Take dictation as required.
    C4. Perform miscellaneous duties as required.
    C5. Make appointments for Director and indicate on calendars.
    C6. Maintain knowledge of placement of information in files and provide to Director upon request.
    C7. Exercise discretion regarding access to director whenever possible, answer questions and handle problems without interrupting Director.

Chart 5.

Position
Secretary 1: Director's Office
Job Summary
This non-exempt position serves as clerical support to the Administrative Assistant and to the Director of Libraries.
Duties and Responsibilities

A. Serve as secretary to the Administrative Assistant and to the Director of Libraries. Performing work in routine secretarial tasks as required.
    A1. Maintains and orders office supplies for complete library, including contracting outside vendors for materials not available locally.
    A2. Types routine correspondence, work orders, reports, and other documents as requested.
    A3. Files correspondence, reports, and other documents according to established procedures.
    A4. Performs other clerical tasks and work as assigned.
B. Compiles and completes monthly required reports, including the completion of other forms and paperwork.
    B1. Receives invoices and prepares requisitions and IDTs according to procedures.
    B2. Compiles leave forms from all staff members, and completes monthly leave and overtime report according to procedures.
    B3. Collects work schedule and hours of library operation through Department Heads and maintains library calendar each quarter.
    B4. Maintains ongoing records of all student workers (approximately 100). Checks, compiles, and completes report for student payroll. Forwards any information regarding procedural changes to appropriate individuals. Also, coordinates workloads and supervises student workers within central library office.
C. Acts as receptionist for Director's office.
    C1. Greets visitors, ascertains nature of business and assists visitors or conducts visitors to appropriate departments.
    C2. Arranges for interviews, meetings, and keeps Director's appointment schedule.
    C3. Answers and screens telephone calls, giving routine information and routing other calls to appropriate person.

- Use of Manuals in-Office
- File Document Manipulation
- Copier Usage

Chart 6 summarizes a data collection checklist for gathering statistical and process information on the office.

Chart 6. Data Collection Checklist of Library Office Processes

Process	Associated Tasks
Calculating	Performing calculations, creating charts and graphs, analyzing statistical data, summarizing statistical data for presentation.
Copying	Copying on and off-site.
Distributing	Collation by hand; collation by machine; binding/stapling; addressing envelopes or routing slips; marking names of recipient on copy; stuffing; delivering.
Errands and Reception	To other departments in the library; out of the building; personal; greeting visitors to the library; escorting visitors; arranging for passes/parking permits
Personnel Related	Processing time sheets; reporting and attendance records; vacation schedules; transfers and promotions; job appraisals; skills updates.
Appointments	Checking calendars; updating calendars; confirming dates; rescheduling.
Travel Arrangements	Reservations; creating travel agendas and meeting schedules; maintaining travel records; arranging for advances; expense statement creation; trip reports.
Incoming Mail	Leave area and pick-up centrally; leave desk and pick up within the library; deliver to staff boxes; open; date stamp; log; preparation of route slips; deliver to mail drops.
Outgoing Mail	Address; fold; stuff; stamp; deliver to addressee; deliver to mailroom; deliver to post-office.
Record Keeping	Post information; fill out forms; track forms; use office reference books; create recaps and summaries; update organizational charts; produce formats; update manuals; produce educational and workshop enrollment forms; update and maintain budget and financial records.
Research and Analysis	Read in office; look up information; use files and periodicals; synthesize and recap; create reports; program archives; standards manuals.
Review and Follow-up	Maintain follow-up file; Review reports for special information; follow-up with others.
Schedule Meetings	Establish date and time; adjust; reserve room; refreshments; contact attendees; audiovisual equipment.
Transmit	Mail; telex; facsimile.
Supplies	Requisition; order; locate and pick up special items; supply room.

Chart 6.   (Continued)

Typing and Transcription	Type from long hand; type from shorthand; self-typing; revision; assemble standardized text; forms.
Proofreading	Spelling; grammar; format; style statistical verification.
Steno—Dictation	Shorthand; machine.
Filing	Prepare index/filing schemes; preparation of folders; retrieval; purge; develop system; bind printouts; label printouts and binders; organize printouts; records retention.
Creation	Hand-write; dictate; use terminal; talk/telephone; think.

SUMMARY

As far back as 1971, Heiliger and Henderson noted that the library is "not one but three systems and the needs and opportunities for mechanization and automation are revealed in:

1. Technical processes that are directly concerned with the acquisition of library materials, their cataloging in preparation for later use, and reference to the accumulated holdings.
2. Control processes that are applied to the resources employed by the library, the handling of library materials, and processing of data through them.
3. Administrative processes concerned with the organizational structure of the library and its operational activities."[13]

They noted that these processes are applicable in every type of library and to every library data system whether manual, mechanized, or automated. While serving as a valuable resource giving basic guidance to automation in the first two areas, technical and control processes, their discussion of a library's administrative process and applicability was somewhat sparse. Simply stated, office automation had not developed to the point it occupies today. While rightly noting that many libraries' automation interests have centered on those facets of library work least familiar to computer people; serials control, cataloging, and circulation, they failed to note that administrative processes normally assumed by the library administrative group have often been the last to be considered for automation.[14]

Where does one go from here? As John Dykeman recently noted: "The old advice is still the best. If you don't know what your office is doing now and you don't have performance standards, get them before you move ahead. Otherwise, you may merely automate chaos."[15] The role of the library manager in an automated environment can be a challenging one indeed. The key issue is understanding the nature of what occurs in the administrative suite; determining how the new office technology can be effectively exploited to support these activities; and managing the process, on an on-going basis, to ensure compliance with the overall mission of the library's administrative function.

NOTES

1. Joe R. Matthews and Joan Frye Williams, "Oh If I'd Only Known: Ten Things You Can Do Today to Prepare for Library Automation Tomorrow," AMERICAN LIBRARIES, 14(6), June, 1983, p. 408.

2. Michael Hammer and Marvin Sirbu, 1980 OFFICE AUTOMATION CONFERENCE DIGEST, 1980, p., 17.

3. Ibid., p. 19.

4. Matthews and Williams, op cit., p. 409.

5. Hammer and Sirbu, op cit., p. 22.

6. William Saffady, INTRODUCTION TO AUTOMATION FOR LIBRARIANS, Chicago: American Library Association, 1983, p. 145–146.

7. Hammer and Sirbu, op. cit., p. 27.

8. Robert J. Kalthoff and Leonard S. Lee, *Productivity and Records Management*, Englewood Cliffs, NJ: Prentice-Hall, Inc. 1981, pp. 79–80.

9. Margrethe H. Olson, "Remote Office Work: Changing Work Patterns in Space and Time," *Communications of the ACM*, 26(3), March 1983, p. 182.

10. John B. Dykeman, "Future Shock is Upon Us," MODERN OFFICE PROCE-DURES, 28(4), April, 1983, p. 14.

11. Len Yencharis, "Office-Automation Technology is Ready; The Definition of the Specific Needs of Workers—From Clerks up Through Executives—Is Next," ELECTRONIC DESIGN, 30(1), January 7, 1982, p. 240.

12. Hammer and Sirbu, op cit p. 28.

13. Edward M. Heiliger and Paul B. Henderson, Jr., LIBRARY AUTOMATION: EX-PERIENCE, METHODOLOGY, AND TECHNOLOGY OF THE LIBRARY AS AN IN-FORMATION SYSTEM, New York: McGraw-Hill, 1971, p. 7.

14. Ibid., p. 13.

15. John B. Dykeman, "Future Shock Is Upon Us," MODERN OFFICE PROCE-DURES, 28(4), April 1983, p. 14.

A SURVEY OF THE SIXTH-YEAR
PROGRAM IN LIBRARY SCHOOLS
OFFERING THE ALA ACCREDITED
MASTER'S DEGREE

Alice Gullen Smith

INTRODUCTION

This paper explores those goals of library education which are relevant
to the sixth-year programs, gives a review of the development of such
programs, presents the data gathered in three important studies of these
programs, and offers a view of the state of the art in the mid-1980s. Conclusions drawn from these studies are purely the judgment of this writer.
If the trends in Library Education suggested by these studies occur, there
will be: (1) a continued leveling of the numbers of students enrolled in
master's degree programs, and (2) a need for a larger variety of kinds of

Advances in Library Administration and Organization
Volume 6, pages 197–220
Copyright © 1986 by JAI Press Inc.
All rights of reproduction in any form reserved.
ISBN: 0-89232-724-3

continuing education. The sixth-year program, which is one form of continuing education, may well be coming into its own.

DEFINITIONS

Practitioners as well as library educators often use terms such as "library school" in a number of different ways which are as confusing to the professional librarian and the library educator as they are to the lay person or to the novice in the field. Some of the disparities in understanding occur because of the growing pains of an evolving discipline. Thus, a "sixth-year degree," for example, has meant different things at different stages of this evolution of education for librarianship. For clarity and communication, it is necessary to define some of the terms which will be used throughout this work. A selected number of these are defined below:

Library School: the unit of an institution of higher education offering a master's program in library science which is accredited by the American Library Association (ALA). The degree offered may vary in acronym: MLS, MA, MSLS, MALS, etc. The important thing is that the program itself is accredited. The school may offer other degree programs such as the sixth-year under discussion or a Ph.D. program, but none of these programs is accredited by the ALA.[1] Danton's study and others have recommended that all library science degrees be accredited, but to date, this has not been implemented.[2]

Associate Library School: a school which has no programs accredited by the American Library Association, but which is an associate member of the Association of American Library and Information Science Education (ALISE).

Sixth-Year Programs not Included in this Study: sixth-year programs in any discipline other than Library/Information Science or sixth-year programs offered by the faculty of an "associate library school." No two-year master's degree programs in library schools are included either. The sixth-year program in a library school offers a certificate or degree at its completion. It is work after and beyond the master's degree, generally, not leading to a doctoral degree. The most drastic change in the nature of six-year programs occurred during the years described in Danton's classic study. These programs, about one-year in length, are typically designed for practitioners who want to improve professional competencies. The variances are discussed in the analysis of offerings reported by the library schools which were surveyed.

HISTORY OF THE SIXTH-YEAR PROGRAM

A review of the history of library education indicated a confusing replication in the use of the term sixth-year degree. In the 1920s, the Board of Education for Librarianship (BEL) approved three types of programs for accreditation (I, II, III). The last of these (III) was a master's degree program of two-year study beyond the baccalaureate designed especially for people intending to work in complicated positions in large institutions. This meant completing six years of higher education. Five schools were accredited to give these "sixth-year" master's degrees.[3] Six other schools had advanced programs, usually consisting of one-year only, which occasionally conferred a master's degree.

In 1947, the University of Denver was approved by BEL for a program leading at the end of one post-baccalaureate year to a master's degree. At that time, other schools were encouraged to implement programs of similar length. This implied condensing the two-year programs. In spite of opposition to the shorter program, by 1955 all master's degree programs were changed to offer only one-year of post-baccalaureate work. By 1960, the last of the original two-year degrees was conferred.

Although a number of schools had programs leading to the doctorate by 1962, only 173 people during a 33-year period had graduated from these programs. The primary purpose of the first doctoral programs in library science was to prepare instructors for library schools. To some extent, as with all doctoral programs, the underlying purpose of research itself and training in research hampered the preparation of instructors. In addition to the program's weakened emphasis on preparing people to teach, upon graduation, Ph.D.s could receive larger salaries at other institutions and sometimes in business than they could in library schools. Thus the objectives of placing persons with Ph.D.s as qualified instructors in library schools was impeded.

There was no halfway house between the master's degree and the Ph.D. to prepare students for more than entrance-level knowledge in librarianship. To fill the gap, in 1961, the library school at Columbia University established the first of the contemporary "sixth-year specialist programs," which involved a year of specialized study beyond the master's degree. Such a degree was needed for continuing education that would give specialization in the areas of the student's choice and focus on advanced professional preparation rather than on pure research and research techniques.

With the advent of Title II B of the Higher Education Act of 1965, the incentive of stipends to qualified students encouraged many people to enter either the Ph.D. or the sixth-year programs. The impact of this motivation and its implications for sixth-year programs through 1969 was examined by J. Periam Danton.

The Danton Study

Danton received the J. Morris Jones–*World Book Encyclopedia* ALA Goals Award for a survey describing educational practice in the then emerging sixth-year specialist program in the library schools which offered programs accredited by the American Library Association.[4] It was carried out under the sponsorship of the committee on accreditation of the American Library Association and published in 1970. This classic study of sixth-year programs is used as a guide in current assessments of such programs.

The Danton study and others which have both preceded it and followed it put emphasis upon the types of sixth-year programs, their origins, the number of schools which offer them, the scope and depth of the programs, their purposes and their achievements or influences. For his data, Danton relied upon a study of the history of library education, reports of current trends by such people as Harrison, and Jack Dalton and a survey which he sent to the directors of library schools offering programs accredited by the American Library Association. He also visited most of the twenty schools which then operated sixth-year programs and sent letters to identifiable employers of eighty-three graduates of some of these programs. The twenty schools included Toronto which then had a program leading to a sixth-year M.L.S. degree rather than to a sixth-year specialist degree. Danton found more than seven purposes of these twenty programs: to update knowledge, to upgrade professional skills, to prepare for teaching in library schools, to prepare for administrative work in libraries, to specialize in information science and automation skills, to specialize in the administration of instructional material centers, to meet the certification requirements of a state (for school media personnel) which went beyond the master's level, to prepare library personnel for community college librarianship and for supervision of technicians or technical assistants in a variety of types of libraries.

Many of the sixth-year degree plans did not begin as fully developed programs with specific criteria for admission, but emerged slowly from the practice of accepting qualified librarians for the pursuit of their own individual interests through advanced graduate study. Both demand from the profession and the increasing availability of HEW funds were factors influencing the design of more formal programs which would cover a year of study and result in a certificate or degree. Although the work could be accomplished in a calendar year, students were often encouraged to undertake study on a part-time basis that would be stretched over five years and in some cases even seven.

In 1976, six years after Danton's report, Rogers used that report as a gridwork in his study for the Library School at Kent State. In his review of the literature published since Danton, he found one book and six relevant articles. The articles were primarily descriptive concerning the programs at Denver, Berkeley, Columbia, Catholic University and Pratt Institute, respectively.[5] The most provocative of the articles called for six-year programs to become integrated with doctoral programs. There are mixed feelings among faculty concerning such integration. Historical practice indicates that a similar indecisiveness has been seen since the first indication of need for an intermediary degree between the one given at the master's level and the degree offered at the doctoral level. Rogers identified 23 library schools offering sixth-year programs in contrast to the 20 identified by Danton. The return of Roger's questionnaire showed wide variation in descriptions and practices of what each school thought of as a sixth-year program.

Although Rogers found sixteen different names for the programs, there was more agreement upon purposes than Danton showed. All agreed on: (1) specialization beyond the master's degree; continuing education, some degree or certification that could be earned. Other purposes indicated were "preparation for administration," and personal needs. The nature of the program was alternately described as: (1) terminal; (2) an alternative to the doctorate; (3) a first step to the doctorate; (4) having no relationship to the doctorate. Admission requirements also varied. The majority of schools required a master's degree from an ALA-accredited program, while others requested only some professional experience. Some stipulations were for adequate scores on tests such as the GRE or Miller analogies, letters of recommendation, statements of purpose, etc. There was variance in a number of other items: course requirements, length of the program in terms of numbers of credit hours required, (some of these were semester hours, others were quarter hours), hours accepted from other disciplines or other institutions. To repeat, the only universal factors were that each program was planned to meet the individual needs of each student; each program was considered a form of continuing education and a degree or certificate could be earned.

Comparing Continuing Education and Sixth-Year Programs

Continuing education, while taking many forms, does overlap with sixth-year programs.[6] Each is concerned with offering students a working knowledge of the new technologies, some impact of world events, or other evolving knowledge with which librarians must continually update or renew themselves. Many aspects of basic education for librarianship quickly become outdated or obsolete, relegating unalert practitioners to unsatisfactory levels of performance. Quick efforts at presenting new information to practitioners are too frequently offered in unrelated discrete units, or in a limited number of courses in sequence which are not linked to preceding courses and may not be relevant to other courses taken as continuing education by any one person.

Sixth-year programs go beyond offering discrete units of unrelated information. They bring new information together in meaningful patterns according to the need of individual students, but of equal importance, they also teach transition relationships from one course to another and coping skills for handling change. These skills will be more effective and longer lasting than clumps of knowledge or information which continue to change and accrue. Sixth-year programs also meet other needs: utilizing input from specialists in related disciplines; furnishing contact with the resources of the regular staff of a library school; giving access to contemporary and traditional scholarly materials; and enabling students to continue association with peer practitioners from a variety of libraries who both seek and share information.[7]

Although a sixth-year program offers incomparably more to a student than fragmented continuing education courses can offer, both are important. It is essential to know the degrees and differences of their importance.

On the other hand, continuing education courses may also be offered in a planned sequence in which one course depends upon another. Many continuing education courses are specifically designed to teach new skills or to advance the use of old skills. They may also be taught in many areas out in the field where it is often impossible for the library school to offer a program course.

A successful sixth-year program, however, gives a focus of interest and study and a continuity of commitment. Each facet of the program integrates the commitment into a meaningful, self-sustaining unit which may involve scholarly work, but which also leads to the fulfillment of some practical goal. It is true that some students are intent only upon a salary increment or a change in position, each of which may be advanced only by the individual's receipt of an advanced certificate or degree. This requirement prohibits the students from taking continuing education courses which cannot be used in a sixth-year program of studies. If the advisor allows these students to take any course in "green stamp" fashion that is conveniently available whether or not it is rewarding in itself; follows a sequential building of knowledge and skills or helps the student become a more effective librarian, the avowed purpose of sixth-year study becomes a travesty.

Both the Danton and Rogers studies offer data to substantiate these differences. Although continuing education in all its forms is needed, studies point out the need for and the growth and development of sixth-year programs with recommendations for continuing the programs. Many of Danton's recommendations are still needed for sixth-year programs.[8] Some recommendations that seemed paramount at the time of the study have become obsolete. For example, the change of university higher education requirements for graduate faculty made a part of Danton's first recommendation impractical. The majority of new faculty for library schools are now selected only from candidates who have an earned doctorate. Thus, using sixth-year programs as training grounds for library school faculty is now futile. This change in university policy meets Danton's eleventh recommendation that faculty be better trained so that instructors would no longer teach students who already have degrees that were higher than those held by the instructors themselves. The fifth recommendation which was also designed to improve the quality of sixth-year program graduates who were to teach in library schools was met by the time of Roger's survey, but not for the original purpose. This requirement was to make certain that enrollees were exposed to the problems inolved in preparing a piece of research. Students now usually receive this indoctrination in the master's degree program with emphasis added in each year of post-master's education.

SMITH'S STUDY

In the fall of 1982, Alice Smith, Professor in the Library School at the University of South Florida at Tampa, began a review of the state of the art of sixth-year programs in the eighties. The review gathered information from: a literature survey, a questionnaire,[9] and a cover letter sent to the 37 library schools (with master's programs accredited by the American Library Association) which were indicated as having sixth-year programs in the March, 1982 listing of Graduate Library Education Programs,[10] and a review of the catalogs as well as other printed or mimeographed materials which the 37 schools had available concerning their offerings, telephone conversations, correspondence and personal interviews. Twenty-four replies (including South Florida) were received by January, 1983. A second copy of the questionnaire with a revised cover letter was sent to the thirteen schools from which replies were desired. During the last week in March, eleven of these schools replied. The remaining two schools were queried by telephone. Therefore, total responses are recorded in the study. All respondents indicated interest in sixth-year programs and an interest in the study.

   Smith's questionnaire asked: date program began, person or persons working with the program, purposes, number of students currently enrolled, number of graduates, required courses, number of hours required (semester or quarter hour credits), length of time needed to complete the program, request for fieldwork or internship hours (if any), methods of evaluation of the program. There was also space to submit a sample program as well as for individual comments of importance to the respondent. Smith's questionnaire repeated some of the same questions asked by Danton and by Rogers but in terms relevant to 1982–1983. It also asked for additional information. Other questions asked:

1. Official name of the library school.
2. Name of the parent institution.
3. A catalog description of the sixth-year program(s).
4. Person(s) responsible for administering the sixth-year program(s).
5. Year program(s) established.
6. Number of specialties within the sixth-year program(s).
7. Total number of students now enrolled.
8. Total number of graduates since the beginning of the program.
9. Total number of hours required.
10. Maximum time required for the completion of the degree.
11. Average number of months or years in which students complete degree.

Further questions asked concerned fieldwork, internship, thesis (essay or report), degree or certification awarded, core courses, purposes, goals and attainments for which students are prepared through the program (e.g., different positions, personal satisfaction, etc.), and evaluation of the program. Items 1–11 with other quantifiable information have been recorded in chart form arranged alphabetically by name of the library school.

Other information is grouped according to the types of programs most commonly offered, the numbers of specialties in programs, the most unusual specialties, interdisciplinary programs, courses offered by all the sixth-year programs, and types of program evaluation.

Samples of three programs are briefly presented as case studies. Three other programs are discussed in terms of their uniqueness in that at the moment of study, no other programs of these kinds are being offered in other sixth-year programs.

Analysis Of The 1983 Survey Chart

In a narrative analysis of the 1983 survey chart, a summation of the data presents a more global review of some aspects of the sixth-year programs. Fifteen of the programs began during the seventies. Five began during the eighties. A few of the schools which began programs in the sixties have also instituted other six-year programs at a more recent date. Often this was ten or more years later. Among these is Pittsburgh, which continues to offer two programs. The 1962 program has 199 graduates with thirteen students currently enrolled. There are sixteen graduates of the newer program with eleven students currently enrolled. Current enrollments in all programs range from zero to 44 people. The dean of one school reports that the faculty members are so involved with both the master's and the doctoral degrees that, even though the sixth-year program is printed in their catalogs as available, there is no time for them to spend on it.

Admission requirements are similar for all of the programs. Each requires a student to have earned a Master's degree. Although the majority of the schools ask for that degree to be from an ALA-accredited program, some suggest that a master's degree in a related field from a regionally accredited institution of higher education is equally acceptable. If the GRE, Miller Analogies, or TOEFL are required by the host institution or for the master's program, then they are also required for a sixth-year program. Acceptable scores on these tests were not presented on the charts. An examination of the catalogs does not locate precise information about this. The majority of programs also require "experience in the field" varying from one to two, or in one case, even three years experience. The chart gives no indication of the firmness with which this criterion is upheld.

Twenty of the schools award a certificate with other schools stating that a certificate is optional. Thirteen give a degree with an additional school reporting that their degree is in education.

Courses of study vary. With the primary purpose earlier stated as "planning a program according to the student's needs," there is little evidence of rigid requirements. Ten schools report that there are no core courses. This is in contrast to findings from an analysis of catalogs and sample programs in which specific individual courses or groups of courses are strongly recommended to students. These courses advance the goals of those students towards such areas as management, special services, specific areas of information science, work with bilingual materials and patrons, etc.

Although they are not labelled as core courses, either fieldwork or internship are required or strongly recommended in about half of the programs. Fifteen require one or the other, while the majority of the other respondents state that such opportunities are "available" or "optional."

Nineteen schools require a final paper, essay or thesis which may or may not be preceded by a number of independent study hours. One of the nineteen respondents specifying the graduate paper requirement does state "paper with independent study."

The number of required hours is similar to that reported by McCrossan.[11] The average required number of hours for graduation is 29 semester hours.

Admission Requirements — Core Courses

Name of School With Sixth-year Program	Year Begun	Number of Grad.	Current Enroll-ment.	GRE	Other Exam	Degree	Work Exper.	None	Other	Internship	Fieldwork	Thesis Essay	Cert.	Degree	No. Hr. Req.
Alabama	1978	28	8			Accred Masters	2yrs.	vary		yes	yes	no	no	Ed.	30
Albany	1978	3	41				2yrs.			no	yes	yes	yes	no	30
Atlanta	1971	19	2			Accred Mas.				no	no	yes	no	yes	30
Buffalo	1981	1	7			Accred Mas.				no	yes	yes	yes	no	30
UC/Berkeley	1973	61	8			Masters	2yrs.	no		no	no	yes	no	yes	30
U.C.L.A.	1968	9	2			Masters		none	paper	yes	no	yes	yes	no	36
Case Western	Inactive at this time														
Catholic	1972	17	30			Masters				yes	no	no	yes	no	24
Chicago	1969	66	6			Masters	2 yrs.	no		no	no	no	yes	no	27
Columbia	1980-81	39	20/4/10			B.A.	vary			no	yes	yes	yes	no	30
Denver	1968	60	5			Masters		3		no	no	no	yes	no	Q45
Drexel	1977	11	7	No		Mast. or Equ.		no	paper	no	no	P.Ind.	St.y	no	32
Emory	1966	42	27			Masters		no		no	no	no	no	yes	30
Florida State	1969	79	4			Masters		no		no	no	no	yes		30
Illinois	1963	94	14			Masters	2yrs.		one	no	yes	no	no		40S
Indiana	1978	14	6			Masters	2 yrs			no	yes	yes	yes	yes	30
Kent	1968	17	2			Masters		no		yes	yes	no	yes	no	24

Long Island	1977	6	3 or 4	Miller Ana.	Masters		no		no	yes	no	yes	no	30
Minnesota	1967	6	44		Masters	2 yrs.	no		no	no	yes	yes	yes	yes	Q44
No. Texas	On the books but not implemented.													
Oklahoma	1982	None	None		Masters	3 yrs	no		available	available	avail.	yes	no	no	30
Pittsburgh	1962/1976	199 old 16 new	11/13		Masters	15 hrs.			available	available	avail.	yes	no	no	24
Queens	1976	4	0		Masters	2 yrs.	2		available	available	yes	yes	yes	no	30
Rhode Island	1981	0	8		Masters		2		no	yes	yes	no	no	yes	30
Rosary	1976	5	17		Masters	2 yrs.	1		no	no	yes	yes	yes	yes	30
Rutgers	1974	13	22		Masters	2 yrs.	2		no	no	yes	yes	yes	yes	24
St. John's	1978	6	7		Masters	yes			no	no	no	yes	yes	no	24
So. Carolina	1977	3	8		Masters		1		yes	no	yes	no	yes	yes	30
So.Connecticut	1979	5	30		Masters	yes/no			yes	yes	yes	yes	yes	no	30
So. Florida	1978	3	12		Masters		2		yes	yes	yes	-	yes	yes	32
Syracuse	1976	2	2		Masters	2 yrs.	0		Opt.	Opt.	no	-	yes	yes	36
Texas at Austin	1978	10	5		Masters		0		no	no		no End of Sp.	no	no	12
	1967	26	6		Masters	2 yrs.	0		available	available	yes	yes	yes	no	30
Texas Women's	Inactive at this time.													
Vanderbilt-Peabody	1957	42	3		Masters		2		no	no	yes	-	yes	yes	30
Wayne State	1972	Inactive at this time.					5					yes	no	no	30
Wisc/Madison	1965	33	2		Masters	experience	0	yes, paper	available	available	yes	yes	yes	no	18
Wisc/Milwaukee	1981	4	10		Masters	2 yrs.	0		available	yes	no	yes	yes	no	24

Twenty-one of the schools require 30 hours for completion. Other requirements range from eighteen to forty semester hours. A few schools require forty-four quarter hours which equate to 29.4 semester hours.

Sample Programs

Interesting examples of individually student-planned programs are shown below. The first example is (A) from a southern library school. It emphasizes work with children and young adults including work with exceptional children, minority and multi-cultural literature and educational dimensions as well as further exposure to a variety of cataloging methods and multi-media software. The last two (B) are from the same northern library school: one indicates a combination of library science computer information, school media and the humanities (including fine arts). The other includes very few pure library science classes, but has heavy emphasis upon automated systems information processing and management.

Each of these programs indicates the need practitioners have for experience with new technologies, new literature, and practice in the utilization of a variety of skills, from those of management to program presentation, appealing to a contemporary recognition of the cultural plurality of the patrons to whom librarians give service.

MOST UNIQUE PROGRAMS

Among the sample programs returned with the survey questionnaires, the most unique programs were found to be in the School of Library Science

A
SAMPLE PROGRAM

Discipline and Course No.	Title of Course
LS 398	Independent Study
LS 352	Storytelling
LS 312	Cataloging Nonprint
Ed 269	Literature and the Exceptional Child
Ed 326	Multi-Cultural Dimensions
	Contemporary Education
LS 315	Bibliography Minority Cultures
LS 355	Services and Materials Utilization for Youth and Adults
Ed 391–A	Methods of Educational Research
LS 310	Cataloging and Classification II
LS 320	Library Materials in Microform
LS 330	Bibliographic Instruction Programs for Libraries

Within the Library School	Within Other Disciplines
No Required Courses	

B
SAMPLE PROGRAMS

Information Studies
Humanities Resources
Analysis and Evaluation of
    Media Centers
Library Automation
Independent Study—research
    and reading in computers,
    curriculum and education
Basics of Information Retrieval
    Systems
Statistics for Research I
Microcomputers and School
    Media Centers
Education
Seminar in Humanities
    Education
Instructional Improvement
    Institute
Fine Arts
Films from Novels

Information Studies
Computer-based Reference Services
Numeric Databases
Information Processing for Managers
Microprocessor-based Information Systems
Network Management
Office Automation
Information Systems Analysis
Management
Marketing Systems
Quantitative Methods for Managers
Introduction to MIS
Accounting
Engineering
Database Management Systems

---

at Columbia University. These are not called sixth-year programs but are "Advanced Certificate Programs." Two of them can be taken as the "sixth-year."[12]

A

Advanced Certificate In Preservation Administration

For those who already hold a master's degree in library science, the preservation administrator program can be taken in one year. The five specialized preservation courses (those in the 5000 and 7000 series) must be taken in SLS regardless of the students' previous course work in these areas. Equivalency for the other required courses in the curriculum will be determined on an individual basis. Established in 1981–1982.

Program Courses:
• Introductory technology and structure of record material
• Protection and care of record materials
• History of books and printing
• Introduction to descriptive bibliography
• Photoreproduction of library materials
• Administration of preservation programs
• Conservation treatment for preservation administrators

- Preservation administration fieldwork
- Preservation of library and archival materials

Recommended Courses:

- Introduction to library administration
- Systems analysis for libraries
- Academic and research libraries
- Library and information networks
- Management of archives and manuscripts collections

Credentials:

- 30 points of credit are required for the post-master's certificate in preservation administration.

B

Advanced Certificate In Information Management

The study and management of information is an increasingly central concern to our society. Major economic activity has shifted to the information sector in the post-industrial society in which we live. The Advanced Certificate in Information Management is designed to provide librarians and information officers who wish to expand and update their backgrounds in information management and technology with the opportunity to do so. While the emphasis is on preparation for positions in the corporate and specialized information sectors, those in academic and research organizations should find the training to be of comparable value in furthering their careers. Established in 1981–1982.

Course of Study:

The thirty point program (usually ten courses) may be taken full-time or part-time or a combination of both. The courses below are suggested. Courses may also be taken in other graduate divisions of the university which offer subjects appropriate to this program.

Background Courses:

- Programming for information systems
- Indexing
- On-line bibliographic data bases
- Records management
- Special libraries
- Literature of various disciplines

Advanced Courses:

- Systems analysis for libraries
- Library personnel administration
- Information systems

- Human factors in information systems
- Data base development and management
- Independent study

C

Conservator Program
(Established in 1980–81)

This is a three year program designed to prepare conservators of library and archival materials in the types of libraries and archives in which the conservator is most likely to be working. Admissions requirements in addition to the general requirements of the school of library science include a specified science background, a portfolio of work demonstrating aptitude in some form of art or craft, and indication of aptitude in manual ability and in perception relevant to the tasks required of a conservator. The book conservator aptitude test is given for such assessment. Two years of specifically designed courses are followed by a two-term full-time internship in a working institutional conservation laboratory. After course work and projects are completed, the student receives the master's degree in library science from the library school at Columbia University. After the internship is completed, a Certificate in Library and Archives Conservation is awarded jointly by Columbia University and New York University. The long list of courses is not presented here. The program is worth studying, although it is not in the generally accepted pattern of a sixth-year program.[13]

D

Specialization In Bibliotherapy In The Sixth-Year Program At The Library School, The University Of South Florida[14]

Course sequences: LEGEND: *required of all students;
                                     **required in bibliotherapy specialization

A. *Survey of library services for special groups
B. *Bibliotherapy I
C. Choose one of the following for the Bibliotherapy sequence:
    1. Guidance techniques (Department of Counselor Education, College of Education) Presentation and practice of counseling skills as needed for work in Bibliotherapy. (To be offered twice each year), or
    2. Techniques in the communication process (Department of Communicology, College of Social & Behavioral Sciences).

D. *Thesis: this comes at the end of the program as the culmination of an internship experience or an in-depth study of some aspect of special services.

E. **Internship-varying credit: 1–9 hrs.

F. *One course in Education Foundations, such as:
    1. Women in Education, or
    2. Education in the Metropolitan Areas, or
    3. Theories of Personality for School Personnel.

G. "Elective" Library Studies Courses: *Adult Services in Libraries; Choose an additional 8 hours from elective courses appropriate to student's needs: Reading Guidance; Story Telling; Selected Topics, such as, Community College Librarianship, or Selection of Materials Suitable for Bibliotherapy. There are at least thirteen other suitable courses in the U.S.F. colleges from which the student may choose one or more, such as: Juvenile Corrections, Social Interactions, Psychological and Sociological Aspects of Aging, etc.

Minor in Bibliotherapy:

Students from other departments, both in the College of Education and other colleges, taking a minor in Bibliotherapy, must take the following library science courses:

- Bibliotherapy I and Bibliotherapy II;
- Basic Information Sources, or
- One of the "Materials" courses for a particular age group or other library science courses such as Reading Guidance;
- Appropriate courses in the Counselor Education Department (a minimum of 4 hrs);
- One or two internships in bibliotherapy under the supervision of the Library, Media, and Information Studies Department, the Counselor Education Department, and the Department of Communicology.

SUMMARY OF THE STUDY

The total study including the data from the chart and the sample programs gives a global view of the status of the programs. Although one program has never been active and two are presently inactive, respondents answer that there is a needed place for these programs in the continuing education of librarians. The range of the most common types of programs gives insight into the general needs of professional librarians around the country. Twenty-eight programs are general in nature with emphasis either upon a specialization such as academic, public, special or school media librarianship. Twenty-five are in some form of management. Thirteen of these are administration and management. The other twelve are information management. There are several unusual types of programs only four of which are described in this chapter.

Interdisciplinary programs include business and management, psychology and human relations, international studies, instructional technology, communication arts, college of education and others. The range is enlarged from earlier programs. They may be interdepartmental, with other colleges within the same university, sometimes with another university or other institutions.

The total number of reported graduates is 943. The numbers enrolled each year are few, and some of these do not complete the degree. Many of those who graduate take two or more years to complete their studies. In spite of the relatively small enrollments, respondents are interested in the programs and discuss them in a fashion which indicates commitment.

Letters, conversations and other written material included with the returns also show a commitment to internship, observation visits and other forms of fieldwork. A review of the literature of such working experiences gives an interesting historical note in which library educators are often reluctant to admit an innate belief in the importance of such work during a program of higher education. Much of the pejorative connotation stems from the struggle to elevate library education beyond the status of a skills training program and to build a body of knowledge based on theory. Williamson (1923), Danton, Leigh (1954) and Rothstein (1968)[15] have promoted the idea that preparation in other professions "calls for a major share of the student's study be given to practical work," and that "experience shows the value of properly handled practice work." The examples cited by respondents in the 1983 study uphold these viewpoints.

Evaluation

Evaluation is carried out in many ways in both informal and formal arrangements:

1. Quizzes, tests, examinations.
2. Supervision in practicum or field experiences.
3. Developing computer efficiency or other types of on-line skills.
4. A terminal project which may be library research and a paper; fieldwork and field study with final paper, etc.

A terminal project sums up the total program. For example, at the University of South Florida the student is required to complete a project in the field (usually earning nine semester hours credit) which culminates in an essay. This involves a proposal written according to university guidelines. The proposal is first approved by the advisor and then submitted to the University Graduate Office for refusal/revision/acceptance before the deep involvement in action for the project is begun. The essay itself is also written according to graduate office guidelines and in the same fashion as the proposal, is sent to the Graduate Officer after its acceptance by the department. There is a right of refusal.

COMPARISON OF THE DANTON AND THE SMITH STUDIES

Five out of the eleven of Danton's major concerns have resolved themselves. The first is preparation of library school faculty. In the 1960s, sixth-year programs were perceived as training situations for library school instructors. As the eighties advance, an earned doctorate has become almost a universal criterion for appointment as a tenured library school faculty member. In part, this is due to pressures from the parent institutions of higher education of which library schools are a part. Other factors, of course, have contributed to both the effectiveness and the educational level of library school faculty. Library school faculty members rank with other members of the graduate faculties of their parent institutions of higher education.

The second concern was the need for professionals to understand research, to be able to implement the results, to be able to do research for a profession which is still building its own body of knowledge. This, too, has resolved itself. Introductory research courses are now standard in library science master's degree programs. More advanced research is recommended in all of the sixth-year programs. Granted, the depth of statistical method necessary for a Ph.D. dissertation is not required of a student in sixth-year programs, but the techniques for understanding and, in some measure, for design are offered.

The third was a recommendation that an admissions criterion for all sixth-year programs be "one or two years of experience" in the profession. The 1983 chart (Smith) indicates that the majority of programs suggest this as a criterion for admission. There is no indication of the extent to which this is enforced.

The fourth recommendation that an award such as a certificate or degree be given at the end of the sixth-year program is met. However, the fifth recommendation, that the award be the same in each school, has not been met. As the chart shows, in the majority of schools it is either a certificate or a degree with very little choice given to the student.

Danton's eleven recommendations are not all based upon his quantitative findings. They come from discussions, correspondence, responses to his questionnaire and interviews. They are not the unsupported opinion of the investigator. In spite of an evident consensus, three recommendations are not within the prerogative of such a group to decide. The first is a recommendation that some school in the Northwest area of the United States implement a sixth-year program to be designed especially to meet the need of preparing library school instructors or specialists in information science, junior college libraries or instructional materials. This has not been implemented. No question was asked in the 1983 survey (Smith) to discover if there had been interest in or work done towards this goal.

In relation to the recommendation concerning rewards given by employers for sixth-year study, because of the practical structure of various institutions, no library school can establish appropriate positions, classifications and salary schedules of benefit to the graduates of sixth-year programs. This is done by the employing institution. Considering some of the other recommendations, COA does not coordinate, monitor or arrange to accredit any program of library science other than the master's level program. Finally, the ideal of a common sixth-year program could undoubtedly never be met because if programs are designed to meet individual needs or regional needs, or have some specific goal such as preparing for library service to populations of specific ethnic mix, then individual needs are more important than needs in common.

Recommendation for program improvement towards meeting student expectations appears to be internal and a part of each library school's own self-evaluation. The answers to the survey questionnaire specify no definite form of evaluation commonly used and no examples were forthcoming.

The growth in the number of programs and the longevity of many of them are strong indicators of need for these programs. It is possible that there may never be a "standard" or "all-purpose" sixth-year program as is required in programs offering the basic rudiments of librarianship. If the programs fulfill the needs of library professionals and enable them to become more efficient because of this diversity of thrust, then there is a rightful place for the program.

CRITICISMS OF SIXTH-YEAR PROGRAMS

Criticisms of sixth-year programs come from the literature and interviews rather than from the survey or the material submitted by the schools. The two largest complaints concern funding of the program itself and reward for the graduates by employers. In most institutions, there appear to be no systems of cost-accounting to ascertain in how to budget specifically for a sixth-year degree or certificate program. In many schools, both doctoral and/or master's students may be enrolled in the same classes as the sixth-year program students. Although few schools agree that a towards a doctoral program, there are instances in which this is indeed the practice. Those courses designated solely for sixth-year students often have low enrollment. In those schools in which an FTE allottment ratio is a part of the fiscal rule, the low enrollment courses are "permitted" to be taught because other courses are more heavily enrolled and "carry" the small classes by "earning enough of the apportionment" so that there is an appropriate over-all number of students. At other times, professors teach the desired course in addition to their other courses with no extra emolument, but as a "part of the load." Whatever the method used for support, the library schools offering sixth-year programs are continuing to teach the courses.

As for the second complaint, although library institutions and agencies around the country vary in terms of pay scale and classifications, it is possible that an *ad hoc* committee within ALA state or regional professional organizations could take unification of these matters as a task which may well be a part of setting professional standards for types of libraries. School systems appear to increase salaries according to levels of education between the master's degree and the doctorate. Some academic libraries require a second master's degree (often in a discipline other than library science) or an "equivalent" advanced degree at a level before the doctorate. Job descriptions for supervisory positions in some libraries specify "specialized training" for appointment and advancement. Others ask for a specialty in "work with children," with the aging, with other populations with specific needs. Completion of the sixth-year program of advanced study usually meets these needs. The means by which advancement and/ or higher pay scales for such positions are devised could well be a part of a study in unifying and advancing the professional value of a sixth-year degree or certificate.

Other criticisms involve the content of the programs. Many of these criticisms or suggestions involve individual programs or one specific institution. These are handled internally. More widespread suggestions concern internships and other forms of practice work. There are strong arguments both for and against practice work.

Practice Work in Libraries

Witucke (1981) documents the resurgence of a variety of forms of practice work in formal library education.[16] By the 1980–1981 school year, only one library school did not offer some form of field or practice work. This was because of that school's extensive work study program. The practice work discussed here does not include pre-professional experience outside of the library school. It does include practicum internships, some forms of field trips and observations. These may be modules or single courses, separate courses, or long-term controlled experiences on a full work-week basis in specially selected libraries. There may be rigid guidelines to follow and evaluations to complete by both student and supervisor.

In the other literature about this topic, various people such as Williamson (1923), Leigh (1954), Rothstein (1968),[17] and Monroe (1981)[18] give descriptions and definitions of "practice" as well as arguments supporting the value of these experiences. Once again, the brevity of the one-year master's degree program does not allow time for sustained practice in a variety of circumstances. A sixth-year program gives opportunity to practice in new fields or to acquire depth or new dimensions in one's own field.

ACQUIRING AND IMPLEMENTING A SIXTH-YEAR PROGRAM IN A UNIVERSITY

Universities have their own rules and regulations which must be followed before any program of higher education is established. These are in addition to the designing of the proposal which also must follow specific rules of format and categories of content to be covered. This step could include the use of data from a variety of surveys ranging from opinions of faculty, students, alumni, potential employers, the community at large and demographic statistics of a local, state and national level. Depending upon the kind of system under which a particular university operates, an even longer and more cumbersome procedure evolves.

The state of Florida may be an example of requirements within a planned State University System (SUS) in which one Board of Regents is the governing body for the entire system and is responsible for all final decision of policy and actual implementation of a program or refusal of that program. The process involves departmental/division/college review and decision making before the proposal is sent to that area of the university administration which is responsible for graduate education. This process may involve review by a number of committees, some of which will be interdisciplinary. It may also entail revision and/or defense of the proposal. The same procedure is repeated with an administrative committee before recommendation is made by the president of the university to send the proposal to the Board of Regents. The board may decide that all other programs of the same or a related discipline need to be aware of the proposal. In some cases this involves a review by the concerned parties and even a defense by the unit offering the proposal before the Board of Regents. The entire process may take place in a time frame ranging from one year to three or sometimes even longer. The library school faculty must feel a strong commitment to the program in order to carry out the process necessary for receiving approval.

Criteria For The Success Of A Sixth-Year Program

1. Strong sense of commitment from faculty and the university: From the faculty, for ensuring worthwhile courses for teaching, and for proper (adequate) advising to ensure that students were guided away from the "Green stamp" planning of programs. From the university, to see that faculty, materials and accomodations were available.
2. Strong sense of purpose: A universal purpose gives the best opportunity for specializing.
3. Separate identity from that of doctoral programs.
4. Unique potentials beyond the general potentials for specialization.
5. European needs are different from the American. This is due to the lattice or step classification of professional library positions. An individual (through education) can proceed from one position to another.

SUMMARY

This paper has placed heavy emphasis upon the Danton study with a look at changes which have taken place over the years from 1970–1983, and the state of the art of the sixth-year program at present. In the years which have elapsed, there has been an irregular acceleration both in the number of ALA-accredited master's degree programs as well as in the number of sixth-year programs. The rapid program acceleration of the 1970s is beginning to slow down and all programs are under stringent review, as economic conditions and fluctuating populations change the locations of educational and library needs. Technological change has played a great part in this. All of these influences are seen in the numbers, locations, and purposes of sixth-year programs. Although there are many programs which reflect technological and informational needs, others concentrate on ethnic plurality of population, concern for today's children, and other humanistic values ranging from the preservation of cultural and historical volumes of rarity and antiquity, through programs of appreciation for the visual arts to the mental health and other personal needs of such diverse groups of patrons as the juvenile, the aging, the institutionalized, etc.

It is apparent that the brevity of an already crowded master's degree program cannot offer the depth or the varieties of specialized study that a sixth-year program can. While some of the additional dimensions found in sixth-year study can be and are offered through sequential "general" continuing education courses not leading to a degree or certificate or through those occasional one-of-a-kind courses of continuing education, the thrust or impact of a planned program around a specific purpose appears to provide the most useful and satisfactory accomplishment of individual professional goals. It also appears that the demands of a doctoral program structured on the Germanic model of rigid research of a primarily theoretical nature, while useful for constructing an ideological body of knowledge as well as discovering new directions which practitioners may explore, does not fulfill the advanced educational needs of the practitioner who needs a specialized course of study consistent with his/her own professional demands.

The need continues to exist for individually planned programs which advance personal and professional development, but are not as narrow as doctoral programs. The practitioner wishes to learn new methods which are at a higher level than learning rote skills, but which do not depend on hours of acquiring and applying mathematical formulae.

It would be well for someone to formally investigate the recognition of these programs as helpful in advancing the needs of employers in the field. This would require an analysis of the impact such education has already made on the work sector as well as the assessment of the graduates of these programs. This is done for the graduates of accredited master's programs. Schools preparing for such accreditation might use that opportunity for a similar assessment of sixth-year program graduates. The concept of well-planned and supervised segments of practice work might also be pursued at greater depth. Surveys such as those by Danton, Witucke, Smith and others reveal the existence of both practice and need.

As greater numbers of people each year are growing into the gray area of senior citizenship, their needs are becoming greater. Assuaging these needs may be attempted by some practical application of information sciences, but the needs themselves must be met on a human, personalized basis. This involves one to one and group contacts with opportunities for retaining usefulness to society and a sustained feeling of self-respect. At the opposite end of the spectrum youth, too, have disparate needs intensified by nuclear threats and fluctuating family patterns. They, too, need more specially planned library programming. Little of this is done at the master's level of work. Here, too, are unique but widespread opportunities for study and practice. The field is wide and demanding.

NOTES AND REFERENCES

1. Agnes Reagan, Professor, Graduate School of Library and Information Science, University of Texas at Austin. In correspondence with Alice G. Smith. November, 1982.

2. J. Periam Danton. Between M.L.S. and Ph.D.: *a Study of Sixth Year Specialist Programs in Accredited Library Schools.* Chicago: American Library Association, 1970, pp. 1–6.

3. Ibid., pp. 1–6.

4. Ibid., p. 6.

5. Robert Rogers. "Report on Six-year Programs in the United States." *Journal of Education for Librarianship,* 20 (Winter, 1979), p. 250.

6. Marvin Mounce in his chapter of this book discusses these forms and offers working definitions of Continuing Education which are practical for an understanding of the issue at hand.

7. Jo Ann Bell. "The Role of Library School in Providing Continuing Education for the Profession." *Journal of Education for Librarianship*, 20 (Winter, 1979), p. 250.

8. Danton, pp. 80–81.

9. Alice G. Smith, Professor, University of South Florida School of Library and Information Science. "Questionnaire on Six Year Programs in Accredited Library Schools." Tampa, Florida: University of South Florida, November, 1982.

10. *Graduate Library Education Programs,* Accredited by the *American Library Association under Standards for Accreditation, 1972.* Chicago: American Library Association, March, 1982.

11. John A. McCrossan. "Beyond the Master's Program: Library Schools and Continuing Education of Library, Media and Information Professionals." *In Advances in Librarianship,* Vol. 12, Wesley Simonton, editor. New York: Academic Press, 1982.

12. Richard L. Darling, Dean, School of Library Service, Columbia University. In an explanatory attachment to his response to "Questionnaire on Six Year Programs in Accredited Library Schools," unpublished survey sent by the University of South Florida, Winter, 1982.

13. Columbia University School of Library Service, *Bulletin,* 1983–1984. New York: Columbia University, 1983, p. 11, 36–37.

14. University of South Florida School of Library and Information Science, *Bulletin: Education Specialist,* "Education Specialist in Curriculum and Instruction with a Specialization in Library and Information Science with Concentration on Library Service to Special Groups." Tampa, Florida: University of South Florida, 1978.

15. Williamson, Danton, Leigh and Rothstein are cited in *Library Education, an International Survey.* Larry Earl Bone, editor, Urbana, IL. University of Illinois Graduate School of Library Science, 1968.

16. A. Virginia Witucke. "The Place of Library Experience in Library Education: Trends and Current Status." *Journal of Education for Librarianship,* 22 (Summer/Fall, 1981), pp. 74–88.

17. Williamson, Leigh and Rothstein are cited in *Library Education: An International Survey,* Larry Earl Bone, editor. Urbana, IL: University of Illinois Graduate School of Library Science, 1968.

18. Margaret E. Monroe. "Issues in Field Experience as an element in the Library School Curriculum." *Journal of Education for Librarianship,* 22 (Summer/Fall, 1981), pp. 57–73.

THE EVOLUTION OF AN ENDANGERED SPECIES:

CENTRALIZED PROCESSING CENTERS AND THE CASE OF THE UNIVERSITY OF SOUTH CAROLINA

Charmaine B. Tomczyk and Linda K. Allman

INTRODUCTION

The disappearance, or sometimes publicized death, of processing centers transpired as swiftly as their spontaneous birth. Their emergence was prompted by necessity, but their continuance was plagued by many internal and external factors. Survival depended partially upon the application of sound management principles, including long-range planning, especially in the area of automation, budgeting, cost-effectiveness and sensitivity to

Advances in Library Administration and Organization
Volume 6, pages 221–240
Copyright © 1986 by JAI Press Inc.
All rights of reproduction in any form reserved.
ISBN: 0-89232-724-3

clients' needs. Competition in the processing marketplace contributed to the failure of centers. While some of these factors have been individually labelled as bringing about the downfall of centers, their collective application to provide services to libraries has caused their evolution. Perhaps library processing centers have not disappeared; only changed shape and nomenclature. In the *ALA Yearbook,* Simpson asserts that "the year 1977 has provided a mere taste of changes to come in bibliographic processing centers. [See also Networks]" (57). The *1985 American Library Directory* lists nineteen pages of networks, consortia and other cooperative library organizations. This article will attempt to review what shaped the processing center concept, why some centers did not survive and, finally, how some centers, in particular the Library Processing Center of the University and Four Year Campuses of the University of South Carolina, still endure and thrive.

THE EMERGENCE OF CENTERS

Centralized processing burst upon the scene in about 1960. Not until 1958 did library literature even indicate a heading that suggested centralization or cooperation in cataloging by separate units (Hunt 54). The propagation of centers throughout the sixties can be partially credited to sunny economic climates. The baby boom generation assisted in fueling healthy budgets for libraries. The base year for the Consumer Price Index was 1967 when $1.00 was equal to $1.00 of buying power. In contrast, the dollar as of August 1985 is worth about $.30. Opportunities to purchase large quantities of library materials were available. However, the mechanisms to expedite ordering, cataloging and physical preparation, namely the technical services departments, were neither equipped nor staffed to handle increased workloads. The emergence of centralized processing centers fulfilled this need for rapid growth by providing a quick growth medium. Their numbers were further boosted by the Library Services Act (LSA) of 1956 that provided funding for such cooperative efforts. The State Plans under the LSA 1960 Supplement further encouraged centralized processing activities.

Described as "a current dynamic and explosive idea" (Hunt 54), processing centers were seriously considered by many libraries and library systems. Feasibility studies were prolific. The State University of New York contracted Arthur D. Little, Inc. to devise a plan for a center that would accommodate their predicted one million volumes by 1970. Their plan's objective expressed foresight in considering current technology and known trends. The major advantage was cost savings. "The savings from center purchasing and processing both repay the current operating cost and amortize the capital investment" (Little 6). Rothines Associates conducted a feasibility study for state regional area processing centers in 1971 (Roth). The study was intended to show the need for more than a processing center network. It wanted to establish basic agencies to unify library service, with an interlibrary loan component and statewide borrowers' cards. The study recommended centralization for libraries in Indiana. Another feasibility study was conducted by James Fry in 1977 for some Pennsylvania libraries to consolidate or coordinate technical services countywide. A 1980 study of the then existing Illinois Libraries Materials Processing Center cited as one major conclusion, "the potential market for processing center services has not been realized" (Highum 1).

The University of South Carolina (USC) System and Centralized Library Processing

The baby-boom generation pumped dollars into higher education. To accommodate the demands for college degrees, universities developed systems of branches, regionals, or satellite campuses at distances from the main campus. The USC system expanded in this way. Prior to 1957, when a student who was not on the main Columbia campus needed a course, the only two avenues available were to take a correspondence or field course, or to enroll in Columbia. The offering of courses distant from the Columbia campus evolved as a result of a response to needs voiced by community members and leaders. The first USC off-campus offerings in 1957 were held in Florence, about 75 miles from the Columbia campus. The basement of the Florence County Library then sufficed as classroom and library space (the Florence branch is now Francis Marion College). A brief two years later, courses were offered in Beaufort, South Carolina along the southern coast. During the next decade, six more campuses were established at Lancaster, Conway, Aiken, Union, Salkehatchie and Spartanburg. The final addition was the Sumter campus, completing a USC Regional Campus system of eight sites. From a few course offerings in the 1960s, the number of students and their needs for additional courses increased dramatically. Today the USC system includes the main campus, three Four Year campuses and five Two Year campuses.

As each campus was formed, written contracts were formulated between the University and the local entities or commissions. The University assumed all administrative authority, including policies, staffing and academic instruction. The local county board's chief responsibilities were to provide the physical facilities and equipment (books were designated as equipment). These written agreements were adhered to until 1967, when the State no longer permitted the University to spend significant amounts of State funds on facilities not owned by the State. The original contracts remain, but they have little relevancy to today's University and Four Year Campus System. Yet even today, the University of South Carolina still lists books as equipment (Duffy).

It is important to review the early history of the USC Extension Division to understand the eventual evolution of today's Library Processing Center (LPC) of the University. The Extension Division Library supported field and correspondence courses aimed primarily at public school teachers needing to update certification. The Extension Division's mission extended the Columbia resident student's privileges to remote areas of the State. Professors affiliated with the University of South Carolina on a full or part-time basis traveled once or twice weekly to these areas distant from the Columbia campus to teach. Usually, the professors selected library materials from the Extension Division collections to distribute to students enrolled in field courses. Correspondence enrollees wrote to the Extension Division for materials. From 1945 to 1958, the Extension Division Library's purpose was to order, catalog, and physically prepare materials for the Extension Division programs. In addition, two full-time staff and a handful of students compiled catalogues of plays and assembled groups of books, pamphlets, and magazines pertaining to specific subject areas for the Package Library Service. These materials and bibliographies were packaged and made available by mail or pick-up to students and faculty distant from the Columbia campus. There was a scarcity of money for building these collections. As one early staff member, Marie Hallman (1985), of the Division stated, "You just had to care". The small Division collection contained only 2,000 books that were classified according to Dewey Decimal Classification. Each catalog card was manually typed. In 1958, Dr. Nicholas P. Mitchell was appointed Director of the Extension Services. One of his major goals included the concept of offering University classes at permanent facilities around the State and hiring professors whenever possible from the local communities.

As classes augmented, the need for library resources did likewise. Eventually, the necessity for local library facilities was required for accreditation by the Southern Association of Colleges and Schools. To upgrade the regional campus libraries to accreditation standards, each library had to own 20,000 volumes. The University appropriated $250,000.00 of state funds in 1966 to bring library collections in line with standards (Toombs). Thousands of new books had to be shelf-ready in just 18 months.

Effective September 1, 1967, a new library director for McKissick Memorial Library on the Columbia campus, Mr. Kenneth Toombs, was appointed. For the first time, the Director supervised all library activities throughout the University system, including the RegionalCampuses. He implemented such improvements as ordering books and periodicals from jobbers, requesting books pre-processed whenever possible (until SO-LINET was available), reproducing cards sets on a Xerox machine adapted for card stock, and applying typed Se-Lin labels to the spines of books, replacing the stylus method. To begin the work of building library collections at the various campuses, Mr. Alfred Rawlinson, previous Director of Libraries at USC, and Toombs selected titles for each of the eight campuses. They selected approximately 25,000 titles, matching them against holdings in the Columbia undergraduate library and against the titles in *Books for College Libraries*. Book vendors were asked to provide computer lists of their inventories. In addition, the serials librarian at Columbia, assisted in compiling a core list of periodical titles essential to support the disciplines taught at each campus. The list designated which titles were to be bound or microfilmed and which required purchase of backfiles. Careful consideration was given to titles' probable usage and their storage and space requirements. Rawlinson worked with serial and book jobbers for the Regional Campuses' purchases until his retirement in 1968. Toombs negotiated a contract for book binding of all USC libraries' collections.

For the task of cataloging, the Director of Libraries purchased a Xerox machine for reproduction of catalog cards. A Polaroid camera was used to enlarge the catalog entry found in NUC. The Polaroid picture was taped to a blank catalog card and the call number typed in the upper left-hand corner. When the entry was not an exact match, an electric erasure eradicated the incorrect information to allow for correct re-typing. Call numbers were originally inscribed on book spines using an electric stylus. Toombs worked with Gaylord Library Supplies to develop the Se-Lin labelling system. The campuses received books irregularly by truck or, if someone happened to be traveling to the other campuses, processed books were added to their journey. Using streamlined processing techniques, a small staff of clerks and students assisted Hallman and Rawlinson to catalog and process 31,140 volumes from July 1, 1967 to June 30, 1968, nearly doubling their holdings in one year to 77,549. As many as 3,000 volumes per week were purchased, processed and delivered to the Regional Campus libraries for less than $7.00 per volume. A bookkeeper was hired to pay invoices and maintain ledgers of encumbrances and expenditures for the campus libraries and the Extension Division Library. The number of books prepared each day was so numerous as to justify the purchase of a van to deliver the processed books to each campus. During the following year, 1968–1969, the number of volumes held collectively by the campuses increased to 115,449. Although the campus libraries did not reach the hoped for 20,000 volume per library goal before the accreditation team arrived, the intentions were visible to the team, and accreditation by the Southern Association of Colleges and Schools was granted in April 1968 (Toombs).

Between 1967 and 1972, Toombs's role encompassed additional responsibilities for Regional Campus libraries such as preparing for and assisting with the Southern Association of Colleges and Schools' accreditation visit (announced in 1966), advising campus librarians on their administrative concerns and policies, designing and planning new library facilities at Aiken, Conway (known as the Coastal Carolina campus), Lancaster, and Spartanburg campuses, and talking to local community leaders to solicit funds for new buildings and to increase the library materials budgets, staff and equipment, (Toombs). Realizing the importance of easy access to library materials, Toombs decided that all library materials at every location in the USC system were to be reclassified to the Library of Congress Classification system, starting April 1, 1968. By the end of 1970, Extension Division Library personnel had reclassified all the volumes held by Regional Campus Libraries, as well as the holdings of the Extension Division Library.

A major reorganization in the University's administrative structure occurred in 1972. The Associate Provost for Regional Campuses became solely responsible for the Regional Campus Processing Center (RCPC) operation. The Director of Libraries' official duties were then confined to the Columbia campus libraries; however, his expertise continued to be sought frequently by the librarians and the Associate Provost.

As part of the university's reorganization in 1972, a separate department for processing Regional Campus Libraries' materials was created from the General Studies Library, the former Extension Library, which continued to be administered by Hallman. This separate department was the Regional Campus Processing Center, later to be named the Library Processing Center. In September 1971, Linda Allman, a former librarian at the Florence Regional Campus and zip cataloger at the McKissick Library on the Columbia campus, was hired to supervise the Regional Campus Processing Center (RCPC). At the time of this division, the staff of the RCPC consisted of Allman, who was the head librarian, Susan Kennedy, serving as an assistant librarian, and several student assistants. The first few years were spent working to eliminate the cataloging backlog accrued during the push for accreditation. During the period 1973 to 1975 the staff expanded from two full-time staff members with a few students to seven full-time staff, and in 1975, to over 12,000 hours of student help (USC. Regional Campus Processing Center 6). In 1973, the Center adopted an automated acquisitions system developed several years earlier by the Columbia campus library. With the implementation of this system, called the Monograph Processing System (USC. University Libraries, 1974, 30), three staff members were added to keypunch, to verify book orders, and to maintain accounting for the campuses. In early 1975, the RCPC joined SOLINET, as part of the Columbia libraries' membership, to serve the

Regional Campuses, (USC. University Libraries, 1975, 20). This was instrumental in eliminating the cataloging backlog and establishing a valuable cluster for machine-readable data. SOLINET ended the manual searching for cataloging entries in the National Union Catalogs (NUC). Sumter, a former Clemson University branch, and the last campus to join the Regional Campus system, stopped local processing within a few years of entering the system. From October 1975 to December 1984, Mary Ann Camp served as Director. Her nine years of leadership expanded services to include reference assistance and interlibrary loan (ILL) in 1977 (USC. Two and Four Year Campus Libraries 4), a shuttle delivery system in 1979 that now provides service twice a week to each campus, and an electronic mail system in 1984 (USC. Library Processing Center 13).

Coastal Carolina Campus at Conway became the first campus to be awarded Four Year status in 1974 with the Spartanburg campus following later that same year. Aiken attained Four Year status in 1975. Coastal's material budget increased by 485%. The reverse happened to the Spartanburg budget which decreased by 7%. Coastal's dramatically increased materials' budget resulted in only a 62% increase for the Regional Campus Processing Center's operating budget. Although materials' budgets for most of the Four Year Campus libraries increased substantially for many years, the rapid expansion in curriculum proved difficult to support adequately. During this period, the Two Year campuses enjoyed small increases. By fiscal year 1981, all the Four Year campuses and some of the Two Year campuses suffered substantial budgetary decreases due to the recession. After fiscal year 1981, all libraries experienced decreases almost yearly. Only two of the Two Year campuses have risen to their 1981 allotment, while only one of the Four Year campuses has done so. These budgetary constraints reinforced the conclusion reached by librarians nationwide; namely, that the dream to purchase every title needed was impractical. Furthermore it was realized that resource sharing, such as interlibrary loan, and cooperative efforts, such as collection development, were valuable and necessary collective goals.

IDENTIFICATION OF CENTRALIZED PROCESSING CENTERS

In their heyday, an estimated 200 processing centers were in operation. An exact count of current centers is unknown. The American Library Association's Resources and Technical Services Division (ALA RTSD) Discussion Group on Processing Centers, which now has 76 members, is preparing an update to their revised 1979 listing of centers. In the *1977 ALA Yearbook* Simpson reports 160 centers in 1961 and 70 centers in 1977

(55). However, another report in 1970 indicates 422 centers (Hendricks). Many of these 422 were school and public libraries, and only three were academic libraries. A 1964 article by James R. Hunt lists only 48 centers. These variances may be a result of an unclear definition of what constitutes a processing center. RTSD broadly defines it as "an agency ordering, receiving, cataloging and preparing materials for two or more libraries" (ALA. RTSD. 233). Evelyn Mullen's "Guidelines for establishing a centralized Library Processing Center" define a center as "a single agency which processes materials for a wider group of libraries" (Anderson 8). Overall, the literature on processing centers "does not support a systematic or comprehensive definition of what they are or what they do" (Anderson 10).

The discrepancies in the total number of operating centers also testifies to the volatile, erratic growth of centralization. Throughout the past two decades, many closings have been suspected, while a few have been documented. Using the 1966 RTSD preliminary list of 59, researchers at the University of Illinois mailed questionnaires to these centers and found that five of the nineteen total respondents were no longer in operation or otherwise ineligible (Polich). Another study (Camp & Tomczyk), using the 1977 update to the preliminary list, queried 23 centers of which 21 responded. Of this 21, seven or 33% had ceased and two others did not consider themselves processing centers. In the late 1970s, *Library Journal* repeatedly reported the woes of struggling statewide processing centers. Reports were also made of terminations.

REASONS FOR CLOSINGS

Mechanization and Customization

Just as the economic need for centers came from outside its structure, so did its decline and often demise. Rapid technological change and commercial competition outpaced the evolution of some centers. Early cost estimates were based on manual systems whose costs escalated as computer systems in outside sectors brought reduced unit costs. Early studies budgeted high for space and staff. When it became apparent that automated procedures would be cost-effective, centers' budgets could hardly bear the expense of the equipment, let alone the hiring of trained staff. Commercial operations (jobbers) had the financial base to invest in automation and the development of software options. Their processing fees were less than that of the processing centers. In Clayton Highum's study of the Illinois Libraries Materials Processing Center, he stated: "The opportunity for significant cost reduction is limited without substantial mechanization and computerization" (19). "Any increase in the volume of business [at the Processing Center] must be coordinated with appropriate adjustments in the price structure and/or the subsidy in order to avoid further deterioration of the financial condition of the Center" (2). In 1977, Simpson writes: "Some centers have closed because they have been unable to make the transition from mechanization to automation or could not remain competitive with services provided by the commercial sectors" (55).

Providing processing that is tailored to libraries' requests gobbled up profits. Few library operations offer such a myriad of standards than those of technical services, and in particular cataloging. Any special request that veered from the centers' standardized process expended additional staff time. The premise of centralization presumed a uniformity of procedures as a basis for savings. To centralize is to "bring into one system, or under one control", (Webster 436). According to Harold Roth (1971), many centers failed to insist on standardization to reduce unit cost under the pressure of member libraries who demanded customization. His study for Indiana libraries recommended no provision for customized cataloging; it was "actively discouraged" (iii). Further, many librarians do not realize the cost of processing nor general cost analyses in order to recognize a fair price for services. In any case, it is believed that "tailored" cataloging did not ultimately benefit the library patron, (Hendricks, 1985). Just the contrary, it may have hurt the patron due to delays in the books' availability. In one effort to save the Rhode Island processing center, suggestions were to avoid "custom cataloging" and eliminate non-essential elements on the catalog card, (*Library Journal,* 1976, 851). Even for those libraries that did not request tailored cataloging outright, it is suspected that these libraries would make their own adjustments in-house after receipt of the center's cataloging (Hendricks, 1985). This additional processing only added to the overall processing cost per item. The quest for standardized cataloging does not obviate the situation. Even today, "Standards applied to USMARC and AACR2 vary so much that although format may be standardized, its application is not" (McCombs).

Costs and Fees

Processing costs crept higher and higher as centers hesitated to increase fees. In one 1983 study (Camp & Tomczyk), unit costs ranged from $1.28 to $7.00, while the unit fees for the same group ranged from $.20 to $3.30. In all cases, costs were higher by at least 42%. The average unit cost was $3.66; the average unit fee charged was $1.81. In that same study, approximately 50% of the centers polled had never done a cost analysis of their operation and could, therefore, not answer the unit cost questions.

The lack of cost analysis applications in processing centers is also evidenced in Anderson's study (1980), where almost half of the libraries gave no answer to his unit charge question (19). Results of another questionnaire survey of 59 processing centers conducted in late 1979 showed a mean fee per item of $.92 with a range of $.20 to $1.60 using four valid cases. The survey noted a mean cost per item of $3.46 with a range of $1.50 to $6.75 using twelve valid cases (Polich 7). The Highum study showed one center's cost per product serviced was $2.74 for already cataloged trade titles. However, a trade title that needed original cataloging had a unit cost of $10.77. This category was between 5 and 6% of the books processed. One center's feasibility study projected an estimated savings of $.84 to $5.61 per volume with a $1.05 per volume charge. However, the actual fee charged when this center was in operation was a minimum of $2.25 (Davis). Similarly, the Colorado Academic Libraries Book Processing Center (CALBPC) underestimated the cost per volume in early studies. Donald Riggs' literature review in 1975 showed no evidence of application of management systems to processing centers. He states: "Apparently, the new processing centers have been developed without much thought given to the benefits of new management systems [such as PPBS and MBO]" (20). As the above cases illustrate, improved long-range planning and budgeting were needed for processing centers to survive financially, and processing centers did not charge enough for their services.

Even with increased unit charges, a cost recovery system would not guarantee the survival of processing centers as their overhead costs escalated and federal and state funding diminished. Several state and regional centers were largely federally-funded. When these subsidies diminished, many centers found it difficult to stay afloat. The Nassau County Library System credited its longevity to its state funding. In 1977, its director admitted that state funding was the only way a processing center could "make a go of it" (*Library Journal,* 1977, 2389). Further, he contended that if centers tried to recover costs by charging for their work, libraries would more than likely drop out and do their own processing to avoid out-of-pocket expenses. The measure of federal and state subsidies played a major role in some centers' survival. The North Carolina Community College system's Media Processing Center (Raleigh, N.C.) is subsidized through state funds. Its director feels that this valuable support has continued the existence of the Center (Doyle).

Competition in the Marketplace

Another threat to processing centers' survival, as Goetz realized in his 1979 suggestion to close a Maryland center, was the competitive pricing and services of commercial vendors. "Before jobber processing became so cheap and easy, the Maryland Center was the only way small systems could hope to cope" (Goetz). *Library Journal* reported in a 1977 article, entitled "Iowa's processing center skirts bankruptcy", that a drop in business from participating libraries was causing their plight. Due to fewer federal dollars to buy books coupled with less purchasing power, a recduction in the use of processing centers resulted. It was reported that many of Iowa's participants sent less than half of their books to the center for processing. With the closing of the Florida State Library's Bureau of Book Processing, the State Librarian then cited commercial vendors as attracting the Bureau's potential customers by offering processing services at a much lower cost (*Library Journal*, 1976, 2418). In the same article the Bureau Chief stated that cost-conscious librarians were switching to lower-priced commercial services, even at the sacrifice of quality. Yet Cuyahoga County's (OH) decision to end its services in 1982 was based on a cost analysis study in 1979 that concluded operating costs could be cut while improving service to its 26 branches. The county found that "by banding together into a consortium" and contracting with a vendor for processing services, they were able to pay less (*Library Journal*, 1982, 392). One respondent to the Camp and Tomczyk questionnaire stated that his eventual decision to close a processing center and de-centralize services had saved the 19 county systems "well over $100,000.00 a year in excessive processing fees" (Goetz).

Not only were jobber prices better, but they provided a faster turnaround time (Hendricks, 1985). In terms of priorities, libraries tend to rank speed in delivery higher than cost of service (Markuson). Of course, many processing centers themselves utilized the services of commercial vendors, but center customers felt that more time could be saved by dealing directly with the jobber, thereby eliminating one middleman. These libraries inevitably lost some book discounts from reduced volume of orders, but gained faster services in return. Moreover the *sine qua non* in library schools' technical services training, according to Barbara Evans Markuson, is that each professional will have his/her own complete, self-sufficient technical services department. Claiming independence from a center was considered a natural progression for many processing center members. There was a tendency within libraries to assume that they could do it better themselves than an outside agency could. However, this stance could not be substantiated by the authors who suspect the opposite may be true.

CONTINUING ROLE OF CENTERS RESHAPED

According to Markuson, Director of INCOLSA, contracting one's services is, as many businesses have learned, more effective than doing them in-house. Few businesses, she contends, would consider doing their own payroll when outside agencies can provide this service. Many repetitive, labor-intensive tasks are candidates for outside contracts. The processing center concept continues to offer an alternative to in-house processing. By removing this function from libraries, time is released for other responsibilities, such as administrative, public services and other professional pursuits. Centralized centers offer shared human resources through professional expertise in cataloging, consulting and reference assistance that may not be available locally. Expensive equipment is also shared by many. New technologies beyond the budgetary reach of smaller libraries can be made available through processing centers.

Some new technologies have encouraged de-centralization. Microcomputer software packages offer data base management systems (DBMS) for in-house operations. CARDS, a collection of computer programs for catalog card production, aids in the maintenance of a manual catalog. CALM is another software package for catalog cards, cards and pocket labels and spine label production. Several other micro programs have been incorporated into technical services to save with local operations.[1] Yet libraries have a larger responsibility to the creation and maintenance of bibliographic records, which is the basis for information transfer. Today, this requires machine-readable formats. In-house or contracted-out card production will be obsolete for a national approach dedicated to resource sharing. Conversion of records into machine-readable format has revolutionized technical services processes. Converting bibliographic records into machine-readable format is an expensive undertaking that has resurrected centralized efforts in the shape of online utilities. Clustering has grown in popularity as did cooperative efforts for retrospective conversion (RECON).

ADVANTAGES OF PROCESSING CENTERS AND TECHNOLOGICAL IMPACT

Early on, the University of South Carolina recognized the need for a formal mechanism for the satellite campuses of USC to tap the vast research collections on the Columbia campus. The time was right for cooperative efforts with the arrival in 1977 of a new University President, Dr. James B. Holderman, who orchestrated important changes for the campus system. He viewed the campuses as an integral and equal part of the University system. He accomplished this by a number of organizational changes throughout the University system: "members of county commissions, those units that share in the governance of campuses outside Columbia, will attend meetings of the Board of Trustees; . . . admission and recruitment functions will similarly be meshed . . . [and] an organizational change has elevated the position of associate provost for regional campuses [Dr. John J. Duffy] to Vice President of all two-year campuses and continuing education for the entire system" (*Carolina Plan*, 1977, 4) Holderman discouraged the nomenclature of "branches" or "regional campuses" and preferred instead "Two and Four Year Campuses", which eventually evolved to the present day "University and Four Year Campuses". He emphasized quick access by students, faculty and the community to all library materials within the nine campus system. Duffy now serves as Vice President for University Campuses and Continuing Education. His association with the campuses spans 26 years. Although the Four Year campuses now report directly to the Office of the President, informal lines of communication to the Vice President are frequently utilized. He has been administratively responsible for the campus system from its genesis, through its turbulent, formative years to today's period of growth. On July 1, 1985, Linda Allman again accepted the challenge of administrating the LPC. As a candidate for the directorship, she was intrigued by the enthusiasm exhibited by the University and Four Year campus librarians and the LPC staff towards such challenges as the RE-CON project, the University-wide investigation of online catalog systems and the librarians' visions for the future. Allman felt she "would be in the forefront of information technology, contributing to a significant organization." Under the guidance of Holderman, the University is constantly forward-thinking and forging plans for the future.[2] Clearly, the firm financial base and the strong administrative structure of the University assisted in the success of the LPC.

Since the inception of the campuses, intralibrary loan among them existed in small measure. If one campus librarian suspected that needed materials were owned by another, an inquiry by letter or telephone followed. The Library Processing Center (LPC), formerly called the Regional Campus Processing Center, was recognized as the central agency that could best facilitate and coordinate reference and interlibrary loan among campuses by utilizing its union title file maintained and housed at LPC in Columbia. On September 1, 1977, the Interlibrary Loan (ILL) Service was implemented, and Linda Holderfield was hired as the ILL Librarian. Her appointment increased the number of professionals on the LPC staff to two. Requests are received and searched in the union title file daily. Although the primary need was the Two and Four Year Campuses' ability to access the Columbia libraries, interlibrary loan usage by the Columbia libraries to the Regional Campus libraries showed significant use of books and periodicals. In the first year of ILL activity, 1,270 requests were received by LPC. Of these requests, 67.8% of the article requests and 84.6% of the book requests were filled. Of the articles requested 79.6% of them received replies within 24 hours, and 84.1% of the books within 24 hours. The second year of ILL activity showed 2,715 requests, an increase of over 100%. In May of 1979, LPC began participation in the OCLC ILL Subsystem, which decreased user waiting time and library clerical time. At the end of the third year of ILL service, there was a 40% increase in the total number of requests received. Between 40% to 48% of the journal article requests were filled by Thomas Cooper Library, the main Columbia library, and other research libraries on the Columbia campus. The use of these automated systems enabled the USC system to better identify and access its total resources.

Being a part of a large university system has its obvious advantages for library research. The USC LPC expands those advantages by facilitating the use of online systems and the resources of the University's Columbia libraries. Aside from an LPC professional's quick access to the ILL subsystem, an electronic mail system was created that further facilitates the ILL requests to and from satellite campuses. LPC staff in cooperation with the University's Computer Services Division, planned and designed an online electronic mail system for sending ILL requests between the campuses and the LPC. The campus librarians can check on a request's status from initiation through completion of the loan. With the use of the electronic mail system, the length of time to fill a request is considerably shortened. Librarians no longer have to telephone or wait for the shuttle to place their requests. Books and articles found at the Columbia research libraries are returned on the next scheduled shuttle. On-Line literature searches, conducted by an experienced LPC professional, are also available through Lockheed's DIALOG service which was added on a one-year trial basis in 1982. The research interview is conducted at the campus library while the actual search later takes place at the LPC. The patron is charged for the search, telecommunications, and a small service fee depending on the database used. In the first year, 35 searches were performed using 39 data bases. Usage continues with the ERIC data base receiving the highest use. Although the smaller libraries in the system cannot afford to purchase these services for their patrons on-site, it is anticipated that the larger Four Year campuses will all eventually subscribe to bibliographic data bases for literature searching. This will likely increase the ILL requests to the Columbia campus libraries. However, the increase that this would produce will reinforce campuses' dependency on the overall library system.

In general, processing centers became valuable for smaller libraries who could take advantage of the same quality and depth of cataloging as larger ones by subscribing to online memberships (Markuson). However, startup costs are high. In late 1982 Aiken, a Four Year campus of USC, and Sumter, a Two Year University campus, presented studies that outlined minimal capital outlay if their campuses had to assume total responsibility for the acquisitions, cataloging, physical processing, shuttle, ILL and reference services now provided by the Library Processing Center. The Sumter study showed that over $82,000.00 in start-up funds would be needed, but that "no improvements or advances would result" (Ferguson, 1982). The Aiken Director estimated "the cost of assuming services now rendered by the LPC the first year alone would cost $83,602.00. Eliminating one-time expenditures, which total $13,335.00, would result in an annual expenditure of $70,267.00, assuming all costs remain stable" (Cubbedge). In contrast, the Aiken campus paid only $10,167.00 that year in direct charges for LPC services. A total of $56,146.00 would be needed for the first year to assume the cataloging function alone for one year. Start-up costs included new staff, equipment and membership fees and other SO-LINET charges, such as FTUs for one year. This estimate by Cubbedge did not assess overhead costs of personnel, space or utilities. These cost estimates for on-site SOLINET service alone proved the fiscal advantage of continuing centralized services at the LPC that serves all satellite campuses. A direct charge to each University and Four Year campus is assessed for administrative, financial aid, and library services rendered through the offices of the Vice-President for University Campuses and Continuing Education, Dr. John J. Duffy, who also served as the Associate Provost for the LPC when called the Regional Campus Processing Center. The charge is based on the percentage of each campuses' total appropriated monies and fees. Few campuses pay the full assessment since the projected overhead is offset by fees collected from the Graduate Regional Studies Program, placing the final assessment between 4% to 9% per campus (Duffy). Fees for Indiana University Library's Regional Processing Division's services are also accrued by its administration based on a formula of campus appropriated monies and projected supply costs and overhead (Hauser).

Assistance with local, original cataloging is provided by the USC Library Processing Center (LPC) staff with the additional cooperation, when needed, of professionals from the main library of the Columbia campus. The centralization of valuable human resources, skilled in cataloging and bibliographic verification are advantageous for the campus libraries. Centralized cataloging reaps other benefits. While it is proven that smaller libraries do have many unique titles (and this is beneficial for ILL), the majority of acquisitions from the USC satellite undergraduate libraries continue to be popular or standard college titles. Centralized cataloging and processing of these duplicate titles saves money. Anderson's technical report for OCLC cites that processing centers comprise "a disproportionately larger number of large users of the OCLC system" (6). Furthermore, processing centers catalog a larger number of duplicate items, and therefore, Anderson found that they had a lower than normal percentage of billable first time uses (FTUs).

By centrally acquiring duplicate titles, the time and expense of generating and handling multiple billings is avoided. A title is cataloged once for many libraries' use. Standing order titles are also ordered collectively by the USC LPC. This concentration of orders gives the Center leverage in vendor and publisher relations. Problems with orders of exact titles can be handled together. This eliminates duplication of work by member libraries. Establishing discounts with jobbers is better negotiated from the LPC that handles the larger volume of all campuses' orders. A recent trial by one campus with a new jobber brought satisfying results except for poor discounts, and in some cases, the lack of discounts. The jobber's response to these results was that a better discount could be given if other campuses in the system would also use them, thereby increasing the number of orders placed. Overall, a central acquisitions unit streamlines the operation by consolidating buying. Weekly, the LPC supplies each campus library with an in-process list of all books for all the regional libraries in a fiche format. When the fiche is used as part of the pre-order searching procedure, it is a useful tool in avoiding duplication of expensive items.

Like any successful business, the LPC recognizes the need to monitor its progress, to critique its plans and to create a forum for new ideas. USC's campus librarians have formed an Assembly of Librarians for these purposes. Annual meetings between the campus librarians and LPC staff had been held since 1971 to discuss areas of mutual concern. As more and more professional librarians were hired at the campuses, their interests and concerns "became increasingly sophisticated [resulting in] more demands for services" (Duffy). In 1976, the Two and Four Year Campus Librarians and the LPC staff organized into a formal structure designated as the Assembly of Two and Four Year Campus Librarians. The October 1984 By-Laws of the body state their purpose "shall be to provide a central vehicle for discussion and resolution of its common problems and professional concerns to promote the interests of the membership. The Assembly shall have the power to collect and disseminiate statistics and other information, to pursue matters of mutual concern, to present recommendations and/or conclusions to USC administrators and/or non-USC entities". The major issues addressed by the Assembly over the years have been faculty rank/status, retrospective conversion of approximately 180,000 titles, cooperative buying, interlibrary loan, copyright issues, electronic mail, serials project and, within an University-wide committee, an online catalog.

The support of USC's administration is a key factor in the Assembly's success. Dr. John J. Duffy, Vice President for University Campuses and Continuing Education views the Assembly as a significant organization that effectively presents professional issues to the administration. "By forming together as an Assembly, the librarians have raised their own

expectations as well as the level of understanding of the entire University"
(Duffy).

THE FUTURE OF LIBRARY PROCESSING CENTERS

Polich's survey listed the following topics as the top four facing cooperative
processing centers in 1979 for the next 10 years; (1) Inflation, Rising Costs,
Reduced Budgets, and Controlling Costs, (2) Integration of Technology
into operations, (3) Providing processing that is tailored to libraries' needs,
and (4) AACR2, Integrating Cataloging Changes and Closing the Catalog
(10). There is no dispute that book and serial prices will rise. A closer
look at why budgets are decreasing may spark new fund-raising ventures,
or at the very least, wiser expenditures of precious dollars, which might
include cooperative buying agreements. Technology is advancing rapidly
as is further evidenced by Compact Disks with Read Only Memory (CD
ROM). The storage capacity of these disks may quickly make microtext
format obsolete. Publishing and indexing and abstracting services are
considering CDs to replace online data bases. This will further encourage
de-centralization of library systems. Information could be accessed in-
house without costly telecommunication charges. However, creating records for national resource sharing remains a cooperative effort. The necessity for standardized cataloging, authority control and MARC format
will be ever-present in the online catalog. It is interesting that one library
in Polich's survey noted "integrating cataloging changes", since global
change is now an important function of online systems.

With new advances come new problems. Rapid proliferation of data
base systems has created a variety of machine-readable systems. A new
challenge for processing centers is handling the complexities of data base
management. For example, the quality control of a central machine-readable source will be difficult to maintain when member libraries have contracted with different commercial vendors, e.g., OCLC, REMARC, for
their raw products into which a meaningful database system must be derived for users. Markuson of INCOLSA sees a new role for processing
centers as trying to mesh this downloaded data into some workable format
for all libraries. The importance of this task is exemplified in the Linked
Systems Project of RLIN. The future will see additional application of
OSI (open systems interconnection) models that allow communication between different types of computer hardware and systems. As more libraries
acquire integrated online library systems, the task of linking these various
systems becomes more complex. The marketplace for turnkey vendors
is competitive and may be unlikely to invest in cooperative linkages.

The USC Library Processing Center, the University and the Four Year

Campus Libraries are represented on a University-wide committee to investigate online cataloging systems. The future holds promise of continuing cooperation to mesh library records throughout the USC system. Once online, the sharing of resources will be further facilitated, and interdependency will be strengthened.

Attempts have been made by USC campus libraries to exercise their autonomy from LPC. In fiscal year 1979, Spartanburg requested approval for a CRT to order books. The orders were to link with the Library Processing Center's data. Since 1979, the Four Year campus at Spartanburg no longer orders through the LPC batch acquisitions system. An attempt to increase efficiency was made by Aiken in 1981/1982 to develop a local online acquisitions system. Its primary advantage would be to improve turnaround time. It was implemented in late summer of 1982, substantially expediting the ordering of 1,650 books. However, changes in the terminal brand required a new software program. In addition, staff demand on the Computer Services Division impeded the project with the result of its being shelved. These local projects to improve library processing will continue, especially with the increased use of microcomputers in-house. Beyond that, there will be more and better software products to purchase and online services to access for technical services departments. The prospects for facsimile transmission may be promising for special ILL document delivery among libraries. Unlike Audrey Hauser's (1985) prediction that Indiana's four year campuses will eventually have their own technical services facilities, the authors do not predict such a breakaway. The LPC offers such a diversity of service, not just technical service, that it is not now foreseeable that campuses would divorce themselves from the LPC. The authors do concur with Hauser that the two year campuses will need centralized technical processing for a long time hence. The economic fortunes of the University of South Carolina will dictate to a certain extent the continued total participation of the Four Year campuses. As the libraries' budgets expand, the choice to control all of their processes in-house may be seen as desirable. This may depend somewhat on the LPC's ability to provide fast, efficient, cost-effective services. Although the Four Year campuses have been supportive of the LPC's DIALOG service, Spartanburg and Coastal Carolina campuses now have their own subscriptions to DIALOG due to heavy usage. The LPC strives to be responsive to all campuses' needs whenever possible, but it must assess the economic and staffing impact of each service on the Center.

SUMMARY

The role of processing centers has expanded. It is not enough to provide ordering, cataloging and book preparation. Centers provide reference service, ILL, and online data base searching. They also served as an information broker. In USC's case, the LPC serves as a support system for all library concerns bringing strength in numbers. Processing centers were the catalyst for library networks. They forged the spirit of cooperation towards collective pursuits to gain more than could be attained by libraries individually. Integrated online systems, which also burst upon the library scene, carry with them many of the same sensitivities as early processing center operations, such as competition in the marketplace, an urgency to automate, and a need for cost and value analyses (as with RFPs).

The USC LPC has increased its efficiency through technology and expanded its services to meet the needs of its customers. To remain viable the LPC must continue to stay abreast of change. Continued administrative and campus library support will carry the LPC into further advances. A strong university-wide "systems" approach will reinforce participation by USC satellite libraries. Centralization works well at USC, and though it had meager beginnings, it has gained the ingredients for success.

NOTES

1. See *Small Computers for Libraries* 5 (1985). For more information on software packages available for microcomputers used for processing see other issues of this journal.

2. Since the publication of the *Carolina Plan* in December of 1977, President Holderman has presented updated plans, eg. *Carolina Plan II* (1978) and most recently a "2001 Plan".

WORKS CITED

American Library Association. Resources and Technical Services Division. Regional Processing Committee. "Guidelines for Centralized Technical Services." *Library Resources and Technical Services* 10 (1966): 233–240.

Anderson, Carl A. *Technical Report on Processing Centers.* OCLC Report DD/TR–80/2. Columbus, OH: OCLC, 1980.

The Carolina Plan; A Prospectus. Summary of a report from the President to the Board of Trustees. n.p.: University of South Carolina, 1977.

Cattell (Jacques) Press, ed. *American Library Directory* 38th ed. New York: Bowker, 1985.

Camp, Mary Ann and Charmaine B. Tomczyk. "Advantages and Disadvantages to Library Processing Centers" unpublished questionnaire, 1983.

"Closing R.I. Processing Center Will Hurt Small Libraries" *Library Journal* 1 April 1976:851.

Cubbedge, Frankie H. "Direct charges for Services—USC-Columbia" Memorandum to O. Joseph Harm, Vice Chancellor, USC-Aiken, 16 June 1982.

"Cuyahoga County, Ohio Drops Processing Operation" *Library Journal* 15 February 1982: 392.

Davis, Hillis Dwight. "The Cooperative College Library Center, Inc: and Historical Perspective." *New Dimensions for Academic Library Service.* Ed. E.J. Josey. Metuchen, NJ: Scarecrow, 1975. 268–287.

Doyle, Pamela B. Telephone interview. 8 Oct. 1985.

Duffy, John J. Personal interview. 9 October 1985.

Ferguson, Jane, Charmaine Tomczyk and Elizabeth Mulligan. "The Advantages of Centralized Library Processing System to the Regional Campuses of the University of South

Carolina." Annual Conference of Regional Campus Administrators. Pennsylvania State University, University Park. 13 June 1983.

Ferguson, Jane. "Impact Statement: USC-Sumter/Sumter Tech Library Merger". Sumter, SC.: USC-Sumter Library, December 1982.

"Florida State Library to Scrap Processing Center" *Library Journal* 1 Dec. 1976:2418.

Fry, James W. *A Feasibility Study for Consolidating and/or Coordinating Technical Processes in Beaver County Pennsylvania Libraries*. Harrisburg: State Library of Pennsylvania, 1977. ERIC ED 148 363.

Goetz, Arthur H. Correspondence. 8 Feb. 1983.

Hallman, Marie. Personal interview. 16 October 1985.

Hauser, Audrey. Telephone interview. 30 Oct. 1985.

Hendricks, Donald Duane. *Centralized Processing and Regional Library Development: The Midwestern Regional Library System: Kitchener, Ontario*. Kitchener, Ontario: Midwestern Regional Library System, 1970. ERIC ED 050 780.

———. "Comparative Costs of Book Processing in a Book Processing Center". Diss. U. of Illinois, 1966.

———. Telephone interview. 9 Oct. 1985.

Highum, Clayton, et al. *The Illinois Library Materials Processing Center: a Study* Illinois State Library Report 5. Springfield: Illinois State Library, 1980.

Hunt, James R. "The Historical Development of Processing Centers in the United States". *Library Resources and Technical Services* 8 (1964):54–62.

"Iowa's Processing Center Skirts Bankruptcy". *Library Journal* 1 Oct. 1977:1981.

Little (Arthur D.) Inc. *A Plan for a Library Processing Center for the State University of New York* Report to the Office of Educational Communications at the SUNY. Cambridge, MA: Arthur D. Little Inc., 1967.

Markuson, Barbara Evans. Telephone interview. 16 Oct. 1985.

McCombs, Gillian. Personal correspondence. 7 Oct. 1985.

Polich, Deborah. "Survey of Centralized Processing Centers." Urbana, IL: University of Illinois. Library Research Center. Responses tabulated as of 29 Nov. 1979.

Riggs, Donald E. *Centralized Technical Processing and PPBS: A Literature Review*. ERIC 1975. ED 108 688.

Roth, Harold, L., Theodore C. Hines, and Jessica L. Harris. *Centralized Processing for Indiana Libraries*. Indiana Library Studies Report 13. Bloomington: Indiana University, 1971.

Simpson, Donald B. "Bibliographic Processing Centers". *The ALA Yearbook: A Review of Library Events, 1977*. Chicago: ALA, 1978. 55–57.

"Some Processing Centers Getting $$ Help". *Library Journal* 1 Dec. 1977:2389.

Toombs, Kenneth E. Personal interview. 9 October 1985.

University of South Carolina. Assembly of University and Four Year Campus Librarians. *By-Laws*. n.p.: n.p., Oct. 1984.

University of South Carolina. Library Processing Center and Libraries of the University Campus System. *Annual Report of the Director, July 1984 to June 1985* [Columbia, SC]: n.p., 1985.

University of South Carolina. Regional Campus Processing Center. *Annual Report, July 1974–July 1975*. [Columbia, SC]: n.p., 1975.

University of South Carolina. Two and Four Year Campus Processing Center. *Annual Report, July 1977 to June 1978*. [Columbia, SC]: n.p., 1978.

University of South Carolina. University Libraries. *Report of the Director July 1973 to July 1974*. Columbia, SC: n.p., 1974.

Webster's New International Dictionary of the English Language. 2d. Unabridged. Ed. William Allan Neilson. Springfield, MA: Merriam, 1959.

LIBRARIES AND DISABLED PERSONS:

A REVIEW OF SELECTED RESEARCH

Marilyn H. Karrenbrock and Linda Lucas

INTRODUCTION

The importance of research as a tool for administrative planning and implementation is well-recognized in the field of librarianship. Research can provide the data needed to maintain old programs and justify new ones. It can be used to identify needs, evaluate practices, and select courses of action from among alternative solutions to problems. Although it is often necessary for librarians to conduct their own research, knowledge of studies already conducted in the area of interest is of great importance. Librarians, like most people, have no desire to reinvent the wheel. They often, however, have difficulties in identifying and locating research that has already been done. Reviews of research studies in particular areas of librarianship have become increasingly necessary and useful in recent years.

Advances in Library Administration and Organization
Volume 6, pages 241–306
Copyright © 1986 by JAI Press Inc.
All rights of reproduction in any form reserved.
ISBN: 0-89232-724-3

Several years ago, while writing a book on library services to disabled children (Lucas & Karrenbrock, 1983), the authors were frustrated by the lack of bibliographic control of research about library services to disabled persons. At that time, the need for such services was becoming increasingly apparent to both librarians and the public, due to efforts such as the International Year of Disabled Persons and, in the United States, increasing federal legislation which mandated that facilities and programs must be accessible to disabled persons. Librarians implementing programs for disabled persons needed accurate information about their special, sometimes unusual, and often varied needs for services, equipment, material formats, and access to facilities. Appropriately conducted and reported research provides such information, but published studies were difficult to locate and apparently few in number, indicating a clear need for a review of the research in this area. Such a review might provide a beginning point both for administrators who are interested in planning programs for disabled persons and for researchers who are planning further study in this area. This article is a review of research studies concerning library services and disabled persons.

Studies included in this review were conducted throughout the world, but only those published in English (including translations from other languages) are included. No time limit was imposed on the search. The earliest study located was done in 1903, and research reported through early 1985 is included. Although some were obtained through personal contacts with the investigators responsible, many of the studies are readily available in the United States. Studies were primarily identified through searches of ERIC, LISA, NTIS, *Dissertation Abstracts International,* and *Library Literature,* although a few were located using various other databases, indexes, and sources. Whenever possible, computer searches were used, but because of difficulty in selecting appropriate descriptors, they were often supplemented by manual search and retrieval processes. We consider the resulting list of research studies to be extensive, but make no claim that it is exhaustive.

A broad definition of research was used in order to include as many studies as possible which potentially might provide information useful for making informed decisions about library services to disabled persons. Studies are reported here if they include: (a) the collection of data (generally through surveys) and/or the compilation of information (often through historical research, description, or literature review) about the state of library service and disabled persons in the past or present; the information, format, service, or physical access needs of disabled persons; or user interests in library materials; or (b) the systematic collection of data (including surveys, case studies, and experimental research) which might be employed to evaluate or modify library services to disabled persons or to develop model library programs for this population. In order for a study to be included, some analysis of the data was required. (Surveys which resulted in an unanalyzed compendium of information, such as a directory of services or a bibliography, are not included in the body of this paper, but selected examples of these are listed in Appendix A for the convenience of the readers.) Many of the studies utilized descriptive research designs. Many might appropriately be labeled feasibility studies, program evaluations, or analyses of model programs. All studies which fit the above criteria were included, without regard to the type or quality of the research design or its implementation.

All studies reported here were examined by the authors, with the exception of a few dissertations which were not available through interlibrary loan or personal contact with the authors. In these cases, the materials were reviewed from the information supplied in *Dissertation Abstracts International*. Studies which appeared to meet inclusion criteria and would have been included had they been available (including, for example, studies from foreign countries which are not available on interlibrary loan, or uncirculated theses) are listed in Appendix B.

Although most of the studies reported here are directly related to libraries, a few studies of reading habits, information and format needs, and information-seeking behavior of disabled persons were included from other fields. The inclusion of such research demonstrates the interdisciplinary nature of disability research which might be of interest to librarians. Research and development reports concerned with the development of new equipment or formats which will provide increased information accessibility to disabled persons have usually not been included. Such reports are primarily of interest to specialized organizations who provide equipment or materials to the disabled, or to specialized libraries, such as the National Library Service for the Blind and Physically Handicapped of the Library of Congress, which do the same. These studies were only included if they provided information which might be applicable in public, academic, institutional, or school libraries which serve disabled patrons.

SURVEYS OF LIBRARY SERVICE TO DISABLED PERSONS IN THE UNITED STATES

Most of the studies discussed in this review are surveys, and the majority of the surveys which are available in English have been conducted in the United States. The patterns of research in this area have been heavily influenced by the history of library service to disabled patrons and the legislation which has made it possible, factors which are of course specific to this country. Therefore, the library surveys from the United States are discussed first. These studies generally fall into recognizable groups based upon type of disability and/or type of library, and will be discussed under these topics. It will be noted that the term "services" in nearly all these studies means either provision of materials or provision of barrier-free facilities. In each section, studies will be listed chronologically, except in the case of historical research where the period studied differs significantly from the date of the research. In this case, the study will be placed chronologically with the period being studied.

Public and State Library Services to Persons Who are Visually Disabled

Research surveys of library services to visually disabled persons form a pattern which reflects the history of service to this population. Of all disabilities, blindness and severe visual disability have been perceived as those most likely to preclude use of library materials. Perhaps because of this, library service to such persons was established earlier and has received more support, especially at the federal level, than has service to those with other disabilities. Public library service to visually impaired individuals began at the Boston Public Library in 1868. Federal funding for the American Printing House for the Blind, which had been chartered by the state of Kentucky to produce reading material in braille and other accessible formats, was begun in 1879. Early service to blind persons was provided at the local and state level in many areas, although free postage for reading material for blind people was instituted in 1904. In 1931, the Pratt-Smoot Act established service to blind adults at the national level through the Division for the Blind of the Library of Congress and the system of regional libraries associated with it. In 1952, service to blind children was added, and in 1966 the target group was enlarged to include persons who are unable to use normal reading materials because of physical disability. This Library of Congress service was known as the Division for the Blind and Physically Handicapped (DBPH) until 1973, when it was renamed the National Library Service for the Blind and Physically Handicapped (NLS). Also in 1966, Title IV–B of the Library Services and Construction Act (LSCA) authorized payments to states for establishing and improving library service to physically handicapped persons. Services were also affected by the issuance of standards. The first standards for library service to those who were blind had been issued by the American Library Association in 1961. In 1967, new standards were issued by the Commission on Standards and Accreditation of Services for the Blind (COMSTAC). The American Library Association issued standards again in 1979 and in 1984. Many research studies have examined how service in public and state libraries has been affected by federal legislation and library standards.

The earliest research into library service to blind persons was conducted in 1929 by Irwin, who surveyed blind adults in the United States and Canada under the auspices of the American Foundation for the Blind. No final results were reported in the literature, but the study is said to have been a factor in the passage of the Pratt-Smoot Act two years later.

C. S. Green (1967) traced the early development of library service to blind people in the United States until 1931. Starting with a discussion of the care and treatment of blind persons in ancient times, she related early library service in the United States to education of persons who were blind, showing that a regional distribution system for materials was virtually inevitable. The study's focus was on an overall view of library work with blind persons, but examples from individual libraries were included to illustrate the ways service had evolved.

Bond (1932) surveyed the services of state libraries to persons who were blind. She found that materials were provided by 10 state libraries. Although collections ranged from 50 to 28,279 volumes, only four libraries had more than 500 volumes and served more than 25 borrowers. Many circulation procedures were similar to those used for seeing borrowers.

Grafton, in a 1940 literature review, studied library services to blind individuals in the Midwest. She wanted to show the development of service patterns of federal, state and local agencies which supplied reading materials to adult blind readers. Statistics on book availability and use in 1931 (just before the passage of the Pratt-Smoot Act) and in 1938 were contrasted. Trends were noted: a move from private to public sponsorship, an assumption of service by increasingly higher levels of government, increased federal aid and systematic organization of service at the national level through a network of regional libraries. Grafton's recommendations included federal funding for adequate staff in the regional libraries, development of specialized collections, better selection of titles to be recorded, better distribution of talking book machines, catalogs in braille and recorded formats, and federal aid for operating costs as well as for books. It is interesting to note that Grafton felt that "In general, young people ought not to be encouraged to use talking-books, as they are able to learn to read raised print" (p. 112).

Three studies in the early 1950s, by Sullivan, Sheffield, and Goldstein, described services to blind persons at three large public libraries. Sullivan (1950) used interviews, observations, and a literature review in a study which emphasized progress since the beginning of federal participation in 1931. The study included historical background on the development of reading matter, printing houses and libraries for blind people; of national and state participation in library service; and of the Books for the Blind program at the Free Library of Philadelphia. Sullivan also described the status of that program in 1950, including staffing, collection, cataloging, procedures for working with readers, and reader statistics.

Sheffield (1951) used interviews and a literature review to describe the history of library service to blind people, with emphasis on the history of the program at Cleveland Public Library. She discussed the impact of federal participation after twenty years and made projections for the future.

The Library for the Blind of the New York Public Library was examined by Goldstein (1953). The study's first section was primarily a history of the library, including scattered information about patrons and services. The second part described processing and services at the time, and the last section described special collections and services, such as the children's collection and special bibliographies.

Wellons (1966) surveyed public libraries in Kansas to determine existing services. She concluded that the "public library's role in services to the blind is one of interpretation of materials, funneling of services from other agencies, and reader's advisory services similar to those provided for sighted patrons" (p. 11). Librarians were said to need bibliographies, information about agencies providing special services, and regional workshops.

Soon after the passage of Title IV–B of the Library Services and Construction Act in 1966, which authorized funds for state use in extending library services to physically handicapped persons, three state surveys were conducted by Swank; Arthur D. Little, Inc.; and McCrossan, Swank, and Yacuzzo. Swank (1967) prepared a survey for the California State Library which reviewed existing library service to blind and physically handicapped persons in the state and made suggestions for long-term planning to improve services. The study recommended a full range of service comparable in quality to that offered to sighted persons. Such a program of service could not be accomplished by the two DBPH regional libraries of the state alone: Swank emphasized the need for personal assistance at the community level. A statewide network was recommended, with personalized services at the community level and major collections provided by the regional centers. The state library would handle specialized requests and oversee the system.

Arthur D. Little, Inc. (Little, 1967) conducted a two-part evaluation of general library resources in Vermont and of current procedures in library service to persons who were handicapped. At that time, service to disabled readers in the state was provided by the regional library in Albany, New York. Little, Inc., estimated that within three years, Vermont would have the 1000 handicapped readers necessary to set up its own regional library. Until that time, it was recommended that the New York State Library should be reimbursed on a per capita basis for services provided to citizens of Vermont. The Vermont Free Public Library Service was advised to begin at once to plan for needed physical facilities and funding for its own regional library. Many provisions for increased service were suggested, such as purchase of materials not provided by DBPH, publicity for the service, provision of a catalog of holdings to all libraries in the state, an interlibrary loan and reserve system, and increased service at the local level.

McCrossan, Swank, and Yacuzzo (1968) conducted a survey for the state library of Ohio in order to estimate the number of handicapped people in the state, provide a description of current library service to them, and draw up tentative recommendations for library service under Title IV–B. A basic goal recommended in the study was provision of the same range and quality of service to handicapped as to nonhandicapped patrons. More direct personal assistance at the local level was recommended, including reference and reader's guidance, home visits and book delivery; expansion and diversification of library resources in special media; and bibliographic control of resources through a union catalog and interlibrary referral services. It was suggested that community services be supported by a system of regional libraries within the same system as cooperative library services in general, and that local responsibility (municipal, county, and state) be developed with the LSCA contribution used as seed money. The distribution and repair of talking book machines was seen as the responsibility of the regional centers.

Two studies in 1973, by Masek and Johns, investigated library services to blind and physically handicapped patrons in public libraries. Masek provided introductory essays and annotated bibliographies in three areas: public library services currently available, problems in extending service to blind and physically handicapped people, and future trends in service. She concluded that public library service was limited because the NLS distribution system bypassed public libraries.

Johns (1973) described the development of library services to handicapped people in Northern Ohio, reviewed the events which led to the formulation of the COMSTAC Standards in 1966, and examined the services of the Braille and Talking Book Department of the Cleveland Public Library to determine the extent to which services met COMSTAC standards. She concluded that the library could not meet COMSTAC standards because of the inapplicability of the standards themselves. The standards recommended that materials and services for handicapped people should duplicate those available to nonhandicapped patrons even though this would require considerable extra effort and expense. (Recommended per capita spending was five to seven times that for a nonhandicapped patron, for instance.)

Services of the NLS System

The NLS system, which began with 11 regional libraries in 1931, has grown to include 56 regional libraries, 4 multistate centers, and numerous subregional libraries in 1985. NLS has been diligent in conducting research into its operations. Several studies, both by NLS and other agencies, have investigated services offered by the system or its component libraries.

In 1957, St. John conducted a survey for the American Foundation for the Blind "to assess the professional effectiveness of the special library facilities and programs established to serve blind individuals" (p. 2). One questionnaire was sent to the 28 regional libraries then in operation, and another to the 50-odd agencies that distributed talking book machines. Interviews were also conducted at the regional libraries. Extensive recommendations emphasized service, but included all phases of operation, including: finance, organization, staff, physical conditions, records, book selection, communication, talking book machines, technical problems, and publicity. This study was influential in establishing the need for standards, which led to the 1961 standards mentioned earlier.

Four surveys (by Martin; Allen; Wessells, Smith, and Rawles; and Rice) described certain regional libraries. Martin (1970) described Maine's services as part of the national network. He discussed both Maine's handicapped population and the agencies which participated in providing library service in Maine. He concluded that the number of talking book users, braille readers, and users of other reading aids had all doubled in approximately the previous three years; that there was great potential for future expansion; and that cooperation among agencies was chiefly responsible for the recent growth in service.

Allen (1977) conducted a survey of 400 users of the DuPage (Illinois) Library System Subregional Library for the Blind and Physically Handicapped. A large print questionnaire was used. One purpose of the survey was to test the feasibility of printed surveys with the target population. The 19% response rate was actually higher than expected. The questionnaire gathered information about the readers, the reading formats accessible to them and how these were used, reading interests, problems and satisfactions with service. Results of the study raised questions concerning whether or not physically handicapped readers were adequately served, since only 9.7% of the respondents were not visually handicapped. Physically handicapped subjects also reported that they read very little. Further research into this question was recommended. The printed questionnaire was found to produce a low response rate and it forced the person who could not read it into an undesirable dependency role. It was, however, less expensive to produce than instruments in other formats. Allen concluded that the library must balance past experience, the hardship to readers, and budget limitations to decide whether to use the print questionnaire or another format.

Wessells, Smith, and Rawles (1979) evaluated user satisfaction and cost effectiveness of the computerized systems at the two regional libraries in Ohio (Cleveland and Cincinnati). Methods included a user survey, interviews with librarians and experts serving blind and physically handicapped patrons, discussions at national conventions with other librarians in the field, and a literature survey. A random sample of users was questioned by telephone. The program was rated as excellent by 52%, very good by 32%, and good by 14%. The respondents expressed high satisfaction with the courtesy of librarians (100%), availability of librarians (97%), speed of replacing machines (92%), magazine selection (91%), condition of machines (91%), availability of braille materials (90%) and working of tapes (87%). It was concluded that the program was meeting user needs. The computerized systems of both libraries had been specifically designed for the libraries, and included data bases on circulation of materials and reading interests of users. The systems were judged cost effective, allowing librarians to make service quicker and more efficient. Recommendations included continuation of the current structure of support for computerization in the regional libraries, and conversion of funding by the State Library from a formula-based to a program-based system, which would encourage more evaluation and long-range planning.

A study of the regional library in Missouri was reported by Rice (1983), who described the study as the third in a series, the others having been carried out in 1979 and 1981. The study was conducted to update and revise the user files, measure the quality of specific services and identify areas where change was needed, and to facilitate planning specific activities for the following year in the area of communication with patrons and public. Large print questionnaires were included in the library's large print newsletter, a braille version was mailed with the brailled newsletter, and users of the cassette newsletter were requested to call in responses. Favorable responses were given regarding basic services and the working of the talking book machines. It was reported that few readers who lived in Kansas City visited the deposit collection at the Plaza Branch Library there. Lack of transportation and lack of knowledge of the collection seemed to be important factors.

Smalley and Mendenhall (1983) conducted a full-scale evaluation of NLS and the regional and multistate centers in relation to the 1979 ALA *Standards of Service for Library of Congress Network of Libraries*. Questionnaires were tailored to the type of network unit, and site visits were conducted. Published statistics were analyzed. When the network components were compared to the *Standards,* the results were varied. General recommendations were made relating to areas where the network as a whole was found to be weak. These recommendations were grouped under the categories of organization, administration, budget and planning; personnel and facilities; resource development; user services; and public education and information. Specific recommendations for each regional library, multistate center, and NLS as a whole were included in individual working papers.

Public and State Library Services to Persons with Other Disabilities

A study by Tsao (1967) investigated public library services to "retarded readers," who were defined as "readers whose retardation is caused by physical handicaps, poor reading habits, emotional immaturity, lack of interest in reading, English language barrier of foreign born and lack of education. The mentally ill and blind are excluded from this study" (p. 4). The study was therefore not limited only to persons with a physical or mental disability. In fact, mentally retarded persons were effectively excluded since "it is customary to regard as disabled readers only those whose reading ability is well below their potentialities for learning, as disclosed by intelligence tests" (p. 8). The purpose of the study was to present the status of service, to examine the service as a phase of reader's advisory service, and to present new theories and current developments in this field. It was concluded that few large public libraries had formal remedial programs; a majority provided remedial reading service through cooperation with high schools or social service agencies; most had special collections for remedial reading; librarians preferred to work with individuals rather than classes; and that non-establishment of such programs resulted from lack of funding, trained librarians, and requests for the service.

Four studies (Brewer & McClaskey; Kim; Lewis; Jahoda & Needham) have investigated services of public and state libraries to persons with hearing disabilities. The last of these studies included those with visual and mobility disabilities as well.

Brewer and McClaskey (1976) surveyed the status of library service to deaf persons through a questionnaire sent to the 50 state library agencies. They studied attitudes toward deaf persons and the state library's role in developing library service to this group. Over half the respondents felt that deaf individuals were not severely handicapped, but over 60% felt that library services in their states were inadequate. The researchers concluded that few public library services were being provided, that failure to provide services resulted from a general lack of awareness about the needs of deaf persons, that librarians were unaware of available resources which could help them serve deaf populations, and that libraries favor cooperating with other agencies in developing library services to the target group.

Kim's (1976) study is essentially a survey of library literature, pointing out communication needs of deaf and hearing impaired people and the library's role in meeting these needs. Kim pointed out that many important materials were already in library collections and that valuable programs could be implemented within existing budgets. However, special materials and equipment might require special funds. She concluded that public library service to those who were hearing impaired was a valid and needed service which had recently become of interest and which could be expected to increase.

Lewis (1978) also conducted a literature review, bringing together suggestions for adaptations, ideas from model programs, and other information about public library services to deaf persons. The need for evaluation of library projects and programs was emphasized.

In 1980, Jahoda and Needham surveyed library services to physically disabled persons, those disabled in vision, hearing, or mobility. Questionnaires were sent to about one-third of the public libraries in the United States which served more than 25,000 persons, all public libraries that are also NLS network libraries, and all state libraries. User input was obtained through organizations for handicapped people. Library service to hearing impaired persons was found to be in greatest need of improvement, but better resources, facilities, and services were needed for all who were disabled. The biggest challenges were seen to be identifying potential users, determining their information needs, and involving them in planning and evaluation. The researchers also recommended a study of the relationships between public libraries and the NLS network, since NLS provides materials, but not a full range of services. They felt that new technologies should be used to facilitate NLS services and that catalog access and ordering of materials could be accomplished online through the public library. Recommendations included the recruitment of physically handicapped people into the library profession and the study of existing model programs to determine how service might best be provided.

In the final study in this section, both public and academic libraries were included. Pemberton (1982) surveyed 209 public and academic libraries in Tennessee to determine the extent of services offered to physically disabled persons. Questionnaires were returned by 125 libraries (83 public and 42 academic), a return rate of 60%. Of these, 70.4% had three or fewer staff members; 5.6% had 25 or more staff members. Ten libraries reported having done a community analysis to identify the number of disabled persons in the potential user population, and 16 libraries (12 public and 4 academic) had written policy statements concerning service to disabled individuals. Only 4.8% of the libraries reported substantial demand for service by disabled persons. Three public and five academic libraries reported a staff member professionally trained to offer service to disabled patrons, and nine public and seven academic libraries had one or more disabled persons on the staff. Of materials for visually disabled persons, 66.4% of the libraries had large print books, but braille and audiotaped books were each held by 14.4% of the libraries. Almost no periodicals for blind patrons were held by libraries; the Bible was the most frequently held reference book (in 18.5% of the libraries). Few libraries had materials or equipment for deaf persons, but four public and eight academic libraries reported a staff member who could communicate in sign language. Physical access was also limited, with public libraries more likely to be accessible than academic ones. Pemberton concluded that public libraries in Tennessee were generally more active in service to disabled persons than were academic libraries, and that although larger libraries tended to be more active than smaller ones, many smaller libraries responded positively to many of the questions.

Library Services to Physically Disabled University Students

In addition to the Pemberton study just discussed, several surveys have studied library services offered to physically handicapped students by college and university libraries. Early studies concerned only service to blind students, but most of the later studies have included all physical disabilities. Studies have often concentrated on the accessibility of library facilities, especially since the passage of the Rehabilitation Act of 1973 and the 1977 issuance of regulations for implementation of its Section 504. The Rehabilitation Act of 1973, among other things, mandated accessible facilities in all new public buildings which received federal funding and in existing buildings within three years. Not only facilities, but programs were to be made accessible under the law.

Services to blind university students were studied by Parkin (1974), who first surveyed services in four-year universities in eight intermountain states. He found that most universities did not offer many of the recommended services. For instance, 78% did not have a special catalog of media for blind students, 75% had no librarian assigned to work with these students, 78% had no reference materials in braille and 92% had no reference materials in other media. However, nearly half the libraries did have private study areas, listening rooms, and tape recording equipment available to blind students, and 64% reported ground level access to the building. Parkin followed up this part of the study with a user's survey, interviewing blind students at Brigham Young University to determine personal needs and to evaluate library services at BYU. He found most blind students used the BYU library frequently and found its services generally adequate. Overall recommendations were made for university libraries with both minimum and more extensive budgets or space.

Major's (1978) study is a user's study, rather than a library survey, but is included here because she based it upon students using, or eligible to use, the library for blind students which had been established at The Ohio State University. Her intention was to learn how well the library was serving its clientele and to provide useful information for other academic librarians serving this population. She found that blind students were more receptive than partially sighted ones to catalogs of available materials, recreational reading material, reference material and to a register of local readers and transcribers. Partially sighted students were more receptive to optical aids. Both groups were interested in information on local and state services and in special reading and listening rooms. Students reported needing a variety of reading aids, but few of them had used the equipment already provided. Major concluded that librarians must understand the differing needs of blind and partially sighted students; that they need to know what patron group they will be serving; that catalog files in appropriate formats should be provided; that reading rooms and information on federal, state, and local services must be provided; and that a full-time staff member should be assigned to aid disabled students.

Goss (1978) investigated library services for hearing handicapped students at the Clearwater Campus of St. Petersburg Junior College (Florida), and developed a model program for library orientation for this population. A questionnaire was administered simultaneously to 39 deaf students, with the aid of an interpreter for the deaf. Goss then developed an alternative teaching technique for presenting library orientation to a deaf audience, utilizing narrative, videotape, graphics, reference books, and an interpreter. Students used the material independently and at their own pace. An evaluative questionnaire was administered at the end of the program. Goss saw a need for special counseling early in high school for students with demonstrated academic ability, for special counseling and special library services in community colleges, for greater attention by librarians to the needs of students with hearing impairment, and for at least one library staff member who knew American Sign Language. She recommended a revised library orientation program on videotape, in-service training for librarians, and establishment of guidelines for developing additional special programs for hearing impaired students.

In 1978, J. Thomas published *College and University Library Services to the Handicapped Student in Texas,* a directory of services (see Appendix A). In a later article (1980), he analyzed the data from the survey, which covered special services, specialized equipment, accessibility to buildings, and problems in meeting needs of handicapped students. He found that 51% of the institutions offered some special services, 82% had some specialized equipment, 85% of the buildings had an entrance at ground level and 70% had a ramp. Facilities within the libraries were less favorable, with only 49% having wide bathroom stalls with grab bars and

23% having extended handrails in stairways. Thomas concluded that librarians must become more informed about needs of handicapped users, more equipment must be purchased in advance of need, accessibility standards must be followed and the needs of the handicapped students must be met.

In a further study, J. Thomas and C. Thomas (1983) surveyed all college and university library directors in the United States and outlying areas (Canal Zone, Pacific islands, Puerto Rico, and the Virgin Islands). Their purpose was to provide information to handicapped students making educational plans and to provide information to library personnel to help them in planning. Again, most buildings were accessible from the outside, but inside accessibility was more limited. Equipment was generally not well provided, although 73% had tape recorders/players. Special services were provided by 82% of the libraries reporting.

Two studies in 1982 investigated accessibility of academic libraries. DeVeaux conducted a literature review to identify special programs for disabled students, and surveyed academic library directors about the accessibility of facilities and programs. She found that physical barriers were less limiting than attitudinal ones. Administrative policies were restrictive and little equipment was available. She recommended written policy statements about service to disabled students, establishment of working relationships with other campus organizations serving the target group, public relations and publicity techniques to bring library services to the attention of these students, better physical access, provision of volunteer readers and interpreters, input about and evaluation of services by the disabled students, flexible policies and more services for disabled students served, and the hiring of handicapped librarians.

Jackson, also in 1982, used existing printed sources to investigate accessibility of academic programs and facilities. In libraries built between 1973 and 1977 (after the passage of the Rehabilitation Act but before the 504 regulations were issued), the least accessible features were fountains, telephones, and bookstack aisles; the most accessible were ramps, ground level entrances, elevators, wide and easily opened doors, restrooms, and parking. Buildings built in 1978–1980 were more accessible, but primarily in programs, not in facilities. In both time periods, there were no significant differences in the accessibility of new buildings and of those added to or those both renovated and added to. Hierarchical regression analysis was used to determine variables which might predict the degree of accessibility. Size of the parent institution was the principal variable contributing to total, physical, and program accessibility. The period of construction, scholastic level (whether or not the institution had a graduate program), and type of sponsorship (public or private) were also factors in total accessibility. Period of construction and scholastic level of the institution also contributed to program accessibility. Scholastic level and period of construction contributed to physical accessibility, but this equation explained much less of the variance than did the ones for total and program accessibility. Amount of federal financial aid received also contributed to physical accessibility, but this factor was dropped from the regression equation because of the abnormality of its distribution and the lack of goodness of fit of the regression line.

Bowen, Self, Broadway, Abbott, and Swetnam (1983) interviewed 53 vision, hearing, or mobility impaired students at Florida State University to evaluate the university library's services to disabled students. A semistructured questionnaire was pretested, revised, and used in the interviews. The library was used daily to weekly by 68% of the mobility impaired students, by 37.5% of those who were hearing impaired, and by 14% of visually impaired students. All of the remaining mobility and hearing impaired students used the library monthly or infrequently, but 21% of the visually impaired students never used a campus library. Graduate students used the library more often than undergraduates, and all used it primarily for educational purposes. Physical access was difficult for many of the mobility and vision impaired students; 50% of the wheelchair users reported problems with low tables and carrels. Half the students rated the staff and services favorably, but others complained of insensitivity on the part of librarians. The researchers concluded that visually impaired students needed special equipment and materials and more direct information delivery than the typical academic reference service provides, and mobility impaired students needed assistance in using the card catalog and in retrieving materials from the stacks. Visual and hearing impaired students preferred individual library use instruction, but those who were motor impaired preferred mainstreamed library use instruction. Recommendations included modifying doors for easier use, publicizing information about the location of emergency exits, a limited number of tables and carrels on each floor modified for use by patrons in wheelchairs, provision of special photocopy services, modified library instruction, in-service training to sensitize staff to the problems of disabled students, and the designation of a resource librarian to coordinate services to disabled persons. The researchers also included advice for others interested in doing a similar study in their own library.

Langan (1984) studied the Oberlin College Library's capabilities for service to blind and physically handicapped students by surveying public service staff and disabled students. Evaluations and recommendations are made in the areas of campus relations, physical access, copyright, policy statement, public services, student recommendations, equipment, and collection development.

Services to Students in School Library Media Centers

Library services to disabled students in elementary and secondary schools have depended upon two historical developments; the establishment of school libraries and the evolution of education for disabled children. The number of school libraries grew rapidly in the 1950s and 1960s, aided by an expanding economy and by passage of the National Defense Education Act in 1957 and the Elementary and Secondary Education Act in 1963. Education for disabled children was expanding, principally through special classes, at the same time. The most significant legislation for education of handicapped children in general and for school library service to disabled children in particular was the Education of All Handicapped Children Act (Public Law 94–142) in 1975.

Vinson (1983) used historical and descriptive research methodologies to trace the history of school library media center services for handicapped students from 1950 to 1980. She concluded that there was little evidence of planned programs for disabled children until the 1970s; that litigation and legislation brought about awareness of the needs of disabled children; and that sources of free materials, such as NLS, aided in the development of services. Vinson also investigated school library media services to disabled students in 1979–1980 through a questionnaire sent to a nationwide random sample of 1000 school library directors. She found that by 1980, P.L. 94–142 had not yet had much impact on school library media services, but librarians were becoming advocates for disabled students, and individualized education was becoming institutionalized through the use of Individualized Education Plans (IEPs) mandated by the law. A wide variety of material formats was provided. Thirty-five services specifically for disabled students were reported, along with 13 others in which these children participated. Factors which contributed to problems in serving disabled children included the lack of consistency and commitment to funding. Factors contributing to success included effective communication and rapport with other school personnel, awareness and understanding of the needs of handicapped children, and a positive atmosphere in the library media center.

Buckley (1978/1979) surveyed a stratified random sample of one-tenth of the public school library media specialists in Alabama, Kentucky, Louisiana, Mississippi, and Tennessee. The purpose of the study was to investigate the status of library media services for exceptional students; ascertain opinions about the education needed by media specialists serving exceptional children; and explore the relationships between adequacy of resources and frequency of services and selected characteristics of media specialists and schools. Library media specialists rated their collections as moderately adequate. They provided media services to exceptional students occasionally, and their facilities generally lacked adaptations of facilities for physically handicapped children. Media specialists perceived a need for training in special education and preferred continuing education programs at the school/district level along with integration of special education into existing library science courses. Regression analysis showed that the variables of perceived adequacy of resources and the number and frequency of services provided for exceptional children were related to professional experience, length of experience in present position, and per pupil expenditure, but were not related to the percentage of exceptional students enrolled, the media specialist's education, and the size of the media staff. Buckley concluded that media specialists need to develop an awareness of the educational needs of exceptional children and master the skills necessary to serve them, and library education must develop strategies for providing the preparation which in-service and pre-service personnel require.

Davie (1980) studied the nature and extent of school library media resources in Florida public schools and the provisions made for using these resources for exceptional students. She concluded that appropriate materials and equipment are generally available, but additional and more varied materials are needed to allow longer loan periods and improved circulation patterns. Also needed were appropriate furnishings, more certified media personnel to allow for individualized instruction, more clerical staff, more volunteer help, more publicity aimed at students and teachers, more use of the resources of the Florida Learning Resource System and of interlibrary loans with community libraries and the Florida NLS system, and more pre-service and in-service training. Media specialists were seen as having made such adaptations in equipment, materials, and facilities as were possible within the limits of budget, personnel, and time available. They were receptive to suggestions for improvement, recognized the need for individualization, and expressed generally positive attitudes about working with exceptional children.

Library Services in Schools for the Deaf

Unlike blind people and, more recently, those who are physically disabled, deaf and hearing impaired persons have seldom been served directly through federally funded library programs. The principal federal program has been Captioned Films for the Deaf, which loans materials to schools and libraries. Local libraries have also been slow in providing special services to deaf persons, because these individuals have been perceived as capable of using ordinary library materials, despite the fact that language and reading impairments are common among them. However, schools for the deaf, both publicly and privately supported, have a long history in the United States, and such schools have often been important purveyors of library materials to deaf children. Therefore, much of the research on library services to deaf and hearing impaired individuals has concentrated on library services in schools for the deaf.

The earliest research into library services for persons with any disability which was located for this study was Kennedy's 1903 survey of libraries in state schools for the deaf. In the first section of her paper, she described administration, materials, and services; gave funding and circulation statistics; and discussed treatment and instruction of deaf students. Special mention was made of Baker Library at Gallaudet College. The second part of the study primarily concerns ways to promote reading, stressing the importance of the library and the need for a trained librarian. Section three is a list of books popular with deaf students. Subjective comments are inserted throughout the narrative.

More than 60 years later, research into library services in schools for the deaf resumed with Cory's (1966) survey of the status of libraries in schools for the deaf. This study, commissioned by the Convention of American Instructors of the Deaf and funded by the Office of Captioned Films for the Deaf, led to the publication of *Standards for Library-Media Centers in Schools for the Deaf* the next year. Thirty schools were visited in this study, and their library media programs were examined in light of the 1960 *Standards for School Library Programs* published by the American Library Association. Cory found that no school met the ALA standards in every area, although one qualified in everything except physical facilities. A few schools came close to meeting the lower ranges of the ALA standards. Ten schools offered services that might be called "superior" in relation to those of the other 20 schools.

Opocensky (1975/1976) studied 60 public residential schools for the deaf to evaluate their library media centers in relation to the 1967 *Standards for Library-Media Centers in Schools for the Deaf*. She found that the library media centers "are not equipped with facilities, collection, personnel, equipment or budget to serve the educational program to the degree anticipated by the authors of the Standards" (p. 218). Facilities were considered at least adequate by 60% of the media specialists, yet only six schools met or exceeded the recommendations of the standards. Although facilities for the use of nonprint in the libraries were often inadequate, print and nonprint materials had been integrated into most catalogs. Personnel were generally well qualified, but were often doing clerical work. Programs were generally good, but there was a need for more hours of access and more individualized and group work. Professional collections were minimal, and book collections for students were far below the numbers which the standards recommended. Captioned films, filmstrips, and transparencies were in good supply. Only three of the larger schools spent within the budget ranges recommended by the standards. One exceeded the upper limit.

In a similar study, Carter (1982/1983) surveyed library media centers in public day schools in light of the *Standards for Library-Media Centers in Schools for the Deaf.* He found that 56% of the schools which responded had media centers. Half of the library media centers had personnel who met the educational requirements of the standards, but only one-third employed clerical personnel. Minimum standards for expenditures were met by 43%; only one exceeded the upper limits of the standards. Most of the facilities met the standards in seating capacity, but not in overall area. Collections varied widely, but generally did not meet the recommendations of the standards. Recommended programs, however, were generally available.

Library Services to Homebound and Institutionalized Disabled Persons

Several studies have investigated services to persons who were homebound, hospitalized, or institutionalized in nursing homes, mental institutions or other specialized situations. In an early study, Woodman (1933) surveyed institution libraries (state hospitals, state schools, and licensed private sanatoriums) in New York state. He reported that all the "well established" (p. 63) state hospitals and schools had libraries varying from a few hundred to 6,274 volumes; most materials were donated; and there was a general shortage of current magazines. The person in charge of the library varied from "an intelligent patient" (p. 64) to a trained librarian. Subjective comments on the history of hospital libraries and the author's personal beliefs are included.

Yockey (1949) gives an account of the Frederick and Henryett Slocum Judd Fund, which supported the Cleveland Public Library's service to "the old, the crippled, and the ill in institutions or in their own homes" (p. iii). The report gives historical information on outreach service in general and especially in Cleveland, where the Judd fund began in 1941. A reading interest survey conducted in 1943 was reported; fiction, history and biography were most popular, and current events, European royalty, travel, and best sellers were also liked. Yockey saw the future of library service to handicapped persons consisting of book circulation to shut-ins for pleasure reading, the circulation of books that have potential value as medical treatment, and the provision of materials to help those in need of rehabilitation to live as fully as possible.

Strong (1974) investigated services to homebound adults in 10 selected communities in each of the New England states. She found that most of the libraries served homebound individuals, but only to the extent of delivering materials. Several libraries maintained telephone contact with homebound patrons. Funds were usually limited, and seldom constituted a separate budget item. Most homebound patrons were elderly, and were referred by friends and neighbors. Seventy percent of the libraries served people who were temporarily ill, and 56% served people who had transportation problems. Home visits, not just book delivery, were considered important, and 95% of the libraries have lent special materials (large print, talking books, braille). Over half the libraries regularly served not more than 25 homebound patrons.

Korlaske (1974) studied library policies and services in six Missouri state mental institutions. Most of the institutions had a separate library department, but none of those designated as "librarians" had a library degree. These people attended the same state library workshops, which may have accounted for the fact that their libraries had similar policies and procedures. Only one library had a written selection policy. An LSCA grant permitted books to be centrally processed. The type and quality of service varied, and there were few special programs or attempts at library instruction. There was little cooperation between the librarians and staff at each institution, and little cooperation among the six libraries. Traditional book collections, rather than media, were provided for recreation. Korlaske recommended user studies to determine the extent of reading and the needed types of materials.

Waddicor (1975) interviewed 80 librarians, nursing home administrators, registered nurses, and occupational therapists in the Providence, Rhode Island area. Seven public libraries served 14 of 60 institutions in their communities. Overall, 25% of the patients in the homes with library service were actual readers; 719 out of 2,500 patients in the 60 institutions had service. Waddicor's report included quotes from interviews and much anecdotal material with no real analysis. He saw the major obstacles to extending service as lack of awareness on the part of librarians that patients desire and need service, lack of understanding on the part of nursing home administrators that service to private institutions is within the proper domain of the public library, and fear on the part of these administrators that they would be held responsible for lost books.

SURVEYS OF LIBRARY SERVICE TO DISABLED PERSONS IN OTHER COUNTRIES

Although a number of English-language surveys in countries other than the United States are listed in indexing and abstracting services, copies for examination are difficult to locate or not available through interlibrary loan (see Appendix B). Most of the available studies come from countries which use English extensively: the United Kingdom, Australia, Canada,

Nigeria. A few studies from Scandinavian countries have been translated into English. Many untranslated studies have been published in various languages, but these are outside the scope of this paper. Two international surveys have been identified and are discussed first. Other studies in this section are arranged alphabetically by country of origin.

International

Schauder and Cram (1977) brought together information on policies and practices in libraries for the blind in nearly 30 countries. The United States (which has been most heavily documented), and Britain and South Africa (where the researchers had professional ties) received the most extensive coverage. The report concentrated on services to adults rather than children, and on talking book services rather than embossed media. Each chapter covers a separate topic, including reading media, financial and administrative responsibility, centralization or decentralization, selection, production and acquisition of materials, organization, printed catalogs and bibliographic current awareness, bibliographic control, personnel, study and vocational materials, use made of facilities and reading media, cooperation, and new technology. In each chapter, practices are given for each country, with the United States listed first, Britain last, and other countries alphabetically between. Because the scope is so broad, many topics cannot be covered in great depth, but the study brings together a great mass of material that would otherwise be unavailable. There is an extensive bibliography of published and unpublished material.

Mayer and Cylke (1979) prepared a study of 52 African countries to determine the extent of braille facilities for blind persons, with the aim of choosing a location for a central braille-producing facility. Factors considered included ease of communication (central location), political stability (in 1978–1979), and the extent of already-existing organizations for the target group. Tanzania and Kenya had the highest estimated blind population; Swaziland and Kenya, the highest literacy rates; Swaziland and the Ivory Coast, the highest per capita incomes; Tanzania, Senegal, and Kenya, the most libraries for those who are sighted; and Tanzania, Gambia, Ivory Coast, Kenya, and Liberia were strongest politically. Tanzania, Ivory Coast, and Kenya were recommended as the best sites for a braille production facility. Much of the report is a cost analysis of braille production methods.

Australia

Six reports of surveys of library service in Australia were examined. In 1978, the National Library of Australia published the first comprehensive investigation of library services for blind and physically handicapped persons in Australia. A questionnaire was sent to all organizations working with handicapped people. Questionnaires were also sent to state libraries, other public libraries, university and selected college libraries, school libraries, and government departmental libraries. Services were found to be fragmentary and inadequate, with the level of service far below that provided to nondisabled individuals. An almost complete lack of serial and foreign language materials for handicapped people existed. There was, however, a growing awareness of the needs of handicapped people, and a desire to improve service.

Thorn (1978) discussed the same National Survey in a paper given at a National Consultative Seminar on Library Services for the Handicapped. The author noted that it was "extremely difficult to obtain any useful statistics, principally because of the difficulties in obtaining satisfactory definitions which can be easily applied for statistical purposes" (p. 21).

Another report by the National Library of Australia's Working Party on Library Services for the Handicapped was published in 1979. Its purpose was "to investigate and recommend on library services for the handicapped including the possibility of mounting a national conference or seminar of organizations interested in the question" (p. 5). The report concentrated on information from the National Survey and the National Consultative Seminar discussed above. Recommendations included establishment of a national program operating on three levels: national, state, and local; service provided from public libraries to whatever extent was possible; inclusion of services to handicapped patrons in standards; establishment of cooperative production and distribution of special materials; and adequate accessibility to buildings and facilities. The report includes numerous recommendations for special services to be provided by the National Library.

Gorman (1980) studied the needs of disabled library users at Monash University. The survey was part of Project MIND (Meeting the Information Needs of the Disabled), which was established in 1979 by the University and College Libraries Section of the Library Association of Australia. Questionnaires were distributed to disabled students. (Although technically this is a user's study, it is included here because it concentrates on services of a particular library.) Students with a clearly visible disability (such as paraplegia) were most satisfied with library service; those with less visible disabilities were more critical of service. Except for the coordinator for disabled users, library staff members were found to lack an understanding of the needs of disabled students, of special facilities in the library which were available for them, and of good communication techniques to use with disabled persons. The most serious problem students mentioned was obtaining books when they were needed and being able to borrow them for a long enough period. Students also mentioned problems with shelf height, type size, and various architectural barriers. There was a lack of sufficient publicity for special equipment and facilities available in the library. Gorman concluded that the most urgent need was for more on-going training and sensitizing for all staff members whom disabled students might encounter. Administrative flexibility was seen as needed to respond to student needs.

Hillman (1982) also studied disabled students' perceptions of library services in an academic library, the Robertson Library of the Western Australia Institute of Technology. The problems identified appeared to be specific to the respondent's disability: access problems, problems using library tools or arranging for readers, problems with heavy items. One student with epilepsy found fluorescent lighting, especially if it was flickering, a problem. The students noted some failure of the library staff to communicate. The library resources the students appreciated most were lifts, automatic doors, special study/reading rooms, helpful staff, and microfiche catalogs. Student reactions to library service were generally positive, but both students and staff lacked awareness of the services and facilities available.

Moon (1983) surveyed public, academic, and special libraries in New South Wales, as well as the state library, to determine the level of service provided to persons with all types of disabilities (visual, intellectual, physical, and hearing). The questionnaire used in the National Library of Australia (1978) study listed above was used, after being modified for all handicaps. Levels of service were "essentially fragmentary and inadequate" (p. 59). Large print and talking books were readily available in public libraries, but elsewhere, special formats were mostly lacking. A few libraries had special materials and services, special reading rooms and extra reference services. In such libraries, a staff facilitator was usually appointed to help disabled patrons. Gaps in service noted were absence of policy statements, budget allocations, special format materials, individualized services such as volunteer readers, modified reference services, and materials in languages other than English. There was a limited range of periodicals and local information in special formats; and limited and uneven levels of service, outreach, and resource sharing. The state was judged as not yet anywhere near its goal of providing any book in any format or language needed by the disabled user.

Canada

Dale and Dewdney (1972) surveyed a selected group of public libraries across Canada to learn what resources and services were available for physically handicapped people. They recommended examining facilities for accessibility, publicizing services to organizations for handicapped persons, publicizing needs to library boards in order to get budget authorization for services, and in-service training. They also recommended encouraging social action programs by government and local groups, cable television and other media programs for shut-ins, closer cooperation with city departments and service clubs who work with disabled persons, and familiarity with services offered by other institutions and agencies in the community.

Denmark

Petersen has reported two Danish studies. The earlier, "De lasehandicappede og bibliotekerne" ("The Handicapped in Reading and the Libraries") was conducted by the Danish Institute for Social Research. This study is only briefly mentioned in another paper (Petersen, 1979), and the population of the study is not clear. Petersen reported that 48% of the adult population (16 years or older) used the public library at the time of the study, 28% had visited a library at some time, and 24% had never used one. The actual use was seen as slightly higher because some persons used library books and recordings borrowed from the library by friends and family members. The figures for this adjusted use were 52% who used the library, 25% who had previously visited it, and 23% who had never used a library. The public library was used by 37% of children 6 years of age and younger, and by 76–79% of those 7 to 15 years of age.

Petersen (1983) also reported on two committee reports on library services to the visually disabled, one on services in Denmark, the other in Sweden. Each paper was originally published in the native language of its country of origin. (The Swedish paper will be discussed below.) The Danish paper (title in English translation: "Library Service for the Blind and Weak-Sighted. Report of the Committee on Library Service for the Blind and Weak-Sighted Appointed by the Ministry of Culture, Copenhagen, 1982. Report No. 950") makes recommendations for the overall future of library service to the target population. The first section reviews the users, materials, legislation, and present library service. The second section includes recommendations. It was recommended that the service should be decentralized, with more service offered by the local public libraries. The State Library for the Blind (which the committee felt should be part of the public library system) and a central library for blind children should also provide services. Talking books and home visitation should be provided by public libraries. A permanent coordinating committee for the production of talking books was recommended at the national level, but the recording of books requested by individual readers was felt to be best provided in the individual public libraries. Service should also be improved to "others handicapped in reading" (p. 5). The various municipalities were advised to estimate existing needs and plan for centralizing collections. Each municipality was encouraged to start a local talking newspaper, including items for children. It was seen as important that services to disabled persons have a high priority in budgeting.

Nigeria

Atinmo's (1979) study identified existing public and state library services, available resources and the handicapped group(s) they aimed to serve. Existing library services in schools and institutions for handicapped persons were also identified. Finally, Atinmo made recommendations for improved library service. The target population in the study included physically handicapped people in hospitals or prisons or those confined to their immediate environment by physical or mental disability. All state and public libraries were surveyed, as well as schools for handicapped children. Handicapped children integrated into regular schools and those in leprosy settlements were excluded. It was found that only 15% of the state libraries provided services to handicapped persons; no Nigerian librarian had special training in working with those who are handicapped; the only library service provided was lending; and the groups served included prisoners, patients, juvenile delinquents, and "the deaf, dumb, and blind" (p. 444). The schools and institutions for handicapped persons had very inadequate provision for library service. One school provided no library service at all. Only one school, which served deaf children, provided audiovisual materials. Collections were small, and staff members were inadequately trained. Atinmo's recommendations included: a broadened concept of library service; the utilization of outreach, deposit collections, and storybooks for persons with different kinds of handicaps; a full range of library services; increased publicity and trained personnel. Atinmo felt that "emphasis on technical expertise will have to give way to social service . . . understanding people, especially the handicapped, learning about their needs, and responding creatively to them" (p. 448).

Sweden

Petersen's (1983) paper on library services in Denmark and Sweden was mentioned above with discussion of the Danish report. The Swedish report (title in English translation: "Talking Books—Publication and Distribution. Report of the Committee on Talking Books, Stockholm, 1982"), unlike the Danish report, focuses only on talking books. Its purpose was "to present recommendations for effectuating an even greater degree of decentralization of talking book services" (p. 6). The target group included those "handicapped in reading" as well as those who were blind or weaksighted. Decentralization of services was already well advanced in Sweden at the time of the study. The committee recommended that the State Library for the Blind have total responsibility for central production of talking books, but it was felt that users should be able to get services and materials at local public libraries. The committee recommended that county libraries coordinate distribution and ensure service availability. Under this plan, the central library would establish collections of seldom requested titles to be made available through local public libraries. State grants to accelerate decentralization, help local libraries buy talking books, and improve coordination of services were encouraged, but the committee noted that municipalities must put higher priority on the purchase of talking books.

United Kingdom

Armstrong (1967) surveyed public library service to the homebound and hospitalized people in the United Kingdom. Services to hospitals were provided by 36% of the libraries, and 47% provided services to homebound and handicapped persons. Qualified librarians were usually responsible for the services, but visits to homes and hospital wards were more likely to be made by volunteers. Deposit collections were often placed in hospitals and hostels. Eighty-eight percent owned large print materials. Few libraries provided materials in braille, and 34% reported use of National Library for the Blind services. Other special services were limited. Libraries in smaller communities were less likely to provide services, but when they did so, individual contacts tended to be closer. The largest libraries had by far the slightest contact with individuals.

USER INTERESTS AND NEEDS

Fifteen studies have investigated the reading interests of disabled persons, their needs for materials in various formats, and their needs for access to libraries. Eight of the studies investigated the interests and needs of blind readers; five of these were conducted by or for the National Library Service for the Blind and Physically Handicapped. The other seven studies are varied in focus. Only the NLS studies are specific to a particular type of library. Sometimes the studies are about reading in general rather than library use, but they all have implications for libraries. The studies of the reading interests of blind readers will be discussed first, followed by the other seven studies.

The Reading Interests and Format Needs of Blind Readers

Riddell (1940) surveyed the reading interests of blind people. She begins by saying, "We have known for a good many years that reading is the chief leisure-time activity of the blind, to whom so many doors of entertainment are closed" (p. 189) (later researchers would be more hesitant to state such an assumption). The purpose of the study was to discover trends of reading interests of blind persons in the United States. Questionnaires in both braille and print were sent to people on the mailing list of the braille edition of *Reader's Digest*. The respondents were better educated and younger than the general blind population, but the percentage employed was about the same. Two-thirds had read from 1 to 25 books in the past six months. They liked fiction, especially best sellers and books on which movies had been based. Nonfiction was read if it was non-scholarly; nonfiction subjects preferred included biography, history, government, health, and travel. Younger people liked to read drama and books about music; older ones liked religious books. Readers of all ages liked current events and self-help books on improving conversation, getting along with people, becoming more self-confident, and accomplishing more at work. The most popular titles mentioned were generally fiction or on topics of very current interest. As the researcher pointed out, several of these books were already available in braille or as talking books, but many readers would not know this because they had no access to a catalog. Although readers overwhelmingly wanted to read fiction, Riddell noted that it made up only one-third of the books brailled by the Library of Congress between 1931 and 1938. She believed that more emphasis was needed on providing currently popular books. She pointed out that non-fiction books, brailled and recorded, were likewise not in line with reader interests, although she felt the trend seemed to be toward transcribing more titles related to expressed reading interests.

Josephson (1964) brought together the results from several studies conducted by the American Foundation for the Blind. According to these studies, states varied greatly in the number of blind readers who were residents. Blind people were more likely to read, and were heavier readers, than were sighted persons. More than half read using recordings; and more than one-fourth read with the help of sighted readers. The number who could use ordinary print was about the same as the number who read braille. The amount of reading peaked in the group aged 21–39, then declined, and finally rose to a plateau in old age. Reading increased with education level, and family influences were important. The amount of reading increased along with the number of social, medical, and financial services received. In the 21–39 age group, one-third used records and one-fifth, braille; in the group aged 70–79, two-thirds used records. Two-thirds of those who used records, but less than one-half of those who used braille, reported chronic conditions other than blindness. A steady drop in the number of braille readers as blindness has become a phenomenon of old age was noted. The trend was toward a desire for more recorded materials. Few persons were reading as much as they would like, but on the whole they were satisfied with regional library services.

Chandler (1977) surveyed blind attendees at the American Council for the Blind Convention in 1976 and also the readers of *Braille Forum*. The respondents were atypical of the entire blind population, since most were in the age group 20–40, and they were probably more interested in books and reading than the average blind or sighted person. Chandler noted that they might, however, have been representative of active readers. Disk and cassette recordings were both popular with the respondents. Sound sheets (i.e., flexible disks) were judged as satisfactory for periodicals, which are heavily used, but not for books. Large print and jumbo braille materials received low ratings. Braille was popular out of proportion to its use in the blind population at large. Many respondents were not familiar with live reader services. A strong demand for cassettes, disks, and braille was identified. The demand for large print was not adequately tested in this study because of the target group. Respondents showed a high interest in library contact by phone and by braille, something that would require increased budgetary support because of the staff time it would take. Because of the interest in cassettes, it was noted that information was needed about the reliability of various brands of tape and models of equipment and about maintenance of equipment. It was suggested that sound sheets be considered when many copies are needed, when prompt delivery is required, and when durability is of secondary concern.

Since 1969, the Division for the Blind and Physically Handicapped (later called the National Library Service for the Blind and Physically Handicapped) has regularly queried its users about their interests and needs. The first study located (Nelson Associates, 1969) had two purposes: first, to study reading interests and needs of DBPH patrons; secondly, to study circulation procedures used to meet patrons' needs. Forty-three percent of the users were aged 65 or older; nearly one-half of the readers were aged 55 or older when they became unable to use print; and the reading needs and preferences of older people were found to be different, but not sharply different, from those of younger readers. Some rotating collections were reported in schools, hospitals, or homes for the aged, but few were in public libraries. Many readers experienced transportation problems which made mail service preferable. Few readers reported only physical disabilities (that is, most physically disabled persons also reported visual disabilities), and most users first heard of the service through family, friends, or an institution. One recommendation of this study was that patrons who were not clients of a state agency which distributed talking book machines should still be able to obtain a machine easily (at this time, reading machines were not yet distributed by DBPH). Other recommendations included: availability of talking books from either local collections or by mail; recruitment of more not-blind physically handicapped users; and production of more professional and vocational materials, plays, serious fiction, and reference materials. In the study of circulation procedures, 13 regional libraries were visited. Researchers noted a need for uniformity among regional libraries in reporting statistics. It was seen as satisfactory for each regional library to determine its own circulation practices to meet local needs, but workshops and other interactions were recommended to help new regional libraries establish policies and practices.

Evenson (1974) reported on a survey of braille readers conducted for DBPH. The purposes were to learn what kind of books and magazines readers preferred and to obtain information on characteristics of the readers. Braille and print questionnaires were sent to 1,735 readers on the mailing lists of *Braille Book Review, Braille Monitor, Braille Forum,* and *New Outlook for the Blind.* The usable return rate was 40%. The reader profile showed that there were more women than men among braille readers; that 25% were under age 25, 28% were ages 25–39, 38% were ages 40–64, and 9% were 65 or older; 28% were students, 44% were employed, and 15% were retired. Most readers listed their occupations as professional and technical; housewives were second. Although only 28% said that braille was the only reading medium they could use, 51% used it for most of their reading. Respondents were about equally divided on whether they preferred books or magazines, but readers of *Braille Book Review* read more books than did those respondents whose names were obtained from other mailing lists. While 45% reported reading two to six books per month, 51% read two to six magazines in the same period. DBPH service was ranked as adequate by 51%, but 23% said they received too much material. There was more satisfaction with magazine service than book service. The most favored book categories were entertainment, general education, hobbies, and education. Preferred magazine categories were general interest, news, and entertainment. Evenson's recommendations included maintaining or increasing the number of braille titles produced; concentrating on production of popular categories; producing books of varying lengths instead of so many shorter ones; and further evaluation of braille service in the future.

In 1979, a *Survey to Determine the Extent of the Eligible User Population Not Currently Being Served or Not Aware of the Programs of the Library of Congress, National Library Service for the Blind and Physically Handicapped* (the so-called Non-user Survey) was an extensive effort to identify the potential population for NLS service. The purposes of the study were: to learn the size of the eligible population, to understand more fully the social and demographic characteristics and reading habits of the eligible population, and to explore actual and potential utilization of NLS services in institutions and special schools. Several differing methodologies were used. In the household study, a national sample of households was asked about family members' ability to read and use regular print materials; a sample of those identified in the first survey as being in the target population was then asked to take part in a second survey. The institutional study used mail questionnaires and field visits to nursing homes, hospitals, and special schools. Some NLS network librarians were interviewed in the librarian study. It was concluded that only 12% of the target household population and 2–4% of the target institutional population were using NLS services. Awareness of the service, however, was much greater: 57% of target households and 86% of institutional staffs knew about the service. Thus, there appeared to be considerable potential to expand the program among non-users. NLS users were found to be generally younger and better educated than non-users. They were also more likely to be white, legally blind, and without disabilities other than visual ones. It was concluded that NLS should consider expanding present service to include large print, materials for learning disabled persons, and more employment and educationally-oriented materials.

A 1981 study entitled *Readership Characteristics and Attitudes: Service to Blind and Physically Handicapped Users* was conducted to develop a profile of NLS readership and to aid NLS in future planning by identifying reader interests and concerns. User characteristics were found to be similar to those in previous studies. Nearly two-thirds of the respondents reported visual disabilities; 7%, physical disabilities; and 28%, multiple disabilities. NLS users included more older people and more females than the general population, and 93% of the respondents were white. Two-thirds were retired or unemployed, and incomes were limited despite high levels of educational achievement. Braille readers were younger and better educated than talking book users. They were less likely to have other physical handicaps, and more of them were long-term users of NLS. Among current users, 21% had used NLS services for at least 10 years. Respondents were more likely to visit subregional libraries than regional ones. Talking book record players were used by 90% of the respondents, and more than one-half used both record and cassette machines. Older readers were less likely to use cassettes. Although 70% of the users indicated no preference in sex of the narrator, older readers preferred male readers and narrators without regional accents. Older readers also objected to strong language or explicit sexual descriptions in fiction. Readers were less pleased with availability of materials than with the speed with which orders were filled. About 40% used magazines on records, and about 4% could read braille. Only 25% knew of the NLS music service, and about 10% were interested in non-English materials, especially Spanish.

The 1983 *Braille Reader Survey* (Library of Congress, 1983) was conducted to determine the needs and interests of current braille readers, and to help explain why braille readers were borrowing fewer books from NLS.

(Over a 10-year period from 1972 to 1981, the number of braille readers remained fairly constant, but the number of braille books borrowed declined significantly.) The study sample consisted of 500 persons drawn from a pool consisting of the 8,540 persons who receive *Braille Book Review*. The sample was representative of the readers for age and geographic region. Surveys were tabulated for 242 readers, a usable return rate of 48.4%. Totally blind readers made up 77.2% of the respondents, and 90.4% regarded themselves as excellent or good braille readers. Eighty-two percent had learned braille in childhood. Although 71.8% preferred to read braille, only 52.3% read it most frequently. Readers preferred braille for materials which demanded quick access: cookbooks, reference books, the Bible, current events; but they preferred other formats for bestsellers and other fiction. Eighty-five percent of the readers ordered specific titles. Over one-half had never borrowed hand-copied braille; promotion of this service was recommended. In summary, most readers were satisfied with the quality of service; the major difficulty was in receiving, storing, and returning bulky books. There was more dissatisfaction with the choice of braille books available than with the talking book collection, and one-third of the readers did not feel the available books met their needs.

Other Studies of the Interests and Needs of Disabled Persons

Seven other studies present a miscellaneous group, but all deal with the reading interests and the needs (including the needs for materials in particular formats and/or needs related to the physical facilities of the library) of disabled persons other than those who are blind. The two earliest studies discuss the reading interests of institutionalized disabled persons. Spilman (1964) investigated the reading interests of patients at Seton, a private Catholic mental hospital. The study's purpose was "to illustrate the hypothesis that within each medical diagnostic group there is a definite pattern of reading interests, shown by choices made by patients, that is peculiar and distinctive to each group" (p. 1). The patients were acute, not chronic, cases experiencing psychotic, psycho-neurotic, and personality disorders. The subjects' reading choices over a five-year period, as shown on their library cards, were studied. Only cards listing at least five titles were used. Results showed that the frequency of subject choices in all groups correlated closely with the number of books on those subjects held by the library. However, humor and poetry were chosen more often than would be expected based on the number of volumes in the library. Manic depressive patients chose the most books, followed by patients who were alcoholic or schizophrenic. Psychotic depressed patients read the least. Psychotic patients preferred poetry more than did the other patients. Depressed patients chose sports, detective stories, and poetry, but rarely literature. Schizophrenic patients chose religion, self-teaching, poetry, and literature. Manic depressive individuals preferred humor and travel; depressed manic depressive people chose biography and religion. Psychoneurotic patients chose humor and art more often than did those who were psychotic. Passive-aggressive patients chose travel, history, and self-teaching; passive dependent persons chose short stories and humor; and those who were sociopathic chose religion, self-teaching, and art. Alcoholic patients liked detective stories. All patient groups except the depressed manic depressive group chose fiction first, and biography was second in six groups. Spilman interpreted the data in light of the diseases to show why patients chose particular books. For instance, she felt that reading about sports might allow depressed patients to release aggression and hostility, rather than turning it against themselves. She concluded that definite reading patterns could be established for each group on the basis of the mental illnesses diagnosed; and that age, sex, occupation, socioeconomic status, and education were not factors in reading patterns. The patients made reading choices unknowingly to compensate for their illness or to help themselves toward recovery.

Delvalle, Miller, and Saldicco (1966) studied reading patterns of aged persons in a nursing home. The study was conducted in a White Plains, New York nursing facility consisting of an intensive care unit and four therapeutic community groups. The White Plains Public Library provided a mobile circulating library replenished monthly. One-third of the respondents in this study were selected from the intensive care unit and the rest from "the intellectually intact therapeutic community groups" (p. 9). Most of the respondents were women. Approximately one-third of the total nursing home population was found to read. Many had disabilities and had not read for years before the service began. The most frequently read subjects were mystery, autobiography, history, and psychology. The subjects which attracted least interest were nature, religion, animals, sports, westerns, and science fiction. It was noted that the library preselected the 100 books available each month at the nursing home, with an occasional special request honored, and that the activities staff at the nursing home distributed the books. The researchers felt that librarians might have been able to "sell" a greater variety of subjects if they had had direct contact with the residents. On the other hand, the activities staff knew the patients personally, which could be an advantage.

Two studies from Canada collected information through associations working with disabled people, rather than from disabled persons themselves. Ludlow, Henderson, Murray, and Rawkins (1972) surveyed national organizations serving physically handicapped people to discover the effects of various disabilities and the relationships of disabled persons with the library. Telephone interviews were used, following pre-established guidelines. The study concluded that public libraries should give full attention to physical planning; that programs require planning for both content and facilities; and that libraries should make available materials about disabilities, including materials provided by organizations serving handicapped people, as well as costly books and vocational and guidance materials. Libraries should seek out and cooperate with organizations which serve handicapped individuals, including drug and insurance companies which often provide free materials; libraries should take advantage of publicity campaigns of various charity "weeks" by scheduling programs at those times. Finally, organizations for handicapped persons should be informed of library activities so that they can promote library services.

In a similar study, A. Simpson (1972) queried organizations and institutions serving physically disabled people in British Columbia about the characteristics of the persons they served; the reading and listening materials they provided; their interest in provision of materials by the library; their perception of the library's role, and that of volunteers, in developing services; their promotion of library service and referral; and their methods of coordination with other organizations. Simpson identified possible targets for library service as physically disabled people who could use the library if it were accessible, persons in extended care hospitals and rest homes and those who were homebound.

One study addressed the reading interests and needs of deaf persons. McLaughlin and Andrews (1975) studied the extent and nature of reading by deaf persons, noting that reading achievement studies indicate that adult deaf persons usually read at the third to fifth grade level. Using sign language, the researchers interviewed 36 deaf adult members of a church which served as a major social center for members of Baltimore's deaf community. Most of the men had manual jobs; the women were usually housewives. Their education ranged from grade to high school, and their ages from 19 to 69. Most respondents read at least one newspaper a day; the men preferred sports, comics, and the front page, while the women liked the front page, local news, style, and comics. Most regularly bought and read magazines, preferring very popular ones such as *TV Guide, Life, Look,* and *Ladies' Home Journal.* Book reading was less frequent. Less than one-third read books; the Bible was the book most frequently read. Respondents read books which had been made into movies, but few read best sellers. Older people, most of whom were retired, were the most frequent readers in all categories. Those aged 24–49 read least. Most of the respondents who were readers had been educated in schools where manual communication was encouraged. The researchers found many similarities to hearing readers, but deaf persons read less. It was recommended that captioned television and foreign films with English subtitles be used to promote interest in reading, and that topical material from newspapers and magazines be used in teaching reading. The researchers suggested that greater availability of reading material in the home would increase interest in reading.

A British study queried physically disabled persons about their needs for access to and use of library facilities. S. Simpson (1976) drew material related to libraries from a study conducted by the Central Council for the Disabled Fire Research Unit in Great Britain. The full study had examined factors perceived by disabled people as the greatest barriers to their use of public buildings, including libraries. The sample was drawn from members of voluntary and charitable organizations and contained a greater percentage of the disabled population than does the general public. Most respondents were from the 16–49 age group. Simpson reported, "We have not stumbled yet upon any startling new truth" (p. 355). Changes in level, such as steps, stairs, and steep gradients, made up 62% of all complaints about library design. Only 32% of the libraries studied had upper floors accessible to wheelchairs and only 51.5% of the public libraries were accessible to wheelchairs at all. Librarians reported little demand for service from disabled people, but the disabled respondents indicated more interest in using libraries than in most other activities. Simpson noted that fire safety precautions need to be taken into account; heavy firedoors are a common problem for those who are disabled. Smoke and heat activated doors were suggested as a good option where fires are a rare occurrence. The author recommended working with local clubs and voluntary organizations to promote services and explore needs. Librarians were encouraged to cost out desired improvements and to relax formal policies when necessary.

Kenney (1981) investigated the needs of disabled persons engaged in scholarly research. She surveyed scholars with earned doctorates who were listed in *Resource Directory of Handicapped Scientists* (1978) and *Educators with Disabilities: A Resource Guide* (1981). Respondents were asked about their publication record, present position, nature of disability, and how it had affected their work. Findings pertinent to libraries included the following: almost one-half of the respondents reported limited mobility; about 20%, limited vision; one-eighth, limited hearing; and the rest various organic or multiple disabilities. One-third of the respondents needed help with architectural barriers; one-fourth, with transporting books; and one-seventh, with reading research materials. A minority reported using mechanical aids, including tape recorders (one-fourth), special equipment like the Opticon (one-fifth), recorded materials (just over one-tenth), and braille, large print, sign, etc., (just under one-tenth). Specific desirable services in libraries mentioned were making wheelchairs available, as many museums do; help with catalog cards and indexes; help in consulting reference works; and volunteer readers.

LIBRARY MATERIALS FOR DISABLED USERS

Fourteen studies will be discussed which address the selection, provision, and use of various types of materials for disabled persons. Some of the studies specifically discuss library materials; others discuss materials in a more general way, but they provide information which can be used by libraries in serving this population. Ten of the studies discuss particular formats: large print materials, recorded materials (talking books) and tactile materials. The other four studies are a miscellaneous group which address the selection and provision of materials for particular groups of disabled persons.

Material Formats for Disabled Persons

Many visually disabled persons are able to use large print materials. Although NLS does not provide funding for large print books, regional and subregional libraries often provide such materials with other funding. Large print materials are popular in public libraries and may also be found in other types of libraries. Five studies have investigated these materials.

Warner (1965) correlated large print books with the Virginia school curriculum and provided a selected list of such books which could be used by visually disabled children in that state. The annotated booklist included materials for children in grades one through six. The list was intended as a buying guide and reference tool. Warner also discussed previous research on the effect of type-size.

The New York Public Library, Office of Adult Services study of its Large Print Book Project (1967) evaluated use of model collections at three locations: a branch library, a library center, and the Interbranch Loan Office. Special collections were placed in each location, and special registration forms were devised. It was found that at the library center, many registrants came from outside the New York Public Library service area, while at the branch library, most users were from the neighborhood. Many persons with normal sight were found to borrow for homebound friends or relatives. More elderly people used the branch library than the library center. Registrants were asked by questionnaire why they borrowed large print, and what they would like to read in that medium. Circulation records were also studied. At the library center circulation grew steadily, but the branch had much less circulation. There was increased pressure for deposit collections in the branches from the Interbranch Loan Office. Although the deposit collections were small, there was heavy turnover. The study concluded that few visually disabled and elderly patrons borrowed for themselves; they were more likely to depend on friends or relatives. Because many who would benefit from large print were not current library users, it was recognized that there was great potential for expanding service, especially among elderly adults. Since two-thirds of the disabled readers were over 60, emphasis in selection should be on satisfying the reading tastes of senior citizens. Fiction, philosophy, religion, and biography were preferred by older adults, and they liked materials, such as magazines, which can be quickly read. A need for better delivery methods was recognized. A problem for libraries is that special materials in unusual formats, and often in multiple volumes, make library processing difficult.

This two and one-half year Large Print Book Project was further evaluated (New York Public Library, 1969). The project's aim; to provide clear, large-print materials for partially sighted adults; was felt to be largely accomplished. Information had been disseminated, a collection had been established and distributed throughout the branch libraries, and a publicity campaign was mounted to alert potential users to its existence. Among the conclusions of the study were: interest in large print is widespread among librarians; potential readers are difficult to reach; effective publicity is essential; a balanced book collection is difficult to maintain without special funds for reproducing books to order because there are few publishers in the field; outreach is important through mail, rotating deposit collections in nursing homes, hospitals, and community centers, and even messenger service; there is enough material in large print available to begin and maintain adequate service; and large print is best provided through regional, county, or state systems.

Swingle (1978) used a literature review to investigate information about large print books and library collections, paying special attention to NLS libraries, and analyzing two editions of *Large Print Books in Print*. With increased concern for service to disabled populations in the 1960s, there was found to be a sudden surge of enthusiasm for large print books. Large print publishers who marketed their books as useful to disabled readers were more successful than those who marketed them to the general public. Consequently, publishers of large print tended not to market their books through normal advertising and distribution channels, and libraries rather than the general public purchased nearly all those published. The vast majority of large print books published were found to be textbooks for disabled students. At the time of the study, only a few attempts had been made to incorporate large print materials into the NLS system libraries, and it was felt to be unlikely that the materials would be generally accepted unless NLS endorsed them. Librarians were found to realize the need for large print, and many thought that low use was due to the types of books available, but Swingle believed that the most serious problem might be a lack of personal attention on the part of the librarians. Readers of large print required extra time for service. Swingle concluded that more research on large print was needed.

In a British study, Bell (1980) attempted to discover whether present provision of large print materials met user needs, and if not, to recommend changes. Four surveys were made: of librarians and libraries, of large print readers, of the community, and of "linkmen" who connect library services and users. (The first two surveys were of users; the last two of non-users.) She found that libraries generally have small stocks of available titles, making selection too restricted. Print size was found to be the most important factor to readers, and they preferred smaller books. Libraries provided few special and homebound services, and publicity about large print was wholly inadequate. The links between libraries and social service departments were informal when they existed at all. Present users were mostly elderly, and there were more females than males. Librarians were believed to underestimate the number of potential users of large print materials because the problem is invisible. Significant numbers of elderly and visually disabled people did not use libraries and did not know about large print. Many younger readers and many older ones were not interested in the subject range of materials currently available. Bell concluded that most libraries need more large print books and that these books are needed in a wider interest range.

Connor (1981), in evaluating large print and microfiche for low vision students, sought "to compare reading performance of visually handicapped students under a variety of circumstances, such as positive or negative images, high or low light intensity, contrasting screen tints, varying print sizes, traditional large type on paper, and all combinations of these" (p. 33). Thirteen students read under each experimental condition. Treatments were randomized, and a z-score was derived for each child. Reading speed was the criterion measure. Results indicated that visually handicapped students performed better using microfiche than using large type on paper. Conner believed that this might be because rear illumination of the microfiche image creates less glare than does front lighted inkprint on paper. Only two variables had a significant effect on reading performance. Positive microfiche was significantly better, as was 24 point type size. There were individual differences on other variables, but Conner cautioned that these differences might not be consistent for individuals over time. He concluded that it is important to provide all available options for visually handicapped students in order to best support their learning.

Three studies (by Walker, Jurrist, and Hviid) investigated use of talking books. Walker (1961), combining questionnaires, interviews, a literature review, and observation of the North Carolina Library for the Blind, surveyed the use of talking books in the NLS regional libraries that then existed in the Southeast (i.e., in Maryland, Virginia, North Carolina, Georgia, Alabama, and Florida). She found that staff and book collections were adequate for serving registered patrons, but the variety of materials was limited. Technical processing and regulations for borrowers were similar in all regional libraries, and all served mainly elderly patrons. The libraries used telephone and mail service to contact patrons, and all libraries showed increased circulation of talking books. There were few juvenile borrowers and few juvenile books in the collections. Periodicals were popular, but few were available. Most readers preferred devotional, recreational, or escapist reading. More staff in the libraries and more research into needs of blind readers were recommended.

Jurrist (1970) used questionnaires and interviews to examine the Nassau (New York) Library System's service to disabled readers. This service, which included a deposit collection of talking books, was developed in response to the 1966 amendment to the Pratt-Smoot Act which authorized service to physically handicapped persons. Most of the borrowers were found to be visually impaired, and 41% were over 65. The major limitations to service were found to be inadequate publicity, homebound service in only 27% of the libraries, and barrier-free facilities in only one-half of the buildings.

Hviid (1983) studied children's use of talking books in Denmark. This study is not specific to disabled children, but includes all children who use talking books. (In Denmark, copyright restrictions limit access to some talking books to those who are visually or reading disabled, but there is free access to other talking books.) The study is included here because the findings have implications for talking book use by disabled children as well as by nondisabled ones. Interviews were used to collect data. Children aged 9 to 13 were found to be the heaviest users of both print and talking books. They preferred recorded versions of books with which they were already familiar or of titles recommended by friends, although parents often guided their selection. Parents who previously read aloud to their children continued to do so when the children began to use talking books. Many children preferred to borrow both the printed and recorded version of a book at the same time. Although the reading speed of the recorded book was frequently too fast for the child to follow in the written text, they liked to have the book in their hands as they listened. Children often did other things while they listened, such as playing games or drawing. Hviid concluded that talking books were a good supplement to children's media consumption, and that many children borrowed talking books which, in print form, would have been considered too advanced for their age level.

A final format study (Nolan, 1976a) addressed tactile map reading by blind persons. The purposes of the study were to identify map reading skills used by good map readers, to determine if brief periods of training were effective in increasing tactile map reading of visually handicapped students, to determine if map reading skills used by good map readers can be taught to poor map readers, and to explore the efficacy of different tactile map designs in improving map reading skills. An experimental design was used. It was found that good map readers were more likely to trace lines and recognize shapes than poor readers. Specific instructions on how to search the display facilitated performance of children in grades 4–6, but had no effect or interfered with performance in grades 7–12. This suggests that training in spatial concepts and the scanning of tactile displays is more effective for younger children who have not yet developed search strategies of their own. Tactile map reading can be significantly improved with short periods of training, including both line tracing and the strategy of locating distinctive features; students need to learn to be analytical, systematic, and complete in exploring the tactile environment. Broad raised lines were found to be easier to read than narrow or incised lines; textured backgrounds (previously thought to be helpful in differentiating large areas such as countries) proved to be distracting. This study can have implications for selection of materials in libraries.

Miscellaneous Studies on the Selection and Provision of Materials for Disabled Persons

Four miscellaneous studies (by Gallimore, Wilson, Latham, and Hebert and Noel) included research on materials. These studies investigate the selection and provision of materials for various special groups of disabled persons.

Gallimore (1973) explored the selection and evaluation of materials for mentally retarded adolescents and adults, with the intent to stimulate further research and develop workable criteria. This is primarily a state-of-the-art study which synthesized the various criteria currently in use. Gallimore concluded that little had been published as definite working criteria. Many libraries had developed their own standards through experience. The criteria used generally included simple vocabulary, theme, and illustration; and there was acknowledgement of the need for materials on subjects familiar to retarded persons. Gallimore noted that federally funded regional centers (see the study by Latham below) were not evaluating materials for severely and profoundly retarded persons, which meant that librarians and others working in institutional settings must continue to develop their own criteria by trial and error. A great need for exchange of criteria and other information was perceived. It was noted that the audience for special materials is increasing, and more materials will be needed. Gallimore recommended more adequate field testing by publishers, as well as a uniform format for recommended reading lists which include basic vocabulary and controlled field test results.

B. L. Wilson (1976) reported on a study conducted by the Library Services to the Blind and Physically Handicapped Section, Health and Rehabilitative Services Division of the American Library Association. This study attempted "to determine how many employed handicapped persons need vocational reading matter in formats other than ink print and what they need in order to perform their jobs or advance in them" (p. 10). Questionnaires were sent to public libraries with annual book budgets in excess of $25,000, rehabilitation counsellors in the southeastern United States, DBPH regional libraries, and disabled persons who used Recording for the Blind. The public library survey was the least successful. Most libraries were unable to report the number of patrons with various handicaps because they did not keep such statistics. Most public libraries reported that they used regional libraries first to locate materials, then DBPH, then their state library. Many also cited vocational rehabilitation agencies, large print publishers, and instructional materials centers as sources. The most needed formats indicated were (in order of need): cassettes, large print, records, braille, regular print, and captioned film. Rehabilitation counsellors showed varying degrees of awareness of resources. Public and academic libraries tied as their first choice for resources, with regional libraries of DBPH a close second. Cassettes were the preferred format, with regular print a strong second. Many counsellors emphasized a need for materials with low reading levels. Employed disabled persons worked in a wide range of occupations. Nearly every standard reference book was cited by one of them as a resource. They agreed that an enormous list of reading matter was needed, but not available in a format they could use. Most of them used paid readers. Open-reel tape was the most frequently used format, followed by cassettes and records (a tie), braille, large print, and captioned film. The most preferred formats were cassettes, open-reel tape, braille, and records. A low rate of success in getting material in other than ink formats was reported. Sources searched included Recording for the Blind, LCDBPH, regional libraries of DBPH, American Printing House for the Blind and public libraries.

Latham (1976) investigated teacher use of the federally funded regional Instructional Materials Centers and Learning Resource Centers (IMC/LRCs) which had been established with ESEA funds to serve special education teachers. The study involved 1150 special education teachers and 25 IMC/LRCs. Three methods of data collection were used: a survey of material evaluation cards (filled out by teachers who used the materials), teacher interviews, and on-site visits to IMC/LRCs. Latham found that 70–80% of the materials had been checked out only once or not at all in any one year; one-third of the materials had never been checked out. The size of the collection was found to be irrelevant as long as it contained materials the teachers found useful. Reading and language materials were the most often used (55–65%); arithmetic (15–20%) and social studies (10–

15%) materials were next. Except for visually and auditorially impaired students, the type of disability was not important in choosing materials. Materials which were considered appropriate were those that supported the instructional effort in subject areas, not those which matched the unique characteristics of the learner. Materials were described positively by 90.7% of the teachers. Several factors were found to influence use. The collection was more likely to be used if the teachers were close by. The proximity of the collection was unimportant, however, if there was good delivery of materials; the preferred methods of delivery (in order of preference) were: delivery by IMC/LRC staff, district courier, and mail (the last was felt to be cost prohibitive). Knowledge of the collection by the IMC/LRC staff and by the teachers increased use. Materials already known to the teachers were more likely to be used, especially if the teacher had suggested the purchase. Promotional efforts increased use of the collection, as did adequate facilities with easy access (e.g., convenient parking, no stairs). Materials were most likely to be used if they were readily available and in good condition. The factors which influenced purchase of particular materials included the availability of funds, the instructional needs of the teachers, IMC/LRC staff awareness of the material's availability for purchase, and the per-item cost of the material as a function of the size and age of the collection.

Hebert and Noel (1982) carried out an international survey of copyright laws and their application in providing materials for disabled persons. They discussed general background and specific information on copyright: the handicapped population; social consequences of copyright; production of materials for handicapped persons (braille, audiotape, large print); copyright and materials for the handicapped (permission for original transcription and for redissemination); copyright legislation (existing copyright legislation, special provision for analogous purposes); legal mechanisms (e.g., exceptions, compulsory license, arbitration); international activities; and international copyright conventions. "Few countries have enacted special provisions for the handicapped in their copyright laws. Those special provisions which do exist differ greatly in the activities which they cover, the rights which they affect, and the conditions within which they operate" (p. 63). General recommendations included an international effort to determine the number of persons unable to read normal print, adoption of the standard definition "unable to read print because of a physical handicap" (p. 65), worldwide exchange of materials in special formats via interlibrary loan, and national union catalogs of special format materials. Copyright recommendations included, among others, recognition of the right of handicapped people to access to published information and the right of the copyright owner to remuneration. Hebert and Noel emphasized the necessity for agreement and action by the library community at both the national and international level, in order to improve access to materials through copyright provision for handicapped individuals.

TECHNOLOGY

This section includes research studies which investigated uses of technology to aid disabled library patrons. Two studies which investigate the use of technology for library operations in NLS system libraries are also included.

Technology to Aid Disabled Library Patrons

Three of these studies; by Stetten, Stetten and McElhaney, and Pors; are specifically addressed to libraries. The other studies are general ones which might have applications to libraries.

Stetten (1976) reported on a limited experimental application of a new method for electronic delivery of talking book services to the home. Telebook uses inexpensive bandwidth telecommunications to play recorded information directly to a person's home. The system utilizes centralized playback equipment and recordings along with a means for the operator to select and restart recordings upon individual request. Telebook provides immediate access to a large library of recorded material and eliminates delays in mail service, excessive handling of materials, shipping errors, and long waits for popular books. It also permits browsing and allows sighted operators to help patrons peruse the catalog. It was concluded that NLS would realize savings through centralization. The study was conducted in the Washington, D.C. area for 12 weeks. The operators were high school and college students who kept logs of transactions, a card file which showed where to restart books for each listener and a multi-indexed list of annotated books. Readers were given a subject indexed catalog of available books and a telephone amplifier. Telebook was also installed in about 20 institutions such as nursing homes and hospitals. Readers preferred books 10 to 1 over periodicals, and most readers listened for an hour at a time. Afternoons were the most popular listening time. It was concluded that the service was feasible technically and economically, and that it could be adequately staffed. Home users found Telebook convenient, simple to use, and quick to react to needs; 87% liked the service. All users could be instructed in proper use of the system without home visits. The system was little used in institutions, however. Major disadvantages in institutions were tying up telephone lines and the limited number of books available. Stetten believed both problems could be eliminated in a mature system.

Stetten and McElhaney (1978) reported on the third phase of the Telebook project. (A report on Phase II, which was the design for a larger and more sophisticated system, was not located.) In the third phase, Telebook service was offered to all qualified users in Franklin County, Ohio for nine months. The purpose was to determine the long-range feasibility of the Telebook System with special emphasis on long-term costs, user and institutional acceptability, and technical performance. The report was primarily a handbook and reference document for later users. Operating procedures for staff and cost projections were included. It was stated that most user information and conclusions on the overall utility, desirability, and feasibility would be issued later by the Library of Congress.

A study from Denmark (Pors, 1980) examined the extent to which persons with visual disabilities could use closed-circuit television for their reading and evaluated the extent to which the service should be provided in public libraries. The Frederiksberg Public Library in Copenhagen provided the service for a six week period. It was widely advertised in the mass media and through eye specialists and teachers. Librarians worked five hours a day to instruct patrons in use of the equipment and the library's resources. Over half of the 106 persons who used the service were aged 60 or older; 59 of them were female. Many came more than once, traveled long distances, and brought personal materials to read. Trials lasted from 15 to 60 minutes and included instruction in use of the equipment, a test of the patron's ability to use it, and individual use by the patron. Librarians completed information sheets after each trial. All of the persons who could read either regular print or large print could use the system. The majority preferred inverse video (white on black) and most magnification ranged from 2.0–6.0 mm. The 16 patrons who could not use the system included persons with very limited vision, persons who had lost the ability to read through lack of practice, and those who could not manage movement of the platform which held the material. However, only 58% indicated that they would use the system if it were regularly available; the rest either could still read print materials or had transportation problems that would preclude their coming to the library on a regular basis.

The remaining studies of technology for use by disabled persons are not library specific, but they have been included here to alert librarians to research in related fields which may be applicable in libraries.

Nolan (1976b) reported on three related experimental studies evaluating tonal-code systems which could be used for indexing audio recorded materials. In the first study, 100 sighted college students were used as subjects. Codes included long and short tones, low and high pitched tones, ascending and descending tones, a combination of the first two, and a combination of all three. Each group of 20 students was taught one code; the criterion for learning was two consecutive errorless trials. Long and short tones were far easier to learn than any of the others. In the second study, 21 braille or large print readers in grades 7–12 were taught to use the long and short tone codes in locating material in textbooks. The criterion was ability to locate exact book parts with 92% accuracy within an average time of two minutes. All students were able to learn to use the codes within 40 trials; the median was 11 trials. In the third study, three vocal index systems were tested for ease of use on cassette recordings: index information on the same track as the text content, use of parallel tracks on a four-track system, and use of Zindex (numeral announced on separate track). Subjects were 24 visually impaired students in grades 7–12. They received one hour of training in each system and were then tested on their ability to locate material. The index and text on the same track was most successful, but all systems were satisfactory for practical use.

Kerr, Hiltz, Whitescarver, and Prince (1979) reported on the first 10 months of a pilot study to test the feasibility of computerized conferencing to aid disadvantaged people; to discover the changes required in system features, user interface, and teaching procedures; and to assess social impact. A computer terminal was installed at the Cerebral Palsy Center of Belleville, New Jersey. Computer conferencing, as a tool of rehabilitation, was seen as potentially contributing to overall adjustment and as helping persons function productively in society. Computer conferencing links persons who are communicatively isolated; eliminates many potential communication problems, such as confusing nonverbal cues; and is interactive, thus promoting "connectedness". It was concluded that there is a high probability that computerized communication/information systems will neither be made available to nor designed for the needs of disabled persons. These field trials indicated, however, that such individuals would greatly profit from using these systems.

Cylke, Deschere, Evenson, and Gibson (1980) presented a review of research aimed at developing information service aids and programs for handicapped individuals. Three major research areas were discussed: electromechanical technology, tactile technology, and transfer devices and tools for hearing impaired individuals. The review focuses on the technologies, describes what was available at that time, and points out the need for an appropriate mechanism to disseminate information. The researchers suggest a diffusion network which includes existing information/data centers and the creation of research utilization laboratories and demonstration sites. They also suggest a need for articles on information technology in journals read by handicapped persons.

Green and Hopkins (1984) report on communication and telecommunication needs of cerebral palsied people in Canada. This is one of a series of Canadian studies about communication services for disabled persons. The other studies include *Communication and the Handicapped* (1978), *Communication Needs of the Deaf and Hard of Hearing* (1980), *Telecommunication Needs of the Blind and Otherwise Print Handicapped* (1981), and *Communication and Telecommunication Needs of the Speech-Impaired* (1983). The aims of the study discussed here were to identify Canadians who are communication impaired by cerebral palsy, to review the literature related to technology and the communication impaired, to survey those who use augmentative communication systems about current services, and to recommend government policy. Methodology included surveys of professionals, interviews with users of augmentative communication systems, and interviews with parents and teachers. The needs of the group were found to be similar to those of the population in general, but were more difficult to fulfill. The needs also overlapped with those of people with other disabilities. The cerebral palsied person was found to need a desire to communicate, a means to communicate, something to say, and a social setting in which to interact. To ensure the best possible service, the following interrelated aspects need to be considered: provision of information, resources, education, communication links, research, and community awareness. The establishment of regional communication resource centers was recommended.

Technology for Library Operations in the NLS System

Two studies of automated circulation systems in the NLS System appeared in 1981. Haaf, Wanger, and Cuadra reported the results of a survey on book circulation. NLS circulation differs from that in public libraries in two main ways: books are circulated by mail, and they are selected for the readers. The NLS regional libraries therefore have many unique problems. Many of these libraries undertook their own automation projects in the 1970s. The report included information on numbers of staff at the libraries, numbers of active borrowers, numbers of titles and copies/items, and annual circulation. Service objectives and system requirements for circulation systems were discussed, and suggestions for using a computerized materials selection system are given.

Wanger, Haaf, and Cuadra (1981) also prepared a report based on personal interviews with 19 network libraries (14 which had operational circulation systems in place and 5 which were well on the way to automation). The report focused on the general background of each library and its automation experience, and gave information about system capabilities. The automated libraries were generally well established and among the largest of the regional libraries. Three automation methods were discussed: systems purchased from commercial vendors, software packages developed under the direction of the regional library, or software acquired from another regional library and modified as needed. The report identified and described a master set of major circulation system requirements and design considerations and illustrated various implementations of these requirements in currently operational systems.

LIBRARY PROGRAMS FOR DISABLED PERSONS

This section discusses research on library programs for disabled persons. Although the total library program includes the provision of special materials, facilities, staff, and other resources, most of the studies in this section are limited to those which examine services offered to patrons to assist them in using the library and its materials. Most studies which examine the total program, or several of its components, are general surveys of particular libraries or library systems, and were discussed in the first section of this paper. Research on special materials and their provision was also separately discussed above. Five of the seven studies in this section concern programs for mentally retarded persons, and one concerns those who are developmentally disabled. (Developmental disability is a term often used synonymously with mental retardation, although it also includes other severe disabilities which occur during the developmental period.) The last study in this section discusses a reading program for blind children.

Sze (1976) developed a model for a public library program for slow learners aged 3–19. The slow learner was defined as "an intellectually subnormal person, whose mental slowness is the result of hereditary and/ or environmental causes during the developmental period" (p. vi). Program objectives were to help slow learners develop a sense of value, personal integrity and honesty; to help them achieve happiness through constructive use of powers, and develop a sense of pride in a task; and to help them develop such attributes as confidence, self-esteem, and self-direction. Provisions for access, facilities, personnel, materials, and program activities were included. These provisions were assigned to three levels of priority, based on costs, availability, and inclusiveness. The model was tested at three public library systems in the Chicago area to see if the services were currently being provided or were very likely to be provided in the future. All three systems provided, or expected to provide within two years, most of the first priority services. The library systems had few projections for new services in their long-range plans. The site criterion was perceived as too costly to carry out, and bookmobiles were rejected, probably because the model provided for each bookmobile to be devoted to a particular subject.

Ownby and Braun (1979) reported on a demonstration project whose purpose was "to design a replicable model for library service for the severely and profoundly mentally retarded" (p. i). The sample included 32 clients at a training center for mentally retarded persons. Of these, 8 were over age 21 (4 were moderately mentally retarded and 4, severely mentally retarded), and 24 were under 21 (12 were severely mentally retarded and 12, profoundly mentally retarded). Two clients were later dropped from the project for medical reasons. Individualized library programs were developed based on each client's Individualized Educational Program (IEP), which is required under the Education for All Handicapped Children Act (P.L.94–142). Each client spent 30 minutes per week in the program. Programs were defined as "teaching" and included work with fine-motor skills, attention span, communication skills and cognitive skills. Reinforcement was based upon the client's individual preference, and included praise, food, magazines, and records. Volunteers conducted about half the sessions. The authors concluded that individual programming in a library setting was moderately successful, and the residential care staff saw it as successful. Client and staff interest in the library increased. Problems encountered included client absenteeism and behavior problems, difficulties in transporting clients to the library, and volunteer turnover. The study recommended more training for volunteers and closer communication (including better feedback) with the supervisor.

Thwaits (1979) reported on a library instruction course, combined with a reading skills class, for developmentally disabled adults served by the College for Living Program at Colorado State University. This program offered courses through the University's Center for Continuing Education. The class was taught by volunteers, with a maximum of ten students and a minimum of two instructors per class. Objectives were for the student to: understand the function of the library; be able to check out and return materials; learn to locate basic information using dictionaries, encyclopedias, and almanacs; look up topics using subject, author, and title cards and locate material on shelves; look up a periodical and locate it. Pre and post-tests were given, but there was no control group. All students were "good" readers; they had finished the 12th grade in special education. The report is primarily an analysis of the progress of two students in a case study format. The researcher concluded that the students did learn to locate books with guidance. The time factor was seen as prohibitive because students needed extra time. Although the two courses worked well together, combining library instruction with reading meant that time for each was limited. Lack of appropriate (simple) reading material in a research library was a problem. It was felt that the course would work better in a public library.

Another model program ("Developing a Public Library-Type Service," 1977). was developed at Pennhurst Center (Pennsylvania). A school library on the premises was changed into a public library-type facility for all ages. The program's objectives were to develop a library to which the mentally retarded citizens of the center would come on their own to choose, borrow, and return materials; to gain understanding of literature through reading, looking at pictures, hearing books read, and witnessing program presentations; to locate and make some use of reference books; and to exhibit more normal, mature behavior. Use of the library by staff members of the center was also an objective. The program involved 23 regularly scheduled 45-minute classes per week (seven were held in residential areas for those who could not come to the library). There were also 18 hours a week of open time, including some hours on Saturdays and in the evening. The program was judged successful in providing an atmosphere of enrichment, creativity, and enjoyment of literature, art, music, and nature. Citizens exhibited responsibility in borrowing and use of materials. Spot checks of comprehension showed that only 2% had no comprehension of the material at all, 13% knew the title, 65% had some knowledge of the content, and 20% had a thorough understanding of the content.

Newberry (1980) reported a model program (Project Leisure-Time Alternatives) at Sunland-Marianna, a Florida institution for mentally retarded persons. The aims of the program were to acquaint residents with library services, equipment, and materials; and to train and inspire them to make decisions about their use of leisure time. Audiovisual materials and equipment, games, puzzles, magazines, books, and pets were purchased for the project. Three-week orientation programs were provided for all residents. The first week was spent with high interest recreational activities, and the second in learning equipment use. Attendance, enthusiasm, and equipment competence were recorded. Nonscheduled library use was encouraged, but such library use was confusing to institutional staff as they planned activities. Clients exhibited passivity, but there were no serious behavior problems. The author concluded that a market does exist for traditional and innovative library services in institutions for mentally retarded persons.

Breivik (1981) reported on a Norwegian project in Tromso County Library. The project included building a collection of media, testing it, and planning for its use with mentally retarded individuals. A permanent collection was maintained at the County library and duplicates were placed in schools and institutions. The materials were mostly books and slides to use with picture books. Aims in testing the material included connecting books with a library setting, kindling interest in books, and teaching how to use the library. Books were introduced to mentally retarded persons (all ages) and those which the clients chose and ignored were observed. Picture books were popular; those without pictures had little or no appeal. Simple easy-reading books were not usually selected unless they were presented and recommended by the librarian. Fairytales were popular, as were nonfiction books with good pictures and books in large format. Picture books with slides taken from their illustrations were popular. Finding suitable books for adults and young adults was the most difficult problem. Clients in schools and institutions were given systematic instruction in how to borrow books and attempts were made to motivate them to use the library. Public librarians also visited classes. After the training was completed, the mentally retarded clients visited the public library and were encouraged to return again on their own. The author's observation was that the program was a success. Prior planning, systematic planning, and cooperation were rated as very important.

Lee (1981) compared two READ-a-thon programs at the Tennessee School for the Blind. She compared a Multiple Sclerosis READ-a-thon program carried out in 1978 at the school with an experimental READ-a-thon program developed specially for the school in 1980. She concluded that both programs stimulated greater interest in pleasure reading, but there was no clear indication that experimental project collection in large print, braille and recordings was "an indispensable ingredient" (p. 61). She discovered that short, high interest stories were needed because of the great incidence of multiply handicapped readers at the school.

ATTITUDES TOWARD DISABLED PERSONS

Attitude is one of the major barriers which disabled persons face: their own attitude toward their disabilities, and the attitudes of other persons toward them. Two studies have studied attitude toward disabled persons in a library context.

An empirical study by Dequin and Faibisoff (1981) used the Attitudes Toward Disabled Persons (ATDP) scale developed by Harold Yukor to compare the attitudes of librarians toward disabled people with the attitudes of other professionals. The survey was conducted among able-bodied librarians in public libraries of Illinois. The effects of age, close contact with persons with disabilities, and attendance at workshops and seminars about disability were correlated with the results of the attitudinal survey. General attitudes about disabled persons were positive. Men were slightly more positive than women, and younger respondents than older ones. Persons with no contact with disabled people were as positive as those with one or more contacts, although persons with disabled family members had more positive attitudes than persons with disabled friends. Attendance at workshops and seminars did not affect respondents' attitudes.

Dresang (1981) studied the effects of media upon students' attitudes toward disabled persons. In a pre and post-test experimental design, 120 sixth-grade students were randomly assigned to six groups. The students were presented with media about mainstreaming and disabilities. Independent variables were method (communication conditions) and material (media in relation to selection conditions). Material was presented under two communication conditions: user input or no user input prior to media selection. Material was chosen under three selection conditions: choice of materials based on student-expressed interests, choice based on teacher and librarian perception of student interests, and choice unrelated to student interests. Dependent variables were information retention (checked with multiple choice test), positive difference in attitude (as shown by Semantic Differential test), and positive difference in intended behavioral change (shown with Sociometric test). In an exploratory follow-up phase of the study, 16 students were interviewed to determine uses they had for information presented in the media. Groups receiving media based on student-expressed interests exhibited more positive attitudes toward disability; the results were statistically significant ($p<.05$). Dresang attributed the absence of positive attitudes toward mainstreaming to a lack of available material on this subject. Although communication conditions did not yield significant results, the exploratory data suggested that such conditions did have an impact. The study emphasized the role of the librarian as media and communication specialist.

LIBRARY PERSONNEL AND DISABILITY

Seven studies have investigated library personnel in relation to disabilities. Two of these reports have studied personnel in libraries which serve disabled persons. The other five have studied employment of librarians who are themselves disabled.

A survey of resource center personnel in schools for the deaf was made by Huff (1974). This was the first project of the Association of Resource Personnel Serving the Hearing Impaired. The purposes of the study were to provide information for administrators in comparing their schools to others, to establish a basis for formulating standards of certification, and to point out training needs. A questionnaire was sent to 130 residential and day schools in the United States; the 67% response rate included most of the largest and/or best known schools. There were more responses from public schools, both residential and day, than from private ones. A wide divergence in the number of personnel was found. Larger schools, as would be expected, employed more personnel; public residential schools employed more people than did public day schools, and private schools employed fewer. The best situations were two schools with seven full-time employees. Schools reported that 60% of the personnel were professionals, and 30% were part-time. Of the 74 librarians, 7 had library science degrees (level was not specified) and 21 others had studied some library science. Most had been educated in the field of deaf education; 46% had the B.S. degree in some area, 45% the M.S., and 9% had no degree.

Applied Management Sciences, Inc. (1980) evaluated the use of volunteers in the NLS system. Data was collected through a mail survey of each network agency. Information included the number of volumes held by the library, number of hours donated by volunteers, cost assessments, and conformity to ALA standards. Telephone interviews with staff of network agencies gave added information on the characteristics of effective programs and problems associated with volunteers. The report showed that 76.6% of the agencies used a total of 10,937 volunteers in production, repair, circulation and maintenance, reader services, outreach, and administration. The estimated value of their time was $3,940,121 in 1979. The net value of the NLS volunteer program, after deduction of $1,000,808 in administrative costs, was $2,939,313. Over half of the ALA standards were met by 50% of the agencies. The highest ratio of volunteer time versus cost was in reader services, including such activities as reading in homes, delivering materials, and transporting patrons. Volunteers were also efficient in repair work, in tape inspection, and in narration and monitoring of the production of recordings in large libraries. The least effective use of volunteers was in production of materials in libraries with less than 1000 readers. Optimum use of volunteers in any category depended on their training and supervision by regular staff. It was recommended that NLS review its overall strategy for providing technical assistance to network agencies in the area of volunteers. NLS expertise in publicity to attract volunteers, management and supervision, and in the production of training materials could be of great help to the network libraries. Twelve other recommendations concerned methods for carrying out the previous recommendations.

Studies by Pritchard; Bryan; Wilson; the President's Committee on the Employment of the Handicapped; and Warren have explored the employment of disabled persons as librarians. Pritchard (1937) tried to find out if a blind person could become a librarian in a library for the blind where the materials were all in braille. She sent out letters to library schools, public libraries, and the Library of Congress. Two of 24 library schools reported having one blind student each in one or two classes. Responses regarding professional education ranged from seeing complete training as a librarian as impractical but favoring a special course emphasizing books in braille, to recommending private tutoring, to suggesting on-the-job training. Three public libraries reported that they currently employed or had previously employed a blind staff member in their library for the blind. They noted advantages in contacts with the blind community, demonstrations of reading braille, proofreading braille materials, operating talking books, and in using a blind person as a stenographer or an executive. The Library of Congress Service to the Blind was not able at that time to use blind staff because of the detailed record keeping necessary in a format requiring sight. At Britain's National Library for the Blind, all seven employees, except the director, were blind. All records were kept in braille. The chief librarian of the Canadian National Institute for the Blind was blind, and saw administration as no problem, although he felt that efficiency might be reduced in handling books and ink correspondence. The Library of the Valentin Hauy Association for the Blind in Paris reported only one sighted employee. Pritchard concluded that positions were available for blind librarians in libraries for the blind; that they were more likely to be employed in institutions for the blind than in public libraries serving the blind; that there were some advantages to having a blind administrator, but at least one sighted person was needed on the staff; a college education was needed; and that at that time library education had been best achieved on the job.

Bryan (1952), in a study of public librarians carried out for ALA, studied employment of handicapped persons. Special attention was given to disabled veterans. Library administrators at two-fifths of the libraries reported no stated policy regarding the employment of disabled veterans, and 36% of the libraries had none with regard to handicapped nonveterans. All but one metropolitan library reported no policy for employment of handicapped persons. Even fewer small libraries had policies; in some cases, the director indicated this was because no disabled person had ever applied. About one-sixth of the libraries reporting had policies precluding the hiring of any handicapped person. Only one library gave preference to disabled veterans. About two-fifths of the libraries said they employed the best qualified person, whether handicapped or not. Two-thirds of the libraries had no employees who were handicapped enough to "materially interfere with efficient service" (p. 190). Employees who were physically handicapped "to the detriment of service" were reported by 16% of the libraries, and 22% reported employing persons who were mentally handicapped to this extent. Both professional and subprofessional employees were included in this assessment. Administrators reported that they had difficulty in supervising employees who were emotionally disturbed, because they feared that the employees might claim that they had been unfairly treated.

E. C. Wilson (1962) sought to determine the extent to which academic librarians would consider hiring professional librarians who were physically disabled "provided that their disabilities would not interfere with performance" (p. ii), what types of disabled persons they would employ and in what positions. She hypothesized that most colleges and universities had no official policy on hiring disabled people, that larger libraries with more specialization were more likely to hire disabled librarians, and that most libraries preferred to place their disabled employees behind the scenes. Wilson found that 84% of the respondents said they would hire disabled persons, and 8% said they would not. Disabled persons were currently employed or had been employed by 23% of the reporting libraries. Persons with the following disabilities were most often hired or most likely to be hired: diabetes; disability of one foot, leg, hand, or arm; heart disease; arrested tuberculosis; or partial deafness. The greatest employment opportunities were in behind-the-scenes positions rather than in administration or public services. All hypotheses were thus confirmed.

A study conducted by the President's Committee on Employment of the Handicapped ("Handicapped Working in Libraries," 1976) reported that handicapped people worked in libraries in positions ranging from director to page. A total of 1,399 libraries (public, academic, and regional) reported 907 full-time and 358 part-time disabled employees in 607 libraries. The survey found that "libraries go beyond local or state Merit or Civil Service registers to recruit personnel" (p. 657).

Warren (1979) studied the effects of physical and psychological barriers on the professional careers of physically handicapped librarians in the Southeastern United States. Subjects included 48 librarians in 30 libraries which had at least 20 professionals on the staff. Warren found that one out of five handicapped librarians had been denied a position because of disability; for those who were hearing impaired, the figure nearly doubled. The librarians worked in all aspects of library service and were active in continuing education. They were typically aggressive, optimistic, and self-confident. Many had held administrative positions, and a majority would choose the career again. Psychological barriers were thought to be as important as physical barriers in their careers. Only nominal expenditures had been necessary to accommodate the physical needs of the respondents in their positions. Warren concluded that the attitudes of many library directors must change; "library administrators must accept responsibility for many of the handicapped librarians' problems" (p. 117).

MISCELLANEOUS STUDIES

One study was located which does not fit into any of the previous categories. It concerns the problem of identifying disabled populations. In Nebraska, Sallach (1967) surveyed physicians, nursing homes, and county welfare offices to determine the number and distribution of handicapped persons eligible for library services. A high percentage of the physically handicapped youth of the state were located in metropolitan areas; more women than men were handicapped among older citizens, but fewer women were handicapped among the younger group; older persons were more likely to be institutionalized; and there were more physically handicapped persons per 10,000 population in smaller communities than in larger ones.

CONCLUSIONS

This paper has reviewed research concerned with library services and disabled persons. In conclusion, general characteristics of this research will be discussed, as well as certain problems connected with it.

Characteristics of the Research

Most of the research concerned with library services and disabled persons is descriptive in nature. The most common methodology used in these studies was that of the survey. Slightly over half of the research studies discussed in this paper reported findings generated by surveys of library services to disabled patrons conducted at the local, state or province, national, or international levels. Survey methodology was also used extensively in most other areas including user needs and interests, library materials and formats, and personnel. Examples of other research designs, such as the experimental, were seldom found; hypotheses were only occasionally explicitly postulated; and statistical analysis beyond the descriptive level (such as percentages, frequency distributions, and histograms) was rarely utilized. With the exception of research conducted by and for NLS and its predecessor DBPH, few studies were designed to replicate or expand upon previous work, in an attempt either to lend further support to prior findings or to produce evidence leading towards revision, expansion, or rejection of those findings.

One-third of the research originated as studies performed to meet academic requirements: doctoral dissertations, master's and specialist's theses, and student papers. The majority of this work was performed in Library Science departments, but approximately half of the dissertations were done in departments of Education. There are also a number of studies conducted or funded by various departments of the United States Government, especially the Library of Congress and the Office of Education. A limited number of such studies were funded by various state governments, national governments of other countries, and international organizations such as UNESCO. In addition, library organizations and organizations specifically concerned with disabled persons (such as the American Foundation for the Blind) have provided a limited amount of sponsorship. A large amount of work has been performed as projects of individuals or individual libraries, without external funding or official sponsorship.

Most of the research concerned with library services and disabled persons has been performed in recent years. Although the earliest study was reported in 1903, it was more than a quarter-century before another study appeared, and only 11.4% of the reported research took place before 1960. The next decade produced 15.8% of the studies; 41.2% appeared in the 1970s, and 31.6% was reported from 1980 to 1984. This pattern is consistent with the growth in recent years of library research and with the current interest, at both the national and international levels, in all kinds of services for disabled persons. As already mentioned, research activity in the United States is also consistent with Federal legislation which has affected library services to disabled persons: the passage of the Pratt-Smoot Act in 1931; the increase of service to physically disabled persons in 1966, due to the extension of service to this population by the Library of Congress and at the state level through LSCA Title IV–B; the passage of the Rehabilitation Act of 1973 and the regulations for implementation of its Section 504 which were issued in 1977; and the passage of the Education of All Handicapped Children Act in 1975.

Problems Relating to the Research

Certain problems arise when one attempts to locate and utilize the findings of the research reviewed here. One problem is simply the lack of such reported research. Less than 115 studies were located. A related problem is that existing research is concentrated in certain areas, while other and perhaps equally important topics are virtually ignored. Surveys of library service, current or past, make up half of the research. Services in NLS system libraries, public libraries, and academic libraries have been most thoroughly investigated. Surprisingly, given the large body of existing educational research dealing with the needs of disabled children, very few surveys have attempted to examine services in school library media centers. In the United States, more than half the surveys which did deal with school library media centers involved those in schools for the deaf. Studies of user interests and format needs, and of library materials for disabled persons made up 25% of the studies. Almost all the studies were limited to those individuals with physical disabilities: blindness and visual impairments, deafness and hearing impairments, and mobility and dexterity impairments. Rarely have studies endeavored to address problems of library services to those with mental disabilities, except in the area of library programming. Unfortunately, those are limited almost entirely to programming for mentally retarded persons, and are further limited by focusing almost entirely upon those in institutions. One very important area which has been virtually ignored in terms of formal structured investigation is that of attitudes toward disabled patrons.

Another problem is the general lack of bibliographic control of the research dealing with library services and disabled persons. It is very difficult to locate materials in this area, and the serendipity factor can quickly assume major proportions. The many ways of describing disabilities and the lack of standardized terminology create great difficulty in locating relevant information. In addition, the retrieval process is further exacerbated by the lack of a comprehensive source which might collect the research reports which are currently scattered throughout many databases, indexes, abstracts, and bibliographies. Finally, and perhaps most discouraging, many studies are simply not listed at all. Locating the research often seems comparable to solving a mystery; one never knows when a fresh and frustrating clue will crop up. For example, when this paper was nearly complete, the authors came upon a reference (in Thorn, 1978) to a Canadian survey of library services which formed the basis for the 1978 Australian National Survey of Library Services for Handicapped People. Despite concerted effort, no further information about the Canadian survey was located.

The lack of dissemination of research is a related problem. Only one-third of the reported research located had been published as journal articles, and of these, many appeared in specialized and occasionally obscure journals which are often difficult to locate. One-fourth of the studies were available as ERIC microfiche; in a few cases, the ERIC microfiche duplicated research reports available in journal articles. Fully 40% of the research which was located is available only in limited distribution: dissertations and unpublished master's and specialist's theses, which may or may not be available through interlibrary loan; unpublished studies or ones which had limited distribution, usually sponsored by NLS, other governmental bodies, or private organizations and foundations which may still have copies available; and unpublished papers done by individuals and individual libraries, which can sometimes be obtained from the authors.

Undoubtedly, the most serious problem, both for persons wishing to use the research in future studies and those interested in utilizing the original study, is an extreme lack of quality control. The studies conducted by or for NLS and most of those funded by other governmental bodies, both in the United States and abroad, are generally large, well-conducted studies by capable researchers. Other appropriately designed, conducted, and reported studies can be found. However, many studies exhibit substantially lower quality. Studies are generally noncumulative; they do not build upon previous research or test conclusions drawn by other researchers. Much research is highly localized without adequate sample description, and therefore not generalizable to other situations. Although the research is often undertaken to meet a specific need, its use as the basis for action is problematic, since there are very rarely any reports of implementation of its recommendations or of further research on the situation. Weak or inappropriate research design is often found. Frequently found problems, including a lack of hypotheses, poorly described population samples, undefined or indistinct terminology and variables, lack of validated instruments, unsophisticated or unsuitable statistical methods, unwarranted assumptions, inappropriate generalizations, lack of objectivity, and poor reporting of the research, result in a considerable body of seriously flawed research. Users of research must therefore carefully evaluate the research which is reported before utilizing the results.

The low quality of much of the research is due to the fact that many persons interested in the field commonly have little knowledge of research methods. As already stated, one-third of the studies were originated by students as part of the requirements for a course or a degree. Few students, even at the doctoral level, are knowledgeable enough to produce exemplary research. Unfortunately, the faculty members who direct student research may also lack needed expertise. Most library science faculties have at most one or two members who are interested in and knowledgeable about library services and disabled persons. These faculty members may or may not be well-versed in research methodology; lack of such expertise was especially common in the past, when fewer faculty members held doctoral degrees. In the case of doctoral dissertations, the problem is compounded, since half the degrees are earned in departments of Education (usually in educational administration), where faculty members may know little or nothing about the unique environments and requirements of libraries.

The second group of people who are likely to undertake research in this field are practitioners who work with disabled patrons or who are themselves disabled. These persons also may have had little or no training in research design and in addition, may have had only very limited opportunities to develop such expertise in the field. More significantly, however, they are likely to be strong advocates for library services for disabled persons. This can be an advantage, but it can also lead to bias in designing research instruments or interpreting the findings. All too often, the advocacy role of librarians in the field does not allow for the neutrality, objectivity, patience and willingness which is required if one is to subject cherished ideas to the tests of rigorous research.

A final problem is the *ad hoc* nature of the research. There is no tradition of systematic research in the field and no generally agreed-upon framework or agenda which determines research needs and priorities. There is a general lack of interest in and support of research in this field. In times of tight budgets, administrators are often reluctant to fund studies which are perceived as benefitting only a limited group. This is an area in which the strong advocacy role of librarians in the field could be of value. The high motivation of these librarians, when combined with training in and a strong commitment to appropriate research methods, could produce the quality which is needed in the research to justify and improve programs and services for disabled persons. Many of the studies reported in this paper raise interesting questions which should be investigated further. Research concerning library services and disabled persons is still very sparse; the field certainly invites further and more rigorous study.

REFERENCES

Research Reports:

Allen, A. (1977). Survey results: DuPage Library System Subregional Library for the Blind and Physically Handicapped. *Illinois Libraries, 59,* 269–271.

Applied Management Sciences, Inc. (1980). *An evaluation of volunteers in the National Library Service for the Blind and Physically Handicapped. Final report.* Silver Springs, MD: Author. (ERIC Document Reproduction Service No. ED 197 731)

Armstrong, D. J. (1967). Survey of public library service to hospitals, the homebound and prisons. *Library and Information Bulletin, 1*(4), 113–118.

Atinmo, M. I. (1979). Public and school library services to the physically handicapped in Nigeria: An evaluation. *International Library Review, 11,* 441–449.

Bell, L. J. (1980). *The large print book and its user.* London: Library Association.

Bond, E. G. (1932). *Service to the blind by state libraries.* Unpublished master's thesis, Columbia University, New York.

Bowen, D., Self, S., Broadway, M., Abbott, J., & Swetnam, M. L. (1983, May). *Library needs and uses by disabled students at the Florida State University: A survey.* Paper presented at the Conference on Academic Library Services to Disabled Students, Tallahassee, FL. (ERIC Document Reproduction Service No. ED 240 756)

Breivik, M. (1981). Use of books and libraries give greater possibilities to mentally retarded children, young people and adults. *Scandinavian Public Library Quarterly, 14,* 46–49.

Brewer, K., & McClaskey, H. (1976, Spring). Survey of state library agencies. *HRLSD Journal,* pp. 15–16.

Bryan, A. I. (1952). *The public librarian.* New York: Columbia University Press.

Buckley, C. W. (1978/1979). Media services for exceptional students: An exploratory study of the practices and perceptions of library media specialists in selected Southern states. From *Dissertation Abstracts International, 39,* 5781A.

Carter, W. A. (1982/1983). Library media centers in public day schools for the deaf (Doctoral dissertation, University of Oklahoma, 1982). *Dissertation Abstracts International, 43,* 2861A.

Chandler, J. G. (1977, June). ACB reader survey: Statistical findings. *Braille Forum, 15,* 16–18.

Connor, A. (1981, November). A comparison of traditional large type and microfiche as reading modes for low vision students. *Journal of Micrographics, 14,* 32–38.

Cory, P. B. (1966). *Report on phase 1—School library programs in schools for the deaf* (Contract No. OEC04–19–066). Convention of the American Instructors for the Deaf. (ERIC Document Reproduction Service No. ED 031 833)

Cylke, F. K., Deschere, A. R., Evenson, R. H., & Gibson, M. C. (1980). Research to develop information service aids and programs for handicapped individuals. *Drexel Library Quarterly, 16*(2), 59–72.

Dale, B., & Dewdney, P. (1972). Canadian public libraries and the physically handicapped. *Canadian Library Journal, 29*, 231–236. Also in: *Public library service for the physically handicapped*. Ottawa: Canadian Library Association. (ERIC Document Reproduction Service No. ED 067 797)

Davie, J. F. (1980, Fall). A survey of school library media resources for exceptional students in Florida public schools. *Florida Media Quarterly, 6*, 9–13. Also from *Dissertation Abstracts International, 40*, 4786A.

Delvalle, J., Miller, D. B., & Saldicco, M. (1966). Reading patterns of the aged in a nursing home environment. *AHIL Quarterly, 6*, 8–11.

Dequin, H., & Faibisoff, S. (1981, July). Results of an attitudinal survey. In K. Kraus & E. Biscoe (Eds.), *Summary proceedings of a symposium on educating librarians and information scientists to provide information and library services to blind and physically handicapped individuals* (pp. 6–9). Washington, D.C.: National Library Service for the Blind and Physically Handicapped, Library of Congress. Also: (ERIC Document Reproduction Service No. ED 214 504)

DeVeaux, P. (1982). Academic library service to handicapped college and university students (Doctoral dissertation, George Peabody College for Teachers of Vanderbilt University, 1982). *Dissertation Abstracts International, 43*, 1849A.

Developing a public library type service adapted for mentally retarded citizens. Final report. (1977). Spring City, PA: Pennhurst Center. (ERIC Document Reproduction Service No. ED 167 142)

Dresang, E. T. (1981). Communication conditions and media influence on attitudes and information uses: the effects of library materials selected in response to student interest about mainstreaming and disabilities. From *Dissertation Abstracts International, 43*, 294A.

Evenson, R. H. (1974). *Report on Braille Reader Survey*. Washington, D.C.: Library of Congress, Division for the Blind and Physically Handicapped. (ERIC Document Reproduction Service No. ED 100 320)

Gallimore, J. E. (1973). *Criteria for the selection and evaluation of book and non-book materials for mentally retarded adolescents and adults*. Unpublished master's thesis, California State University, San Jose.

Goldstein, D. (1953). *The Library for the Blind of the New York Public Library*. Unpublished master's thesis, Drexel Institute of Technology, Philadelphia.

Gorman, P. (1980). Disabled library users at Monash University. *Australian Academic Research Libraries, 11*, 111–123.

Goss, T. C. (1978). *Model library services for the hearing handicapped*. Nova University. (ERIC Document Reproduction Service No. ED 167 163)

Grafton, C. E. (1940). *Library service to the adult blind in the Midwestern States*. Unpublished master's thesis, University of Chicago.

Green, C. S. (1967). *Library service to the blind in the United States: Origins and development to 1931*. Unpublished master's thesis, University of Chicago.

Green, J. R., & Hopkins, B. J. (1984). *Communication and telecommunication needs of the cerebral palsied population in Canada*. Government of Canada, Department of Communications, Ottawa.

Haaf, J. W., Wanger, J., & Cuadra, R. N. (1981). Report on automation in libraries serving the blind and physically handicapped. *ASIS Conference Proceedings, 18*, 74–76.

Handicapped working in libraries. (1976). *Library Journal, 101*, 657.

Hebert, F. & Noel, W. (1982). *Copyright and library material for the handicapped: A study prepared for the International Federation of Library Associations and Institutions*. New York: K. G. Saur Munchen.

Hillman, J. (1982). Services for disabled users in the Robertson Library. *Australian Academic Research Libraries, 13*, 113–122.

Huff, A. (1974). Personnel survey of resource centers in schools for the deaf. *American Annals for the Deaf, 119,* 358–360.

Hviid, I. (1983). Children's use of talking books. *Scandinavian Public Library Quarterly, 16,* 97–98.

Irwin, R. B. (1929). Survey of library work for the blind in the United States and Canada. *ALA Bulletin, 23,* 250–252.

Jackson, K. M. (1982). A study of the accessibility of college and university libraries to handicapped students since passage of the Rehabilitation Act of 1973. College Station: Texas A & M University. *Dissertation Abstracts International, 43,* 1851A.

Jahoda, G., & Needham, W. L. (1980). *The current state of public library service to physically handicapped persons.* Unpublished manuscript, Florida State University, Tallahassee.

Johns, J. J. (1973). *Services of Cleveland Public Library's Braille and Talking Book Department compared with standards formulated by the Commission on Standards and Accreditation of Services for the Blind.* Unpublished master's thesis, Kent State University, Kent, OH.

Josephson, E. (1964). A study of blind readers. *ALA Bulletin, 58,* 543–547.

Jurrist, B. (1970). *The Talking Book and its use in the libraries of Nassau County, New York.* Unpublished master's thesis, Long Island University, Greenville, NY.

Kennedy, H. T. (1903). *Libraries in state schools for the deaf.* Unpublished bachelor's thesis, University of Illinois, Urbana.

Kenney, A. P. (1981, October). Independent minds: Scholarship and disability. *Scholarly Publishing, 13,* 79–91.

Kerr, E. B., Hiltz, S. R., Whitescarver, J., & Prince, S. (1979). Applications of computer conferencing to the disadvantaged: Preliminary results of field trials with handicapped children. *ASIS Conference Proceedings, 16,* 149–158.

Kim, R. A. (1976). *Public library service to the deaf and hearing impaired.* Unpublished master's thesis, University of Missouri, Columbia.

Korlaske, R. (1974). *An analysis of library policies and services in six Missouri state mental institutions.* Unpublished master's thesis, University of Missouri, Columbia.

Langan, K. M. (1984). *Assessment of the provision of library services to the blind and physically handicapped.* Unpublished manuscript, Oberlin College, Oberlin, OH.

Latham, Glenn. (1976). *Teacher use of instructional materials and other matters related to special education IMC/LRC collections.* (Theoretical Paper No. 59). Madison: Wisconsin University, Research & Development Center for Cognitive Learning. (ERIC Document Reproduction Service No. ED 126 663)

Lee, L. S. (1981). *A comparison of two Read-a-thon programs at the Tennessee School for the Blind.* Unpublished specialist's thesis, George Peabody College for Teachers, Vanderbilt University, Nashville, TN.

Lewis, F. (1978). *Serving deaf people in the public library.* Unpublished manuscript. State University of New York, Albany.

Library of Congress, National Library Service for the Blind and Physically Handicapped. (1983). *Braille reader survey: Survey findings.* Washington, D.C.: Author. (ERIC Document Reproduction Service No. ED 234 522)

Little, Arthur D., Inc. (1967). *A plan for library cooperation in Vermont. Report to the Vermont Free Public Library Service* (Report No. C69224). Boston, MA: Author. (ERIC Document Reproduction Service No. ED 030 450)

Ludlow, F., Henderson, J., Murray, L. & Rawkins, R. (1972). A survey of national organizations for the handicapped, based in Toronto. *Canadian Library Journal, 29,* 310–318. Also in: *Public library services for the physically handicapped.* Ottawa: Canadian Library Association. (ERIC Document Reproduction Service No. ED 067 797)

Major, J. A. (1978, May). The visually impaired reader in the academic library. *College and Research Libraries. 39,* 191–196.

Martin, P. (1970). *Library services for the handicapped in Maine: A state of the art report.* Unpublished master's thesis, Catholic University, Washington, D.C.

Masek, E. L. (1973). *Public library services to the blind and partially sighted in the United States and Canada: An annotated bibliography.* Unpublished master's thesis, Kent State University, Kent, OH.

Mayer, M., & Cylke, F. K. (1979). *African braille production: A statistical review and evaluation of countries and costs* (Contract No. UNESCO594960). Washington, DC: Library of Congress, Division for the Blind and Physically Handicapped. (ERIC Document Service No. 176 770)

McCrossan, J., Swank, R., & Yacuzzo, D. (1968). *Library services for the handicapped in Ohio.* Kent, OH: Kent State University, School of Library Science. (ERIC Document Reproduction Service No. ED 020 758)

McLaughlin, J., & Andrews, J. (1975). The reading habits of deaf adults in Baltimore. *American Annals of the Deaf, 120,* 497–501.

Moon, V. (1983). *Report on library services to disabled persons in New South Wales, 1983* (Report No. ISBN0–7305–0095–0). Sydney: Library Council of New South Wales. (ERIC Document Service No. 249 721)

National Library of Australia. (1978). *Report on the National Survey of Library Services for Handicapped People.* Canberra: Author.

National Library of Australia, Working Party on Library Services for the Handicapped. (1979). *Report of the Working Party on Library Services for the Handicapped, April, 1979.* Canberra: Author.

Nelson Associates. (1969). *Division for the Blind and Physically Handicapped, Library of Congress. A survey of reader characteristics, reading interests, and equipment preferences; A study of circulation systems in selected regional libraries.* New York: Author.

New York Public Library. (1969). *Large print book project: A report.* New York: Author.

New York Public Library, Office of Adult Services, Large-Print Book Project. (1967). *Annual report of administrative assistant, June 15, 1966–June 14, 1967.* Unpublished manuscript.

Newberry, W. F. (1980). The last unserved: Are public libraries ready to mainstream mentally retarded patrons? *American Libraries, 11*(4), 218–220.

Nolan, C. Y. (1976a). *Facilitating the education of the visually handicapped through research in communications: 15 November 1972–30 April 1976. Final report. Part three: Facilitating tactile map reading* (Grant No. OEG0–73–0642). Louisville, KY: American Printing House for the Blind. (ERIC Document Reproduction Service No. ED 133 926)

Nolan, C. Y. (1976b). *Facilitating the education of the visually handicapped through research in communications: 15 November 1972–30 April 1976. Final report. Part two: Index for tape recordings* (Grant No. OEG–0–73–0642). Louisville, KY: American Printing House for the Blind. (ERIC Document Reproduction Service No. ED 133 925)

Opocensky, V. L. (1975/1976). A comparison of library-media centers in public residential schools for the deaf with *Standards for Library-Media Centers in Schools for the Deaf.* (Doctoral dissertation, University of Nebraska, 1975). *Dissertation Abstracts International, 36,* 7820A.

Ownby, M., & Braun, S. (1979). *A demonstration project of model library programs for institutionalized mentally retarded and multiply handicapped persons* (Grant No. 6007801812). Fairfax, VA: Northern Virginia Training Center for the Mentally Retarded. (ERIC Document Reproduction Service No. ED 183 169)

Parkin, D. (1974). *The university library: A study of services offered the blind.* Provo, UT: Brigham Young University, Graduate School of Library and Information Science. (ERIC Document Reproduction Service No. ED 102 972)

Pemberton, J. M. (1982). Services to the disabled in Tennessee libraries. *Tennessee Librarian, 34,* 20–37.

Petersen, J. (1979, August). *The handicapped in reading and the public library.* Paper presented at the Conference of the International Federation of Library Associations and Institutions, 45th, Copenhagen, Denmark. (ERIC Document Reproduction Service No. ED 185 993)

Petersen, J. (1983). Library service for the blind in Denmark and Sweden. *Scandinavian Public Library Quarterly, 16,* 2–7.

Pors, B. (1980). Experimental provision of closed circuit television at a public library. *Visual Impairment and Blindness, 74,* 102–104.

Pritchard, M. C. (1937). Vocation for the blind. *Library Journal, 62,* 579–581.

Readership characteristics and attitudes: Service to blind and physically handicapped users. (1981). Washington, DC: Public Sector Research Group of Market Facts, Inc.

Rice, C. (1983, August). Wolfner Memorial Library user survey, 1983. *Show-Me-Libraries,* 27–30.

Riddell, M. (1940). A survey of the reading interests of the blind. *Library Journal, 65,* 189–192.

St. John, F. R. (1957). *Survey of Library Service for the Blind 1956.* New York: American Foundation for the Blind.

Sallach, D. (1967). *A survey of the physically handicapped of Nebraska, the parameters of expanded library service.* Lincoln, NE: Public Library Commission. (ERIC Document Reproduction Service No. ED 025 275).

Schauder, D. E., and Cram, M. D. (1977). *Libraries for the blind—An international study of policies and practices.* Stevenage, England: Peter Peregrinus.

Sheffield, H. G. (1951). *A report on the history and development of the Library for the Blind of the Cleveland Public Library.* Unpublished master's thesis, Western Reserve University, Cleveland, OH.

Simpson, A. (1972). A survey of organizations and institutions serving the physically handicapped in British Columbia. *Canadian Library Journal, 29,* 319–326. Also in: *Public library services for the physically handicapped.* Ottawa: Canadian Library Association. (ERIC Document Reproduction Service No. ED 067 797)

Simpson, S. (1976). Promoting services for the physically handicapped—No startling new truth. *Library Association Record, 78,* 356,370.

Smalley, A. W., & Mendenhall, K. (1983). *Final report on the State-of-the-Network: An evaluation of NLS, the Regional Libraries, and the Multistate Centers in relation to ALA Standards of Service for Blind and Physically Handicapped.* Columbus, OH: Battelle.

Spilman, E. (1964). *Reading choices of the patients of the Seton Psychiatric Institute.* Unpublished master's thesis, Catholic University, Washington, DC.

Stetten, K. J. (1976). *Telebook Center of the Blind: Phase 1, Final Report.* Washington, DC: Mitre Corporation. Also: (ERIC Document Reproduction Service No. ED 117 932)

Stetten, K. J., & McElhaney, W. E. (1978). *The Columbus, Ohio, experiment with advanced Telebook system.* McLean, VA: Mitre Corporation. (ERIC Document Reproduction Service No. ED 160 532)

Strong, R. K. (1974). *A study of public library service to homebound adults in ten selected communities in each of the New England States.* Unpublished master's thesis, Southern Connecticut State College, New Haven.

Sullivan, E. R. (1950). *The administration of "Books for the Blind" at the Free Library of Philadelphia.* Unpublished master's thesis, Drexel Institute of Technology, Philadelphia, PA.

Survey to determine the extent of the eligible user population not currently being served or not aware of the programs of the Library of Congress, National Library Service for the Blind and Physically Handicapped. (1979). (Vols. 1–5). New York: American Foundation for the Blind. Volume 5 reprinted in: Berkowitz, M., Hiatt, L. G., de Toledo,

P., Shapiro, J., & Lurie, M. (1979). *Design and execution of a study of reading with print limitations*. New York: American Foundation for the Blind. (ERIC Document Reproduction Service No. ED 197 754)

Swank, R. C. (1967). *Library service for the visually and physically handicapped. A report to the California State Library*. Sacramento: California State Library. (ERIC Document Reproduction Service No. ED 024 426)

Swingle, V. B. (1978). *An investigation of large print publishing in relation to library services for the handicapped*. Unpublished doctoral dissertation, University of Chicago.

Sze, E. C. (1976). *A public library program for slow learners from three to nineteen years old*. Unpublished master's thesis, University of Chicago.

Thomas, J. L. (1980, Winter). College and university library services for the handicapped student in Texas: Selected findings from a survey. *Texas Library Journal, 56,* 12–14.

Thomas, J. L. & Thomas, C. H. (1983, Winter). A report of the findings from the survey *Academic Library Facilities and Services for the Handicapped Student in the United States. Dikta,* 109–121.

Thorn, W. D. (1978, August). Australia: Results from the National Survey of Library Services for Handicapped People. In National Library of Australia, *Library Services for the Handicapped. Development of Resource Sharing Networks, Network Study No. 9. A National Consultative Seminar* (pp. 21–27). Canberra: Author. (ERIC Document Reproduction Service No. ED 178 035)

Thwaits, M. B. (1979). *Academic library instruction program for developmentally disabled adults*. Fort Collins: Colorado State University, Libraries. (ERIC Document Reproduction Service No. ED 205 220)

Tsao, J. J. C. (1967). *Public library service to retarded readers*. Unpublished master's thesis, San Jose State College.

Vinson, R. J. (1983). School library media center service for handicapped students 1950–1980. (Doctoral dissertation, Southern Illinois University at Carbondale, 1983). *Dissertation Abstracts International, 44,* 1231A.

Waddicor, J. (1975). Library service to nursing homes: A regional study. *Library Journal, 100,* 1892–1895.

Walker, F. R. (1961). *The Talking Book and its use in selected Southeastern Regional Libraries serving the blind*. Unpublished master's thesis, University of North Carolina, Chapel Hill.

Wanger, J., Haaf, J. W., & Cuadra, R. N. (1981). *Automated circulation systems in libraries serving the blind and physically handicapped: A reference guide for planning* (Contract No. LC2347). Santa Monica, CA: Cuadra Associates. (ERIC Document Service Reproduction No. ED 205 221)

Warner, E. E. (1965). *A selected bibliography of books in large print for the visually limited child, which are correlative to the Virginia school curriculum*. Unpublished master's thesis, Catholic University, Washington, DC.

Warren, G. G. (1979). *The handicapped librarian: A study in barriers*. Metuchen, NJ: Scarecrow Press. Also: Warren, G. G. (1978/1979). The career of the handicapped librarian: A study into the effects of physical and psychological barriers. (Doctoral dissertation, Florida State University, Tallahassee). *Dissertation Abstracts International, 39,* 3199A.

Wellons, J. (1966, Fall/Winter). Service to blind, sometimes. *Kansas Library Bulletin, 35,* 10–11.

Wessells, M. B., Smith, A. E., & Rawles, B. A. (1979). *A Study of the Braille and Talking Book Programs in Ohio. Final report*. Columbus, OH: Battelle Memorial Institute. (ERIC Document Reproduction Services No. ED 174 230)

Wilson, B. L. (1976). Vocational materials: Needs assessment—An interim report. *HRLSD Journal, 2*(2), 9–12.

Wilson, E. C. (1962). *Employment of physically handicapped librarians in Southern colleges and universities.* Unpublished master's thesis, Emory University, Atlanta, GA.

Woodman, R. (1933). State institution libraries. *Library Journal, 58,* 62–67.

Yockey, Robert. (1949). *The winged bequest: An account of the Cleveland Public Library's service to the incapacitated.* Unpublished master's thesis, Western Reserve University, Cleveland, OH.

Other Sources Cited in Text:

American Association of School Librarians. (1960). *Standards for school library programs.* Chicago: American Library Association.

American Library Association, Association of Specialized and Cooperative Library Agencies, Standards for Library Service to the Blind and Physically Handicapped Subcommittee. (1979). *Standards of service for the Library of Congress Network of Libraries for the Blind and Physically Handicapped.* Chicago: American Library Association.

Communication and the handicapped. (1978). Government of Canada, Department of Communications, Ottawa.

Communication and telecommunication needs of the speech-impaired. (1983). Government of Canada, Department of Communications, Ottawa.

Communication needs of the deaf and hard of hearing. (1980). Government of Canada, Department of Communications. Ottawa.

Cory, P. B. (1967). *Standards for library-media centers in schools for the deaf: A handbook for the development of library-media programs.* Washington, D.C.: The American Instructors of the Deaf.

Gilmore, J. (1981). *Educators with disabilities: A resource guide.* Washington, DC: U. S. Department of Education.

Lucas, L., & Karrenbrock, M. H. (1983). *The disabled child in the library: Moving into the mainstream.* Littleton, CO: Libraries Unlimited.

Owens, J. A., Redden, M. R., & Brown, J. W., eds. (1978). *Resource directory of handicapped scientists.* Washington, D.C.: American Association for the Advancement of Science, Office of Opportunities in Science.

Telecommunication needs of the blind and otherwise print handicapped. (1981). Government of Canada, Department of Communications, Ottawa.

APPENDIX A

Bibliographies and Directories

The first item listed below is a master's thesis, an annotated bibliography which is not included elsewhere in this paper because it includes no analysis. The other items are selected directories which were compiled through surveys but which also contain no analysis of the data.

Huffman, E. S. (1980). *Library services for deaf, blind, and physically disabled people in the United States, 1977–1979: An annotated bibliography.* Unpublished master's thesis, University of North Carolina, Chapel Hill. Also: (ERIC Document Reproduction Service No. ED 189 816)

Libraries for college students with handicaps: A directory of academic library resources and services in Ohio. (1977) Columbus: The State Library of Ohio.

Library of Congress, National Library Service for the Blind and Physically Handicapped. (1983). *Library resources for the blind and physically handicapped: A directory with FY1982 statistics on readership, circulation, budget, staff, and collections.* Washington, DC: Author. (ERIC Document Reproduction Service No. ED 240 755)

Ploeg, T. A., & Murphy, J. M., Eds. (1978). *Access II: A guide to Massachusetts post-secondary facility libraries serving persons with special needs.* Boston: Massachusetts Board of Library Commissioners. (ERIC Document Reproduction Service No. ED 169 707)

Thomas, J. L., Ed. (1978). *College and university library services for the handicapped student in Texas.* Denton: North Texas State University. (ERIC Document Reproduction Service No. ED 167 165)

Thomas, J. (1981). *Academic library facilities and services for the handicapped student in the United States.* Phoenix, AR: Oryx Press.

APPENDIX B

Copies of the following studies could not be located or were unavailable through interlibrary loan. Available information about these papers suggest that they meet the criteria used by the authors in selecting research studies for this review, and would therefore have been included if they had been available.

Bell, L. (1980). The large print book and its reader. *Oculus, 4*(3), 45–52.

Cooper, S. E. (1980). *An investigation into the provision of information to disabled people in Leicestershire.* Unpublished master's thesis, Loughborough University of Technology, Loughborough, England.

Crook, D. A. (1980). *The provision of information to people approaching retirement, with particular reference to the role of libraries.* Unpublished master's thesis, University of Sheffield, Sheffield, England.

Cross, D. E. (1971). *Library materials and services for the emotionally disturbed and brain injured child.* Unpublished manuscript, State University of New York, Albany.

Gray, P. G. (1968). *Mobility and reading habits of the blind.* London: HMSO).

Herbert, D. A. (1982). *An appraisal of library services for the blind and partially sighted.* Unpublished master's thesis. Loughborough University of Technology, Department of Library and Information Studies, Loughborough, England.

Hunt, A. T. (1939). *Survey conducted at the Braille Institute Library in Los Angeles.*

Jeffers, M. (1980). *Academic library services for the handicapped in Northern Ireland.* Unpublished master's thesis, Loughborough University of Technology, Loughborough, England.

Krishnan, B. (1983). *The wheelchair-bound: Some problems they face in libraries.* Unpublished master's thesis, Loughborough University of Technology, Department of Library and Information Studies, Loughborough, England.

Lewis, M. J. (1974). *The elderly reader: A study of the reading needs of, and the scope for library services, the elderly.* Unpublished fellowship thesis, The Library Association, London.

National Deaf Literacy Scheme. (1976). *A report on the National Deaf Literacy Scheme: A pilot project, September 1975–March 1976.* London: Author.

Newell, M. M. *The development of library services to the blind in the United States*. Unpublished master's thesis, Southern Connecticut State College, New Haven.

Smith, E. L. (1953). *The development and extent of library service to the blind in the United States*. Unpublished master's thesis, Carnegie Institute of Technology, Pittsburgh, PA.

Swindley, R., & Kidd, B. (1981). *Library services for disabled people. A report to the nation.* Melbourne: Australian Library Promotion Council.

Tuttle, D. W. (1972). *A comparison of three reading media for the blind: Braille, normal recording and compressed speech.* Unpublished doctoral dissertation, University of California, Berkeley.

The use of public library provision by the children of Byker, an Education Priority Area in Newcastle upon Tyne: A project carried out by students of the Department of Librarianship, Newcastle upon Tyne Polytechnic, in April, 1975. (1975). Newcastle upon Tyne: Newcastle upon Tyne Polytechnic, England.

West Midlands Branch. (1970). *Report on library services to hospitals and handicapped people.* Birmingham, England: Library Association, West Midlands Branch.

Young, Arthur, and Company. (1979). *Library for the blind and physically handicapped of Southern Ohio; An independent evaluation of the ABCD Project.* Cincinnati: Author.

BIOGRAPHICAL SKETCHES OF THE CONTRIBUTORS

LINDA K. ALLMAN, Director of the University of South Carolina's Library Processing Center, is a former chair of the Technical Services section, SCLA. Her current interests center on the implementation of online catalogs and their impact. Another recent paper "Automated Standing Order List Utilizing Listhandler" appeared in *Small Computers in Libraries,* October, 1984.

CAROL E. CHAMBERLAIN, Head Acquisition Librarian of the Pennsylvania State University Libraries, has been a frequent speaker on acquisition matters at various conferences. A recent publication is "Automating Acquisitions: A Perspective from the Inside" in *Library Hi Tech,* September 1985. Serials management and automation are major interests as reflected in her papers and presentations.

DEBRA DECKER, Serials Coordinator in the Clarion University Libraries, teaches General Studies 110, The Student and the University. A former elementary school teacher, her interests in addition to serials librarianship include computer related activities especially in adapting microcomputer capacities to both teaching and library applications.

ROBERT E. DUGAN, Head of Planning and Development for the Massachusetts Board of Library Commissioners, is responsible for the planning, management, and evaluation of library development for Massachusetts. Formerly Director of Boxford Town Library, he has been a speaker on automated resource sharing efforts in Massachusetts. He has been a participant on ALA programs and assisted in planning programs on fees and microcomputers. Other publications include "Micros in Libraries" in *Year of the Oceans: Science of Information Handling,* edited by R.L. Grundy and R.T. Ford, 1985. Other interests of his include statistical analysis and evaluation, library resource sharing, and computer hardware and software.

JOHN N. GARDNER is Associate Vice President for University Campuses and Continuing Education at the University of South Carolina. Co-author with A. Jerome Jeweler of "College is Only the Beginning," Wadsworth, 1985, he is also author of a recent article "The Freshman Year Experience: Where are the Collegiate Registrars and Admissions Officers?" which appeared in *College and University,* summer 1986. He is Director of the University 101 Program, the University of South Carolina's freshmen seminar program. He is recognized as a national authority on the freshmen year experience, and in 1982 participated in the organization of the first national conference on The Freshman Orientation Course/Freshman Seminar Concept, and has organized successive national conferences on the freshman year experience. He has also participated in organizing international conferences on the freshman year experience which have been and will be held in Great Britain. In 1985 he was a key note speaker at the National Forum of the College Board in San Francisco and also at the 6th Annual Conference on Learning in Higher Education at the University of Wisconsin in Kenosha. In 1975 he was awarded the Amoco Foundation Outstanding Teaching Award for the University of South Carolina's Columbia Campus.

EDWARD D. GARTEN, Director of University Libraries at the University of Dayton, is active in the Library Administration and Management Association. He is editor of the *LAMA Newsletter* and editor-designate of the Association's forthcoming new journal *Library Administration and Management.* A recent publication is "50 Best Database and File Management Packages for Academic Libraries" which appeared in *Library Software Review,* March/April 1985. Other major interests of Garten's include the change process in academic libraries and higher education, organizational development, and staff development.

MARILYN H. KARRENBROCK, Assistant Professor in the Graduate School of Library and Information Science, University of Tennessee, is the co-author of *Disabled Child in the Library: Moving into the Mainstream,* Libraries Unlimited, 1983, and has written several articles on children's authors for *Dictionary of Literary Biography,* Gale, 1985 and 1986. Her major professional interests are in children's and young adult materials, reading, and services in school and public libraries, and she teaches on these subjects in the Graduate School. In the American Library Association, she is active in the Young Adult Services Division, and the American Association of School Librarians. The President's Committee on Employment of the Handicapped named *Disabled Child in the Library* to its "Recommended Books" list in 1985.

LINDA LUCAS, an Associate Professor in the College of Library and Information Science, University of South Carolina, teaches in areas of adult services and services and materials for the institutionalized and disabled. She is the author of "Educating Librarians to Provide User Education to Disabled Students," in Teaching the Teachers: *On-the-job Education for Bibliographic Instruction,* Scarecrow 1986, and "Library Service and the Generation Gap Among Older Adults" appearing in the *Journal of Educational Media and Library Science.* She is co-author of *Disabled Child in the Library: Moving into the Mainstream,* Libraries Unlimited, 1983; this book was named in 1985 to the "Recommended Books" list of the President's Committee on Employment of the Handicapped. She is active in the Association of Specialized and Cooperative Library Agencies, American Library Association.

FRANCINE G. McNAIRY, Dean of Academic Support Services at Clarion University, manages the Support Services Division overseeing the student retention and testing programs, academic advising, and coordinates the faculty development program. She is the author of "The Minority Student on Campus" in *College is Only the Beginning,* Wadsworth Publishing Company, 1984.

CHARLES B. OSBURN, Dean of Libraries of the University of Alabama, is a member of the Advisory Board on Scholarly Communications, American Council of Learned Societies. Another recent publication is "Issues of Structure and Control in the Scholarly Communication System" *Library*

Quarterly, January, 1984. His interest in the subject of scholarly communication is reflected not only in this publication but also in his work for the ACLS noted above, and his chairing the Association of Research Libraries Task Force on Scholarly Communication.

BRIAN A. REYNOLDS, Siskiyou County, California librarian, has had service in other public libraries in California, Illinois, and Central America. Active in the California Library Association, his particular interests are rural librarianship and development of leadership in librarians for the improvement of library services.

ALICE GULLEN SMITH, Professor of Library Science at the University of South Florida, has been active as a teacher and author in the field of children's literature. At South Florida, she was chair of the Department of Library Science prior to its elevation to school status. She is active in ALA, ASCLA, and the Florida Library Association. In addition to children's and young adult literature, she has a major interest in bibliotherapy and has published on that subject.

CHARMAINE B. TOMCZYK, Associate Librarian for Technical Services at the Coastal Carolina Campus of the University of South Carolina, is the author of "Journal and Book De-Selection at USC—Coastal Carolina," published in the *South Carolina Librarian,* fall, 1982. While the subject of networking is a major professional concern, conservation of materials is also a serious professional interest for her. She is a former chair of SCLA's Technical Services section and has spoken on technical services topics at workshops and conferences.

MARYANN TRICARICO, Director of the Peabody Institute Library, Massachusetts, was formerly Assistant Director of the Lynn Public Library. Active in professional associations, she is chairperson of the Conference Committee, Massachusetts Library Association. Author of "Dialing for Dollars," Grants Magazine 1986, she is a consultant for library development to health and human service groups.

AUTHOR INDEX

SUBJECT INDEX

Advanced Certificate in Information Management, 210
Alabama, 21, 256, 277
ALA (see American Library Association)
ALA Yearbook, 227
Albany, New York, 246
ALISE (see Association of American Library and Information Science Education)
Allman, Linda, 226, 233
American College Testing Service, 157
American Council on Education, 160
American Foundation for the Blind, 244, 245, 248, 267
American Library Association, 7, 54, 198, 200, 244
American Library Association, Committee on Accreditation, 215
American Library Association Resources and Technical Services Division. Discussion Group on Processing Centers, 227
American Library Directory, 222

American Printing House for the Blind, 244
Amherst College, 83, 102, 161
Andover, 103
Arlington Heights, Illinois Public Library, 21
Arthur D. Little, Inc., 222
Attila the Hun, 23
Argyris, Chris, 35
Assembly of Librarians, 236
Associate Library School [definition], 198
Association of American Library and Information Science Education, 198
Association of American Colleges, 154
Association of Resource Personnel Serving the Hearing Impaired, 290
Astin, Alexander, 157
Australia, 154, 261
Automated Resource Sharing in Massachusetts, A Plan, 88

Baltimore Public Library, 49
Baumol, William, 19
Berelson, Bernard, 59

317

FOUNDATIONS IN LIBRARY AND INFORMATION SCIENCE
A Series of Monographs, Texts and Treatises

Series Editors: **Evelyn Daniel,** Dean
School of Library and Information Science
Simmons College

Robert D. Stueart, Dean
Graduate School of Library and Information Science
University of North Carolina

The Mexican American: A Critical Guide to Research Aids
Barbara J. Robinson and J. Cordell Robinson

A Practical Approach to Serials Cataloging
Lynn S. Smith

The Microform Revolution in Libraries
Michael R. Gabriel and Dorothy P. Ladd

China in Books: A Basic Bibliography in Western Language
Norman E. Tanis, David L. Perkins and Justine Pinto

Budgetary Control in Academic Libraries
Murray S. Martin

Cost Analysis of Library Functions: A Total Systems Approach
Betty Jo Mitchell, Norman E. Tanis and Jack Jaffe

Management of a Public Library
Harold R. Jenkins

Collection Development in Libraries: A Treatise (2 vols.)
Edited by Robert D. Stueart and George B. Miller, Jr.

Introduction to Serials Management
Marcia Tuttle

Developing Collections of U.S. Government Publications
Peter Hernon and Gary R. Purcell

Library Management Without Bias
Ching-Chih Chen

Issues in Personnel Management in Academic Libraries
Murray S. Martin

Information Needs of the 80s: Library and Information Services' Role in "Bringing Information to People" Based on the Deliberations of the White House Conference on Library and Information Services
Edited by Robert D. Stueart

ALMS: A Budget Based Library Management System
Betty Jo Mitchell

Options for the 80s: Proceedings of the Second National Conference of The Association of College and Research Libraries (2 vols.)
Edited by Michael D. Kathman and Virgil F. Massman

The Library Services and Construction Act:
An Historical Overview from the Viewpoint of Major Participants
Edward G. Holley and Robert F. Schremser

Changing Technology and Education for Librarianship and Information Science
Edited by Basil Stuart-Stubbs

Videotex and Teletext: New Online Resources for Libraries
Michael B. Binder

Research Libraries and Their Implementation of AACR2
Edited by Judith Hopkins and John A. Edens

Brochure Available Upon Request

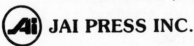 **JAI PRESS INC.**

ADVANCES IN SERIALS MANAGEMENT, Volume 1

Edited by   **Marcia Tuttle**, *University of North Carolina*
at Chapel Hill
Jean G. Cook, *Iowa State University*

In the light of the growing recognition of the place of serials in today's research and leisure environment, it is appropriate that an annual publication be devoted to librarians' work with these materials. The purpose of *Advances in Serials Management* is to monitor and publicize trends in acquiring, processing, and making available library materials issued in serials format. This series will enable serials librarians to understand what is happening in our professional world — what we need to know, what changes are occurring (or should occur), what we need to do to prepare for the future.

ADVANCES IN LIBRARY AUTOMATION AND NETWORKING, Volume 1

Editor   **Joe A. Hewitt**, *University of North Carolina*
at Chapel Hill

The purpose of this series is to present a broad spectrum of in-depth, analytical articles on the technical, organizational, and policy aspects of library automation and networking. The series will include detailed examinations and evaluations of particular computer applications in libraries, status surveys, and perspective papers on the implications of various computing and networking technologies for library services and management. The emphasis will be on the information and policy frameworks needed for librarians and administrators to make informed decisions related to developing or acquiring automated systems and network services with special attention to maximizing the positive effects of these technologies on library organizations.